Reggae Routes

The Story of Jamaican Music

Kevin O'Brien Chang

Wayne Chen

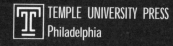 TEMPLE UNIVERSITY PRESS
Philadelphia

First published in the USA 1998 by
Temple University Press
Philadelphia 19122

ISBN 1-56639-629-8 softcover

Cataloging-in-Publication Data is
available from the Library of Congress

Design by Prodesign Ltd, Red Gal Ring,
Kingston, Jamaica, W.I.

Printed and bound in the USA

Acknowledgements
Cover photo of Bob Marley by Adrian Boot.
The publishers are indebted to the artists, record companies
and producers who granted permission to reproduce
the songs and illustrative material used in this book.

'I hope Jamaicans don't ever forget that reggae is a culture.
It's not just a music, it's a culture belonging to us, created by us,
and we must take care of it.'

Alton Ellis

The lyrics you can analyse
The riddim you must feel

Ghetto Bard Wayne, dub poet

Yes I was from before
Christopher Columbus
And I was from before
The Arawak Indians
Trod in creation
Before this nation
I'll always remember
I can't forget
And I never weary yet

'Never Get Weary'
Toots and The Maytals

Contents

The History

The Sounds

Appendices

Acknowledgements

We wish to thank all those who helped make this book possible. Thanks especially to David McLeod, book designer and editor, for giving it final shape. Thanks also to Frankie Campbell for making available his music charts from 1960 to 1973 which, as far as we know, exist nowhere else. To Margaret McLaughlin for proof reading and permissions research. To Bob Clarke for checking historical accuracy and advice on the reggae all-time hits list. To Carolyn Cooper for her preliminary reading and final title suggestion. And to Ekpedeme Otuokon, Tomlin Ellis, Michael Barnett, Olivia 'Babsy' Grange, Neville Lee, Eddie Lee, Byron Lee Jr, Richard Burgess, Ronnie Nasralla, Joan Richards, Richard Chen, Denise Davis, Nugent Richards, Jenny Lyons, Pamela Douglas, Stephanie Chen-See, Cindy Gaussen, Tammy Sasso, Ann Chen, Denise Chang, Vincent and Gloria Chen, and Bobby and Angela Chang.

This book is our small contribution to Jamaican music and culture and salutes those who continue to educate the public and keep the music alive, including Olive Lewin, Bunny Goodison, Winston 'Merritone' Blake, Dermot Hussey, Roger Steffens and Chris Wilson.

Above all, Thanks and Praise to the Most High.

Wilfed 'Jackie' Edwards

Preface

Why another book on reggae? Well, apart from *Bob Marley: Reggae King of The World*, no book about Jamaican music has been written from a Jamaican point of view. And existing books about reggae tend to concentrate on the 'rasta roots' period from say 1975 to 1980, which represents only one aspect of the music. More importantly, those who helped establish the music are not getting any younger. Quite a few 'foundation figures' have passed away in the last few years and pretty soon none of those who created reggae will be around to help tell its story. But this is above all a labour of love. We 'born and grow' with reggae and it has always been a part of our lives. The men and women who sang and played and produced it have given us countless moments of joy. In a way this is our small token of thanks for the real happiness they brought into our lives.

Yet we have more than just an emotional attachment to Jamaican music. Reggae is one of the world's few living folk musics. It remains a genuinely popular sound spontaneously generated by a people's experiences, emotions and traditions without the outside interference of multinational marketers, press agents and spin doctors. Since its birth reggae has been the Jamaican nation's main collective emotional outlet, and this remains its chief *raison d'etre*. Reggae's international earning abilities matter very little in the dance hall. But who knows how long this situation will last? Reggae might well go the way of most indigenous cultural forms in the video age and become an ostentatiously mannered, tourist oriented, emotionally gutted affectation. If it does, we hope this book will serve as a document preserving a lost but significant moment in time. Not that it is intended to be a sociological tract; reggae is a supremely life-loving music, and we have tried to reflect this 'glad to be alive' outlook.

While we write from a Jamaican perspective, we have tried to avoid being parochial. Our intended audience is any person interested in an intelligent discussion of reggae music and Jamaica. We hope to be both accessible to the neophyte and satisfying to the connoisseur. While the book attempts to give a broad introduction to reggae, it's also a look at Jamaica through its music. So the songs we have written about are not necessarily the best reggae singles of all time, although none is a bad tune. Each song was chosen because it either highlights an important artist, is socially significant, evokes a particular time or has a nice story.

As a listener's guide we have included a list of what we consider the best reggae singles (see page 232). How did we arrive at this? Having grown up with the music, read widely on the subject and talked to a lot of people in the business, we should have a fair idea of what a good reggae song is. Perhaps a thousand or so tunes fall into this category. Over the five years it took to write this book we listened to these repeatedly. The less we got tired of hearing a song, the higher we rated it.

All good music pleases both heart and head. But we view reggae as essentially an intuitive folk music where visceral and emotional appeals take precedence over intellectual attractions. Ezra Pound said music decays when it strays too far from dance, and this is especially true of reggae. Some people equate musical excellence with 'conscious lyrics'. Intelligent and well-expressed verses do add charm to a song, but what's the point of wonderful lyrics if the melody and rhythm put you to sleep? Unless a song's words are so childish or pretentious as to interrupt mood and atmosphere, lyrics are usually of secondary interest. As W. H. Auden puts it, 'people do not sing when they are feeling sensible'. Very little reggae, or pop music in general, stands up to textual analysis. Music is music and poetry is poetry, and rarely do the twain meet. The greatest music ever composed for the human voice came from the pens of Verdi and Mozart, but neither wrote a line of their librettos. And who remembers the names of their librettists?

Every significant musical form gives the listener certain unique experiences and has its special competitive advantage, something it does better than the rest. Reggae is just one music among many and is certainly not a universe unto itself, able to evoke every possible musical sensation. We find Jamaican music most intriguing when it doesn't quite sound like anything else, when it arouses emotions that no other type of music does, when it gives us something we can't get anywhere else. This book is also a search for, and an attempt to define, such moments, a quest for the essence of reggae. People who listen mainly to reggae or pop might have formed different opinions.

But there are many mansions in the father's house. While we have listened to a lot of different types of music, we make no claim to musical omniscience since there is much we know nothing about. But we're willing to reveal our prejudices up front and confess that we prefer Mozart to Bach, Verdi to Wagner, Carmen to Beethoven's Fifth Symphony, Leroy Carr to Robert Johnson, Louis Armstrong to Bing Crosby, Muddy Waters to Elvis Presley, Patsy Cline to Diana Ross, The Drifters to The Four Tops, The Rolling Stones to Earth Wind and Fire, Stax to Motown, Van Morrison to Jim Morrison, Public Enemy to Hammer, Lyle Lovett to Garth Brooks, 'Take the A Train' to 'Rock Around The Clock', 'I'm So Lonesome I Could Cry' to 'Dock Of The Bay', 'Amazing Grace' to 'My Way', 'When a Man Loves a Woman' to 'Yesterday'. *De gustibus non disputandum* – there is no disputing taste.

A definition

Reggae has two meanings. It is a generic name for all Jamaican popular music since 1960 – 'West Indian style of music with a strongly accented subsidiary beat' according to the *Concise Oxford Dictionary*. But reggae can also refer to the particular beat that was popular in Jamaica from about 1969 to 1983.

Jamaican popular music since 1960 can be roughly divided into four eras each of which had a distinctive beat – ska, rocksteady, reggae, and dancehall. Ska dated from about 1960 to mid 1966. Rocksteady lasted from late 1966 to late 1968. The popular beat from 1969 to about 1983 was named reggae and had two phases 'early reggae', from about 1969 to 1974, and 'roots reggae', from about 1975 to 1983. From 1983 onwards the prevalent sound has been called dancehall.

Just as the ska beat is different from the rocksteady beat, so is the dancehall beat different from the reggae beat. Outside of Jamaica dancehall is often called 'ragga' or 'dub', but in Jamaica 'dub' usually refers specifically to bass-heavy instrumentals created by mixing out other instruments and leaving the drum and bass only. Dub was especially popular here in the 1970s.

The History

Introduction

∙∙∙∙∙∙∙∙∙∙∙∙∙∙∙∙∙∙∙∙∙∙∙∙∙∙∙∙∙∙∙∙∙∙∙∙∙

'Man, if you have to ask, you'll never know.'[1] Maybe Louis Armstrong was just tired, maybe someone asked 'What is jazz?' once too often or maybe he was just telling it like it is. Perhaps jazz, or blues or opera or classical music or rock or reggae, can only be experienced, never explained.

No one actually knows why certain combinations of notes sound better than others. All we really understand about music is its effect on us, and most people are happy to leave it at 'I know what I like!' – which often means 'I like what I know'. But if you're going to analyse musical preferences, you have to at least attempt definitions. So what is reggae?

We view reggae as music created by Jamaicans to satisfy their spiritual and emotional needs. Styles and trends may shift and turn, but this yardstick definition remains incontrovertible. You can classify the various eras of reggae, but it's nonsense to say the music being made today in Jamaica is not reggae but something entirely different. The name has changed over the years (mento, ska, rocksteady, dub, dancehall, ragga) but the tradition in which the music is created and enjoyed has not. Reggae is not and never was designed to suit a specific formula or espouse a given political view. Nor was it thrust upon the masses by slick corporate hype or central planning committees. Reggae has grown directly out of the experiences of Jamaican people and all discussions must begin there.

What makes reggae so fascinating, even to people who don't like it, is its singular global popularity. Other vital indigenous music like Trinidadian Calypso, Dominican Meringue, Zairean Rumba (Soukous) or Brazilian Samba haven't attracted the same attention or exerted similar influence. In parts of Africa and Brazil, reggae is actually displacing native music. Reggae is probably the only music not of European or American origin which can be heard in every country on earth, and is arguably the first example in modern times of a third world country exporting its culture to such a diverse audience.

Some years ago CNN carried a story of an astronomer in the American midwest who was trying to make contact with extraterrestrial life by beaming radio signals into outer space. His music of choice was reggae, because of its universal appeal. Also a few years ago a TV advertisement for the Goodwill Games (whose avowed purpose is to bridge global ideological divides) used a version of 'Many Rivers To Cross'. There was no commentary. Apparently the song alone was deemed enough to suggest worldwide brotherhood.

Jamaica has less than one-twentieth of one percent of the world's population and produces even less of its wealth. Geographically, it has no special strategic value. No event of major military, technological or historical significance has ever taken place here. By any measure it should be an obscure country with little influence on the rest of the world. Why is its music so popular?

Maybe Jamaica is just special – 'We likkle, but we tallawah,' Jamaicans like to say – we are small, but exceptional. Living here you accept reggae as only part of a culture as distinctive as any to be found. Life expectancy is about 74 years (not much less than that of the U.S. overall and greater than that for African-Americans), so Jamaica is relatively blessed. But it's still a third world country with more than its share of poverty and violence.

In terms of popular music though, it's the most fortunate nation on earth. Like everything else, reggae has had to adapt to a faster moving world. But it remains inarguably Jamaican, a rhythm in tune with its people, not only listened to all over the globe but still listening to itself. Most commentators understandably focus on the music's extraordinary international popularity. Yet, in many ways, reggae's most impressive achievement is to have retained its popularity among its own people amidst the unfettered cultural imperialism of the mass communication age. American and British commercial music may be overwhelming indigenous song elsewhere, but reggae today is at once more distinctly Jamaican and more popular among Jamaicans than at any time in its history.

No one moving through the island can avoid being struck by reggae's prevalence. From dance hall to street corner to bar, sound systems and tape players and radios blare out the rugged beat sent forth from yard to conquer the world. This is not a music which has to be artificially preserved by official sanction; nor an 'authentic' song tradition heard only at respectfully observed festivals; or 'festival' music like Trinidad's calypso which is truly popular only for a brief period each year. Ninety percent of the records on local top 40 charts are reggae tunes. In an increasingly homogeneous 'global music village' dominated by the industrially processed

and hyped offerings of the Michael Jacksons, Madonnas and Garth Brooks, reggae's position is, if not unique, at least remarkable.

The vitality of a native music is surely a sign of a people's self-confidence. Jamaicans have always welcomed new ideas, habits and styles from other lands while maintaining their distinctive lifestyle. Small wonder that many countries have adopted reggae music as a bastion against blanket 'westernization'. Reggae has provided musical inspiration for many third world liberation movements. Bob Marley was an honoured musical guest at Zimbabwe's 1980 Independence celebrations because of the inspiration his music had given to freedom fighters in the bush. Chinese students used The Wailers' 'Get Up Stand Up' as their marching song in the 1989 Tienanmen Square demonstrations. In the Nicaraguan civil war Marley's music was immensely popular with both 'Contras' and 'Sandanistas' – each side saw itself as fighting oppression.[2] When the Berlin Wall fell, celebrants stood on the remains singing Marley's 'Three Little Birds' for hours.

Probably no country on earth devotes a greater percentage of income to music than Jamaica. Music here is profoundly woven into the fabric of society, still giving voice to the collective feelings of the community, a function it has lost in a lot of places. Musicologist Pamela O'Gorman once noted that Jamaican 'folk music' audiences are not passive recipients, but active participants who dance, clap, sing and provide verbal encouragement to performers. They listen to music not only for its own sake but as part of a unifying communal activity where threatening forces are described, emotions openly expressed and passions shared.[3] Now perhaps this is the way it was, or should have been. But 'folk music' in the stylised, costumed, rustic, traditional sense is as dead in Jamaica as in the rest of the world. How can a largely pre-industrial musical form infused with mostly rural experiences appeal to the primarily urban sensibility of the late 20th century?

Yet the picture she paints is a strikingly accurate description of a dancehall stage show or sound system crowd in Jamaica today. The outward form of Jamaican music may have changed, but reggae remains every bit as emotionally important to its audience as 'folk' music was to their ancestors. In the crucial sense of genuinely popular performers addressing audiences' direct concerns in their own language, reggae is one of the world's few living 'folk music' forms.

The export of its music has earned Jamaica an exceptional global prominence. No country of comparable size has had such an impact on international popular culture. Only a handful of countries, all much larger, can surpass Jamaica's influence on the late twentieth century's psyche.

To millions the world over, reggae is more than a music. It gives voice to their cultural aspirations and is a lifestyle, a mindset, even a philosophy. A startlingly varied range of communities have adopted reggae as an expression of something deeper than mere 'entertainment' – Hopi and Havasupai Indians in Arizona, Palenquero Maroons in Colombia, urban youths in Nigeria and South Africa, working-class skinheads in Britain, Maoris in New Zealand, and aboriginal Australians, to name a few.[4]

Language explains a lot of reggae's worldwide appeal. English is the *de facto* universal language of our age and Jamaica, although small, is the world's most populous predominantly non-white, solely English-speaking country. Most Jamaicans are West African in descent, our ancestors being forced here as part of the 17th- and 18th-century slave trade with the Americas, which was concentrated on the West African coast.[5] Jamaicans are proud of their African ancestry and many deeply rooted customs remain, but time and distance have made the links to the mother continent unavoidably

Music and dance were ways of resisting the hardships of slavery and creating a new cultural identity.

fragile. Cultural traditions cannot long survive loss of language, and the nation's legal, governmental and educational systems are all based on English models established through the hegemony of the British Empire. The island has, in a sense, been the scene of a unique social experiment – the head-on collision of modern western culture and African sensibilities. The Africans that came resisted the conditions of slavery from day one, and the terms and shape of their struggle has produced a unique society. The distinct forms of Jamaican-English and patois that developed reflect the rich diversity in our heritage. This linguistic aspect of reggae's composition goes some way to explaining its global mobility and metaphorical muscle.

Jamaicans and African-Americans share this African-English heritage. But the former have always been a majority in their own country, the latter usually a minority. This difference in historical experience may partly explain their often divergent outlooks. In the U.S. some African-Americans resent Jamaican immigrants' conservative bourgeois leanings. The popular musical tastes of both groups have certainly drifted apart over the years. They were very similar before 1960, when there was no such thing as Jamaican recorded music.

Today very few songs from the Billboard Top 100 or R&B charts become hits in Jamaica and those that do are always slow, syrupy, soul love ballads. Faster American dance tunes almost never appear on Jamaican charts. Rap and dancehall may be obvious cousins, and rap enjoys some popularity among Jamaican teenagers. But rap songs almost never crack the Jamaican Top 40. American blacks in the past returned the compliment by completely ignoring reggae. During his lifetime Bob Marley had almost no following among African-Americans.

But reggae and dancehall in the 1990s have made significant inroads into black and white American markets. Many Jamaican deejays have 'crossed over' with rap versions of local hits, and featured on remixes of rap hits. And the recent influx of cable TV into the island may well pull Jamaican musical tastes back towards those of black America. No one can predict what the future holds. Let us keep that in mind as we begin the story of reggae.

Olive Lewin and the Jamaican Folk Singers have won awards all over the world, keeping Jamaica's traditional music forms alive and vital.

The Heartbeat of a People

Reggae is many things to different people – 'conscious' music dealing with social and racial issues; a reawakened African art form; just another danceable Caribbean rhythm. The music's ability to satisfy such a varied spectrum of needs explains much of its widespread popularity. And each definition has some validity. Given Jamaica's history, themes of social change and racial awareness have an obvious appeal. Jamaicans are mainly of African descent, so their music is naturally Afrocentric. And of course Jamaicans have little use for music you can't dance to.

This last fact is a central reality of Jamaican popular music which too many observers ignore. Reggae has always been based on a dance beat. Coxsone Dodd, one of its progenitors, states frankly that ska developed from attempts to find a sound which was popular in Jamaican dance halls.[1] And as Lovindeer, reggae artist and social commentator, says: 'A lot of people expect that reggae has to have a message. Rubbish. Reggae is a beat. You can put a message on top of it, you can put gospel, you can put on slackness, you can put on pop. But reggae is a beat, and a lot of us are losing sight of that fact.'[2]

With the beat came a sense of conviction, lack of pretense, and natural intensity which made the music attractive to millions who were never part of the intended audience. Yet reggae remains essential to Jamaicans not because it can be heard in every country on earth, but because it continues to move them deeply, to express their feelings, to mirror their everyday reality. Reggae's creators set out to do nothing more or less than make music which fellow Jamaicans liked. You don't have to be Jamaican to appreciate it any more than you have to be Italian to appreciate opera. But let's not read into reggae things which were never intended. The genesis of Jamaican music had nothing to do with preconceived notions of universal appeal.

Through all its stylistic changes, reggae in its purest arena – the dance halls – has retained the essential bond of shared emotional experience. Performer and audience implicitly assume a common language, culture and musical heritage. Foreign reggae artists have never gained large followings here. Though Lucky Dube has been well-received at Reggae Sunsplash, only a relatively few musical sophisticates know anything about him or other African reggae stars like Alpha Blondy and Majek Fashek. Even native-born and bred Jamaicans who migrate tend to lose touch musically with their homeland. Jamaicans are proud of stars like Jimmy Cliff, Burning Spear and Culture, but their current music no longer has widespread grassroots popularity.

Out of sight, out of mind? Foreign-based reggae artists, like Burning Spear and Culture, often lose popularity in Jamaica.

At the Sting Christmas reggae concert in 1988 Maxi Priest, fresh from a number one hit in England, was pelted with oranges by an audience impatient for dancehall stars. Bunny Wailer suffered a worse fate when he was 'bottled' in 1990. The 'massive's' behaviour was indefensible, but clearly they felt that wealthy, internationally orientated stars could not speak for them or share their concerns and outlook. While discussing The Wailers, Joe Higgs addressed this same issue in a different context: 'The heavier albums were the earlier ones, "Catch a Fire" and "Burnin", dealing with experiences totally. Confrontation, truth and rights. No compromise. You can only imagine those albums now, because that experience was not to be experienced anymore, only to be thought of. You could only imagine afterward what it was like to be sad. Those days . . . was what it is.'[3]

Authenticity is no guarantee of musical excellence, but it's a necessary condition. A little technique coupled with real feeling can go a long way towards producing profound music. But if the heart is missing, all the technique in the world can never touch the soul. Compare rock and roll music to the delta blues from which it sprang. The great practitioners of the post-war blues – Muddy Waters, Howling Wolf, Sonny Boy Williamson – could never compare in musicianship with their acolytes such as The Rolling Stones, The Beatles and Led Zeppelin. But they produced a music of infinitely deeper feeling. Willie Dixon, the great blues song writer, mused about this: 'The ability to deliver the blues with this depth of feeling can't be learned from books or schools. You can find people who can play rings around these blues artists, and have better voices, but they can't duplicate that real, inherited soul.'[4]

It's not difficult to imagine reggae suffering the same fate as the delta blues – co-opted by commercial popular music, its roots insidiously and inevitably gnawed away, and its greatest practitioners lured away from the source of their inspiration. The separation of artistic ability and emotional depth is always a cultural tragedy.

How many great blues were written after rock and roll became popular in the mid 1950s?

Perhaps it's no accident that the vast majority of great reggae songs were made before 1975 or so, before reggae became a large scale, commercially viable music. Reggae's new found international appeal meant that Jamaican artists could generally earn far more money abroad than at home, so the cream of Jamaica's musicians began spending most of their time touring overseas. One could hardly blame them, but it did mean a diminished contact with their roots and, some say, a consequent loss of instinctive vigour.

Can Jamaican music resist being swallowed by the sheer forces of economics and population? International pop is already co-opting the sound. The 'Abbaesque' dancehall of Ace of Base sold in the tens of millions, and the ska-based sounds of groups like The Mighty Mighty Bosstones and No Doubt enjoyed tremendous success in 1996 – the Bosstones sold 7 million albums in the US alone the same year. Apache Indian, the 'bhangramuffin' deejay, became one of the biggest pop stars in India; Majek Fashek claims that reggae originated in Africa, not Jamaica; and dancehall

Apache Indian, part of the new wave of International Reggae

is commonly referred to abroad as 'Jamaican Reggae Rap', which is a little like calling rhythm and blues 'black rock and roll'.

In the nineties Jamaican reggae artists are experiencing unprecedented sustained international success. Dancehall has made larger inroads into popular music abroad than even Bob Marley did while alive. Shabba Ranks appeared in *Time* and *Newsweek* magazines and shared a number one hit on the American rap charts in 1995. Snow, a white Canadian dancehall artist, took 'Informer' to number one in America and Britain. Chaka Demus and Pliers had a number one hit in the U.K. with 'Twist and Shout'. Ini Kamoze's 'Here Comes The Hot Stepper' topped the U.S. Billboard Singles charts in late 1994 and was one of the year's biggest selling records.

Inner Circle's 'Bad Boys' not only served as an American television theme song, it inspired a 1995 hit movie of the same name. Diana King's 'Shy Guy', used in the 'Bad Boys' movie sound-track, made the Billboard top ten and her album

'Tougher Than Love' reportedly sold over a million copies. Shaggy, who topped the U.K. charts in 1993 with 'Oh Carolina', is probably the biggest selling reggae artist of all. His two-sided 'Boombastic/Summertime' hit #3 in the U.S. charts in mid 1995 and debuted at #1 in the U.K. charts. The Grammy winning 'Boombastic' album went gold.

All this causes talk about watered down music. Purists grumbled that reggae's best talents virtually stopped making records for the local market, that the quality of music on Jamaican charts had fallen, that the spring was drying up and the river would soon cease to flow. But reggae has shown remarkable resilience in resisting ruinous over-commercialisation through the years. Music may be a mass-produced consumer product in some places, but here it remains the defining cornerstone of national identity.

Perhaps in time a dancehall genius will weave the undeniably compelling

Buju Banton, one of those holding the key to reggae's future

Clockwise from top left, *Luciano, Diana King, Beenie Man and Shaggy, defining the cutting-edge of reggae's development.*

rhythms of the sound systems into lasting and memorable music. Some older performers are going from strength to strength, like Beres Hammond, who enjoyed a sell-out European tour in 1997. Garnett Silk suggested great things before his untimely death in 1994, while artists like Shaggy, Beenie Man, Tony Rebel, Buju Banton and Luciano give hope for the future. Indeed many critics saw Buju's 1995 album 'Til Shiloh' as the genre's first masterpiece and compared the single 'Untold Stories' to 'Redemption Song'. Some boldly acclaimed him the greatest Jamaican musical artist since Bob Marley. More recently, similar accolades have been hailed on Luciano, who was the subject of a glowing review in *Time* magazine early in 1997, suggesting he might be headed for levels stratospheric.

What's to come is always unsure. Perhaps the prophets of musical doom will for once be correct. Or maybe reggae is enjoying a halcyon age. Whatever its ultimate destiny, we will always be able to savour the golden high points of the beat 'sent forth from yard to conquer the world', the music that Jamaicans can forever boast as 'fe we own'.

Roots Music

• •

KUMINA, QUADRILLE, MENTO, BLUES AND JAZZ

Some romantics say Jamaican folk culture is chiefly African in origin and evolved in remote villages uncorrupted by Europe. But though mainly of African descent, Jamaicans speak only English. So the question arises: which is the main social determinant – race or language? Noted social commentator Professor Rex Nettleford sees language, the transmitter of culture, as 'the primary bearer of social genes', and says of the Jamaican experience:

'Africa is indeed tolerated in spurts of syncretised or reinterpreted folk-lore – a little bit of dance, a little bit of music, a little bit of story telling, and a few words lacing the Anglo-Saxon tongue with exotic tone and colour. But our formal education system, our accepted belief system, our art, law and morals, the legitimate customs and so many of our habits and perceived capabilities – all indices of a so-called cultural sense are dominated by the European heritage.'[1]

His main argument is irrefutable, but the 'little bit of [African] music' is debatable. As Pamela O'Gorman points out, the performance style of authentic folk music in Jamaica is African, no matter what the origin of the music. This is readily seen in Rastafarian or Revival performances of European hymns – the percussive accompaniments and use of complicated rhythmic figures, the syncopated treatment of melodies that were originally written in equal note values, the absence of variety in dynamics and the tendency to adhere strictly to meter and tempo. But what makes these performances unmistakably African in style is the open, somewhat relaxed vocal timbre obtained by directing the sound to the face rather than the head.[2]

One African legacy extremely common in Jamaican music is the 'call and answer' group vocal technique, which has been called 'the most salient characteristic of African, or at least West African music.'[3] And as musicologist Garth White points out, in both Africa and Jamaica virtually all music is conceived vocally and the human voice is of overriding importance. Even ordinary speech has a relationship to African music and there is often a 'sing-talk' style of rendering which is reminiscent of dancehall deejays.[4] Then there is the interest in improvisation, and the tendency to use a variety of tone colours in the vocal technique, especially harsh, throaty singing – again African characteristics. Many of these features in Jamaican music follow very closely those listed by Bruno Nettl as having been carried into the New World.[5] Quite a few are found in in ska, rocksteady and reggae, though they are present more as Jamaican characteristics individualised in rural folk music and later incorporated into popular music.[6] The traditional view is that all persisting African cultural retentions come from the plantation slave period. But this ignores the influx of over 8,000 Yoruba and Central African immigrants who came to Jamaica between 1841 and 1865 as indentured labourers and settled mostly in the St Thomas area. Historian Monica Schuler describes the impact on Jamaica of these post-emancipation Africans in her study, *Alas, Alas, Kongo*.[7] The most prominent cultural legacy of these 'direct' African migrants is Pocomania, or Kumina, an African ancestor worship cult emphasising both singing and dancing.

Pocomania also has antecedents in the Myal cult, an African religion which survived among slaves and whose followers were sometimes called Native Baptists. Myalism played a prominent part in a number of slave revolts, and laws enacted in 1774 prescribed death for anyone attending these ceremonies.[8] Zion Revival or Zionism, is similar to Pocomania but more Christian oriented. The term pocomania is sometimes said to be a corruption of *poco mania*, Spanish for 'little madness'. Edward Seaga opposes this and considers it a derivative of Pu-Kumina.[9] Leonard Barrett traces the term Kumina to two Ashanti Twi words: *akom*, 'to be possessed', and *ana*, 'by an ancestor'. (Obeah is another word of Ashanti derivation, combining *Oba*, 'a child', and *Yi*, 'to take'.) Pocomania first became prominent in the 1860s when the great religious revival, which began in Ireland, swept through the anglophone world. The spiritual intensity of the Great Revival, where worshippers physically experienced the Holy Spirit, infused Afro-Jamaican beliefs with a religious fervour which expressed itself in ecstatic music and dance.[11] In 1988 Leonard Barrett identified three types Afro-Christian sects – Pukimina is mostly African in its rituals and beliefs, Revival Zion is primarily Christian, and Revivalism mixes both.[12] But nowadays most Jamaicans use

Pocomania performance

Kumina performance

the term Pocomania, Revivalism, Zionism, Pukimina and Kumina interchangeably.

The most African form of the cult survives in the eastern parish of St Thomas. Followers refer to themselves as 'Africans' and members of the 'Bongo' nation. Like Rastafarians they consider themselves exiles, but look not to Ethiopia but to the Congo-Angola region of Central Africa and the Guinea Coast of West Africa as the homeland of their ancestors.[13] Early Rastafarians are known to have adopted the music of St Thomas Revivalists, and Kumina drumming recorded in 1953 has been shown to be indistinguishable from what Rastafarians now call 'Nyabinghi'.[14] Here then is a clearly direct African influence on popular Jamaican song.

In addition there is no denying that European influences have crept into Pocomania, notably the ubiquitous 'Sankeys', a term applied to a large variety of hymns, some of which were learned from the popular 19th-century hymnal published by evangelist Ira David Sankey.[15] (Hence Lovindeer's 1991 political parody 'Light a candle, sing a Sankey'.) In Revival singing, short verses from orthodox hymnals are repeated constantly, with ornamentation. Often a line is spoken by one person and then sung by the group. This 'tracking' is purely functional in origin, since many members could not read. The singing is normally accompanied by a bass drum and a rattling drum, suspended from the neck and shoulder and played by sticks. A familiar aspect of Revivalism is possession by spirits and a consequent ecstatic 'speaking in unknown tongues'.[16]

Pocomania, however, is not the only African derived music extant here. Others survive in

The Maroons were also a source of authentic African music. A 1924 study identifies African-derived work and grave songs in western Jamaica's Cockpit Country as featuring part singing, antiphonal call-response chanting, and the repetition of single, short musical phrases – all of which are characteristics of reggae. The researchers collected songs (called Coromantee songs by the Maroons) that speak of venerable African story figures like Anansi the spider and Jesta the trickster.[18] Then there is Jon Canoe (variously spelt Junkanoo, John Canoe, Juncunnu), a holiday tradition in which small bands of costumed musicians roam the streets playing for passers-by. Some say the custom has its roots in African fertility festivals. Its impact on mento, especially the use of the flute, fife and side drum, is unmistakable.[19]

Jamaican popular music has always mixed 'the rhythm of Africa and the melody of Europe'.[20] For all their obvious differences, African and European music have much in common, certainly more than either has with say Oriental music. And the first widespread native song form was dubbed quadrille. Quadrille in Jamaica probably originated like 'bluegrass music' in America, with black country ensembles trying to reproduce the stylish European dance music of the mid-nineteenth century such as the French quadrille, the Scottish reel, the waltz and polka. Four distinctive types of quadrille dances seem to have developed – the formal 'Ballroom' in urban Kingston and St Andrew, the robust 'camp style' in rural St Andrew and Portland, the intricate 'virtuoso' in Clarendon, Manchester and Trelawny, and the 'Scottish reel' in the west.[21]

various forms across the island, including Brukins Party in Portland, Nago in Westmoreland, Etu in Hanover, Gumbay in St Elizabeth, Tambo in Trelawny, Dinkie-minnie in the east, and Gerrah in the western part of the island. Many of these traditional forms are linked to 'Nine-night' funeral celebrations.[17]

Top, at more than 80-years-old, Blue Queen Miss gets down at a Brukins party in Portland in 1982; and left, an old-timer demonstrates some wicked Dinkie-minnie moves.

As Stephen Davis points out in his Marley biography, probably the earliest music Bob Marley ever heard was his great uncle's band playing quadrille tunes based on native Jamaican melodies, songs like 'Titanic' or 'Jane and Louisa'.[22] Quadrille song and dance groups are still part of official national heritage festivals in which both children and adults take part. The usual quadrille group today has two guitars, a fife and a four-stringed banjo, with a fiddle and

ur, or sometimes five, contreda
contredanse (q.v.), the quadrille
nore on the cooperative executi
ing·figures, or floor patterns, tha
stepwork. Each of the quadrille'
is danced with prescribed com
igures, such as the *tour de deux n*
ind turn"), in which the couple

Grooving to the quadrille at an American colonial ball.

rumba box being added for special occasions.[23] Some consider mento a variation of quadrille created by adding an extra figure, just as many regard early ska as New Orleans R&B with added emphasis on the off-notes.

Other influences came to bear on the music. As Jamaican-born Harvard sociologist Orlando Patterson points out, Jamaicans are among the most travelled people in the world and have been widely dispersed since the 19th century. Constantly moving back and forth and exposed to different cultures, they try to reproduce them locally.[24] In the 1880s migration to Central America reached an estimated 1,000 a month.[25] Many stayed for good, and communities of

Jamaicans may still be found in Cuba, Nicaragua, Panama and Costa Rica. But other migrants only worked temporarily, and returned home with new cultural habits. For example, Jamaican speech is said to have speeded up when Panama Canal workers came home copying the fast Spanish style of speaking.

Cuba is Jamaica's closest geographic neighbour, only 90 miles away, and it's not surprising that the basic mento bass-drum rhythm is similar to that of Cuban rumba (the English term for what Cubans call son). Significantly, one of the most important instruments in mento is called a 'rhumba box.' Laurel Aitken, arguably the most important Jamaican recording artist of the 1950s, was actually born in Cuba from a Cuban mother and Jamaican father. Aitken moved to Jamaica in 1938 at age 11, and at one time performed under the name 'Cubbana'.[26] Yet there is a notable difference between the musics of the ex-English colonies and their Latin counterparts. While the former (R&B, calypso, reggae) usually focus on a heavy, central beat, the latter (samba, meringue, rumba) tend to be highly polyrhythmic, and some say, more African. This distinction may well be a result of varying colonial outlooks at the very beginning of the African Diaspora.

Slaves in the Latin Caribbean and South America were supposedly more often kept as tribal units and allowed to maintain their social identity and culture. In the English-speaking colonies most instruments were either banned or abandoned during the journey, and Africans had to re-create a folk tradition using improvised instruments.[27] Possibly the British colonists banned drums because they saw them as a means by which slaves could send messages across and between plantations.[28]

Probably an even stronger factor was the early abolition of the slave trade by Britain. While African slave importation to British colonies ended in 1807, Latin colonies continued to receive slaves – and fresh infusions of African culture – through the 1860s.[29] Perhaps this explains why Cuban son more closely resembles

Brazilian samba than Jamaican reggae, even though Cuba is over 1,000 miles distant from Brazil and only 90 miles from Jamaica, and why reggae has more in common with calypso than either when Trinidad is also 1,000 miles away.

Calypso's impact on Jamaican music is quite obvious. Geographically remote and with a considerably different racial composition, Trinidad, along with Barbados, is still the country most socially similar to Jamaica. Linked by language and cricket, they have always interacted culturally, a tradition continuing with soca and reggae. The older and more highly developed musical form of calypso must have greatly affected Jamaican popular music. Some people, not all Trinidadians, argue that mento was nothing but a Jamaican imitation of calypso. And it's worthwhile to note that two of ska's 'foundation' members were the Barbadian Jackie Opel and the Trinidadian Kenrick 'Lord Creator' Patrick.

Whatever its origins, mento was the dominant music of Jamaica from its first appearance in the late 19th century up to the 1930s, and was especially popular in rural areas. Even now mento is regarded ambivalently as 'country' music, somewhat crude and unsophisticated but hearkening back to days of lost, rustic innocence. Like most folk music, mento was a blend of music and dance, with songs mixing narrative and topical commentary. Mento has a clear, strong fourth beat in a bar of four beats and closely follows local speech patterns.[30]

Mento songs are accompanied by various combinations of piccolo, bamboo fife, guitar, rhumba box, fiddle, banjo, shakers and scrapers. Instruments are often home-made from materials like bamboo, calabashes, seeds, metal graters and even PVC piping. One of the best-known mento stars of yesteryear was 'Sugar Belly' Walker, famous for his use of the bamboo fife and saxophone.[31] The Jolly Boys, who began playing in Portland over 40 years ago, were perhaps the longest lived of all mento ensembles. As recently as 1990 they recorded the 'Touch Me Tomato' album, and even toured internationally to support it.

Sugar Belly Walker

Mento retained its rural importance until the 1950s. However observers noted urban Jamaica's waning affection for traditional music as early as 1920. Mento's gradually diminishing importance mirrored population shifts from village to city. Young migrants attracted to the bright lights of big city Kingston associated mento with the harsh deprivations of farm life. (A similar attitude towards the delta blues was noted in the 1950s among American blacks who had 'migrated' from the rural South to northern cities like Chicago.) Mento became progressively marginalised to rural festivities and tourist hotels as the capital's cultural dominance increased, and the number of mento artists declined sharply in the 1950s. In Kingston the musicians who congregated in bars on Princess Street found only occasional employment. By 1960 the only real demand for mento musicians was in the growing north coast tourist industry.

But mento, a most resilient traditional music, continues to exert a direct influence even today. A number of dancehall 'riddims' are based on traditional tunes like 'Sixpence' and 'Dog War a

Matches Lane'. A number of authentic 'non-tourist' bands still exist, like the Blue Glades, St Christopher and Lititz Mento Bands. These play at annual festival celebrations often accompanying quadrille dancers. The Jamaica Cultural Development Commission has launched a Mento Music Development Project and the Jamaican Music Awards included a mento category in 1996.[32]

Mento made one more lasting contribution. International interest in calypso spurred local entrepreneurs Ken Khouri, Stanley Motta and Stanley Chin into recording mento. And these tentative efforts gave birth to the Jamaican recording industry. The first commercial record made in Jamaica is said to be Lord Fly's (real name Bertie Lyons) 'Whai! Ay!' Returning from a north coast engagement with a carload of other musicians, Lord Fly suffered a series of punctured tyres. He penned his laments on the spot and recorded 'Whai! Ay!' at Stanley Motta's.[33]

Paradoxically, mento became a national music just as it went into inexorable decline. Most performers were previously known only to live local audiences, but radio made them famous islandwide. Among those who cut mento records were Count Lasher, Lord Flea, Lord Fly, Laurel Aitken, Baba Motta, Bedasse Calypso Quintet, Lord Composer, Lord La Rue, Lord Messam, Lord Tanamo, Lord Power, Hubert Porter, Reynolds Calypso Clippers, and Harold Richardson and The Ticklers. Topical humour was a favourite theme, but some songs contained veiled social commentary and others reworked old digging songs and ring-play tunes. But a large, and perhaps the most popular, part of the output consisted of bawdy, suggestive songs.[34, 35] One of the first really big Jamaican hit records was the famous 'Healing In The Balm Yard'. Of course the raunchier material was heard only in the privacy of homes or on sound systems. (Some basic elements of Jamaican music have never changed.)

But no longer satisfied with mento, the urban masses increasingly turned to the rhythm and blues of black America. According to music historian Robert Witmer (who differentiates between 'urban mass popular culture' and 'rural folk culture'), printed documents and oral testimony suggest that Kingston's popular music has been closely tied to that of North America since at least the late 19th century. The songs of Slim and Sam, the last and best remembered of the itinerant songster-troubadours active in Kingston in the 1920s and 1930s, were often called 'blues'. Witmer infers that Jamaicans came in contact with a specifically African-American vein of American music, not merely mainstream popular fare, almost from the moment it became available.[36]

Yet Slim Beckford and Sam Blackwood are widely remembered as purveyors of primarily Jamaican music. A number of so-called 'traditional' Jamaican songs were created, or at least given a lasting arrangement, by this duo. Sir Philip Sherlock recalls that Slim, who was long and 'mawga' with a mouth that seemed slightly twisted, sang 'first voice'. Sam, shorter and chubby with one slightly cast eye, sang 'second'.

Slim and Sam

They were walking newscasts in the days before radio and captured events, rumours, love affairs, domestic scandals, and murders such as that committed by Louise Walker, reputedly the first woman in Jamaica to murder a man. Eyewitnesses of their performances remember above all the infectious laughter and two-way flow of excitement between performers and audience.[37]

Slim and Sam first appeared in Kingston in 1929, and generally performed at Parade or near Coronation Market and Solas Market. But they did not attract media attention until Randolph 'Ranny' Williams (later to become beloved in Jamaica as the comedian 'Mas Ran') wrote an article about them in 1939: '. . . they hold to their line with the adhesiveness of a postage stamp. Folklore is their business. All the incidents that have happened and are happening in Jamaica, they record in songs that for plain broad humour, telling expression and true character study, cannot be beaten anywhere. The customs, whims, wiles and living conditions of the masses of the island are an open book in their hands, as "The Balm Yard Blues", "Go Tell The Chauffeur Me Naw Go Back", "Watch You Puddin", "Shephard Gone", "The Nine/Night Blues", "The Labour Strike", "Madda Bulliten", and "Salt Lane Gal Mento" all show.'[38]

Clearly Slim and Sam were not mere imitators of foreign music. North America seems to have influenced Jamaican music then as it would later, (and as European music did before) providing an existing base which was reworked into distinctly Jamaican idioms.

The annual Pantomime at the Ward Theatre in Kingston also played a part in shaping the nation's musical taste. Some of Jamaica's most popular traditional songs, like 'Linstead Market', were written for this yearly musical and theatrical offering, and the 'hit' songs from 'Panto' undoubtedly caught on with the populace. And of course Jamaica has a rich body of folk songs which every child used to grow up singing – tunes like 'Sly Mongoose', 'Chi Chi Bud', 'Evening Time', 'Solas Market', 'Sammy Dead Oh' and 'Long Time Gal'. (Queen

Mas Ran with Miss Lou.

Elizabeth II was so taken with this last song that when she visited the island in the early 1980s after a long absence during the 'socialist' 1970s, she requested that 'Long Time Gal' be played on her arrival.)

Printed records sometimes suggest that Jamaicans heavily favoured big band swing music in the 1930s, 1940s and 1950s. However the hotels and dance halls where such bands played were patronised only by the upper and upper middle classes. The mass of the population could never have got near such places except as musicians or waiters. 'Big' Bands were an exclusively 'up-up town' phenomenon and only a very blinkered social outlook could describe them as the prevailing popular sound of the day. They probably had little effect on reggae's development, except as training grounds for musicians.[39]

The popular Eric Deans Orchestra, contained no less than five future members of The Skatalites – Baba Brooks, Don Drummond, Ernie Ranglin, Roland Alphonso and Tommy McCook.[40] And many big band leaders and musicians – who included Val Bennett, Sonny Bradshaw, Roy Coburn, Redver Cook, Eric Deans, Wilton Gaynair, Bertie King, Milt McPherson, Babba Motta, George Moxey and Luther Williams – played important behind-the-scene roles in the fledgling recording industry.[41]

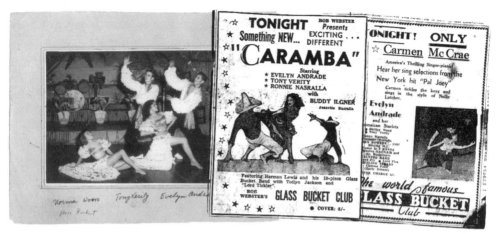

The Glass Bucket was a popular spot for jazz and the big bands with a Latin flavour in the late fifties

Jazz in Jamaica was always a minor substream. As Robert Witmer points out, the small jazz musician community and a dearth of bona fide jazz events indicate restricted dissemination and interest.[42] However, only a narrow minority had access to the media and production facilities in the early days of Jamaican recording, and a tiny group of people had a hugely disproportionate influence on early local musical output. Many of these were jazz fans, including Coxsone Dodd and most of the 20 or so studio musicians who played on nearly all early Jamaican records. So even though jazz musicians and their audience were limited in numbers, jazz had an unmistakably strong influence on ska. Some ska songs, like The Skatalite's 'Music is My Occupation' and 'Eastern Standard Time', can almost be considered danceable jazz.

Radio, as it did everywhere else, changed music in Jamaica. (Local radio broadcasting dates from 17 November 1939. The new shortwave station ZQI used equipment donated to the government by local businessman John Grinan when the war broke out. ZQI was on the air one hour per week in 1940. At first it was used to give out prices and information but soon it began playing classical music. Later programming was mostly BBC relays. In 1947 it was still only broadcasting four hours daily and the signal could not be heard after dark. The impact of station ZQI on local music culture was minimal as there were only 22,920 radio sets in 1950 and the estimated listening audience never exceeded 100,000 by much.)[43, 44] The first commercial broadcasting company, Radio Jamaica and Rediffusion (RJR), came on air in July 1950. In November 1956 RJR had a 'total average listenership' of about 600,000, approximately 50 per cent of the population over 9-years-old. Programming was heavily middle class and did not reflect popular preferences. RJR's most popular musical program-mes for 1956 (in order of decreasing popularity) were: Calypso Corner; Treasure Isle Time; Geddes Grant Hour of Music; Reynolds

Hour of Music; Les Paul and Mary Ford; Bing [Crosby] Sings; Sweet and Swing; [Nat] King Cole's Count; Hit of the Day; Music by Mantovani.[45] And this was a time when rhythm and blues was the dominant sound in the land!

People always complained that Jamaican radio did not play what the public really wanted – though the coming of IRIE FM in 1990 changed the situation. Graham Fowler, an Australian engineer who worked with local radio in that era, tells an interesting story related to this. 'One day I was with Ken Khouri and Byron Lee at Federal Records and Ken called up his friend, Bob Lightbourne. Lightbourne got on to Wills O. Isaacs, and Isaacs told the radio stations that if they didn't play at least 'pro-rata' of foreign music to local music according to sales, they would lose their licence.'[46]

Robbie Shakespeare gives a first-hand listener's account of early radio: 'When I was young I listened to country and western and blues a lot; at first all you could get in Jamaica was one radio station, and that's what they played . . . Jamaicans love sad music, music that makes us want to cry. So the singers with feeling were the ones we liked when we were growing up, everybody from Marty Robbins to Frankie Lane and Bobby "Blue" Bland.'[47]

Since the local radio stations in the 1950s were not playing the rhythm and blues they wanted to hear, Jamaicans naturally looked for other sources. They could pick up Southern U.S. R&B radio stations like WINZ in Miami, but only at nights, and clear reception was not always possible. So most turned to the sound systems.

Sound System Days and Nights

Sound systems – essentially large, mobile discotheques playing at dances, house parties, fairs and nightclubs – were born of economic necessity. In 1950, a modest home record playback system which cost an American 5 percent of his yearly pay required roughly a full year's wages from the average Jamaican. Few among the poorer classes could afford any stereo system, much less one powerful enough to approximate the volume and fidelity of live performances.[1]

As the only survivor of that early period, Clement 'Coxsone' Dodd is often said to have invented the sound system concept. But according to the late Count Matchukie, the first real dancehall sound system was Tom 'the Great' Sebastien, the 'nom de record' of the Chinese hardware merchant Thomas Wong: 'There were other sets playing about the place, but Tom was the first sound with an amplifier properly balanced for the dancehall.'[2]

Tom 'the Great' Sebastien started getting competition from Sir Coxsone Downbeat, Duke Reid 'the Trojan', and Lloyd 'the Matador' Daley. Tom was turned off by the violent rivalry among systems downtown and opened The Silver Slipper Club at Cross Roads. One day he committed suicide by gassing himself in his car, supposedly over financial troubles. Shortly after the Silver Slipper Club burnt to the ground.[3]

The demand for sound systems stemmed from the escalation in temporary migration from Jamaica to the U.S. in the late 1940s. Migrant sugar cane cutters, contracted for six months to a year in the American south, introduced rhythm and blues to Jamaica and it proved hugely popular with the local public. Clement Dodd, an early 'cane cutter', saw the demand and bought his sound system equipment on his first trip. The new venture proved successful and on succeeding trips he enlarged his record collection and equipment, eventually setting up Sir Coxsone's Downbeat sound system, at the corner of Beeston Street and Love Lane in the heart of the inner city.

Coxsone recalls: 'There were 14 dance halls on Maxfield Avenue alone. All those guys who hustled at the wharf used to come to those dances. People came from all Montego Bay to hear the sounds. Duke Reid and me were good friends at times, but he used to buy his guys too much liquor and cause all kinds of fights. Sometimes I had up to 5 different sets playing the same night at different places in the city. Admission was about 2s 6d.'[4]

Chris Blackwell gives an active player's view: 'At about the time "Oh Carolina" was released the sound systems were really burgeoning. They drove the Jamaican recording business, with their need to have the hottest records. When I went to New York in those days I used to buy the latest, most obscure 78s and cross off the labels and sell them to sound systems for vastly inflated amounts: the sound system that had the greatest records drew the biggest crowds.'[5]

There was intense rivalry between sounds, especially Downbeat and Trojan. To protect their exclusives, each set scratched off the title and artist on the record labels. Naturally competitor 'spies' tried to identify popular new records. Coxsone had a very popular theme song

An early Coxsone session

which dance fans called 'Coxsone's Hop', but rival sets were unable to identify the real title. Duke Reid supposedly made 15 trips abroad before he found the record, 'Later for Gator'. When Coxsone heard Duke play the song, so the story goes, he passed out in shock. But there was a dark side to these dances. Rival sets were said to hire 'dance crashers' to 'mash up' the competition by starting fights at their dances and giving them a bad name.[6]

Popular 'sounds' of the fifties included Duke Reid The Trojan, Tom the Great Sebastien, Downbeat or Coxsone (Clement Dodd), Count P or Count Boysie, Lloyd The Matador, Sir Nick The Champ, Count Smith the Blues Blaster, Goodies', Admiral Cosmic and Count John The Lion. Systems played at big dances held in open spaces called 'lawns' (a term still in use today) in downtown Kingston: places like Carnival on North Street, Pioneer in Jones Town, Forrester's Hall at the junction of North Street and Love Lane, Chocomo on Wellington Street, Jubilee on

King Street, Barbeque on Fleet and Tower Streets, and Marcus Garvey's former lodge Liberty Hall. Sounds often purchased records from returning cane cutters or American seamen.[7, 8]

With individual Jamaicans largely unable to afford a record playback system, the sound system was in effect a giant community record player. Chances are this collective listening environment shaped Jamaicans' musical tastes. Groups and individuals often prefer different types of music. And the same song can engender completely different feelings depending on whether it's heard while sitting still in the privacy of one's home or while dancing in the communal outdoors. Financial constraints have more than once forced Jamaican music into new and ultimately fruitful directions.

Sound systems in the 1950s played mainly American rhythm and blues. R&B's appeal to the Jamaican masses is easy to understand. Southern U.S. blacks and Jamaicans had both endured plantation slavery, and in the 1950s were experiencing similar social changes, such as the mass migration from country to city. Plus the average Jamaican could, to a great extent, identify with black R&B artists. Cultural historian Dick Hedbidge notes that the relaxed, loping style seemed to cater to the West Indian taste for unhurried rhythms. The R&B produced in the southern states of America had an almost Caribbean tinge and tended to be much less frantic than black ghetto music from the north.[9]

Jamaicans preferred the 'harder' R&B tunes, says Garth White, especially the crisp, sweet bands of New Orleans and their locomotive rhythm sections. Popular artists included Fats Domino, Shirley and Lee, Bill Doggett, Roscoe Gordon, Chuck Berry, Ernie Freeman, and probably the most influential, Louis Jordan.[10] Interestingly, the electrified delta blues of Muddy Waters, Howling Wolf, or even B. B. King never was popular here. Maybe it was just geographic accident – Mississippi and Chicago being outside Jamaican travel routes at the time. It might be a matter of national psyche.

Jamaicans have never been a brooding or introspective people and the general pessimism of the delta blues apparently strikes no chord within. Even today blues gets very little airplay in Jamaica. In fact 'blues' in Jamaica, while usually referring to rhythm and blues, can mean anything. The 'Yellowman Sings The Blues' album included versions of Kenny Rogers' 'The Gambler' and 'Coward Of The County'.

In the late 1950s black music in American music began to change, for the worse as far as Jamaicans were concerned. The golden age of R&B was ending as the rock and roll era began. Black American records became increasingly slick, self-conscious and soft in the attempt to 'cross over' and appeal to white audiences. The driving beat which moved the sound session dancers was weakening. Not that Jamaicans rejected R&B completely – Sam Cooke, The Drifters and The Impressions were and still are tremendously popular. But 'hard' tunes were becoming scarce and business began dropping at the dances.

In Coxsone's words: 'American music started to change from rhythm and blues to rock and roll but Jamaicans didn't like rock and roll much. I searched the U.S. but the R&B supply was drying up. So I decided to record my own music starting with Roland Alphonso at Federal. I had a couple of sessions, basically tango and calypso and some rhythm and blues inclined sounds. I think the first one was 'Shuffling Jug' by Clue J and the Blue Blasters, a kind of calypso. After the first three or four sessions the feedback was really good because the people started dancing. Basically we found a sound that was popular with the dance crowd in Jamaica and worked from there. The songs were really based on dancing.'[11]

Other sound system operators also cut their own tunes to try and satisfy their restless

Roland Alphonso

Some Federal Records workers relaxing outside the studio

customers. Most early recordings were done at Ken Khouri's Federal Records, then the only studio in the island. Federal recorded almost anyone who wandered in. All you needed was a reasonably good song, a creditable voice and a producer to put up the money. The producer paid for the session time and hired the session musicians. After paying the singer perhaps twenty pounds and a master, the finished product was the producer's property. An unreasonable arrangement? The producer did take the entire risk.

Almost without exception, Jamaican musicians regard producers as crooks. Bitter stories abound, especially the one that runs to the tune of 'I get ten pound for the record and it sell twenty thousand copies!' Of course, no one remembers the songs they were paid for which never sold a single copy. According to Coxsone Dodd, about 60 percent of the records he produced were never released.[12] Exploitation and mistreatment were probably as common as in the music business anywhere, but it's unlikely there was much money in the Jamaican recording industry before foreign markets opened up. A poor country of two million people and limited resources could never realistically support a large body of professional musicians.

As Alton Ellis says: 'I said this and that then but now I think twice. Because the business wasn't that strong then. There was some money but not enough to go around or to satisfy the producer. Studio time was four pounds an hour and the musicians usually get fifteen pounds a song. You have to be god blessed to pick up any royalties, otherwise you keep singing every week for fifteen pounds a song. So sometimes I said I wasn't paid, but there wasn't a lot of money in it. You learn as you get older and realise.'[13] All in all, it could be asserted that older Jamaican musicians have been treated very shabbily

Alton Ellis

by the business – when Jamaican records did begin selling abroad, very little of the proceeds made their way back to the persons who actually created the music – and more than a few reggae legends who continue to be lionised here and abroad have to eke out a hand to mouth existence.

The sound system operators had no intention of selling records when they began producing music. They simply wanted 'hard' tunes for their system dances, records which people would dance to. Naturally they attempted to reproduce the R&B sound popular at dance halls, but some calypso-mento type music was also tried. The earliest records are hard to define. As Clement Dodd puts it: 'After a couple of times in the studio I found a sound that was popular with the dance crowd in Jamaica, and we worked from there.'[14]

According to Garth White, Jamaican music of the late 50s 'proto-ska' period did not merely imitate R&B. Many songs of early artists like Cluet Johnson, Owen Grey, Wilfred Edwards, The Mellow Larks, The Magic Notes, The Maytals and Baba Brooks were clearly in the mento and Jamaica revivalist stream. Even when an R&B format was used, a very strong indigenous ele-ment is heard – as in the music of Bunny (Robinson) and Scully (Simms), Alton (Ellis) and Enid (Perkins), Keith (Stewart) and Enid (Cumberland), Prince Buster, Derrick Morgan, Monty Morris, Theophilus Beckford, Neville Eason and The Jiving Juniors.[15]

In 1958 former prime minister and current opposition leader Edward Seaga started WIRL (West Indies Recording Limited), issuing songs by popular local performers. Seaga had received an anthropology degree at Harvard in 1952 and had researched Kumina, Pocomania and Obeah practices. He supervised the sessions of a 1955 album of cult music for New York based Ethnic Folkways label and then moved into more commercial territory. WIRL's records copied the dominant American models: rhythmic ballads and jumping boogies. Seaga's recorded artists included Wilfred 'Jackie' Edwards, Owen Gray,

Edward Seaga in his young days as a producer

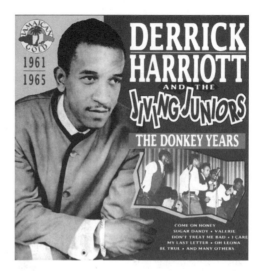

the Jiving Juniors (who included Derrick Harriot and Count Prince Miller as members) and the duo (Joe) Higgs and (Roy) Wilson. Higgs and Wilson's 'Manny O' was a huge hit in 1960, selling a reported 30,000 copies. Seaga had other acts under contract, including Slim Smith and Byron Lee, who had a hit on the WIRL label with his debut single 'Dumplings'. According to Joe Higgs: 'He was the best manager we ever had – we always got paid!'[16]

Duke Reid and Clement Dodd held their first recording sessions in 1959. Reid's artists included the duo Chuck and Dobby, the Jiving Juniors, Derrick Morgan and Eric 'Monty' Morris. Dodd recorded over a dozen tracks with singers like Alton (Ellis) and Eddie (Perkins), Beresford Ricketts, Lascelles Perkins and Theophilus Beckford.[17] Alton Ellis recalls: 'Eddie and I was about the ninth singer in Jamaica to be

recorded. The others were Bunny and Scully, Laurel Aitken, Lord Tanamo, Owen Grey, Wilfred Edwards, Higgs and Wilson, 'Easy Snappin' (Theophilus Beckford), and myself and Eddie . . . we were maybe seventh or eighth, but not more than ninth.'[18]

The first JBC record chart came out in August 1959 and all the entries were foreign. The first local record to make the charts was Laurel Aitken's 'Boogie Rock' which debuted at number 18 on October 9. Two weeks later it moved to number one. The first ten local songs to chart were in order 'Boogie Rock', 'Comeback Jeannie', 'Little Sheila', 'Boogie In My Bones' (all by Laurel Aitken), 'Manny O' (Higgs and Wilson), 'Honey Girls' (Laurel Aitken), 'Dumplings' (Byron Lee), 'We're Gonna Love' (Wilfred Edwards), 'Please Let Me Go' (Owen Gray) and 'I For Love' (Owen Gray).[19]

'Boogie in My Bones' and 'Little Sheila' were A and B sides of the same record. Cut in one of Chris Blackwell's first production efforts, these songs are said to have spent over 12 months in the Jamaican charts.[20] Other hit songs of the times were Derrick Morgan's 'Now We Know', the Mellow Cats' 'Rock A Man Soul'

Young Chris Blackwell

and the key transitional tune 'Easy Snappin'. Sung and played by Theophilus Beckford who was better known then and later as a piano player, 'Easy Snappin' was a huge hit whose 'oh so lazy' feel and emphasis on the off-beat were widely emulated and influential. It wasn't quite ska but neither was it just imitation R&B. Local records, through popular demand, finally began getting airplay. 'Teenage Dance Party', produced by Jazz musician Sonny Bradshaw and originally playing only R&B, began to include local tunes.[21]

Laurel Aitken, who once earned a living with the Jamaican Tourist Board, singing calypso to visitors alighting at Kingston Harbour, was the most important Jamaican singer of the pre-ska era and reflected all the developmental stages of the infant music. He first recorded with Stanley Motta's Caribbean Recording Company, cutting some calypso sides, the spiritual 'Roll Jordan Roll', and 'Boogie Rock'. His late 1950s tunes, like 'Boogie Rock', 'Boogie in My Bones', 'Comeback Jeannie', and 'More Whisky', were heavily R&B influenced (his group was once called the Boogie Cats), but couched in Jamaican accents.

Laurel Aitken

These accents were more pronounced in other early hits like 'Little Sheila' and 'Judgment Day', a key blend of Afro-Jamaican religious music, mento and R&B. He also performed songs rooted in Jamaican folk realities like 'Baba Kill Me Goat A Line'. Garth White considers his mento off-time, 'Nightfall', a transitional record to the modern era.[22] Aitken went to London in the early sixties along with other popular performers like Millie Small and Jackie Edwards, and became quite popular during the skinhead and Mod revivals of the late 1960s. He was still recording in the 1980s.

Derrick Morgan was another big star of the time whose songs changed as the experimental music sought its own

Derrick Morgan

identity. He did the Latin tinged 'Fat Man' (1960), the Gospel oriented 'I Pray For You' (1961), the shuffling R&B 'Forward March' (1962), and settled into ska with 'Shake a Leg' and 'Blazing Fire'.

While Jamaican nationalists insist that ska grew directly out of mento, many musicians and sound system operators considered R&B their virtual model and jazz their spiritual guide. But as Garth White says, neither extreme view can be coherently defended, and the truth is found between these varying poles. Many studio musicians did come out of a mento background. And audiences were not 'digging' only Louis Jordan, because several early local recordings were mento-revivalist songs. On the other hand, Jamaican youths of the time saw mento as outdated 'country' music. Yet if early Jamaican records were merely straight R&B covers, why did they sound strange even to blacks in the US? Clearly both types of music were incorporated into ska, the degree of emphasis depending on the performing artists.[23]

Pamela O'Gorman sees a strong current of rural folk music, including mento and the revival strain, running through our popular music. To her, a song like 'Shanty Town' is based almost entirely on a work-song form, with the sophisticated use of responsorial patterns successfully obscuring its rural background.[24]

Jimmy Cliff confirms these influences: 'I used to sing calypso in school as well as mento and other folklore music, for in the country you have like digging songs, burial songs, wedding songs – there were songs for every occasion. These kind of things seems to be dying out which is a pity, because it's such an integral part of our culture. All these things and people were my inspiration in writing songs.'[25]

Rhythm and Blues

•••

RASTA AND OH CAROLINA

While there were some mento and calypso influenced releases, the vast majority of records produced in the early years were American R&B covers. Heeding their dancehall audiences' complaints about 'soft' R&B songs, the producers started making local versions of these 'soft' tunes, but with a crisper beat. In essence they were trying to reproduce the sound their audiences were used to, not attempting to create anything new. And most early Jamaican records sound exactly like second-rate imitations. Relatively few of the hundreds of records produced in the pre-independence era are worth listening to today. Only a Nostradamus could have predicted that this fitful reproduction of a dying sound would give birth to a totally distinctive and universally popular musical form.

Jamaica was hardly the only country in the world which had become attracted to black American music and tried to duplicate it locally. But only Jamaica developed a sound so different from the original model that it warranted recognition in its own right. Why? Robert Witmer's answer is succinct: 'Unless we hypothesize the existence in Jamaica of a rich and vibrant – but almost completely undocumented – Afro-Jamaican folk or traditional music culture running parallel to the mainstream urban popular music, the rise of distinctive indigenous Jamaican forms in the 1960s remains inexplicable.'[1]

Apparently Jamaican folk traditions were so strongly embedded that they unconsciously influenced local musicians even when they were playing something completely unrelated.

The root cause of the imitation attempts was Jamaicans' cultural stubbornness. Other peoples accepted the lighter sound of the changing R&B beat and kept dancing to it. The reaction of Jamaicans was to reject the altered music and try to recreate the sound they liked. It was a typical response. Modification by their own volition is one thing – Jamaican music has certainly not remained static – but change imposed from without is another.

Jamaicans have always been and continue to be an essentially conservative people. They eagerly embrace technological advances, but loathe change for the sake of change. Once firmly established, their preferences are not easily altered. Something as logically ridiculous as a constitutional monarchy, with a foreign white queen 5,000 miles away being the official head of state of this predominantly black country, survives because that is the way it has always been and the populace sees no reason to alter the 'status quo'. Music is no exception to the general rule – Sam Cooke, Nat King Cole, Jim Reeves and The Drifters (as a group) have all been dead for over 30 years, but in Jamaica they remain extremely popular.

The country's economic position was also a factor. Because of limited resources and outdated equipment, Jamaican producers were never able to precisely duplicate the foreign sound. (Economic constraints have often dictated the direction the music followed. Horns later vanished because they were too expensive.) A richer country, such as Japan today, might have more faithfully reproduced the desired R&B sound, and of course would have created nothing new.

Rastafarianism, which had its genesis in the 1930s, was another great influence on the early music. The worldwide decolonisation movements of the 1950s, and the resulting resurgence of racial consciousness, focused local attention on this sect which had always stressed black pride. It began to attract an unprecedented number of adherents and sympathisers, especially among the socially dispossessed in the Kingston ghettos.

British colonial authorities and the local establishment viewed the Rastafarians' forthright espousal of black unity and pride, and their unconventional appearance and customs, as threats to the existing social order. Rastafarians were treated as outcasts, despised by society and often victimised by police. But their confident independence came to be much admired in the ghetto, and the elders were often regarded as sages by rootless youngsters.

At the Rastafarian campsites and meetings, music and dance were used to give 'thanks and praise' (Satta Ammassagana) to Jah and to 'chant down Babylon'. Babylon was the Rastafarians' derisive name for western imperialism and the oppressions and degradations of colonialism. They likened their position to that of the biblical Israelites. For just as the Jews had been sold into Babylonian captivity, so had Africans been taken from their homelands and forced into foreign slavery.

George Simpson, an eyewitness to the Rastafari Movement in West Kingston in the early 1950s, says the general attitude of middle-class Jamaicans, English citizens and Americans living in Jamaica towards Rastafarians was one of contempt and disgust. There seemed to be no fear of rebellion, but many believed that

Revivalist drumming

Rastafarians were hooligans, psychopaths or dangerous criminals. Frequently they were referred to as 'those dreadful people', a view shared by some police officers. Actually, the movement attracted many types within the Jamaican lower- and lower-middle-classes as well as some students and professional persons.

Though Revivalists and Rastafarians often shared similar social and economic environments at the time, Revivalists were engrossed mainly in the quest for personal salvation and the satisfaction gained from ritual observances. Rastafarians, by contrast, were very vocal about economic hardships and racial discrimination. Although many Rastafarians in the 1950s had been involved in Revivalism, subsequently most of them became hostile to these religious groups. Drumming, rejoicing, spiritual dancing and possession trances, invariably features of Revivalism, were regarded by Rastafarians as backward and never occurred in their gatherings. Yet Rastafarian music and Revival music shared a common focus on Sankey and other Christian hymns, the latter adapted to suit Rastafarian ideology. Unlike later years, drums were totally absent from Rastafarian meetings in West Kingston in 1953. Instead of drums, a rumba box was used.

Simpson adds: 'When I was recording Rasta and Revival music in West Kingston, I also recorded

some Kumina music. Bilby (1986) confirmed that the Kumina music I recorded is indistinguishable from what the Rastafarians would later call Nyabinghi. Moreover, a photograph I took showing three men on drums reveals that the drums and the manner in which they are played is the same as the akete or buru drums, which would later be adopted by Rastafarians under the name of Nyabinghi.'[2] (The term 'Nyabinghi' is often said to be Amharic for 'Death to oppressors!', supposedly the Ethiopian battle cry in the 1936 Italian invasion. But it comes from an East African religio-political cult that resisted colonial domination from the 1890s to about 1928. The word's origin is uncertain, but it may be the name of a Ruandaise princess killed in the resistance and possibly means, 'She who possesses many things'.)[3]

The largest Rastafarian aggregation at this time was the Pinnacle commune outside Kingston, whose leader Leonard Howell used and sanctioned Kumina drumming in his ceremonies. When Pinnacle was broken up by police in 1954 several hundred members dispersed into West Kingston, contributing to the urban spread of the movement and its Kumina derived music.[4]

One of the earliest of Rastafarian Drummers, Count Ossie (Oswald Williams), came under the influence of Brother Job, a master Buru drummer. The Count carried on his explorations at the successive campsites he established in Kingston. These sites were frequented by many top-flight musicians, including established session men like Rico Rodríguez, Roland Alphonso and Johnny Moore, who if not obviously of the Rastafarian faith, were at least very sympathetic to it.[5]

Tommy McCook recalled making regular visits to Ossie's camp beginning in the late 1940s, where he would often sing along with the Rastafarian chants and would sometimes jam on saxophone with the drummers.[6] In time Count

Ossie developed a significant reputation and eventually Prince Buster, then a singer-set deejay-cum-producer in search of a 'different sound', decided to try some of Ossie's rhythms in the studio.

With the three youthful Folkes Brothers on vocals, Ossie and his drummers providing African cross-rhythmic accompaniment and background harmonies, and Owen Gray playing contrasting American styled piano, Buster produced arguably the most famous, influential and important of early Jamaican records, 'Oh Carolina'. This legendary session produced two other popular ska hits, 'They Got To Go' and 'Thirty Pieces of Silver', also known as 'Judas Charmer'.[7, 8]

Count Ossie,
famous Rastafarian drummer

The origins of 'Oh Carolina' are shrouded in controversy. John Folkes, one of the Folkes Brothers who did the song's vocals, says he wrote it and the British High Court supported his claims in November 1994.[9] Prince Buster is adamant that he was the song's creator. The famous 'drop down' opening is definitely copied note for note from the Carla and Rufus Thomas R&B hit 'Cause I Love You', released by Stax Records in August 1960.

Whatever its genesis, 'Oh Carolina' is clearly unlike anything that went before it. Even casual music listeners sat up and took note. Here was something quite out of the ordinary. Ironically it was the only record the Folkes Brothers ever made, and Count Ossie never again had so big a hit, although the 1974 'Grounation' album gained a large cult following.

Prince Buster proved to be a lastingly important figure in Jamaican music. He would later record a very popular body of songs, including 'Wash Wash', 'Wings Of A Dove' and 'Hard Man Fe Dead'. And he produced many significant records, particularly with The Maytals.

In the liner notes to 'Tougher Than Tough' Steve Barrow gives Buster credit for changing the sound of Jamaican music with 'Oh Carolina'. Other Jamaican producers, he says, were simply making copies of R&B, virtually identical to the American model. 'But Buster changed all that. He knew he had to come up with something new, so he had his guitarist Jah Jerry emphasise not the downbeat but the afterbeat. The ramifications of this linger to this day: for, in one way or another, the afterbeat has remained the essential Jamaican syncopation.'[10]

Chris Blackwell makes this interesting comment, 'Count Ossie was a Rastafarian: and

Prince Buster

the main thing the Rastafarian element brought to Jamaica and to Jamaican music was a real recognition and honour of Africa. In American black music there was nothing at that time that was embracing the African heritage, there was very little notion then in America of Afrocentricity. In Jamaica, though, there was a section of the population that was looking to the west and listening to Miami and New Orleans radio, but also there existed the Rastafarian element which was saying that Jamaicans should hang on to our cultural roots. This has been a key dynamic in Jamaican music.'[11]

'Oh Carolina' was an anomaly however, a song years ahead of its time. Most local songs of the day still sounded like poor R&B imitations. A few did stand out like Alton and Eddie's 'Muriel' and Jackie Edwards' 'Tell Me Darling'. But they would have been quite at home in the R&B tradition. The Blues Busters, probably the biggest local stars of the early years, produced excellent music, but in a properly accented American style affecting 'hip' slang.

Gospel was the other great influence on embryonic reggae. (And R&B itself is generally considered a mixture of blues and Gospel music). The Mellow Larks' 'Time to Pray (Allelluia)' was one of the biggest selling records of 1961, topping the JBC charts for six weeks. The Maytals began recording as a gospel group and their first significant record was 'Victory (For Jesus)'. But then nearly all budding Jamaican singers got their start in the 'clap hand' churches. And many Rastafarian songs were derived from Christian hymns.

Early Gospel music in Jamaica was essentially an American bequest, but distinctive local practices made their way into Jamaican churches, most notably Pocomania. Pocomanians are small in numbers, but their unique authenticity and the ecstatic exuberance of their singing and dancing gives them an outsized prominence. Pocomania is still alive and thriving. Both Sly and Robbie, and Steelie and Clevie, currently reggae's most prolific rhythmic creators, admit to being extensively influenced by the Pocomania beat. And as late as 1990 a wave of revival influenced songs swept across the dancehalls, most notably the number one hits 'Pocomania Day' by Lovindeer and 'Chaka On The Move' by Chaka Demus.

Somehow these influences – mento, Rastafarian drumming, Gospel, Pocomania – so impacted on the R&B which producers were trying to duplicate that people began to recognise the new sound as something quite different from its model. It only needed definition.

Ska, Ska, Ska

There seems to have been no conscious attempt to create anything definably Jamaican. The music simply evolved as the subtle difference from R&B became progressively more pronounced. No one can say exactly when the first ska record was created, but at some point it became obvious that the music the session men were playing just didn't sound like 'regular' R&B anymore.

Alton Ellis sums up the process: 'In those days there was nothing special being recorded. We had no general direction, no set pattern. We just recorded anything that sounded good and was saleable. We used to write soft tunes, calypso, blue beat, anything. From there we just progressed a riff onto another riff until we get to where we are. But we usually followed a pattern of the R&B from the States, the boogie-woogie rhythm like Louis Jordan and so forth. We progress from that to ska, and then we go a little slower and get the rocksteady, which is a more relaxed rhythm and more clearly explained itself. From there we progress on and on till we are here.'[1]

Pamela O'Gorman says the main change from R&B to ska was that the characteristic boogie beat of the piano lost its bass notes. To this was added a modified mento-banjo beat, usually taken over by the horns and a syncopated bass on traps.[2]

According to the liner notes of 'Ska Bonanza', ska is a fusion of Jamaican mento rhythm with R&B, with the drum coming on the 2nd and 4th beats and the guitar emphasising the up of the 2nd, 3rd, and 4th beats. The drum therefore is carrying the blues and swing beats of the American music and the guitar expressing the mento sound.[3]

To Garth White the afterbeat, strummed by a rhythm guitar or played on the piano came to be characteristic of the form. No one instrument really predominates – horns and saxes emphasise the guitar chordal beat, the bass often strides in American walking bass fashion and the drum provides the basic 4/4 framework.[4]

Trumpeter Johnny 'Dizzy' Moore has a very interesting insight into the source of the 'ska' beat. He considered the European 'martial' drumming he encountered at Alpha Boys School and in the army as the strongest influence on his playing and one of the key influences on the development of ska.[5]

It's not clear why the new beat was called ska. In *Jah Music*, Sebastien Clarke says Jackie Mittoo insisted that the word 'ska' did not come from slum dwellers or the musicians, who called it 'Staya Staya'. Byron Lee, Mittoo said, introduced the word 'ska'.[6] Ernie Ranglin says the word was coined by musicians 'to talk about the "skat! skat! skat!" scratching guitar strum that goes behind.'[7] One story states that studio double-bassist Cluet 'Clue J' Johnson instructed Ranglin to 'Play it like ska, ska' and the name stuck.[8] Another says ska was an abbreviation of 'skavoovee' a current catch phrase of approval which Clue J was famous for using.[9]

Incidentally, Prince Buster claims there never really was a dance called ska. (Jimmy Cliff concurs: 'It was just a bunch of businessmen coming together to exploit it. Ska was never a dance, just music.') Says Buster, 'The proper dance in Jamaica to ska music was the bebop dance, push and spin, and natural Jamaican things like flashing [snapping] the fingers and pickup moves from Pocomania and mento.'[10]

However it developed, Jamaica's first internationally recognised popular music expression unquestionably emerged from the ghettos of western Kingston, then full of rural 'immigrants' trying to make it in the big town. Most early stars, including Bob Marley, Toots Hibbert and Jimmy Cliff, shared this common background. Cliff, in the movie 'The Harder They Come', gives a completely convincing portrayal of what life must have been like for these newcomers. 'It wasn't an easy road when I come to Kingston. I really didn't know anyone. I was like boarding with some people. I had to feel my way around, and there were some hard times. In the country you can go easily pick a breadfruit or pear or banana and you alright. In the city nobody give you anything, so it was really hard. And then trying to get the songs recorded. You have to go from producer to producer and this one refuse you for whatever reason.'[11]

Many early singers and musicians gained their first public exposure in The Vere Johns Opportunity Hour, a popular talent show broadcast live every Saturday night on RJR.

John Holt was one of them: 'I really started out with Joseph Vere Johns' Opportunity Hour. He's been sort of forgotten, but I haven't forgotten him, because he was the one who took the shakes, the nervousness out of our knees. He's the man who really groomed the Jamaican talent in the early years.'[12]

The programme grew out of the weekly talent shows held downtown at the Majestic, Palace and Ambassador Theatres. The show offered instant celebrity to the winners, who were

Young Jimmy Cliff

Opportunity Hour now in 25th

THIS YEAR m...
the 25th an...
sary of Oppor...
Hour, a talent
programme w...
started on the stag...
the Palace theatre
May 1939 when Mar-
garet Lillian Johns an-

Joseph Vere Johns' Opportunity Hour was a stepping stone for many Jamaican artists

selected by the audience. Winners could not re-enter the contest, but Vere Johns would invite favourites back again as special guests, giving them a chance to showcase their latest material.[13]

Jamaica gained political independence from Britain in August 1962 and the national exhilaration gave musicians an extra impetus to create a distinctively Jamaican sound. It was about this time that the term 'ska' became widely popular, although the heavier bass, loping shuffle-rhythm and riffing on the offbeat can be heard in late 1961 and early 1962 recordings.

At first the music appealed only to the ghettos of its birth. But the uptown bands – including Byron Lee and The Dragonaires, The Granville Williams Orchestra, Carlos Malcolm and The Afro-Jamaican Rhythms – soon picked up the sound, attempting to make it respectable by softening the bass line and taking the edge off the ska riff. Such bands, especially Byron Lee's (the only one still in existence) have been criticised for exploiting, 'prettifying' and 'watering down' a music they had done nothing to help create. Lee tells it this way: 'One day, Eddie Seaga called me up. As Minister of Culture and Development, he said that Jamaica needed its own popular music as an independent nation. He had already asked Carlos Malcolm, who had this big hit 'Rukumbine' at the time, to concentrate on promoting mento. He asked me to try and develop the

music called ska being played in West Kingston, his constituency. So you call it partly political, but whatever his motives, you have to give him credit. If it wasn't for him ska might not have become so popular.

'So I went down to Chocomo Lawn and met all these guys like Jimmy Cliff and Derrick Morgan and Monty Morris. People talk about how Byron Lee water down the music, but nothing about ska was known outside of West Kingston at the time. It had been around about 2 or 3 years, but there were no live shows and you never heard it above Half Way Tree. It was a very rough music, a lot of wrong chords and out of tune guitars. Foreigners called it too ethnic. But still, ska had this powerful feeling. So I had my band work on getting a feel for it, worked with the artists. About August 1962 we put on a show at Glass Bucket called "Ska Goes Uptown". We had Monty Morris, Jimmy Cliff, The Blue Busters, Stranger and Patsy and The Maytals. Some high toned people critised us for bringing such low class music uptown, but it was a big success. Radio picked-up on the sound and middle-class Jamaicans started buying ska records. I would never try to take credit for being one of ska's creators. But we helped to shape it as a music and we were the band primarily responsible for spreading it around Kingston and around Jamaica on live shows.'[14]

Scenes from Independence

Winston Barnes says that there were two basic varieties of ska, the original roots oriented music and after a while up-town ska. Barnes thinks that Monty Morris' 'Sammy Dead', a number one hit, actually had two versions – the original, and the softened version probably done with Byron Lee and The Dragonaires. The music acquired a kind of dual nature at this stage – the sound of a Granville Williams Orchestra was not the same as The Skatalites or even Carlos Malcolm and The Afro-Jamaican Rhythms.[15]

Yet as the late Winnie Wright (one of reggae's greatest keyboard players) pointed out, many musicians in Byron Lee's band also played on 'raw' downtown tunes and would let loose when they jammed among themselves. As he put it: 'At Glass Bucket you had to put on suit and tie and play 'Empty Chairs' and 'Elizabeth Serenade'. The crowd there didn't like the music too rough. And no matter where you are, you always have to play to the audience.'[16]

Far from 'taking the pepper out' to make the music more palatable to wider audiences, The Skatalites were 'hotting up' the original sound, giving it a distinctive freshness. The Skatalites contained most of the top session musicians of the day, including the extremely creative but eccentric trombonist, Don Drummond. The Skatalites were formed in 1963. According to bassist Lloyd Brevette, one day in the studio Tommy McCook said 'Gentlemen, we should give ourselves a name. Because people hear us backing all these records and are asking to see us perform live.' All agreed it was a good idea. But what would they name it? The Russians had just launched the Telestar satellite into space, so Lord Tanamo suggested The Satellites. Al-most as a joke Tommy said 'No, let's call it The Skatalites!' And the name stuck.[17] (Jamaica's current prime minister, P.J. Patterson once managed the band. It is interesting to note that two (of six) Jamaican prime ministers have been intimately involved in the music business.)

The few performers who had international impact were not directly associated with The Skatalites. But many of the hit songs which made the newly emerging record charts had The Skatalites as a group or strongly represented as session men – including the songs of The Maytals, Delroy Wilson and The Wailers, to name only a few. The outsized influence of a handful of studio men remains a feature of Jamaican music to this day. Two duos, Sly and Robbie, and Steelie and Clevie, produced almost half of the number one tunes in 1992.

Despite their legendary reputation today, The Skatalites were not necessarily the most popular band of their time. An RJR poll in February 1965 showed them to be only the fourth most popular band in the country. The Mighty Vikings garnered 2,411 votes; Carlos Malcolm's Afro-Jamaican Rhythms got 2,367. Byron Lee and The Dragonaires got 956; Tommy McCook and The Skatalites 273; The Granville Williams Orchestra 20; The Lennie Hibbert Combo 6.[18]

Groupings of outstanding artists usually run into problems, and Don Drummond's increasingly obvious mental problems only exacerbated the normal conflicts. Drummond murdered his girlfriend, famous rhumba dancer Margarita Mahfood, in January 1965 and later that year The Skatalites split up into two groups. Tommy McCook the saxo-phonist formed the Super-sonics and went to Duke Reid, while Coxsone kept Roland Alphonso and his setup the Soul Brothers. The Skatalites had been together less than 18 months, yet they created the best instrumentals in Jamaica's history – songs like 'Man In The Street', 'Eastern Standard Time' and 'Music Is My Occupation'.

Don Drummond

Many early ska hits were traditional folk tunes redone in the new style, most notably 'Penny Reel', 'Sammy Dead Oh' and 'Oil in My Lamp' by Monty Morris and 'Rukumbine' by Carlos Malcom. Tunes seemed easier to come by than lyrics, and more than a few ska hits had almost nonsensical words. As Timothy White pointed out, when it came to lyrics they threw in the kitchen sink: bush parish adages and proverbs, revivalist sermons, biblical verses, soap powder jingles, appliance pitches, movie posters and cereal-box ad-copy, front and sport page head-lines, obeah oaths, folk medicine recipes, snatches of political speeches and Rastafarian doctrine – nothing was off limits so long as it entertained and fit the beat.[19]

Live show promotions helped to establish the fledgling local recording industry as more than just a passing fad. In 1961 Byron Lee, Victor Sampson and Ronnie Nasralla formed a produc-tion company called Lee Enterprises Limited which promoted live shows around the country featuring a variety of local popular talent

Byron Lee Hits The North Coast!!

AGAIN
WITH HIS
GIGANTIC

"SKA
SPECTACULAR"

BYRON LEE
AND THE
DRAGONAIRES

"THE BAND WITH SOUL"
★ ★ ★ ★ ★ ★
GUEST ARTISTS
THE FABULOUS

BLUES BUSTERS
- ON THE BANDSTAND OF -
CLUB MARACAS - Ocho Rios
THIS SATURDAY NIGHT-20th MARCH '65-From 9.00 p.m.
A Swinging Dance Date - Don't Miss It!
Cover ∴ 10/-

PRINTED BY: ASSOCIATED PRINTERS LTD. 149 PRINCESS STREET, KINGSTON - PHONE 26061

musically supported by Byron Lee and The Dragonaires. Shows were held in the island's larger towns like Port Antonio, Port Maria, Old Harbour, Lucea, Grange Hill, Highgate, Spanish Town, Mandeville, Santa Cruz, Montego Bay and Savannah-la-Mar.

The tours started just after the Christmas festivities, when things were slow, and played in halls with a normal capacity of about 1,000. A group consisting of three to four members was paid between sixty and eighty pounds per night and a solo artist would be paid between thirty and forty pounds, less on a bad night. There were two other big promoters: Stephen Hill (who later moved on to manage Marvin Gaye) and Horace Forbes. But most artists pre-ferred working for Lee Enterprises because of their financial reliability.[20]

Three big groups of the pioneer years were The Gaylads, with 'Lady in a Red Dress' and 'Rub it Down'; The Jiving Juniors, whose members included Derrick Harriot and Count Prince Miller, with 'Lollipop Girl', 'Over The River' and 'Sugar Dandy'; and The Blues Busters with 'There's Always Sunshine' and 'Behold'. Duos were very popular – Martin and Derrick, Keith and Enid, Monty and Roy, Alton and Eddie, Stranger and Patsy, Derrick and Patsy, Roy and Millie, Bunny and Skully.

In 1962 there were a lot of big independence songs like 'Independent Jamaica' by Lord Creator, 'Forward March' by Derrick Morgan and 'Independence Is Here' by A.C.T. Joe.

The Gaylads

Other popular early songs included Monty Morris' 'Humpty Dumpty' and 'Money Can't Buy Life', Stranger Cole's 'Rough and Tough', Carlos Malcolm's 'Rukumbine', Desmond Dekker's 'Honour Your Mother and Father', and Baba Brooks' 'River Bank', The Maytals' 'Victory, Alleluia' and 'Six and Seven Books', Jimmy Cliff's 'Miss Jamaica' and 'King of Kings' and Owen Grey's 'Darling Patricia'. Jackie Opel was another early star. Owen Grey is said to be the first Jamaican to record an LP.[21]

Millie Small's 'My Boy Lollipop' (a remake of the 1957 Barbie Gay R&B hit) was the first ska record to make an international impact, being considered Jamaican even though it was cut in England. Its overseas success opened opportunities for Jamaican musicians, and many emigrated to London seeking recording contracts and steady work. Wilfred 'Jackie' Edwards, Owen Gray, Laurel Aitken, and Rico Rodríguez were some of the early pioneers who went abroad and virtually ceased to influence the development of music in Jamaica. Were it not for 'The Harder They Come', Jimmy Cliff might have shared their fate. Certainly his early work alone – pleasant and catchy but with no real depth – would not have ensured him reggae immortality.

Millie Small

He did not record an oustanding song until 'A Hard Road To Travel' in 1967.

One of the first instances of a Jamaican record being covered abroad was the Spencer Davis Group's remake of Jackie Edwards' 'Keep On Running'. Featuring 15-year-old Steve Winwood on keyboards and Chris Blackwell as producer, the song was a British hit. In England ska was sometimes known as Blue Beat, after the name of the foremost U.K. licensing label. But the term was never used in Jamaica.

1964 was the watershed year for Jamaican music. Before this ska was a young music without self-confident traditions. R&b still remained the primary model and provided the integral source material. But the flowering of The Maytals, whose classics like 'It's You', 'Pain in My Belly' and 'Dog War' bore unmistakable mento folk and gospel influences, heralded a new dawn. Here was music completely Jamaican in outlook and sound. Dealing with the realities of ghetto life, The Maytals' sound was clearly rooted in Jamaican rural traditions but completely modern in feeling. The Jamaican public had never heard anything which touched them quite so deeply and Toots and The Maytals became the most popular and biggest selling group Jamaica had ever known till then. If any one man can be said to have made Jamaican popular music a self-perpetuating entity, it is Toots Hibbert.

Yet groups like The Drifters and Impressions still remained the great influences on and main role models for Jamaican groups. The flip side of The Maytals' 'It's You' was an equally impressive but completely different sounding slow R&B tune called 'Daddy'. In fact The Maytals were advertised as the 'Daddy boys'. The Wailers followed up their smash ska hit 'Simmer Down' with the plaintive love ballad 'It Hurts To Be Alone'. They too were national sensations, appealing especially to the 'bad boy' side of ghetto youth with songs like 'Hooligan' and 'Rude Boy Ska'. Alton Ellis says The Wailers actually catered to and encouraged the 'rude boy' mentality.

Of course, The Maytals and Wailers were not the only ones making great music. Justin Hinds produced the superb 'Carry Go Bring Come' and other standouts included Monty Morris' 'Oil In My Lamp' and 'Sammy Dead Oh', Byron Lee's 'Jamaican Ska', Prince Buster's 'Wash Wash' and 'Wings Of A Dove', Roland Alphonso's 'Tear Up' and Don Drummond's beautiful 'Eastern Standard Time'. But ironically the best selling song of 1964 was Carlos Malcolm's 'Bonanza Ska', a ska version of the TV show theme song.

Music in the ghetto was disseminated primarily by record, but live music played a big part in ska's promotion uptown. The Glass Bucket Club and The Sombrero hosted Byron Lee and The Dragonaires and Carlos Malcolm and The Afro-Jamaican Rhythms while The Skatalites were a fixture at the Bournemouth Club in East Kingston. Other prominent local clubs of the time included Silver Slipper, Lins, Johnson's Drive-In, Club Parascene and Magnal House.[22] Traditional Christmas and Boxing Day morning concerts, started in the 1930s, still went on. (Shows like Sting perpetuate the tradition today). But ska now took the place of mento and folk music, with stage shows featuring the more popular bands backing chart topping singers.

The first attempt to market Jamaican music internationally was the brainchild of Minister of Culture (and record company owner) Edward Seaga. Ken Khouri, Paul Marshall, a New York lawyer, Ahmed Ertegun, president of Atlantic Records met at Federal Records and decided to send a promotional group to participate in the 1964 New York World Fair.

The tour was built around two songs by Monty Morris, 'Sammy Dead Oh' and 'Oil In My Lamp'. Ronnie Nasralla choreographed four dancers into an 'exciting demonstration' of ska. The singers consisted of Monty Morris, Jimmy Cliff, Prince Buster and The Blues Busters all backed by Byron Lee and The Dragonaires. The dance promotions apparently went well, Ronnie Nasralla reportedly turning down offers for a performing career. But ska didn't take off. For one thing, the recording quality was unacceptable to American ears.

There are conflicting stories about the circumstances surrounding the tour, particularly the decision to choose Byron Lee as the backing band. According to Coxsone: 'Seaga just board the bandwagon. They send people to represent the ska business who don't even know anything about it.'[23] Garth White makes this judgement: 'They chose wrongly. They left out The Skatalites and Bop and Persian in what seemed to be class bias. There was absolutely no way you could compare Byron Lee as representative of ska with The Skatalites, which was the top and most authentic band of the time.'[24] Jackie Mittoo was more matter of fact: 'They send Byron Lee because The Skatalites smoked ganja.'[25]

Byron Lee himself tells this story:'We (Byron Lee and The Dragonaires) were booked to appear at the Manhattan Centre. The government was planning this ska tour to the World's Fair and heard about our gig, so they asked us if we would back-up the singers since we were already going to be in New York. But we were never paid by the government. We played for free, to help promote ourselves and the music. So all this talk about us getting out The Skatalites is foolishness. Furthermore, at the time we were the number one live backing band in Jamaica. The Skatalites were fantastic in the studio, but they were never a popular live band. We were the backing band

Ronnie Nasralla, left, leading a ska demo in New York

for almost all the live shows. The artists used to ask for us and I got on well with all of them, and still do. We have been in the Jamaican music business for forty-two years. These people who talk about us not being representatives of the music, were they around then? It's true ska was not a dance at first. When we went to the world's fair there were dances all over the place. The Twist, Mashed Potato, Cha Cha Cha, plenty of them. In order to compete and sell our product, we Jamaicans had to have a dance too. That really is how the ska dance came about. In a sense it was Jamaican Twist.'[26]

Problems or not, those who made the effort deserve a lot of credit. The idea of an indigenous Jamaican music industry must have sounded as far fetched an idea then as the large-scale export of local TV programmes would today.

Ska's success overseas was sporadic, but Jamaican music at least established itself at home. Naturally some of the upper class establishment still sneered at this 'buff buff' music. A 1965

Gleaner review called ska 'an ephemeral craze', and asked dismissively: 'What, for example, will the word 'Skatalite' mean to the average Jamaican in a few years time?'[27]

But this was a minority view. Most Jamaicans had come to accept ska not only as their own music, but as something of worth. Byron Lee says it went beyond music: 'At first most of the artists used to copy foreign singers – Marcia Griffiths was Carla Thomas, Bob Marley and the Wailers were Curtis Mayfield and the Impressions, and Jimmy Cliff used to even copy Otis Redding's style of going down on the floor on his knees. Byron Lee and The Dragonaires were sort of a Jamaican Bill Haley and the Comets. Toots and the Maytals really were the first ones to start doing a pure Jamaican music. Eventually everyone started to write their own songs. I saw the transition as the backing band. At one time we were playing only American music, but it gradually changed until it was a Jamaican sound we were playing. It went further than just the music. Before this nobody supported anything local in Jamaica. They only respected something if it was foreign. But once ska became popular all over the island, Jamaicans started to respect other things Jamaican. The music really gave us national pride.'

Yet the sound of ska was shifting even as it cemented its hold on the popular imagination. The break-up of the Skatalites in 1965 (although their various re-combinations continued to provide excellent studio music) perhaps accelerated the process. But in Jamaica, as elsewhere, the times they were a-changing.

Get Ready for Rocksteady

This is Hopeton Lewis' story of how 'Take It Easy' was recorded: 'Lyn Taitt and The Jets was the backing band. I just couldn't keep time and kept singing slower than they were playing. So Mrs Khouri say to them "Well if him say slow it down, then slow it down. If him can't sing it fast then you must slow it down." Lyn Taitt was on guitar. A guy name Freddy was playing drums. Jackie Jackson was the bass player. Gladdy Anderson was on piano. Leslie Butler was in there too. And Ernie Ranglin. And then they slowed the rhythm down. And that's when I could sing within the context of the rhythm. And then I hear Gladdy say "This one rock steady you know. This one a rock steady." And that's when it came into being basically. This was October 1966.

'But I wouldn't consider myself the founder of rocksteady. It's a "buck up" thing really. People

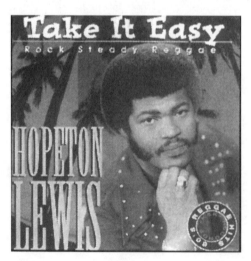

were always looking for a new rhythm with new dance steps. After rocksteady they had "pop a top" and all these different things. There was always a change trying to happen. This just happened to be a big change.'[1]

'Take It Easy' is generally accepted as the first 'rocksteady' song, although others have put forward claims for Roy Shirley's 'Hold Them', Derrick Morgan's 'Tougher Than Tough', Alton Ellis' 'Cry Tough' and 'Girl I've Got A Date', Peter Tosh's 'I'm The Toughest', and The Wailers' 'Put It On'. Alton Ellis' 'Come Do The Rocksteady' was probably the first song to use the actual word. But whether it was the earliest rocksteady tune or not, 'Take It Easy' definitely was the first rocksteady hit and was the song that established the sound.[2]

Of course there were other factors – a general change doesn't come from just one song or person. Bob Marley saw it this way: 'The guys who were in control robbed the older musicians, and they get frustrated and stop playing. So the musicians changed from the older musicians to the younger, hungrier ones who was coming up underneath them. People like I, we love James Brown and we dip into the American bag. We don't want to stand around playing and singing that ska beat anymore. The young musicians, dem have a different beat. It was rocksteady now, eager to go!'[3]

Rocksteady wasn't just slowed-down ska, because not all ska was uptempo music. (Grub Cooper points out that disco deejays have gotten into the habit of playing ska only at 'killdead' speed. So when original cuts are played at original speeds they often sound surprisingly slow.)[4] The major switch was from ska's profusion of percussive instruments, catchy guitar riff and abundance of horns to rocksteady's bold bass lines conveyed in a very laid back fashion. Hence (in another version) the name – you danced by 'rocking steady' in one place. The size of orchestra necessary to produce music also contracted, so production costs became cheaper and record creation more accessible. It's often said that horns disappeared from reggae about this time because they were too expensive. But that explanation is not entirely convincing because a much poorer country like Haiti continues to produce music in which horns are very prominent. Bob Andy gives another perspective: 'There was always tension

between wind and horn section players and singers. Maybe this was partly why singers eventually moved over to pure rhythms, because from that rocksteady era the horns have not been prevalent in our music. Of course

Bob Andy

there's the part about minimising costs. Horn players were always saying how many years they had to go through their discipline and singers could just come up and sing a song and maybe get royalties and make a name for themselves overnight, while they the horn players only get a session fee. But if songs were written to exclude them, and these are just my thoughts, part of the reason might be how difficult they were to get along with.'[5]

Coxsone Dodd has this insight into rocksteady: 'Rocksteady was more like a melodic rhythm. The bass would be playing a steady sort of a melody in the background. We tried to make it rocksteady with a real catchy beat and steady for dancing. Rocksteady was when we realised how important a steady catchy bass line was – just as important as the vocals.'[6]

Leroy Sibbles was an active participant in the mutation: 'Heptones sort of help to start rocksteady. All our songs were slow songs. Like "Ting A Ling" early. Our first album called "Heptones" had pure rocksteady sounding music. Maybe the name come from when they were doing "Take It Easy", but our music was always slower than the fast ska. Even "Fatty Fatty". We helped to change the whole thing from ska to rocksteady. Ska is more uptempo – uh UH uh UH uh UH – and we brought it down to gidgy gidgy boom, gidgy gigdy boom. And that's rocksteady. We brought it down a little slower and added something more to it. It was a little more subtle too and then it came down to one drop. Rocksteady means move steady when you dance.

'The times were responsible for the change from ska to rocksteady. Once upon a time rocksteady was in the air. Everybody is singing what they see and feel and hear and experience. Whenever revolution happens, everyone feels it, no matter where they are. I don't believe things are isolated. When they happen, they happen everywhere.'[7]

The original Heptones

The Jamaican music industry was growing and the number of performers expanded swiftly – groups like The Gaylads, Desmond Dekker and the Aces, The Paragons, and The Techniques emerged and singers like Alton Ellis, Bob Andy, Roy Shirley, Ken Boothe and Delroy Wilson came to the fore. As is usually with such a change, many previously popular performers fell by the wayside. But The Maytals and Wailers retained their pre-eminence.

The Festival Song Competition started in 1966, a contest which provided a vital impetus to the local music industry (at least until the mid-70s, when the contest's musical quality began to decline). The first winning song was The Maytals' 'Bam Bam', a timeless song, cover versions of which hit the charts in the 1970s, 80s and 90s. The contest produced at least two other reggae classics – 'Sweet And Dandy' by The Maytals in 1969, and 'Cherry Oh Baby' by Eric Donaldson in 1971 (later covered by The Rolling Stones and UB40 – interestingly Donaldson has won the contest seven times since those early days, most recently in 1997 with 'Peace and Love'). Other excellent songs were 'Unity' (not a winner) and 'Intensified Festival' by Desmond Dekker in 1967 and 1968 respectively and 'Pomps and Pride' by The Maytals in 1973.

Eric Donaldson performing in 1973 and, inset, laughing with Big Youth in 1997, perhaps about career longevity.

Songs increasingly reflected and commented on social realities of the day. The 'Rudie' mini-epoch was especially fruitful musically. Popular 'Rudie' songs included Desmond Dekker's 'Rude Boy Train', The Clarendonians' 'Rudie Gone a Jail' and 'Rudie Bam Bam', The Wailers' 'Jailhouse', Dandy Livingston's superb 'A Message to You Rudie', and many others. Derrick Morgan's 'Tougher Than Tough' summed up the 'rudie' attitude in one vivid line, 'Rudies don't fear'. (The 'bad boy' strain in current dancehall is clearly nothing new in reggae and merely reflects changing times. Guns for example have replaced ratchet knives.) Prince Buster recorded the admonishing 'Judge Dread' in response to this 'rudie' glorification.

The best and biggest 'rudie' song of all was Desmond Dekker and the Aces 'Shanty Town' in 1967. Alton Ellis was there: 'The bad boy business just sprang up in Jamaica and I couldn't appreciate what's happening. Like when I go to a little dance and want to enjoy myself them fling bottle bout the place and a lot of stupidness. So I write "Dance Crasher" – *Oh dance crasher don't break it up, please don't make a fuss, don't use a knife and take somebody else life.* After that was "Cry Tough" – *Don't you know you're getting old, how can a man be tough, tougher than the world* . . . The situation was confusing and upsetting, Trenchtown, the environment of the guys beginning to act like suddenly something change. Cause I usually walk miles to a dance, and now you scared and you think twice.

'So I was telling the young guys to lay off violence. Because it reach a point where the guys were going with lyrics like "rudie get taller", and "rudie cyan go a jail" and "rudie get bail". Then I got threatened a couple of times. Living in Trench Town and being in that environment amongst the people and being an artist – I'm easy to get at. So I tell Duke Reid I would refrain from singing these types of songs, because it was getting closer and closer to the edge. So I back off from that type of recording and go back to more loving sounds. But of course love is a fact too, and a serious fact.'[8]

Duke Reid's Treasure Isle label dominated the early rocksteady era. Alton Ellis, sometimes backed up by The Flames, released classics such as 'Girl I've Got a Date', 'I'm Just a Guy' and 'Just Another Girl'. John Holt and The Paragons had a string of hits, among them 'Memories By The Score', 'On The Beach', 'Wear You To The Ball', 'Happy Go Lucky Girl' and 'The Tide Is High'. ('The Tide Is High' was covered by Deborah Harris and Blondie in the 1980s and was a worldwide number one hit.) Slim Smith and The Techniques specialised in Curtis Mayfield and Impressions covers like 'Little Did You Know', 'Queen Majesty' (from 'Queen and Minstrel') and 'You Don't Care' (from 'You'll Want Me Back'). The Jamaicans hit with 'Things You Say You Love' and won the Festival Competition in 1967 with 'Ba Ba Boom'. Other big songs for Duke were Dobby Dobson's 'Loving Pauper' and Phylis Dillon's 'Don't Stay Away'.

Leslie Kong held his own with the likes of The Maytals, Derrick Morgan, and Desmond Dekker and The Aces. Byron Lee and The Dragonaires and The Mighty Vikings were the popular live bands, but the hit recordings of the period were done mainly by Duke Reid's Tommy McCook and The Supersonics. Alton Ellis, The Paragons and Techniques were all backed by this combination. Lyn Taitt who helped to fashion the very sound, worked between Sonia Pottinger's 'High Note' label and Duke Reid's 'Treasure Isle', as did Baba Brooks whose horn can be heard on many of The Techniques' hits. Roy Shirley actually mentioned Taitt by name on his 'Get On The Ball'.

Over at Studio One, Leroy Sibbles and The Heptones became headliners, their most memorable hit being the *not fit for airplay* 'Fatty Fatty'. As house bass guitarist, Sibbles played on most Coxsone bestsellers like The Cables' 'Baby Why'. Jackie Mittoo, a former

Skatalite, arranged most of Coxsone's music and often played organ. Mittoo had been taught piano and music reading by his grandmother and had joined Coxsone when only 15 in 1962. His organ led instrumental 'Ram Jam', a wordless version of 'Fatty Fatty', was a big chart hit. 'Full Up' was another big Studio One instrumental. (From 'Full Up' later emerged The Mighty Diamonds' 'Pass The Kutchie' and Musical Youth's big international hit 'Pass The Dutchie'.) Other hits for Coxsone were Ken Boothe's 'Puppet On A String' and 'The Train Is Coming', Delroy Wilson's 'Dancing Mood' and Bob Andy's 'I've Got To Go Back Home'. Andy's 'Song Book' was one of the era's classic albums.

Rocksteady's lyrics, as had mento's, both observed and commented on every aspect of contemporay life. The Ethiopians' 1968 hit 'Everything Crash' addressed the spate of strikes afflicting a country only six years independent – *Watermen strike, down to the policemen too* – and earned the dubious distinction of being perhaps the earliest Jamaican recording without sexually suggestive lyrics to be restricted from airplay. The Maytals' '54-46' combined both personal experience and scathing social commentary. Its searingly raw emotional recap of time spent in prison for supposed ganja possession made it one of the day's biggest hits and an immediate classic.

Many commentators feel that the rocksteady era was the most musically productive period in Jamaica's history, and it's certainly the most fondly remembered. Never before or since, some say, was music at the same time so melodically sweet, rhythmically engrossing and lyrically interesting. Yet it lasted less than three years. The winds of change were already blowing in 1968, and when The Maytals cut 'Do The Reggay' late that year, a new era was christened.

Do the Reggae

· ·

Toots Hibbert has never claimed to be reggae's inventor, even though he was the first to use the term in music and thus, for all intents and purposes, created the name on vinyl. As he tells it: 'Raleigh and me and Jerry were talking some nonsense one day and I just said, "Come on man, let's do the reggae." And later we decide to make a song out of that. It was just a word you would hear on the streets. I don't remember why I apply it to music. But reggae is just a name. Where music is concerned, reggae is a combination of communication. Cause within my music you have gospel, you have country and western, you have blues – a lot of different music goes together in my songs. And reggae means real music, music that tells a good story, music you can relate to, music you can make sense out of.

'At first reggae sort of mean untidy or scruffy. But then it start to mean like coming from the people. Everyday things. From the ghetto. From majority. Things people use everyday like food, we just put music to. Reggae mean regular people who are suffering, and don't have what they want.'[1]

Joe Higgs says 'reggae' came from 'streggae'. Others claim reggae meant ragged or street rough.[2] Certain creative musicologists would later trace the term to 'e rega', which supposedly means 'royal music' in Nigeria. Not being versed in Nigerian languages, Toots is unable to make the connection between the two.

Many observers single out Larry and Alvin's 'Nanny Goat' as the first 'reggae' sounding record. Others cite The Gaylads' 'ABC Rocksteady', The Paragons' 'Wear You To The Ball'

and The Heptones' 'Fatty Fatty'. (Interestingly a very reggae sounding beat can be heard on Don Drummond's 1965 instrumental 'Heavenless'.) According to Coxsone Dodd who produced 'Nanny Goat': 'I had been in England and came back with quite a few gadgets, like a delay, and we made "Nanny Goat". After that we had a series of recordings with the same sound. It was like the guitar on the delay meshed with the organ shuffle. That is where the change came from rocksteady to reggae. You can listen to the guitar change in "Nanny Goat" and quite a few of The Cables' tunes.' – and, he adds wistfully – 'Rocksteady is a beautiful music. You can dance to it, you can rock to it.'[3]

'Do The Reggay' still had a lot of rocksteady mannerisms, but emphasised new aspects of the rhythm. The bass became stronger and more emphatic, driving the beat. This allowed the drummer to play around it a bit more with rim shots and cymbal accents. The guitar was played in a loose, loping strum, with bright, emphasised chords on the head of the upbeat. But the upbeats didn't come as rapidly as in rocksteady. The overall pulse of Jamaican music had slowed again, although certain elements were played faster. The drive came from an unvarying two-chord pattern which provided a persistent counterpoint for the call and response of Toots' chant-like repetition and The Maytals' answering harmonies.[4]

As with ska and rocksteady, the ghetto discovered reggae first. When the music started gaining popularity outside western Kingston, there was confusion about the word's spelling. Following

Toots, uptowners like Byron Lee spelled it 'reggay' at first, but consensus came to rest with 'reggae'.[5] Ernie Ranglin comments: 'I did the lead guitar on the first reggae record, although we called it "raggay" then, because that was what the rhythm sounded like.'[6]

New producers like Bunny Lee, Lee Perry and Clancy Eccles were partly responsible for the shift in beat. Bunny Lee had worked for Duke Reid as salesman and dance promoter and ventured into production for the Caltone Label owned by Ken Lack, one-time road manager for The Skatalites. Perry had been Coxsone's unofficial house producer, supervising many sessions that turned out hits. According to Steve Barrow, Lee and Perry and Eccles couldn't always hire the best musicians, who continued to work for Dodd, Reid and the majors like Federal. So they often used less experienced musicians who were keen to make an impact – players like organist Glen Adams and drummer Leroy 'Horsemouth' Wallace, and bands like The Hippy Boys featuring brothers Carlton and Aston 'Family Man' Barrett. They had no trouble making a completely new rhythm – fast, chugging, tight – which soon got a name. The beat quickly established itself and the major producers of ska and rocksteady – Dodd, Reid, and Leslie Kong – were soon copying their former employees.[7]

In a sense reggae combines all the previous forms of Jamaican popular music – the ska riff on top of a slowed down rocksteady bass line with a dash of mento influence. Rastafarian influences were heard in increasingly pointed spiritual, social and political commentary. Lyrics called attention to the reality of Ghost Town, Denham Town, Trenchtown, Waterhouse. Some analysts have placed a lot of emphasis on this aspect of the music, claiming that 'Reggae is not just a music, more a philosophy, with the advice handed out to a danceable beat.' But history shows the core of Jamaican music is the 'riddim', not the meaning. How it sounds has always been more important than what it says.

Like most of the world's popular music, reggae is in 4/4 time – four beats to a bar of 4/4.

Clancy Eccles

Leslie Kong

However in almost all post-1960 Jamaican music the strongly felt 'downbeats', are not 1 & 3, but 2 & 4. This is one reason why reggae has had difficulty gaining acceptance among many Americans and Europeans, who are used to feeling the downbeat emphasis on 1 & 3 and commonly complain, 'I just don't know how to dance to reggae.'

The bass, reggae's most important instrument, assumed its unique significance in Jamaican music during rocksteady. The Jamaican predisposition for bass is clearly present in mento and predates the arrival of American records and electric instruments. This folk bass culture points to an aesthetic where rhythm takes priority over melody and harmony. The bass is a drum that plays a definite rhythm, but may or may not play a distinct melody line.[8]

In reggae's early days R&B instrumental groups like Booker T and The MGs and the New Orleans group, The Meters, were major influences. The themes from 'Spaghetti' western movies like 'The Good, The Bad and The Ugly' and 'Django' were also a big inspiration, and the spaciousness of Spanish composer Ennnio Moricone's scores had a lasting impact on dub. Reggae's embryonic period was as filled with instrumentals as the ska era had been. 1969's top sellers included The Sound Dimension's 'Musical Scorcher' and the follow-up 'More Scorcher', as well as Roland Alphonso's '1000 Tons of Megaton'.

With the smaller bands and hence lower entry costs, even more producers entered the fray, including Harry Johnson, Joe Gibbs and Harry Moodie. Lee Perry's group The Upsetters was the core of other aggregations like the Bunny Lee All-Stars, the Harry J All Stars, The J Boys and The Hippy Boys. Some old-timers like Byron Lee hung on, but the emphasis was on studio recording groups, which were always in flux. Two of the longer lasting bands to come out of this era were The Soul Syndicate and The Fabulous Five. Fab Five is still going strong today.

A revitalised Jamaican-English music connection appeared as British producers and performers discovered the lucrative West Indian market. Many Jamaican performers got their first taste of overseas experience with the 'Top Of The Pops' television show, among them Max Romeo, Pat Kelly, Bob [Andy] and Marcia [Griffiths], and The Upsetters. Reggae British chart hits included Lee Perry's 'The Return of Django', Bob and Marcia's version of 'Young, Gifted and Black',

Fab Five, more or less

Dave and Ansel's 'Double Barrel' and 'Monkey Spanner', 'How Long' by Pat Kelly, 'The Liquidator' (featuring Winston Wright on keyboard), Ken Boothe's 'Everything I Own' and Pluto Shervington's 'Dat'. Even The Beatles experimented with reggae in late 1968 with 'Ob La Di, Ob La Da'.

The biggest crossover hit of all was Desmond Dekker and The Aces' 1969 worldwide smash, 'Poor Me Israelites', Jamaican music's first significant international hit since 'My Boy Lollipop' in 1964. In 1967 Jimmy Cliff had made the British Top 40 with 'Wonderful World', another Leslie Kong production.

The fruitful years from 1969 to 1971 produced a host of classics like 'Duppy Conqueror', 'Trenchtown Rock', 'Sweet and Dandy', 'Pressure Drop', 'Cherry Oh Baby', and 'Rivers of Babylon'. Yet the most radical and influential song of all was U-Roy's huge 1970 deejay hit 'Wear You To Ball'. Sir Lord Comic had chatted on a rhythm in 'Ska-ing West' in 1966. And King Stitt had a deejay hit in 1969 with 'Fire Corner'. But these were soon forgotten novelties. U-Roy's toasting on Osborne 'King Tubby' Ruddock's dub plates proved more than a fad, and established deejay music as an integral part of Jamaican music.

At one stage in 1970 U-Roy had five records in the top ten. He held the top three spots on both local charts for weeks with 'Wear You To The Ball', 'Wake The Town' and 'Rule The Nation'. On all these songs U-Roy chanted in a

Desmond Dekker on BBC's Top of The Pops

U-Roy was hot in 1970

kind of call and answer arrangement with The Paragons over 'dubbed' instrumental tracks from late 1960s Treasure Isle rocksteady hits. 'Wear You To The Ball' by U-Roy and The Paragons, as the label read, was one of the biggest sellers in reggae history.

King Tubby's redubbings proved revolutionary in their own right. About this time producers began releasing 'versions', placing backing tracks minus the vocals on the 45 flip side. This was originally an economy measure – you could pay studio musicians to record one song and engineer two out of the deal. But other technicians soon picked up on Tubby's experiments with reverbs and remixes, and in time these studio manipulations gave birth to an entirely new branch of Jamaican music – dub. For a time in the late 1970s this bass-heavy instrumental music ruled the land of reggae and eventually had a worldwide impact. Many 1990s international dance music trends like house, techno, industrial and jungle can be traced back to the works of King Tubby, Lee 'Scratch' Perry, Augustus Pablo, Yabby You, Keith Hudson and the other pioneers of dub.

Scratch Perry's propitious combination with The Wailers was another major event of the early reggae era. They first met in 1969 on Orange Street, where most of the studios were located. (Orange Street was known as 'Beat' Street – *Orange Street is the music street / It's the street that sells the beat*, sang Prince Buster in 'Earthquake' in 1968.) 'Beat' Street's high concentration of talent made for many such happy, accidental encounters. In its musically saturated atmosphere artists exchanged and fed off each other's ideas

Dub pioneers: Lee Perry, above, Pablo Moses, top right, and King Tubby

on a daily basis, and this 'hot house' effect accelerated Jamaican music's astonishingly rapid development.

At this time The Wailers had just returned from a European tour with Johnny Nash. In Lee Perry they found a creative producer who afforded them the musical freedom they needed as they drifted towards Rastafarianism and a new, unexplored confidence. Perry's profusion of odd percussion instruments combined with The Wailers' writing talents to create the precursor of the sound that would carry Bob Marley to international stardom. The partnership created the LPs 'Soul Rebels', 'Soul Revolution', 'Soul Revolution II' and 'African Herbsman'. The latter contains the original versions of 'Trenchtown Rock', 'Duppy Conqueror', 'Small Axe', 'Lively Up Yourself' and 'Kaya' plus a medley of The Wailers' Studio One hits and is arguably the strongest collection of Marley songs ever put on one album.

Meanwhile, Toots and The Maytals recorded the outstanding 'Funky Kingston' LP. New stars like Nicki Thomas, Horace Andy, Lorna Bennett and Eric Donaldson climbed the reggae hierarchy. Donaldson, with a unique styling and vocal range, captured the Festival Song in 1971 with 'Cherry Oh Baby', probably the biggest selling record in Jamaica's history. Another big hit was John Holt's 'Stick By Me', a cover of a Shep & The Limelights R&B oldie, produced by Bunny Lee. And the 'Grounation' album by Count Ossie and his group, The Mystic Revelation of Rastafari, proved a very significant record.

Another reggae substream was the 'pop reggae' of performers like Ernie Smith, Pluto Shervington, Zap Pow, Fab Five and Third World, which was primarily popular

DOPPY CONQUER
(B. Marley)

MONO

Irving Music
Inc. BMI
Total–3:21

7309
(45 565090)

Produced by
Lee Perry

BOB MARLEY AND
THE WAILERS

with the 'uptown' rich and middle classes. Ernie Smith, in particular, became one of Jamaica's most popular performers with chart toppers like 'Ride On Sammy', 'Bend Down', 'One Dream' and 'Pitta Patta'. He also wrote and produced Ken Lazarus' 'Hail The Man.' Smith's song 'Life is Just For Living' became a memorable commer-

cial for Red Stripe beer. Possessing a rich, baritone voice, he also had non-reggae hits like 'Footprints on The Ceiling', 'Sunday Morning Coming Down' and 'Tears On My Pillow'. When Smith performed as the opening act for the Johnny Nash Show at the New Kingston hotel he was as popular as any performer in Jamaica and many thought he was the man who would make Jamaican music popular overseas.

Fab Five incidentally was the first reggae band to play on an international hit LP. They backed-up six cuts on Johnny Nash's gold album 'I Can See Clearly Now', which included the Bob Marley compositions 'Stir It Up', 'Guava Jelly', 'More Questions Than Answers' and 'Comma, Comma'. Even before that Fab Five's Frankie Campbell and Grub Cooper had been the first Jamaican group to play reggae in Europe: 'We were called The Reggaes, so I guess you could say we were the world's number one reggae band!'[9]

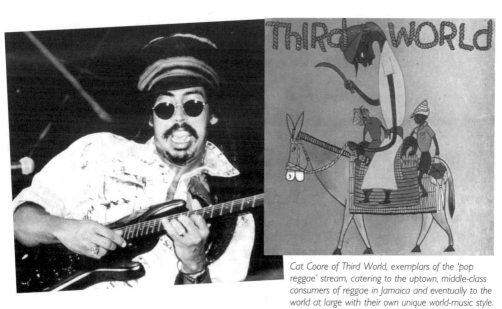

Cat Coore of Third World, exemplars of the 'pop reggae' stream, catering to the uptown, middle-class consumers of reggae in Jamaica and eventually to the world at large with their own unique world-music style.

Reggae International

••

THE HARDER THEY COME AND BOB MARLEY

1972 was a landmark year in politics and music. The People's National Party (PNP) used popular hit songs in their election campaigning, notably Delroy Wilson's 'Better Must Come' and Max Romeo's 'Let The Power Fall On I'. PNP strategists also formed the 'Musical Bandwagon' – a group of popular performers who travelled around the island playing at PNP rallies. Later Third World guitarist David 'Cat' Coore (son of the PNP government's deputy Prime Minister David Coore) remembers: 'Inner Circle were doing the Bandwagon for the PNP – we backed nuff artists like Dennis Brown, Alton Ellis, The Chosen Few, Scotty, Tinga Stewart, Judy Mowatt . . . The election was February '72, but the Bandwagon started about October '71. We played two, three times during the week and at least once on the weekend.'[1]

Bob and Rita Marley also played on the 'Bandwagon' for a few weeks, although they left for England before the elections.[2] Whether because of the music or not, the Michael Manley led PNP swept to a historic victory.

Perry Henzell's movie 'The Harder They Come' was also released in 1972. Other than Bob Marley, this movie was probably the single most powerful purveyor of reggae internationally. It's an excellent film, giving a clear-eyed view of the realities of the Jamaican recording industry and prevailing social conditions in the country.

The sound track featured four of Jimmy Cliff's outstanding songs – 'Many Rivers To Cross', 'The Harder They Come', 'You Can Get It', and 'Sitting In Limbo'. It also included Toots and The Maytals' superb 'Sweet and Dandy' and 'Pressure Drop', plus classics like Desmond Dekker's 'OO7/Shanty Town', The Slickers' 'Johnny Too Bad', The Melodians' 'Rivers of Babylon', and Scotty's 'Draw Your Brakes'. It was the best album Jamaica ever produced, and before Bob Marley's posthumous 'Legend', the biggest selling.

The movie revived interest in Jimmy Cliff the singer. Living and working in Europe for a number of years, Cliff had lost contact with the Jamaican scene. But his 1970 version of Cat Steven's 'Wide World' was popular here and proved a creeping preparation for 'The Harder They Come'. American Johnny Nash, whose pseudo-reggae 'Hold Me Tight' was a big international hit in the late 1960s, had another smash in 1972 with 'I Can See Clearly Now'. The Wailers' Tuff Gong label was also doing well with hits like 'Screw Face' and 'Lively Up yourself'.

Yet Dennis Brown was probably 1972's star performer, with songs such as 'Baby Don't You Do It', 'Silhouettes', 'If I Follow My Heart', 'What About the Half' and 'Money In My Pocket'. A former child prodigy, Brown

Child prodigy Dennis Brown

had developed a commanding new sound and was to prove the most durable and prolific singer in reggae history. Over 20 years and 70 albums later, he remains one of the music's most popular artists. One of the year's top selling songs was the dub instrumental 'Merry Up' by Glen Brown and The Godsons. Other popular tunes were Ken Boothe's 'Silver Words', Pluto Shervington's 'Ram Goat Liver' and Sang Hue and the Lionaire's 'Rasta No Born Ya'.

1973 was the deejay Big Youth's year. Like U-Roy before him, he swept the charts and once had five songs in the top ten. During one stretch different Big Youth songs topped the charts for three straight months. His 'S90 Skank', celebrating the Honda S90 motorcycle created a new dance sensation, and he dominated radio airwaves and sound systems with other hits like 'Chi Chi Run' and 'Cool Breeze'. His

outstanding album was 'Screaming Target' which, like many songs of the day, was named after a movie. U-Roy had given deejays musical credibility; Big Youth established them as social commentators – 'talking gleaners' – and was the biggest local artist until about 1975.

Around Easter 1973 The Wailers released 'Catch A Fire', their first album for Island Records. It was perhaps the first reggae album conceived as a seamless unit and not just a collection of singles arranged around hits. Here for the first time Jamaicans were making music with a foreign audience in mind. Indeed the studio tape of 'Concrete Jungle', the album's opening song, was taken to England and a long guitar solo was added to make the 'product' more accessible to a white rock audience. And while traditional reggae songs were taut and trim three-minute affairs, five of the album's nine cuts were four minutes or longer, allowing The Wailers to cut loose on songs like 'Stir It Up' (all of 5:30).

Dub poet Linton Kwesi Johnson wrote years later of the album's effect: '. . . a whole new style of Jamaican music has come into being. It has a different character, a different sound . . . what I can only describe as 'International Reggae'. It incorporates international elements from popular music: rock and soul, blues and funk. These elements facilitated a breakthrough on the international market . . . Instead of concentrating exclusively on a bottom-heavy sound with emphasis on drum and bass, you had on this

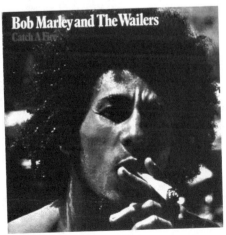

record more of a 'toppy' mix, a lighter sound. The emphasis is more on the guitar and other fillers. No other Jamaican reggae recording . . . had such a clear-cut attempt made to incorporate the modern electronic sounds of metropolitan music.'[3]

Not surprisingly 'Catch A Fire' made little if any impact in Jamaica. Some claim The Wailers refused to release it locally until the heavy bass bottom was mixed in again.[4] Only in hindsight would 'Catch A Fire' be recognised as the beginning of a new era in reggae.

By now The Wailers were a self-contained band, the Barrett Brothers having joined Peter, Bunny and Bob. This ensemble went on promotional tours of England and the U.S., opening in U.S. for Sly and The Family Stone. But Sly fired them because, so it is said, The Wailers were stealing the show. The Wailers' live shows also changed the way reggae music was performed. Stage shows in the past had been a series of tight sets roughly reproducing the vinyl contents live. To Marley's band records became merely points of departure and songs were recreated on stage with long instrumental interludes, vocal improvisation, guitar solos and other features that had long been rock concert staples. When other Jamaican performers went into the international arena, they followed suit.

Bob Marley and The Wailers, as they were soon styled, were rapidly becoming the biggest name in reggae and their subsequent studio albums came to define the decade of the seventies – 'Burnin' (1974), 'Natty Dread' (1975), 'Rastaman Vibration' (1976), 'Exodus' (1977), 'Kaya' (1978), 'Survival' (1979), and 'Uprising' (1980). Each release was eagerly anticipated and fans studied the latest album carefully. And just as many in North America defined the 1960s as the period between Beatlemania and 'Let It Be', so too a lot of Jamaicans saw the 1970s as beginning in retrospect with 'Catch A Fire' and ending with Bob's death in 1981.

'Burnin' was the last collaborative effort between Bob, Peter and Bunny and the only album to feature an outside contributor –

Bunny's girlfriend Jean Small composed 'Hallelujah Time' and 'Pass It On'. Picking up where 'Catch A Fire' left off, 'Burnin' suffered slightly from its inconsistent song quality. Yet it still featured the old classics 'Small Axe' and 'Duppy Conqueror' as well as future standards like 'Get Up Stand Up' and 'I Shot The Sheriff'. Eric Clapton released a version of 'Sheriff' which topped both the U.S. and British charts and helped in no small way to establish both Marley and reggae as forces to be reckoned with worldwide.

'Natty Dread', Bob's first 'solo' album, was an unqualified masterpiece and perhaps his finest album. Its cohesiveness of vision and execution more than made up for the loss of Peter's and Bunny's artistic contributions. It was a continuous tour de force in which every track crackles with the energy of a liberated artist free to chart his own creative destiny. It was received with tumultuous praise in Jamaica, and never before or since has any album been so unanimously admired here.

Bob's long-time Jamaican fans felt that 'Rastaman Vibration' tilted a little too far towards foreign tastes. Nevertheless it was well-received by critics worldwide, making many top ten lists. 'Rastaman Vibration' essentially retraced the footsteps of 'Natty Dread' and evinced little artistic growth. None of its cuts was a failure, but other than 'War' which is perhaps as good a song as Marley ever wrote, the material was not quite up to the standard of its predecessor.

'Exodus' was a triumph. As well as a worldview at once assertive, millenarian and optimistic, the album revealed an expansive musical vision. While the title cut was a martial worldbeat-influenced jam, 'Three Little Birds' and 'One Love' were simple reggae melodies, 'Waiting In Vain' and 'Turn Your Lights Down Low' roots soul ballads, and 'Heathen' a Rastafarian 'grounation chant' evocation. Much of what Bob had previously hinted at came to fruition here as he expanded reggae's boundaries in the full flowering of his talent. This eclectic collection, although not as focused as 'Natty

Dread', possibly represents his strongest work musically.

'Kaya' saw a creative retreat. Its lack of stridency was a disappointment to many – *Rolling Stone* critic Lester Bangs dismissed it as 'weakheart reggae'. But in retrospect 'Kaya', while not his best work, showed another side of Bob which celebrated the herb, love, and Jah's creation. Its introspective meditation was understandable in light of Marley's close brush with death in December 1976 when he survived an assassination attempt. Yet significantly the album ended with 'Time Will Tell', suggesting that even in the midst of reverie he was still aware of life's continuing struggles.

With 'Survival' Bob returned to his old militancy, this time on behalf of African nationalism and the concomitant struggle of oppressed people everywhere. It is his most overtly 'political' album and many European and North American critics found it didactic, feeling that the music had been lost in the message. Yet elsewhere it touched a chord, for here Marley was speaking directly to his African brethren. 'Survival', more than any other album, made Marley an idol of third world revolutionary struggle.

'Uprising' was Marley's swan song, resembling 'Exodus' in philosophy and scope. It saw a return to a wide and varied musical vision, from the disco oriented 'Could You Be Loved' to the hard-core reggae of 'Bad Card' and the acoustic balladry of 'Redemption Song'. It was both a critical and commercial success.

Marley also released two concert albums, 'Live' in 1974 and 'Babylon By Bus' in 1978. The former is widely considered one of the finest live albums in pop music history and contains the definitive version of 'No Woman No Cry'. It was also an international commercial breakthrough and Marley's first album in which sales were commensurate with critical acclaim. 'Babylon By Bus' on the other hand is perhaps Marley's weakest Island LP, with no definitive version of any song. 'Confrontation', the posthumous 1982 work consisted mostly of outtakes from previous projects. 'Legend' attempted the impossible and tried to capture Bob Marley's essence on one album. It did not quite succeed, but nevertheless introduced Marley to millions of new fans and in time became one of the most popular catalogue albums in any music genre.

Chris Blackwell's role in Bob's commercial success has to be acknowledged. Way back in the early 1960s he had seen reggae's potential outside Jamaica. And what he really gave Marley was financial and artistic independence, the freedom to realise his complete musical vision. As Bob later said, Island Records had global clout yet was small enough to allow regular contact with decision makers.

Blackwell actively courted the rock press in his attempt to make reggae 'the next big thing', even bringing in disc jockeys from North America for the launching of 'Catch A Fire'. He employed the best designers in creating the record jacket. The original 'Catch A Fire' album package, in the form of a metallic-blue zippo cigarette lighter which opened to reveal its flame, is a masterpiece of album art. In the charismatic, dreadlocked, half-white Marley he discerned a highly marketable persona who European and North American audiences could embrace as a 'third world' Jimi Hendrix. But little could Blackwell have imagined that Bob Marley would become one of the 20th century's outstanding cultural icons.

Dub and Roots

• •

Politics, music and culture are inextricably intertwined in Jamaica. When the conservative Jamaica Labour Party (JLP), which had ruled since independence in 1962, was replaced by the socialist People's National Party (PNP) in 1972, the entire outlook of the country changed. In very short order Jamaica's traditional pro-western perspective was supplanted by a non-aligned third world stance. Afrocentricity, black consciousness, Rastafarian theology and militant anti-imperialist solidarity all informed a new national zeitgeist.

The 1971 movie 'The Harder They Come' hardly touched on Rastafarianism. And though performers had sometimes adopted Rastafarian beliefs and habits, before 1973 there were virtually no dreadlocked reggae acts. Yet by the end of the 1970s, all the significant reggae performers had sung the praises of Rastafarianism, if indeed they had not actually adopted the faith. The first reggae star to sport dreadlocks on stage was Big Youth. Frankie Campbell remembers what was in retrospect a defining moment not only in reggae, but in Jamaican cultural history: 'It was at the Joe Frazier Revue at Carib Theatre in 1973 that Big Youth first flashed his locks on stage. And it was like everybody's jaw just dropped. People just marveled at what they were seeing.'[1]

And no wonder. Ever since the movement's beginnings in the 1930s the Jamaican establishment and bourgeoisie had

scorned Rastafarians as the 'dregs' of society. After the 1963 Coral Gardens 'uprising' in western Jamaica, where militant Rastafarians violently confronted police, Rastas were commonly vilified as low life criminals. But here, a decade later, the biggest musical celebrity in the land, a man idolised and imitated by the young of all classes, was consciously glorying in the most visible badge of resurgent Rastafarian pride. It was as if a dam had burst, and in seemingly a matter of months, music artists everywhere were 'locksing' on stage, including U-Roy, Third World and later Burning Spear.

The most prominent Rastaman of all time was of course Bob Marley, who was especially identified with by rebellious upper- and middle-class youth. But in 1973 Bob was no 'locksman'. Indeed one can almost trace the growth of his hair through his album record covers. On his last pre-Island album, 'African Herbsman', Marley sported an afro. The promo shots for the 1973 'Catch A Fire' album reveal Bob's locks in bud. 'Burnin' shows his 'picky dreads' still under development. It is not till the aptly named 'Natty Dread' that the leonine locks, so integral a part of the corporate Marley image, are seen in full bloom.

As the prevailing political outlook became more anti-imperialist and socialist, identification with liberation movements, especially left-leaning African ones, became the vogue. The

Channel One Studio band named themselves The Revolutionaries. Their 1976 album featured Che Guevera on the cover and such songs as 'MPLA' (Popular Movement for the Liberation of Angola), 'Angola', 'Che' and 'PLO'.

About this time Burning Spear rejoined the music scene. Spear's initial efforts at Studio One in 1969 had been disappointing – Coxsone Dodd had tried to mould them into a conventional harmony trio. So they simply turned their backs on commercial music and returned to farming in the hills of St Ann. But in 1975 they teamed up with Ocho Rios sound system operator 'Jack Ruby' Lindo and recorded 'Marcus Garvey', an album which many still regard as reggae's finest. With Winston Rodney (who later became Burning Spear) soaring on lead vocal and Rupert Wellington and Delroy Hines chanting in harmony, 'Marcus Garvey' was an unsurpassed statement of forthright black pride.

Like later Burning Spear albums, it drew on childhood experiences, Jamaican folklore and Rastafarian theology. The songs were not lyrically complex and were essentially based on a few phrases chanted and repeated in an almost mantric fashion. Underneath swirled a propulsive rhythm created by the crack session band of Robbie Shakespeare, 'Family Man' Barrett and 'Horsemouth Wallace'. The result was a hypnotic sound never before heard in Jamaica. Toots Hibbert's spare lyrics and gospel charged delivery had preceded 'Marcus Garvey' – 'Bam Bam' and 'Pressure Drop' had already used the same devices to powerful effect. But Burning Spear was more obviously political and championed black consciousness with such titles as 'Marcus Garvey', 'Slavery Days' and 'Red Gold And Green'.

'Spear' did not invent the biblically themed, Afrocentric 'roots reggae' sound. As far back as 1969 The Abyssinnians had cut the seminal 'Satta Massagana'. But Burning Spear's unaffected, folkloric chanting gave an electrifying resonance to the spirit of the times. He would prove second only to Marley in his influence on

Winston Rodney, aka Burning Spear, was to become a one-man music-industry.

reggae in the 1970s, for after him came a flowering of 'roots' performers. The Mighty Diamonds, Ras Michael and The Sons of Negus, Culture, Wailing Souls, The Meditations, The Congoes, The Itals, Israel Vibration, The Royal Rasses, and even Gregory Isaacs can all in a sense be considered disciples of Burning Spear.

But while the ethos of reggae was shifting, the business side of music in Jamaica was also undergoing fundamental change. Recording facilities were becoming cheaper and more widely accessible, with a resulting proliferation of producers and releases. Quality began to suffer as

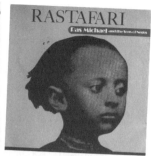

songs were rushed into the marketplace. As a producer remarked 'If you feel you can get a hit by paying four or five musicians and a deejay or singer for a half-hour's work, you are going to at least try.' Kingston studios were now pushing out between three and four dozen releases a week, probably the most per capita in the world.

This easy access to studio facilities coupled with deteriorating economic and social conditions brought a tinge of desperation to the business. Even more so than before uneducated and unemployed ghetto youth saw music as their only possible financial salvation. Roman Stewart's 1975 'Natty Sings Hit Songs' gave a pleading expression to this feeling: *I get up every day, and look into the world / I see big cars, I see pretty girls / I'd be a better man if I get money in my hand / Help me O Jah, I want to come on strong, I want to sing a hit song.*

So many tunes were being cut that outlets were swamped and radio stations were unable to give all of them a fair hearing. The competition for chart songs grew vicious and media employees were threatened. Even Alan 'Skill' Cole, Bob Marley's friend and erstwhile manager, later admitted to such behaviour.[2] In 1974 radio stations discarded their weekly musical charts and they stayed out of charting sales performance for over three years.

But even in these changing times, class remained class. And reggae in the mid-1970s produced no better songs than Toots and The Maytals' 'In The Dark' and The Heptones' 'Book Of Rules'. But about this time The Heptones, one of the greatest Jamaican vocal groups, broke up when lead singer Leroy Sibbles

emigrated to Canada. The group Inner Circle also split, bringing forth another version of Inner Circle and a new group, Third World led by Michael 'Ibo' Cooper and David 'Cat' Coore. Third World signed with Island Records and inherited much of the freedom The Wailers enjoyed. Inner Circle, now based in Miami, and Third World are both still going strong.

In 1975 the Hookim brothers opened their Channel One studio on Maxwell Avenue in Kingston. Their session musicians, led by drummer Lowell 'Sly' Dunbar and bassist Robbie Shakespeare, created the Channel One sound that would dominate reggae in the late 1970s. Later known as The Revolutionaries, although they also recorded for other producers under the names The Professionals and The Mercenaries, these musicians developed a winning formula known as 'rockers'. Often called 'The Skatalites of the seventies', they had many hits with re-recorded and retitled Skatalite compositions and also recorded new versions of many Studio One rocksteady and reggae hits.

Sly and Robbie outside the Channel I studios

The dub phenomenon reached its apotheosis in this period. Since the early 1970s the B-side of Jamaican 45s had mostly consisted of instrumental tracks of the A-side with vocals removed. These 'dub' instrumentals with their deepened bass line caught the public's fancy. There was a time when some dances played strictly dub instrumentals, with extreme dub afficionados threatening to 'mash down' the place if any A-side vocals were played. The 12-inch 45 (the 'disco 45') combined everything – the original song followed by dub and deejay version – and became the popular format of choice. The 1976 hit 'Ya Ho' by The Jays and Ranking Trevor was perhaps the first disco 45 hit. Other classics of the genre were 'Queen Majesty' by The Jays and Ranking Trevor, 'My Number One' by Gregory Isaacs and Trinity and 'How Could I Leave' by Dennis Brown and Prince Mohammed.

Former leader of The Jamaicans, Tommy Cowan turned to producing and one of his prominent artists was the rising star Jacob Miller. As lead singer with Inner Circle he became known for powerful, live sets which rose above the weakness of their recorded output. At the 1978 Peace Concert, perhaps the greatest ever collection of reggae performers, Jacob Miller and Inner Circle easily stood shoulder to shoulder with Peter Tosh and Bob Marley as the night's best performers. Miller never got the chance to fulfil what seemed like unlimited potential, for in 1979 he died tragically young in a car crash.

Winston 'Niney The Observer' Holness was also a major producer of the era, making hits like Dennis Brown's 'Westbound Train' and Ken Boothe's 'Silver Words'. Producer Joe Gibbs, newly ensconced in a modern studio on Retirement Crescent, used many of the Channel One musicians to create his own rockers and enjoyed success in 1976 with the vocal group Culture and the deejay Prince Far I. In 1977 Gibbs topped the UK charts with female deejay duo Althea and Donna's 'Uptown Top Ranking'. Two other big songs of the era were Leroy Smart's 'Ballistic Affair' in 1976 and The Meditations' 'Woman Is Like A Shadow' in 1977.

Jamaica's violent political troubles of the late 1970s spawned songs like Ernie Smith's 'Jah Kingdom Go To Waste', Max Romeo's 'War

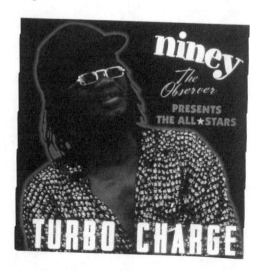

Inna Babylon' and Junior Murvin's 'Police and Thieves'. The apocalyptic tenor of the times found perhaps its most vivid expression in Cultures' 'Two Sevens Clash'. On 7 July, 1977, many Jamaicans stayed at home, fearing to venture outside lest the song's evocation of Marcus Garvey's dire warnings for the 7/7/77 be fulfilled. Sly and Robbie vied with Roots Radics for top rhythm making honours, and new producers like Prince Jammy, Henry 'Junjo' Lawes, his associate Jah Life, and deejay turned producer Jah Thomas competed for record sales.

Sly and Robbie relaunched their Taxi label in 1978 and quickly scored a hit with Gregory Isaacs, the 'cool ruler' who had become the big-gest solo artist in Jamaica. Isaacs' 'Soon Forward' was followed by hits from a new vocal trio, Black Uhuru, who Prince Jammy had discovered in the Waterhouse section of Kingston (dubbed Firehouse by The Wailing Souls). Black Uhuru had a series of hits with Taxi and signed up with Island in 1980, cutting several big selling albums until their break-up in the middle of the decade.

They were for a time reggae's most important act. They won the first reggae Grammy Award with 'Anthem' in 1983, and *Rolling Stone* named 'Red' one of the best albums of the 1980s.

The Wailers' success abroad had made it fashionable for foreign artists like Paul Simon and Eric Clapton to record in Jamaica, while English and American record companies began searching for the next Bob Marley. Their representatives were signing Jamaican acts almost as fast as they could clear

customs. Foremost among these 'searchers' was Virgin Records supremo Richard Branson who, legend has it, came with a briefcase full of money and gave on-the-spot signing bonuses. Chris Black-well had built Island into the largest indepen-dent record company in the world in the late 1960s and early 1970s, and Branson would do the same with Virgin in the late 1970s and early 1980s. With the whole panorama of world music before him, Branson seized upon reggae as a potential gold mine, creating the Front Line label specifically for reggae. Among the artists he signed were The Gladiators, The Mighty Diamonds, U-Roy, Gregory Isaacs, Prince Far I, Big Youth, The Twinkle Brothers, The Abyssinians and Culture.

But foreign blessings were decidedly mixed for reggae artists; many contracts were short-term, covering only one or two albums. Rumour had it that some performers were signed only after agreeing to become dreadlocks, and some who refused were not.

Bob Andy, a Rastafarian him-self, gives some insight into the fashion of the times: 'I was one of those who got lost when Bob Marley became famous. The music went in a Marley direction, and if you weren't looking and sounding and behaving like Marley and Tosh at that time, well . . . I'm not one to follow anybody.'[3]

Frankie Campbell and Grub Cooper of Fab Five tell of their experience: 'Chris Blackwell once wanted to sign us. But only under two conditions. One was that we change the band's name to 'Grub'. That was no problem. But he also wanted us to grow locks and adopt a "roots" image, but we couldn't see with that. It just didn't seem right to pretend to be something we weren't just to sell records.'[4]

Bob Marley's unprecedented success overseas changed the outlook of many Jamaican artists. Their main goal was no longer to make local hits, but to get an international record deal. The music became increasingly formulaic, repetitive and devoid of the animating life force that had made it the sweetest sound on earth. The emphasis was no longer on the 'riddim' but on 'conscious lyrics'. Reggae became a music you listened to, preferably while enveloped in a cloud of sensemilla smoke, rather than one you sang and danced to. Reggae had gone international, but sometimes seemed to have sold its soul.

From its very beginnings Jamaican music has been primarily rhythmically based. The words to a song didn't matter much, but the beat had to be danceable. There have been a lot of number one tunes in Jamaica using nonsensical nursery rhyme based lyrics. As long as the beat was sweet and the words weren't so pretentiously ridiculous as to set you laughing while you sang them, nobody cared. It wasn't what was said, it was how it sounded.

Bob Marley changed all that. For the first time reggae had found a singer whose lyrics were so striking that sometimes you stopped dancing and actually listened to the words. And as he grew more sophisticated and confident of his craft, there was a subtle shift in his music. Rhythm and melody were slowly pushed into the background until lyrics and harmony came to almost completely dominate.

In a word, he intellectualised reggae. And while Bob's splendid talent for melody remained with him throughout and made even his most preachifying and didactic songs danceable and singable, many of his imitators lacked this genius. And in their hands reggae

Yellowman

music often seemed like endlessly repeated statements of 'Remember Marcus Garvey Haille Sellassie Rastafari Fire Pon Babylon Free South Africa, etcetera, etcetera' over soporific, metronomic guitar beats.

Worst of all, many singers lost touch with the everyday concerns of the common man. Rastafarianism and its concerns remained fascinating to outsiders, but its direct appeal to Jamaicans, never that deep or broad, began to fade. Many of the era's sensational selling 'of the moment message songs', like Fred Locks' 'Black Star Liner', now sound dated. Foreigners might be satisfied just listening to 'consciousness', but Jamaicans wanted music they could dance to as well. Roots reggae still had its place, but it became increasingly obvious that it was made with a primarily overseas audience in mind.

And at home reggae found a new set of champions, the deejays. Scorned and reviled they might be for being slack, crude and unmusical in the traditional sense, but it was the deejays who increasingly spoke to the masses. Dillinger, Trinity, Ranking Trevor, U Brown and others had continued the traditions of U-Roy and Big Youth through the late 1970s. And in 1979 the dj duo 'Michigan and Smiley' breathed a new vitality into the sound. For over four years they 'niced up' Jamaica with a string of hits like 'Rub A Dub Style', 'Nice Up The Dance' and 'One Love Jamdown'. When the albino sensation Yellowman completely captured the imagination of the 'massives' with his fearlessly aggressive chanting in the early 1980s, it became clear that deejaying was no longer a 'cult' or 'novelty' which had to take a backseat to 'serious' reggae singing. Deejay music, like ska in the early days, had developed from a crude, almost experimental sound into an arresting experience. And it was given a name – dancehall.

Inna the Dancehall

· ·

Sugar Minott began singing for Coxsone in the mid-1970s. In the late 1970s he formed his own sound system called Youthman Promotion, which he used to promote ghetto talent. Vocalists, including Sugar, would sing 'live' over rhythm track acetates played by the sound system. Steve Barrow says that Sugar Minott's productions, both of himself and singers like Little John, were the the first to be called 'dancehall' music.[1]

Howard McGowan, a leading Jamaican music columnist, gives this convincing version of events: 'In 1983, Michael Thompson, head of Inner City Promotions, coined a show "Dancehall 83". Held at the Harbour View drive-in cinema, it featured the hot deejays of the era such as Yellowman, Charlie Chaplin and General Trees, as well as singers. The particular manner in which this event was marketed caught the attention of the downtowners, the real dance goers, and it almost flattened the venue. A massive crowd turned out, and those of us with experience in the business knew a chord had been struck.

'Because of the impact and success of Inner City's "Dancehall 83", the name "dancehall" started popping up on several shows and dance posters. And

the label went over to the Thursday night segment of "Reggae Sunsplash", which featured mostly deejays and was really starting to gain momentum. A year later Sting, fashioned closely along this line, was born. Because deejay songs virtually ruled the dancehalls, the music played there became known as "dancehall". Soon dancehall no longer meant a place where dances were held, but rather the dominant music form of the day, be it deejays or singers on a popular rhythm.'[2]

A new era had dawned in Jamaican music, where the deejay, not the singer, was king. To be sure a number of vocalists flourished in the dancehall. Singers like Leroy Smart, Beres Hammond, Barrington Levy, Freddie McGregor, Frankie Paul, Carlene Davis, Marcia Griffiths, Half Pint and Coco Tea produced good music through the 1980s up to today. And Gregory Isaacs and Dennis Brown continued to be the biggest 'year to year' stars. But dancehall, first and foremost, meant deejays.

1985 brought another epochal shift in the Jamaican sound. Steve Barrow relates the story: 'The two leading sets of the time, King Jammy and Black Scorpio, were due to clash, and producer Jammy had something special with which to vanquish the opposition. Using a Casio digital keyboard played by Tony Asher, the producer built a rhythm which was to change the future direction of Jamaican music. Jammy emerged victorious, and Wayne Smith's "Under Me Sleng Teng" was the song that did it for him. It also proved to be the sound the people wanted – hundreds of versions of the sparse, driving rhythm were made, as well as many more slight variations. Digital music had arrived in Jamaica.'[3]

Murray Elias, former head of A&R (artists and repertory) for reggae at Profile Records, elaborates: '. . . that was really the first massive drum-machine record where the drum-machine replaced live machines in the studio . . . that record was really a very simple toy Casio, about two feet big. The whole track – the drums, the bass – was one setting on that Casio.'[4]

King Jammy's sound system dominated the early 'computer-riddim' days with artists like Josey Wales, Chaka Demus, Admiral Bailey, Echo Minott, Pinchers and Shabba Ranks. But Jammy was challenged by Winston Riley, a veteran of the 1960s and 1970s whose productions had included the massive 1971 dub hit 'I Care', the flipside of Winston Scotland's 'Buttercup'. Riley's 80s stars included the deejay brothers Red Dragon and Flourgon and the late and lamented Tenor Saw, whose 'Ring The Alarm' became a dancehall anthem.

Pinchers, top, and Josey Wales

Yet another veteran, Augustus 'Gussie' Clark – he had produced Big Youth's 'Screaming Target' album in 1973 (voted as one of the 100 Most Important Albums of All-Time by *Rolling Stone* magazine in 1993) and The Mighty Diamonds' 'Pass The Kutchie' in the late 1970s – came to the

J. C. Lodge

King Jammy

Augustus 'Gussie' Clarke

fore in 1988 with J. C. Lodge's 'Telephone Love' and Gregory Isaacs' 'Rumours'. He also had a big album using the same rhythm. Donovan Germaine's Penthouse Studio also had successes in the late 1980s and early 1990s with singers like Marcia Griffiths and Beres Hammond, either by themselves or in 'combination style' with deejays, a la U-Roy. Increasingly those who created new 'riddims' became the most important men in Jamaican music. Four names above all dominated, 'Sly and Robbie' and 'Steely and Clevie'.

Everything old became new again. Many of the most popular dancehall 'riddims' were basically computer versions of old Studio One rhythms, and a slew of dancehall versions of ska and rocksteady classics became hits including 'Bam Bam', 'Fire Burning' and the UK number one 'Oh Carolina'. Whatever their artistic merits, computerised keyboards did have one undeniably positive commercial effect. While poor recording quality had previously been a big hindrance to Jamaican recordings abroad, the 'cleaner' computer sound allowed dancehall to make new inroads in North American and European dance clubs.

Today, for all intents and purposes, reggae in Jamaica is dancehall. Reggae magazines lavish ecstatic reviews on 'cultural' groups like Israel Vibration, The Congoes and The Itals, but ghetto massives mostly couldn't care a hoot about such music.

Lovindeer put it this way: 'If you go to any reggae concert, people will react to the so-called cultural music. But to see them get into a frenzy and go on bad, put on a deejay. Deejay music just has the power to move those people – it has a force.'[5]

Sly Dunbar has this to say: 'Some of the deejays are really saying something. You cannot say they're not saying anything . . . A lot of the upfront guys weren't doing anything, so the deejays saw the space and came in and filled it up. I wouldn't say that wasn't reggae, because if we take the vocal off and play the rhythm track, that's reggae. You have to give credit where credit is due. Some of them have done a good job, which is to keep the music alive.'[6]

In the country of its birth, reggae is more popular among its people than ever before. Dancehall rules the land and the deejays are its kings.

Scenes from inna the dancehall, where the massive likes to parade its fashions and attitudes.

Dancehall Massive

'Wha dem can do fe stop dancehall music!' The opening salvo of Papa San's 'Dancehall Good To We' isn't a question. It's a statement. Dancehall can be crude, unpleasant and repetitive. But it has undeniable rhythmic potency, brutal vocal power and irresistible visceral appeal. Like a hammering artillery barrage, the endless stream of dancehall tunes from Jamaica has blasted the music into the international pop consciousness.

And the vigour of dancehall on record is far surpassed by live deejays. A stage show with the artists in form and 'mashing down the place' is an unforgettable experience – the audience, deejays and music feeding off each other to produce an almost feverish exhilaration of raw energy. In fact, dancehall is sometimes too exciting for its own good, and violent eruptions, even at big shows like 'Sting' (the annual Boxing Day dancehall extravaganza), are lamentably common.

The *de riguer* dancehall acknowledgement of excellence used to be the victory salute, a round of gunshots fired into the air. Police crackdowns have lessened the practice in recent years, but its violence tinged aura has led many to condemn dancehall as a destructive force in Jamaican society. But a phenomenon that moves a people so profoundly cannot be ignored. Many Jamaicans lament the passing of the days of Bob, Peter, Toots and Jimmy, and maybe the music was better then. But you can't live in the past, or who would listen to anything but Mozart, Beethoven and Verdi? That was then and this is now. Each era must reflect its own dreams and reality, express its own emotions, create its own sound.

When the mood is right and the deejays ride the riddims directly into the bones, the beat envelops mind, body and soul, and the world becomes one big sound system. Commonly underproduced and amateurish, sometimes repetitive and juvenile, dancehall still produces real moments of authenticity like Buju Bantons's 'Murderer' and Tony Rebel's 'One Day' which come straight from the collective Jamaican soul. Then indeed, as Shinehead sings in 'Hello You All', – *not a music in the world sound fresh like this!*

But what is dancehall? Is it just deejay music? Well there are a lot of reggae

high importance, coupled with deviant behaviour allowed by the society and capitalized upon by the musician, may be fairly widespread. It is perhaps one of several which characterizes musicianly behaviour in a broad world area.')[1]

The style of reggae made internationally famous by Bob Marley is no longer the Jamaican public's music of choice. Groups like Third World or Ziggy Marley and The Melody Makers, even living legends like Burning Spear and Toots Hibbert, although popular overseas, do not command a mass following. 'Classic'

singers like Gregory Isaacs, Leroy Smart, Barrington Levy, Beres Hammond, Coco Tea, Half Pint, Frankie Paul and Luciano who are considered dancehall performers. And smooth voiced crooners like Pliers, Richie Stevens, Wayne Wonder or Sanchez doing covers of soul songs are considered an indispensable part of the dancehall scene. But the key element of dancehall is the deejays. Approximations of the other performers might be found elsewhere, but as artists completely in tune with their audience and environment, deejays are unique. They are the biggest stars and biggest draws and there is no dancehall without them.

Deejays attract an enormous amount of media attention and singers seem not to be as conspicuous in the public eye. Perhaps the deejays' theatrical stage names and posturing make people expect a certain amount of outlandish behaviour. And maybe the deejays themselves unconsciously try to live up to these expectations. There is certainly a public fascination with deejays' lifestyles and their frequent brushes with the law usually make front page news. (The observations of ethno-musicologist Alan Merriam seem particularly relevant here: 'There is some evidence to suggest that the pattern of low status and

reggae in Jamaica today is like rock and roll in America – acknowledged as the tradition's foundation, but also yesterday's music, what daddy and mommy used to listen to. Some claim dancehall has moved Jamaican music away from its roots, but Dub Poet Linton Kwesi Johnson disagrees: 'With the discovery of digital recording, an extreme minimalism has emerged – in the music of people like Steelie and Clevie, for example. On the one hand, the music is totally technological; on the other the rhythms are far more Jamaican: they're drawn from Etu, Pocomania, Kumina – African based religious cults who provide the rhythms used by Shabba Ranks or Buju Banton. So despite the extent of the technology being used, the music is becoming even rootsier, with a resonance even for old time listeners, because it echoes back to what they first heard in rural Jamaica.'[2]

Dancehall's roots, like reggae's, were the sound systems of the late 1950s and early 1960s. Sound systems were essentially giant portable record sets. Competition among the various sets was intense, and each had deejays whose job was to get the crowd dance-happy and earn the set an exciting street reputation. Sound system deejaying – where the record selector talked over the records, encouraging dancers to 'move and groove' – was probably a direct offshoot of what Jamaicans heard overseas or at nights on southern U.S. radio stations.

Sir Coxsone Dodd is supposed to have introduced the idea of toasting into the sound system dance halls, instructing his chief deejay Count Matchukie on how to copy the rhyming, jive hipster, bebop sounds of U.S. R&B radio deejays like Douglas 'Jocko' Henderson, Vernon 'Daddy-O' Winslow and Clarence 'Poppa Stoppa' Heyman.[3] Another big influence may have been the American boxer Cassius Clay (later Mohammed Ali, of course). Clay/Ali was extremely popular in Jamaica, achieving an almost heroic status. Jamaicans admired his good looks, style, and refusal to be pushed around by what he considered unjust authorities. His rhymed taunting of opponents (*Archie Moore /*

Will go in four) was widely imitated in the streets and possibly made their way into the dancehall.

So in the beginning it was straight imitation. But as with Jamaican music in general, which started out trying to copy the American R&B sound but created the very different beat of ska, the sound system deejays ended up inventing something quite new. Somewhere along the line the shouted phrases, impromptu scatting, and record sing-a-longs became an essential part of the experience and evolved into a vernacular poetry. Deejays discovered that it wasn't only what was said that counted, but how and when it was said – timing was as important as the patter in exciting the audiences and getting and keeping them on the dance floor.

What started off merely as exhortations to the crowd to dance, became an element in the music itself. People began to vocally compare the deejays' varying abilities to 'rock the crowd'. Soon it became apparent that sound system deejays were no longer only talking on top of the music, but changing the music itself, playing off the song's rhythm to create something completely different from the original. The deejay's art is probably best described as vocal drumming. Steven Davis puts it this way: ' . . . the Jamaican deejay acts as a literal talking drum. He chants rhythmically along with the record, generally entering on anticipatory beats and keying his phrases to rhythms and syncopations . . . He rhymes as much as possible, and often repeats a phrase twice before rhyming it, a device which may derive from blues phrasing . . . Like jazz, where hundreds of tunes and solos have been based on the chord structures of "I Got Rhythm" or "Honeysuckle Rose", hundreds of deejays have chanted over the bass lines to such seminal rocksteady late-60s rhythms as "Satta Amassagana" and "Chiang-Kai-Shek".'[4]

An indirect and often overlooked but immensely important influence on the deejay tradition (some say she founded it), was Louise Bennett, commonly known as Miss Lou. She is perhaps the most broadly popular figure Jamaica has produced, her picture in national dress being

almost the universal symbol of the traditional Jamaican woman. Her only rivals in common affection are Alexander Bustamante, the first prime minister, and Bob Marley. And unlike these, Miss Lou transcended all party, class and religious boundaries.

Born in 1919, she started out as a poet and dramatist. She gained a British Council Scholarship and studied at the Royal Academy of Dramatic Art in the late 1940s. After graduation, she worked in several British repertory companies. On her return home she taught drama, lectured extensively in U.S. and the U.K. and represented Jamaica many times abroad in arts and poetry festivals.[5]

She rose to prominence as a performing artist in Pantomime, the annual play produced each Christmas season at the Ward Theatre. A Jamaican offshoot of the English pantomime, 'Panto' each year showcased the nation's leading performers and songwriters. Miss Lou, almost always playing the laughing, wise, huge-hearted and large-bodied 'Mother Jamaica' was the

Louise Bennett, otherwise known as Miss Lou, a cultural icon of Jamaica and an inspiration to today's deejays.

biggest star it ever produced. In the late 1950s and early 1960s she recreated herself on radio and TV and, along with Ranny 'Mas Ran' Williams, became the island's first native electronic media star.

What made Bennett more than just another popular actor was the true excellence of her poetry. The great feature of her art was that, like Robert Burns, she wrote in dialect – the language of the common man and woman. She is still far and away the biggest selling poet in the country's history and the only one whose books are consistently in print. Many claim she is the only poet who has managed to genuinely capture both the feel of the Jamaican language and the emotions of the people, never becoming mannered or condescending. Yet she was primarily an oral poet and although her poems stood up well on paper, they took on new life when performed by her.

Beneath their proletarian hilarity, her verbal broadsides and monologues at Pantomime contained powerful and authentically poetic rhythms. This, along with her tireless championing of the Jamaican folk customs and song, is credited with having established in the Jamaican populace a respect for their language and tradition – the belief that patois, or 'patwah', wasn't merely corrupted English but a creation of merit and a language of immense vitality, creativity and humour. As she put it: 'Some thought Jamaican-English was vulgar, out-of-order language. It came out of the African heritage and at that time anything African was bad: hair, skin colour, language, music. But I thought it was fascinating. Everything had a rhythm. It was the creation of the people.[6] . . . One reason I persisted writing in dialect in spite of the opposition was because nobody else was doing so and there was such rich material in dialect that I felt I wanted to put on paper some of the wonderful things that people say in dialect. You could never say "look here" as vividly as "kuyah".'[7]

In her 1944 poem 'Bans O' Killing' she laughed at the middle- and upper-class snobbery which denigrated all common Jamaican speech as inferior 'dialect':

. . . Meck me get it straight Mass Charlie
For me no quite undastan,
Yuh gwine kill all English dialect
Or jus Jamaica one?

Ef yuh dah-equal up wid English
Language, den wha meck
Yuh gwine go feel inferior, wen
It come to dialect?

Ef yuh kean sing 'Linstead Market'
An 'Wata come a me y'eye',
Yuh wi haffi tap sing 'Auld lang syne'
An 'Comin thru de rye'

Dah language weh yuh proud o'
Weh yuh honour and respeck
Po' Mass Carlie! Yuh noh know sey
Dat it spring from dialect!'

When deejays started 'bussin dem patwah' the average man, unlike the intellectuals, never doubted that they might have something worthwhile to say, because Miss Lou had been speaking 'patwah poetry' for years. Tony Rebel, who uses Jamaican dialect as effectively as anyone in reggae, acknowledges Miss Lou as his greatest influence. Luciano, currently reggae's most popular singer, says of her: 'She has worked forward into my consciousness that I can be proud of my culture, that I can be proud of myself.'[8]

Rex Nettleford summed up Louise Bennett's accomplishments: 'In a quarter of a century she has carved designs out of the unruly substance that is the Jamaican dialect – the language which most of the Jamaican people speak most of the time – and raised the sing-song patter of the hills and of the towns to an art acceptable to and appreciated by people from all classes in her country.'[9]

Tony Rebel, one of today's performers who acknowledges the influence of Miss Lou.

The Pioneers

COUNT MATCHUKIE AND KING STITT

By all accounts, the first recognised deejay 'star' was the late Winston 'Count Matchukie' Cooper. As there were none before him, Count Matchukie's early days literally constitute the beginnings of dancehall deejaying: 'I got interested in music early. We had two gramophones at home and I started dancing when I was fifteen. After I left school, I didn't work. I became too attached to the music. I couldn't live off it, but the reward was in making people happy. I listened to records from Ella Fitzgerald, Harry James, Lena Horne, Eddie Arnold, Count Basie, Duke Ellington and Charlie Barnett. Don't ask me where my mother got those records.'[1]

He used to walk from corner to corner downtown, listening to the latest records the American ship men brought in. He normally started out at Luke Lane and Charles Street corner where Tom the Great Sebastien had his hardware store. He came on the corner every day, drew a crowd with his dancing, then moved on. 'Tom was the first sound with an amplifier properly balanced for the dancehall. I switched from dancing to selecting when Tom asked me to select one night at Forrester's Hall while he went off to purchase some more liquor for the dance. When he returned, he swore I had brought in records from outside. I explained I was only playing flip sides of his records. Everyone thought they were exclusive new songs and loved them. Things developed from there.

'Tom moved uptown and opened a club, so I joined up with Coxsone, who said he wanted a new selector because the man he had had had burnt up three amplifiers. At first I only selected the records and played them. Then we would announce other dances between the records. Later on I told Coxsone I would make some wisecracks, so it wouldn't seem like is a jukebox we playing.'[2]

Count Matchukie deliberated on the role of the deejay in the dance: 'A deejay then was responsible for conduct and behaviour, and what goes on inside the dancehall. We used the music to control the hearts and minds of the people . . . we didn't realise then that word is power, that the words we used really could control people. We make utterances before a record, introduce

Count Matchukie

the artists, give an idea of the artist's message. And when we find the record wanting, we would inter-serve something like "Get on the ball . . . " and cover the weakness. It was live jive and it really made people happy.'[3]

Some of Count Matchukie's signature phrases like 'It's you I love and not another, you may change but I will never', 'Live the life you love and love the life you live' and 'Whether you young or you old, you just got to let the good time roll' are still heard in the dancehall today. He never recorded, but his descendants U-Roy, King Stitt and Dennis Alcapone all paid tribute to him on record. King Stitt had this to say about him: 'Matchukie is the greatest thing ever handle a microphone. No slackness, just intelligence and real clean fun. No matter what you hear them saying, Matchukie paved the way for all of them, followed by me.'[4]

According to Stitt: 'Him show me a lot of things you know. Like the techniques, how you play a selection, how you must watch the crowd dancing to it.'

And U-Roy says: 'Count Matchukie, well he was a man I used to love to listen to. Whenever you been listening to this man, it was like you never hear anybody like that before. This man phrases his words in time, he doesn't crowd the music when he's talking. You can always hear what the vocalist got to sing. I used to say, I'd like to be like this man.'[5]

Matchukie himself was once quoted as saying that he became a sound system deejay because he wanted to work on radio and figured it was the best place to be discovered. He made no records, but just before he died on 11 November 1994, there was talk of Clement Dodd releasing an album entitled 'Count Matchukie at the Gold Coast Beach'. Life is nothing if not ironic.

The first deejay to go on record was probably Sir Lord Comic in 1966 with 'Ska-ing West' (although Baba Brooks did 'One Eyed Giant', and 'Lawless Street' by the Soul Bros, noted for its vocal scatting riff all the way through, came out about the same time). But his efforts were not very exciting musically, consisting of a few

formulaic rhyming phrases spoken rather flatly over an extended instrumental – *Adam and Eve went up my sleeve / And they never came down till Christmas Eve / Come on you cats we're going west.*

In retrospect these were mere curiosities whose only interest is what came after them, although the salaciousness and boastfulness which were to become deejay staples, were present from the very beginning. You can guess what 'One Eyed Giant' is about, and in 'Ska-ing West' we hear 'Sir Lord Comic is the greatest'.

King Stitt was the first recorded deejay to make an impact on the charts. Stitt started to play sound systems about 1957 with Coxsone, when Coxsone used to set up at the corner of Love Lane and Beeston Street. Stitt started as second to King Sporty (who later recorded in the early 1970s, notably the number one hit 'President A Mash Up The Residence'). When Sporty went to America, Stitt took over. According to Stitt: 'That time it was mostly rhythm and blues, and you had to present some picture to the people. Because some places where you play, the crowd just can't stay outside and know the place is full. So you just use something to draw them in.'

Although he is supposed to have recorded for Coxsone, 'Fire Corner' done for Clancy Eccles in 1969 was his first to be released. His other hits 'Lee Van Cleef', 'Vigorton Two', 'Herbsman Shuffle', 'The Ugly One' – were all done for Eccles. But even Stitt's songs had the feel of novelty, with a usually catchy opening verse followed by a seemingly random series of unconnected catch phrases. The dominant element was still the instrumental track, not Stitt's voice. Today King Stitt is best remembered by the opening rhymes of his biggest hit 'Fire Corner' – *No matter what the people say / This sound leads the way / It's the order of the day / From your boss deejay / I King Stitt / Hit it from the top / To the very last drop.*

Incidentally, King Stitt did establish one lasting deejay tradition. Nicknamed 'the ugly one' because of his front tooth snaggle and generally unattractive appearance, King Stitt was

King Stitt getting down at an early Coxsone session

the first in a long line of unprepossessing dee-jays, establishing a lineage that went through Yellowman, Shabba Ranks and Ninja Man. (Ninja's first stage names were 'Double Ugly' and 'Ugly Man'.) Meanwhile, most reggae singing stars, like popular idols everywhere else are fairly good looking. Some, say Bob Marley and Jimmy Cliff, were legitimately handsome.

Whether it is mere coincidence or a symptom of some deeper meaning, deejaying seems to be the one entertainment field in which a lack of conventional attractiveness is no hindrance to popular success. In fact judging from history, it may be an asset, perhaps lending a 'just one of the regular guys' credence to their image. A 1991 dancehall tune 'Ugly Man Take Over' celebrated

Stitt's, Shabba's and Ninja's simultaneous ugliness and ability to attract flocks of women, attributing this to the fact that 'the pretty boy dem turn lotion man', that is perfumed fops.

King Stitt, left, and Shabba Ranks, above – you don't have to be pretty in the deejay world!

U-Roy the Originator

. . . .

The man who established the deejay style as a legitimate musical form was U-Roy, born Ewart Beckford. Frustrated at seeing crowds respond ecstatically to his art while having nothing to show for it – his best performances vanished into thin air and he was regarded in musical circles as nothing but a glorified record spinner – U-Roy decided to etch his work on vinyl. In late 1969, under the urging of King Tubby, whose set U-Roy was working on, he got some studio time at Duke Reid's and chanted over some old Treasure Isle hits. The result is history.[1]

Within the space of months, the face of Jamaican music was irrevocably altered. U-Roy controlled the top three spots on both RJR and JBC charts simultaneously, an unprecedented feat, with 'Wear You To The Ball', and the presciently titled cuts 'Wake the Town' and 'Rule The Nation'. Spurred by his success, a slew of imitators rushed into the recording studios. Other system deejays like Prince Far I and Dennis Alcapone decided to also put their sounds on record. Catchier and clearer than most of his contemporaries, Dennis Alcapone had a number of hits like 'El Paso', 'Power Version', 'Mosquito One', 'Alcapone Guns Don't Argue', 'Judgement Day' and 'Teach The Children'.

Singers of middling success eyed deejaying as a chance to break through.

One of these Scotty, was the most successful of U-Roy's direct successors, scoring a string of number one hits like 'Skanking in Bed' and 'Sesame Street', the only one well-remembered being the famous 'Draw Your Brakes'.

'Wear You To The Ball' is the most celebrated deejay tune of all time and justifiably so. It was not U-Roy's first hit, 'Wake The Town' came out a few months earlier. But it was 'Wear You To The Ball' which made the greatest impact, and established the deejay sound. The dancehall masses had known about deejaying for years. But being recorded on vinyl meant dissemination to the nation, rural and urban, uptown and downtown. As it had so often before, the sound of the Kingston ghettos spread across the entire Jamaica.

Naturally at the beginning it seemed just another fad, a novelty craze like the twist or cha cha. But the public kept demanding and buying deejay discs and the sound became an established part of local music. Many derided it as 'not really music', a charge you still hear today. But protest as the naysayers might, it became increasingly obvious that the deejay sound of the Jamaican ghetto had developed an almost completely new art form.

Most of the songs didn't make any sense at the start. What was important to the public was a driving beat, bouncy deejaying and a catch phrase – something as trite as Dennis Alcapone's signature 'Ah wa so, El Paso' could make a deejay's reputation and stay on everyone's lips for months. 'Wear You To The Ball' is often cited as the form's apex, but is basically radio deejay patter – a mixture of exhortation, commentary on the song, bragadoccio and nonsense.

What counted was not so much what was said as how it was said. One of the big differences between U-Roy's records and his predecessors' was that he brought all the excitement of his dancehall chanting to vinyl 45, an almost hysterical vocal timbre rising and falling as the song demanded. And he played with the song's rhythms – sometimes bouncing off the beat, sometimes off the singer's voice, sometimes sliding in between both and weaving his voice into the melody and rhythm, sometimes obliterating all background sound with punishing verbal barrages. As U-Roy says to younger deejays who ask advice: 'Be sure that you're not running away from the riddim and the riddim's not running away from you.'[2]

Even though the early recorded deejays, Comic, Stitt and even U-Roy, chanted in the kind of pseudo American accent used by set and radio deejays, it wasn't long before nearly all deejays were toasting in full blooded 'patwah'. The great appeal of deejaying to Jamaicans is that deejaying reproduces habitual, everyday speech mannerisms. Singers are forced to alter their vocal patterns to suit the song's melody – indeed that is what good singing is all about, joining one's voice as closely to the melodic line as possible. So singing produces a sort of generic vocal structure, and national accents tend to virtually disappear in traditional western song.

But the deejays expressed their emotions in the staccato vocal patterns and vernacular language of everyday Jamaican conversation, and this gave their music an unprecedented emotional immediacy. No subconscious translation was needed – the

rhythmic chanting bypassed the conscious ego and went straight to the brain, generating a gripping, visceral excitement not found in 'regular' singing.

This new phenomenon was to have international as well as local repercussions. Once deejaying was established at home, wide-travelling Jamaicans began taking it abroad. And more than most immigrants, Jamaicans bring a part of home to their new surroundings.

Clive Campbell moved to the Bronx in New York with his family in 1967 at the age of twelve. In 1973 he assembled a sound system like the kind he had grown up with in Kingston and began throwing parties. The set was called

U-Roy today

Herculord and Campbell assumed the name Kool DJ Herc. Modeled after the huge sets necessary to compete in the heated sound system battles of Jamaica, Herculord was far more powerful than anything around and blew the competition away, establishing a ghetto wide reputation. He murdered the competition with his 'clean', distortion-free sounds, shattering frequency range, and massive volume.[3]

The exact details and chronology of what came next are lost in the mists of time because no one was really paying attention to what was only one of a million musical trends happening. But Herc probably sensed that while American blacks didn't really respond to the reggae rhythms he and his emcees toasted to, they liked the chanting. Even if they couldn't understand what the Jamaicans were saying and didn't talk like them, something in these verbal broadsides touched a chord. Chanting over funk and disco hits was the next natural step and black American youngsters began adapting the form to their slang and rhythms of speech.

According to Afrika Bambaata: '[Herc] knew that a lot of American blacks were not getting into reggae. He took the same thing that the deejays was doing – toasting – and did it with American records, Latin records or records with a beat. Herc took phrases like what was happening in the streets, new sayings going around like "rock on my mellow", "to the beat y'all", "you don't stop" and just elaborated on that . . . he would call out the names of people who were at the party, just like the microphone personalities who deejayed back in Jamaica.'[4, 5]

Herc began leaving the deejaying to his MC Coke La Rock while concentrating on 'mixing'. Using identical copies of a record on twin turn tables, Herc would cut back and forth on the 'break' part of a song where the instruments jammed. The break was the sonic climax that always sent his listeners wild, but it was too short. By cutting back and forth on his twin turn tables, he created a continuous 'break beat' and thus the first 'hip hop' rhythms. In his book *The New Beats*, S. H. Fernando points out unmistakable similarities between dubbing and sampling and says Kool Herc and Coke La Rock were to the fledgling hip-hop scene what King Tubby and U-Roy were to dancehall in Jamaica.[6]

One amusing aspect of rap's beginnings is how closely it paralleled the early days of Jamaican sound systems. Not only did they use toasters to give dances a live feel, but Kool Herc and his imitators like Afrika Bambaata and Grandmaster Flash would often have system battles where rivals set up near each other and tried to blast away the opposition with superior wattage – shades of Tom The Great, Trojan and Downbeat in the downtown Kingston 1950s! And, hilariously, Herc would often soak his records in water and remove the labels to stymie potential competition![7] Coxsone must have remembered 'Lator For Gator' and chuckled when he heard this. Duke Reid is probably still laughing in his grave.

There's another interesting facet of Herc's early days. As someone who was there notes: 'Nobody ain't never thought of playing no records like he was playing before that. And all of them shits was sitting in your house – all your mom's old and pop's old records. Soon as Kool Herc started playing, every motherlover started robbing his mother and father for records.'[8] It's a very Jamaican trait to keep playing songs you like no matter how old they are.

Curiously, Herc has denied the Jamaican connection with rap: 'Jamaican toasting? Naw, naw. No connection there. I couldn't play reggae in the Bronx. People couldn't accept it. The inspiration for Rap is James Brown and the album "Hustlers Corner" by the Last Poets.'[9] But this album came out in 1973, years after deejaying had been established as a legitimate musical form in Jamaica. And 'Rapper's Delight', the first big rap record, didn't come out until 1979.

It's natural that Herc would wish to be seen as 'an originator, never an imitator' (U-Roy's signature phrase) and that black American kids who had adopted rap as 'their' music should maintain they had created it. But the Jamaican link (and interestingly the earliest of rap stars,

Grandmaster Flash, had Barbadian parents who collected both American swing and West Indian records[10]) aligned with the similarity of musical methods and deejaying's unquestioned chronological precedence, make the conclusion that rap evolved from deejaying undeniable.

Of course some would say that Jamaican deejay music evolved from the southern black R&B radio disc jockeys who in turn developed their style from jazz scat singers. And they may be right. But it was the Jamaican deejays who first turned chanting/toasting/scatting into a commercial musical form that stood on its own and pushed all accompaniment into the background – where people bought the records because of the rhythmic talking.

As many commentators point out, deejaying and rapping can both be considered an extension of the West African oral tradition of the griot or storyteller, who recited the history of his tribal community, sometimes to the accompaniment of talking drums.[11]

Deejay music in Jamaica was going through countless changes in style and form years before rap music was recognised as anything more than a novelty. One thing became clear: the same immediacy that made deejay so potent, also meant it wore badly. More than most other popular music forms, deejay music seems to be a music of the moment and loses its appeal quickly. A smash hit that sounds utterly compelling one month, can wear tiresomely trite the next.

And so it was with deejays too. Indeed the history of nearly every deejay has been one of overnight fame, massive popular appeal and almost complete oblivion. Better management has enabled deejays to last longer of late. Lt Stitchie, Papa San and Admiral Bailey can still pull crowds after almost ten years in the business. But a hot new deejay still begins looking over his shoulder rather quickly.

One offshoot of deejay music which has garnered much interest in academic circles is dub poetry. To quote Jamaican poet, Professor Mervyn Morris, circa 1982: 'The term "dub poetry" was promoted early in 1979 by Oku Onuora to identify work then being presented – often at the Jamaica School of Drama – by himself, Mikey Smith and Noel Walcott. The dub poem, Oku has said, "is not merely putting a piece of poem pon a reggae rhythm; it is a poem that has a built-in reggae rhythm – hence when the poem is read without any reggae rhythm (so to speak) backing, one can distinctly hear the reggae rhythm coming out of the poem". More recently, however, Oku has been arguing that any verse that refers to or incorporates music rhythms belongs in the family, poetry into which music rhythms have been dubbed, so to speak: dub poetry.'[12]

One of Jamaica's best known dub poets at present is Mutabaruka, who is also a healthfood businessman and radio talk-show host. Muta's resonant baritone and striking appearance – his leonine dreadlocks have a natural white streak in front – have gained his work a lot of attention, even though he resists the label of 'dub poet' because it refers to only one aspect of his work. [13]

Linton Kwesi Johnson, who emigrated from Jamaica to England when eleven, is probably the most famous and highly regarded dub poet. LKJ's best work is considered to be 'Dread Beat an' Blood'. According to *The New Trouser Press Record Guide:* '"Dread Beat an' Blood" was a call to arms, a dark commemoration of police harassment and social repression of blacks told in a forceful but strangely spiteless manner. Speaking his poems over absolutely flawless throbbing reggae, Johnson uses the patois of the streets to speak to his audience, calling for brotherhood and vigilance. The clean, supple, vibrant music and incisive pointed words make it a powerful and memorable political statement.' [14]

Linton Kwesi Johnson

Riddim Wild

Musically it was obvious from the beginning that a good deejay tune needed a good rhythm, or 'riddim'. Indifferent riddims inevitably yielded poor songs. The relation between deejay and riddim is like a jockey and race horse – a bad jockey can sometimes win on a good horse but not even the best jockey can win on a bad horse. And it became clear too that somehow different deejays were able to create completely different sounding songs on the same riddim through a process no one quite understands even today.

Clearly riddims were the core of dancehall. The creators of riddims became to the deejays what (to use horse racing terms again) trainers are to jockeys, the most important cog in the wheel of success, though behind-the-scene players. It had always been common practice for producers to re-use well-known reggae riddims. But the primacy of the beat in dancehall, and the myriad uses to which one beat could be put, meant an acceleration of the practice. Inevitably the technician/engineer began reworking old beats into new forms. And what U-Roy was to deejays, King Tubby (Oswald Ruddock) was to these 'riddim makers'.

Tubby ran his own Hometown Hi-Fi sound system in the mid sixties. As he puts it: 'We never really get famous until around May 1968. But I used to fool round sound system from 1964 as a hobby. Coxsone and Duke Reid was still there but them was losing them name. Top sound systems of those days was Sir Mike, Sir George Kelly and Stereo from Spanish Town. Then we came on as Tubby's Hometown Hi Fi. We say we wasn't going in that big, just play in we home town area which was Waterhouse. But eventually we get big.'[1]

He used to cut discs on the side for various producers, mixing two-track tapes with musicians on one track and vocals on the other. To test the quality of the voices, Tubby would drop out the music track for a chorus. When the music dropped back in, Tubby discovered

King Tubby

familiar tunes became even more exciting. He began altering instrumental and vocal tracks – dropping the bass out or bringing it forward, echoing the guitar, using reverb and delayed echo, cutting the vocal in or out.

The resulting sound would in time dominate reggae, particularly the dancehall. In Tubby's words: 'I used to work on the cutter for Duke Reid and once a tape was running on the machine and I just drop off the voice – it was a test cut. We take some of these test cuts and carry them home and the Saturday we was playing out, I decided to test them cause it sounds so exciting the way the records start with the voice, the voice drop out and the rhythm still going. We carry them to the dance and I tell you, about four or five of the tunes keep the dance. Cause is just over and over we have to keep playing them. The crowd wouldn't let us play anything else. We introduce a different thing to the sound system world, with reverb and all that. And it get the people excited and we have a following. And then U-Roy come on with a style . . . .'[2]

To paraphrase Luke Ehrlich in *Reggae International*, 'that moment in a version when the band drops back in from the acapella vocal passage is especially thrilling. Without the band beneath, the vocals by themselves are thin, high and brittle. This rhythmic suspension creates a mounting anticipation in the listener for full body motion. When the driving drum and bass drops back in, he lets himself go with the music and experiences a sort of catharsis.

'Withdrawing and then reintroducing the bass section creates a "plunge". During the acapella vocals, the head is occupied by the singing and the abdomen is not the resonated by the bass. The instrumental "dub" drops back in and shifts the listener's attention to the abdomen at the same time as the cerebral stimulation of the singing ceases.

'As the music plunges, listeners almost feel the ground falling away beneath them – the worries of the mind vanish in the heat of body movement, and you "forget your troubles and dance". Incidentally, "plunges" can be heard in

fleeting moments in other, mostly black, music. "Cool Jerk", a '60s R&B disc by The Capitols, is a good example.'[3]

Apart from this however, the spaces left in the mix when some instrumental tracks were dropped out allowed deejays to stretch out lyrically – thoughts formerly expressed in hurried snatches and phrases could now be elaborated upon, without crowding out the underlying rhythms.

According to Dennis Alcapone, dancehall was really born on that night in 1969 when Tubby brought dubs of four big Treasure Isle hits to his customised echo and reverb equipped set. 'Tubby and [resident deejay] U-Roy open normally, but when U-Roy drop in the remix version of "You Don't Care", the crowd went wild and the place "mash up".'[4]

Dub, as the new sound was called, was to reggae instrumentals what deejaying was to reggae singing – something, if not completely new, not quite like anything ever heard before. What fascinated was that audiences would dance happily for long stretches of time to the same dub plate as long as the deejay varied his style of patter. Having found one it liked, it took far longer than normal for the audience to tire of a popular dub track. Over time this phenomenon became even more pronounced.

Arguably the most distinctive trait of Jamaican music today is the extent to which riddims are extracted, refined and created. There is a paring down process by which the essence of the beat is distilled and everything superfluous discarded. And once a good riddim is created, it can serve as the base for seemingly a countless different number of songs.

In reggae there are certain familiar bass and drum lines that have their own names – Chiang Kai Shek, Charlie Chan, High Fashion, Joe Frazier, Bush Master, Rub-A-Dub, Satta Amassagana. But these are not standardised. A rhythm might be named by any of the records made from it, or just conveyed by the first part of the bass line. Rhythms generally, but not always, stay in the same key as the original version, unless the singer who happens to be working the session can't sing it.[5]

In the field of rhythm creation in Jamaica, one name stands out above all others – Leroy Sibbles of Heptones fame. Many of the seminal bass lines in Jamaican music are the work of Leroy Sibbles, who for a number of years composed the riddims that backed the most influential hits and artists in Jamaica. According to Luke Erlich, this makes Sibbles a true giant in Jamaican music, equal in stature to Bob Marley. Whatever advances The Wailers have made for the vocal consciousness of reggae, Sibbles has done at least as much for the musical development of the music's most important instrument. He brought much of his African heritage as a West Indian to the Jamaican bass style. He is really a one-man bridge between Afro-Jamaican and Afro-American musical values.[6]

Among the riddims Sibbles helped create were 'Full Up', 'Satta Massagana', 'Declaration of Rights', 'No Man Is An Island', 'Ten To One', 'Things A Come To Bump', 'You Mean To Me' or 'Heart and Soul', 'Sweet Talking', 'Freedom Blues' or 'MPLA', 'School Riddims', 'Book Of Rules', 'Midnight', 'Love I Can Feel', 'In Cold Blood', and 'Baby Why'.

To show how entrenched the 'riddim' concept is among Jamaicans, popular RJR deejay Richie B [Burgess] at one time held 'dancehall riddim' contests, playing the popular hits on two different riddims ('Punnany' versus 'Mud Up' for example) throughout his programme, with listeners voting for their favourite by phone.

From very early on 'riddims' have been the core of reggae music, and been seen as reusable. But deejay and later dancehall has taken this tendency to

A youthful Leroy Sibbles, riddim maestro

what some people consider an obsessive extreme. The apotheosis, or nadir, of the recycled riddim came in 1985, the year of 'Sleng Teng', which gave birth to the hard, modern dancehall sound of the computerised, digitalised, drum machines.

Reggae was once again displaying its unsurpassed capacity to absorb new technology without compromising its roots. 'Sleng Teng' was also the example 'par excellence' of the astonishingly varied tunes deejays and dancehall singers are able to create from one riddim and the equally astounding way in which one riddim can so compulsively seize the collective Jamaican imagination. At one time there were something like 20 records in the Top 40 using the 'Sleng Teng' riddim. And although no one could quite keep track, it's estimated that something like a total of 500 versions were done on 'Sleng Teng'.

Sometimes it was difficult to tell one song from another and a lot of it all sounded the same. Yet a good riddim is remarkably addictive and hearing a string of hits on the same riddim can be an amazingly enjoyable experience. And 'Sleng Teng' was only the beginning. Computer driven riddims were the wave of the future – 'Punany', 'Sixpence', 'Mud Up'. The list goes on. Deceptively simple, sounding almost childish at first hearing, such riddims can become hypnotic and strangely comforting.

According to Pamela O'Gorman, 'the riddim is not expected to enhance the words or add expressive meaning. It provides a rhythmic stimulus and a key centre for the voice, and lays down vocal parameters. The riddim's familiarity reassures the listener without drawing attention to itself. Yet when it is withdrawn, and the voice continues alone, the effect is riveting.'[7]

In Luke Erlich's view riddims, like other types of bass playing, give arrangements 'bottom' and complement the chords, melody and lyrics of a song. Yet each riddim has its own strict and distinctive melodic and rhythmic pattern which has a recognisable identity and can be listened to as a separate composition.

Riddims are highly intuitive, delicate and strategic exercises in balancing 'space' (or silence) and 'matter' (or sound) with reference to pitch. The bass 'says' a phrase, then pauses for 'breath' like a person speaking. The pause 'frames' the phrase and gives the mind of the listener time to absorb it. After a string of notes, the listener becomes accustomed to the presence of the bass in his ears and body. At this point, a cleverly placed pause creates a minute 'gap', a momentary emptiness in the bottom of the music, which regains the full attention of the listener.

Physiologically, depending on its pitch and loudness, bass resonates the facial mask, the abdominal cavity and even the pelvic area. Riddims, being low in pitch and under the arrangement, tend to bypass the intellectual mind and communicate directly with the heart by actually massaging it in rhythm.[8]

Talking Gleaners

The deejay's art consists primarily of an ability to 'ride' the riddim, that is to chant in tune with the beat. Next comes a fluency in varying timbre, tone and speed of speech. The knack of creating intelligent and witty lyrics, while always a welcome bonus, seems to rank relatively low in the hierarchy of dancehall skill. Many big deejay hits have been based on nonsense rhymes, and dancehall usually holds up poorly on paper. Indeed many big-name deejays are genuinely illiterate.

As Pamela O'Gorman notes, transcribing deejay songs on paper is a distortion. One cannot convey the rhythmic subtlety or the unorthodox accentuation of words. And the syncopated silences that highlight key words or create a rhythmic push are lost. All these constitute the heart of deejay, which is exclusively an oral art.[1]

Deejays might come and go with dizzying regularity, but deejaying is a surprisingly versatile art form. Not only is it able to accommodate almost any stylistic rhythm changes, a much wider range of topics can be addressed in the form than is possible with singing. Slang phrases that sound ridiculous when sung, gain added potency when bounced off a hard beat. Deejays are almost 'street newspapers' (or in Jamaican terms 'talking gleaners', after the nation's oldest paper *The Gleaner*) giving commentary on almost any topic. Ghetto happenings that never make the official media become nationwide knowledge through the deejays, and some say the Top 40 gives a more accurate reflection than the official media of what's really going on in Jamaica.

In the early 1970s, reggae to the world at large meant 'The Harder They Come', Jimmy Cliff, Toots and The Maytals and Bob Marley. But the combination of dub and deejay was percolating beneath the surface and dominating the ghettos. Deejay music was going through what would become a familiar roller coaster process of dissemination, alternating bursts of hugely popular expansions with sudden mass exodus contractions. After the U-Roy era, it almost went into eclipse.

But in 1973 Manley Buchanan, recording as Big Youth, roared onto the scene and began dominating the Jamaican record charts just like U-Roy before him. At one stage he had five songs

simultaneously in the top ten, songs like 'S-90 Skank', 'Screaming Target', 'Chi Chi Run', 'Cool Breeze'. A lover of jazz, claiming John Coltrane as one of his chief inspirations, Big Youth lasted longer than most deejays, but not very many of his songs stand up well today. 'S-90 Skank', however, remains a classic of the genre. The other big deejays of the era were I-Roy and Prince Jazzbo, the latter remembered for 'School' and 'Crabtalking'.

The Big Youth era lasted for about two years, long by deejay standards. And suddenly deejays began flooding the scene, appearing and vanishing almost simultaneously. Dillinger, hit with 'CB 200' and 'Caymanas Park', Trinity had 'Three Piece Suit', – Jah Thomas, U-Brown, Ranking Trevor, Prince Mohammed, Prince Far I, Ranking Joe, Tappa Zukie, Mikey Dread, Papa Kojak and Liza, Lone Ranger, Eek-a-Mouse – fast they came and furious they went.

In the late 1970s deejay music was again in decline. And wise sages who had all along dismissed it as 'pure foolishness' again nodded heads knowingly and with relief. But dancehall once again found saviours, this time the duo of Papa Michigan and General Smiley (Anthony Fairclough and Errol Bennett). Papa Michy was only an 18-year-old schoolboy and Smiley a 22-year-old accounts student when they had their first big hit in 1978, 'Rub a Dub Style'.

Between them they created some of the most enduring deejay tunes of all time, not only 'Rub a Dub Style' but other dancehall classics like 'One Love Jamdown', 'Nice Up The Dance', and 'Diseases'. Michigan and Smiley accomplished the hitherto unthinkable feat, especially for deejays whose average 'star' lifespan is usually less than two years, of having four consecutive *Gleaner* songs of the year, from

Michigan and Smiley

1978 through 1981.[2] It's hard to define why, but Michigan and Smiley's sing-songy, call and answer, harmony style tunes have held up over the years while other deejays' songs of their era have vanished.

Indeed Yellowman, considered by music writer Howard McGowan as the greatest deejay of all time,[3] is a classic example of the artist who is incomparable live, but whose work on vinyl is forgettable. Yellow exploded on the scene in 1982 and totally dominated Jamaican music for the next few years. In Yellowman's glory days no artist, not even 'superstars' like Dennis Brown or Gregory Isaacs, relished coming on stage immediately before or after him for fear of embarrassment, because impatient audiences wanted only Yellow. His legendary performance in 1984 at Sunsplash when he kept the audience entranced for almost four hours, was the virtual creation of Dancehall Night. And yet one has to comb over Yellow's records to find anything worth listening to – the vast majority have aged poorly. Still, Yellowman almost single-handedly created the coarse, crude and fearlessly direct sound of today's dancehall, a music for which nothing (except religion) – not race, sex, money, love, guns, drugs or politics – is sacred.

(Yellowman rarely performs in Jamaica today. Interestingly, he still enjoys a large following among white American college students, who obviously see a kindred 'party-hearty' spirit in Yellow.)

Yet dancehall was still a 'ghetto' thing. The upper- and middle-class still derided it as 'bhuttu' music (just as their 1960s counterparts had sneered at ska), fit only for the ignorant and uneducated, claiming it was not *Reggae*. But people with open ears could hear that while 'classic' reggae was slipping into ennui and imitative sameness, dancehall was electrifyingly arousing. And when Hurricane Gilbert swept across the island in September 1988, the entire nation, uptown and downtown, laughed away its sorrows in Lloyd Lovindeer's 'Wild Gilbert'. 'Wild Gilbert' was not great music, but it was brilliant social commentary which summed up the experiences and spirit of the nation in disaster and acted as a sort of anesthetic against the reality of the disaster itself. It's the sort of thing that dancehall is uniquely equipped to do.

The barriers to dancehall kept falling. They say nothing can withstand an idea whose time has come, and so it is with a sound that the people want. The upper-classes might be able to keep the sounds out of their houses, but they still had to drive through the streets, where every corner had booming speakers pounding out Josey Wales, Major Mackerel, General Trees, Red Dragon, Flourgon, Ninja, Pinchers, Professor Nuts or Tiger. Then came IRIE FM, the nation's first all-reggae station, on which dancehall was a staple.

Suddenly Jamaicans could enjoy a steady diet of their favourite music rather than just the bits and pieces which RJR and JBC had previously allowed them. Almost immediately IRIE became the nation's second most popular station. Chastened by the market place, its competitors quickly added large doses of dancehall to their format. The defences were breached and Shabba Ranks brought the walls down when he won the Reggae Grammy award in 1992. Nowadays, of course, dancehall is so universally accepted that popular, 'clean'

ROOTS, ROCKING REGGAE, RADIO

Irie FM hit the airwaves in 1990

deejays like Admiral Bailey, Lovindeer, Shinehead, Papa San, Chaka Demus and Lt Stitchie are used extensively in radio and television ads.

An indication of just how deeply dancehall has permeated Jamaican society is the lively 'roots' theatre scene. 'Roots' theatre is a mostly comedic genre celebrating the bawdier elements of Jamaican life while at the same time addressing current social concerns. Writers and actors are mostly middle-class, yet most of the plays get their themes, titles and background music from dancehall hits and current events. Sometimes a play is simply renamed to echo a more current hit, so 'Return of the Don' became 'Trailer Load of Dollars'. Raunchy, full of 'in' jokes and almost incomprehensible to non-Jamaicans, these plays are the cornerstone of a surprisingly vibrant local theatre scene. They are incontrovertible proof that dancehall has become the cultural backbone of the country and is folk music in the real sense of the term, expressing collective emotions and concerns.

The last few years have seen yet another striking change in the dancehall. Ever since Yellowman's heyday, deejays have tended to emphasise 'man and woman business'. Naturally this focus on human relationships often veers off into the salacious and sometimes, as in 1987, 'gal pickney music' and 'slackness' seemed to dominate the airwaves. Then, in 1990, Ninja Man captured public attention with his 'gun talk'. And his 'badmanism', whether it was reflecting social reality or not, sometimes seemed to celebrate violence and instruments of destruction. One

Luciano and Tony Rebel, two exemplars of the new conscious reggae.

could well understand the critics who condemned dancehall for ignoring the spiritual element that had made reggae so unique among the world's popular musics. Of course the deejays' perennial argument, that they were merely reflecting what they saw and heard, was difficult to dismiss.

But about 1993 a shift in values began to take place, spearheaded by the Rastafarian deejay Tony Rebel. Tony Rebel's first big hit had been the love song 'Fresh Vegetable'. But once established he began to openly address larger social issues and spiritual matters. And even if he never gained the popularity of a Shabba, Ninja or Buju, people bought his records and cheered him at stage shows.

Whether through direct or indirect influence, others began following his example. The singer Garnett Silk began bringing back memories of Bob Marley to many, and his tragically premature death

RIP, Garnett Silk

made the comparison even more obvious. Then Buju Banton, deejay of the hour, began growing 'locks' and espousing the tenets of Rastafarianism, and Luciano, in the reggae singer's corner, croons happily and almost exclusively about God and the meaning of life. Suddenly the mid-nineties found the dancehall as full of 'conscious' messages as roots reggae ever was. Heartened by this return to 'spirituality' many former critics have embraced the music, and dancehall is now accepted by a broader cross-section of Jamaicans than at any previous time.

And what does the future hold? Well only the very bold or foolish would try to predict the directions Jamaican music will take. For whatever reggae was, is or will be, its paths are as unpredictable as the people from whence it sprung. Jimmy Cliff's words in 'Sitting In Limbo' say it well: 'I don't know where I'm going. But I know where I've been.'

The Sounds of the Sixties

1960 / **EASY SNAPPIN'**
Theophilus Beckford

'Easy Snappin' was recorded during Coxsone Dodd's first session at Federal. Many people say this is the earliest record with an authentic modern Jamaican feel. It's clearly in the R&B imitation tradition, but the slightly off-main-beat vocals and piano give an inkling of the musical shift underway. At least in retrospect. Who at the time could have imagined that this catchy, good-natured, slow-motion boogie heralded the dawn of a new sound?

Although he continued to play keyboard on many important songs up into the 1980s, Theophilus Beckford never had another hit as a vocalist, but he was known ever after in the business as 'Snappin'. Like most 'foundation members', he has not been treated well by the music industry he helped create. When Beckford heard that 'Easy Snappin' was being used in a European jeans commercial and contacted the company about royalties, executives were astonished to hear he was still alive. They had been told that he had died many years ago. Reportedly the money was being collected by someone closely associated with the song's original release.

1960 / **TELL ME DARLING**
Wilfred 'Jackie' Edwards

The original 'cool ruler', Jackie Edwards was one of the great Jamaican romantic singers and song-writers. 'Tell Me Darling', a Latin tinged, almost but not quite ska ballad, was produced by Chris Blackwell, who Edwards followed to London in 1962. He was head cook and bottle washer in Island Records' early years – not only singing and writing songs but delivering records by bus.

Edwards died in 1992. Outside of Jamaica he is perhaps best known for composing the consecutive UK number one songs 'Keep On Running' and 'Somebody Help Me', both done by the Spencer Davis Group in the sixties. But here it's the bouncy but tender 'Tell Me Darling' which does most to keep his name alive.

FROM ZINC SHACK TO 16-TRACK – EARLY JAMAICAN RECORDING STUDIOS

The first recording studio in Jamaica was Ken Khouri's Federal Records. Khouri had gotten into the area by chance in 1949. He was in a radio shop when a distressed man came in trying to sell a discrecorder to fly back to California. The radio shop declined the offer but Khouri was intrigued and purchased the disc-recorder, a microphone, amplifier, and blanks for $350. He began recording people's voices for 30 shillings and immediately became a music machine Pied Piper, '. . . people used to follow me home and I would record until 2 or 3 a.m.'

Realising the commercial potential Khouri started recording music instead of just voices. He branched out from his home to a club at Red Gal Ring in St Andrew and made an agreement with Decca in London to make records from the discs.

'The first song I did was Lord Flea's "Naughty Little Flea". I contacted Alec Durie of Times Store to help me distribute records and we started the Times Record Label. Durie advertised the records in the Saturday newspapers. This first attempt was a real gamble. But when I got to King Street the Saturday, I saw a line two blocks long. We sold out in less than two weeks. I ordered 5,000 more records and we sold them for between four and five shillings.'

This encouraged Khouri to start manufacturing records himself. He called a factory in California which sold him the machinery and sent an expert to teach him about the recording business. He phased out his furniture store and in 1954 started Records Limited at 129 King Street. He imported two presses and under franchise began pressing for Mercury Records. Then he acquired a mono machine and, with engineer Graham Goodal's help, converted a 'maids quarters' into Jamaica's first recording studio. The small, wooden building with a zinc roof was right beside the pressing plant. Recordings were done mainly at night.

Stanley Motta had previously made a limited number of calypso recordings straight onto discs. Since no processing facilities were then available in Jamaica, all acetates or soft waxes were sent to the U.S. where a stamper was cut and brought back to the island. A few early attempts were also made at JBC and RJR.

In 1957 Records Limited moved to 220 Marcus Garvey Drive and became Federal Record Manufacturing Co. Ltd. Khouri no doubt had the Federation of the West Indies in mind and saw wider Caribbean possibilities. Soon he purchased some old ampex equipment which had a new feature of reverberation. It was still monaural format and everything had to be done in one take. If a singer was recording and an instrumental solo was needed, the singer had to get out of the way quickly and smoothly to allow for the solo.

The musicians who developed the sound in Khouri's studios were Lloyd Knibbs, Drumbago, Lloyd Mason, Lloyd Brevette, Theophilus 'Easy Snappin' Beckford, Ernie Ranglin and Jah Jerry. According to Chris Wilson: 'At first Federal enjoyed a monopoly on record pressing in the island, but they had no mastering capabilities. So songs were sent to New York to be mastered and sent back to Jamaica for pressing. This created a logistical nightmare for independent producers. In fact Coxsone's first session with Roland Alphonso was lost in transit and never found. The producers were also unable to challenge matters like pricing, and this kept releases to a minimum.

'But soon producers like Coxsone were mastering records in Miami, and the reduced distance enabled them to oversee the sound quality of the finished product. Coxsone remembers a young Chris Blackwell stopping by at Studio One, on his way to Miami, and asking if there were any records that he wanted mastered.

'When Caribbean Records started pressing, costs came down by 75 per cent. Caribbean Records was run by Dada Tawari, whose family ran the Regal Theatre. The building was located on Torrington Road, almost across from Record Specialists, but was later torn down after a fire. The lowered price structure resulted in a flood of recordings, and a wealth of material was released during the ska era.'

Another pressing plant came on the scene, West Indies Records, run by Edward Seaga. Then in 1963 Ken Khouri made his next big move and built a super studio. He brought in the first stereo equipment and started making stereo records. Without facilities for cutting stereo mastering had to be done in the U.S.

Byron Lee, leading The Dragonaires, decided that his market was an LP market and cut Jamaica's first stereo LP, 'Joy Ride'. Since there was no stereo cutting facilities, Lee decided to go two ways. The stereo version was cut abroad and a Hi-Fi version at home. The two were differentiated by a sticker on the record jacket. And despite being more expensive the stereo version outsold its counterpart three to one. Other popular bands – Granville Williams, Kes Chin and The Vagabonds, The Caribs, Carlos Malcolm and The Afro-Jamaica Rhythms – realised there was a market for stereo and followed suit.

The music's increasing popularity caused studios to flourish in Jamaica. In 1965 George Benson and Bunny

Mick Jagger at the Dynamic Studios in 1970

Rae acquired West Indies Records from Edward Seaga. West Indies had put in a small studio built by Ronnie Nasralla and managed to lure Byron Lee away from Federal. A year later West Indies plant was destroyed by fire, but the studio was left intact. Lee acquired the company, renaming it Dynamic Sounds.

Then Lee met 'Jeep' Harned. Up till then Harned's chief claim to fame was the installation of a Muzak system at Fort Lauderdale Airport, but he later went on to develop the major recording equipment label MCI. MCI's first ever complete operation of mixer and recorder was installed at Dynamic Sounds. Jamaica now had multi-track recording and overdubbing capabilities. And Lee soon went from 4-track to 8-track sound.

Others entered the multi-track market. Duke Reid built the first independent 2-track studio on the fourth floor of his liquor store. Randy's at Parade also began recording on two tracks, as did Clement Dodd at Studio One. Dodd also first recorded 'Jamaican Stereo', with the band all on one track and the vocals on the other. The age of 'riddims' and 'dub' was at hand.

Most independent producers were content to remain at four or eight tracks. The music they produced was not very sophisticated and did not need much overdubbing. They were dealing mainly with a singles market, so you could lock down all the drums on one track and an organ on the other.

Jamaica began to develop a reputation abroad as a good place to record. For one thing the studio musicians were excellent and demanded much lower wages than their overseas counterparts. Paul Simon visited Dynamic and recorded on eight track. Johnny Nash recorded locally and had a big overseas hit with 'I Can See Clearly Now.' The Rolling Stones' Mick Jagger, on the advice of Lee's friend Ahmed Ertegun, called up Dynamic saying 'Look, I've been hearing a lot about what's happening in Jamaica. I want to come down and do two things – to see if I can cut reggae and see if I can cut my new album. But we need sixteen track equipment.'

In 1970, two weeks before the Rolling Stones arrived, Lee installed a sixteen track machine and MC Board. It was the first in Jamaica, although others soon followed. The Rolling Stones came to Dynamic with a $50,000 budget for three months and recorded 'Goat Head Soup', though they never did any reggae. Their visit paved the way for a flood of foreign talent into Dynamic – Cat Stevens, Garland, Jeffreys, Peter, Paul and Mary, Herbie Mann, Eddie Kendricks, Roberta Flack. Who could ever have dreamed that Ken Khouri's primitive wood and zinc shack studio would lead to all this?

1961 / **OH CAROLINA**
The Folkes Brothers (written by John Folkes)

In 1960 Prince Buster approached the legendary Rastafarian percussionist Count Ossie to record for him. Ossie could hardly believe that middle-class Jamaica wanted anything to do with Rastafarian music. According to Prince Buster 'Count was hesitant to record without the bass guitar and regular band support. However I said "Count, I want you to record just the way you and the group play all the while."' Count Ossie and his drummers had established a camp in Wareika Hills in the early 1950s and some early recordings list his group as Count Ossie and The Wareikers.

Buster booked the one track studio facilities at JBC. But, he says, Duke Reid booked the studio over his head in an attempt to stop him. So Buster had to record in a much smaller temporary studio. Owen Grey played piano, Ronnie

Bop bass drum, Buster did handclaps and imitated horn riffs, all backed up by Count Ossie and his four drummers. Engineered by Cecil Watts, the song was cut in two takes with one mike. Vocals were done by The Folkes Brothers, a trio of teenagers, Miko, John (Jack) and Eric (Junior). It was the only recording they ever did, as Miko, the eldest, migrated shortly after.

The result is arguably the single most important record in Jamaican musical history and probably the most popular Jamaican dance oldie ever. Early Jamaican recorded music was often just an attempt to duplicate American R&B songs. And the usual result was a third-rate copy on fourth-rate equipment of second-rate tunes sung in a quasi-American 'twang'. It's hardly an accident that not many pre-independence Jamaican tunes are played on radio.

But 'Oh Carolina', whether by design or accident, contained distinctive elements not heard in any previous R&B copy. Count Ossie's drum

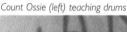

Count Ossie (left) teaching drums

WHO WROTE 'OH CAROLINA'?

This became more than just an historical question when Shaggy had a worldwide million seller in 1993 with a deejay version of the original, topping the charts in a reported 14 countries. Millions in royalties were due to the true author. Prince Buster has always maintained he wrote it. He certainly lifted the famous 'drop down' beginning straight from the Carla and Rufus Thomas R&B hit 'Cause I Love You' (released by Stax Records in August 1960). Virgin Records credited Shaggy, Mancini and Buster on Shaggy's album as writers of the song. Billboard also gave credit to Orville Burrell and W. Riley.

A court case was heard in October 1994 in London to determine the lawful composer of 'Oh Carolina' and to disperse royalty payments for the song. The judge ruled that John Folkes was the real composer. Folkes emigrated to Toronto in 1967, eventually earned a doctorate in literature, and became a high school teacher. He told his story to Roger Steffens (before the court case).

'I composed "Oh Carolina" in 1958 with a pencil on our doorsteps. I knew it was going to be a hit. In the yard they just say "Whoa!". And this was before the drumming or the background or anything, just the tune by itself with the backup with my brothers. When I sang in those days I always got a gathering, and people would do a kind of dip dance to it, not ska, and I realized it was a different kind of song. Even one recording artist who had a big hit previously wanted it. It was that well received then, before I met Count Ossie. And the song was so strong it promoted itself.'

According to him, Prince Buster and Count Ossie were not well-known then – Buster was just a DJ and bouncer with Duke Reid, and Ossie's Nyabinghi drumming was confined to Wareika Hills: 'Mico, Junior and myself had spent time at Duke Reid's rehearsing the song. Prince Buster showed great interest in the song so we decided to cut it with him instead. Count Ossie was very pleasant, a very calm gentleman . . . Owen Grey came up with the piano riff, just cold, from out of nowhere. He had not rehearsed it with us before. A kind of *deus ex machina* event.

'They were playing it up to 15 times a night at Forresters Hall. It got so big, the radio could no longer ignore it. The first time it came over JBC the announcer, Radcliffe Butler, said "Here is a very controversial song." Because "Oh Carolina" was the first song in the history of Jamaica to gave the Rastafarian movement respectability. But in "Oh Carolina" it was just the drums, there were no Rastafarian lyrics. There was no protest, there was no philosophy, no theology. And so it was acceptable as an art form that somehow empowered African roots in a very unintimidating, subtle fashion.'

He says that because of the drums and because Mico wore a full beard, people at first thought the Folkes Brothers were Rastafarians. But they were and still are Christians.

'"Oh Carolina" is not ska; neither is it calypso or rhythm and blues or boogie woogie or mento or even rock n' roll. It is essentially an innovative heritage folk song. But it has echoes of some of the above. It was and still is a party song. It's a powerful thing, not written with any kind of formal tradition, but just powerful feral writing. Plus "Carolina" has a heavy drum sound: primal, ata-vistic, infectious, going back to your roots, but at the same time not making any threatening statement.

'"Oh Carolina" was not a song that gave me much pleasure to think about or much pleasure to talk about, despite it's fame. Sixty pounds was all I got for it, and even that was extracted from Buster under circumstances that were not very pleasant.'

---

group had the most to do with it, but the song's fresh sound wasn't just due to the drumming. What was original was the way the drums played off the other instruments and the singers' voices, trailing just a bit and almost playing call and answer. Combining the energy of R&B with the hypnotic repetition of Rastafarian drumming, the throbbing beat was eminently danceable but not frenetic. It was a happy, accidental melding of the right elements at the right time and place. If one song can be singled out as signifying the birth of reggae, 'Oh Carolina' is it.

1961 / **MURIEL**
Alton and Eddie

Alton Ellis is one of the greatest singers in reggae history. Here he remembers how it all began: 'I started as a dancer on Vere John Opportunity Hour. This was an open contest which took place around Jamaica for a period of six or seven years. Majestic Theatre, Ambassadors Theatre, Palace Theatre were the three main venues but sometimes on the final night it might move to a bigger theatre like Ward Theatre or Carib. I win a couple contests dancing and then switch to singing.

'I was singing on my own and Eddie Parkins asked me to join partner. In those days you have a lot of harmony singers in pair – Higgs and Wilson, Alton and Eddie, Blues Busters, Charmers, Clarendonians, Melodians. So it was Alton and Eddie then. We wrote "Muriel" and went to Coxsone. That was the birth of my career really.'

1961 / OVER THE RIVER
Jiving Juniors

With number one hits like 'Lollipop Girl', 'Over The River' and 'Sugar Dandy', The Jiving Juniors were one of the biggest groups of the immediate pre-ska era. They broke up before ska really developed, but lead singer Derrick Harriot went on to become one of reggae's most consistent hit makers, topping the charts as late as 1985. Another Jiving Junior, Count Prince Miller, had a big number one hit in 1971 with a version of 'Mule Train'.

The Jiving Juniors at work

1960 / WORRIED OVER YOU
Keith (Stewart) and Enid (Cumberland)
1962 / HOUSEWIVES' CHOICE
Derrick and Patsy
1963 / WHEN YOU CALL MY NAME
Stranger (Cole) and Patsy

Listened to in sequence, these 'man-woman call and answer' songs illustrate the transition from R&B imitation to chugging shuffle to hard-edged ska. The similariites are obvious but, although difficult to define, the more important differences in sound and feel are unmistakable.

'Housewives' Choice' was so called because it was heavily requested on Marie Garth's radio show. (This was the first and perhaps the best of the 'man smart, woman smarter' vocal tussles which continue to be popular, *a la* Papa San and Lady G, Beenie Man and Lady Saw.) Keith Stewart went on to become lead singer with Byron Lee during the 1970s and released a number of albums featuring love-ballad covers which were especially popular with the ladies.

Derrick in 'Derrick and Patsy' was Derrick

Morgan, a giant of the early days. The same Patsy sang on both 'Housewives' Choice' and 'When you call my name', her real name being Millicent Todd.

The Stranger was Stranger Cole, a big star of the early ska days who is still going strong today under the name StrangeJah Cole. He relates the following: 'When I was born people say I didn't look like any of my relatives so they called me strange. But now I look like my father who was also a musician, a guitarist. My son Squidly Cole is now a drummer for Ziggy Marley. So I guess you could say music is in my blood.'

Stranger and StrangeJah

1963 / **LION OF JUDAH**
Delroy Wilson
1963 / **KING OF KINGS**
Jimmy Cliff

Two of the earliest reggae songs lauding Haile Selassie. Jimmy Cliff's is a parable: 'The lion say I am king and I reign.' Delroy Wilson is straightforward in praise: 'The lion of Judah shall break every chain.' Interestingly, both were in their early teens when they made these songs.

1963 / **RUKUMBINE**
Carlos Malcolm and The Afro-Jamaican Rhythms

Carlos Malcolm started in the music business in 1960 as a young arranger/producer for the Jamaica Broadcasting Corporation. He was part of the Variety Music Department's original team with the responsibility to develop programmes which would nurture and utilise local talent.

One of the programmes he helped develop was 'The Jamaican Hit Parade' which was presented live from a local theatre and served as an inspiration and push-start for many Jamaican artists who went on to interntional fame. Carlos also wrote incidental music and conducted the tropical music on location for the first James Bond movie, 'Dr No', which was filmed in Jamaica. He also composed full length musicals for the Jamaican theatre.

Carlos Malcolm and The Afro-Jamaican Rhythms, a ten-piece band, blended folk music with modern harmonies. 'Rukumbine', their most famous song, is an old Jamaican folk song with a countless number of bawdy verses. Malcolm's version blended the original mento sound with the hot new ska beat and in his hands 'Rukumbine' sounded like a true original – fresh, modern and 'happening' yet with an unmistakeably authentic Jamaican flavour.

Malcolm migrated to the Bahamas shortly after 'Rukumbine' became a hit. His resident band was still popular with the fans at the Sombrero Club in Kingston. Gradually his contact with Jamaican music faded, but he played on in the U.S. until the early seventies.

1963 / **DON'T STAY OUT LATE**
Kenrick Patrick
1963 / **ROUGH AND TOUGH**
Stranger Cole

Kenrick Patrick, also sang under the name Lord Creator. Born in Trinidad, he reportedly came to Jamaica on holiday and liked it so much he stayed for good. His 'Independent Jamaica' was the biggest selling record of 1962 and in 1963 he topped the yearly charts again with 'The End'. He had a lot of other hits like 'Evening News', 'Golden Love' and later on 'Kingston Town'.

Lord Creator was basically a balladier, and while 'Don't Stay Out Late' has a lot of ska in the beat, the singing is strictly smooth crooning. It contrasts strongly with 'Rough and Tough', another big hit of 1963.

Stranger Cole's rugged stop and start vocals, without a trace of any 'pseudo American accent', showed clearly that ska was not just an R&B variation but a new and unmistakably Jamaican style of music.

1964 / SAMMY DEAD OH
1964 / OIL IN MY LAMP
Monty Morris

When the Jamaican musical entourage went to the New York World's Fair in 1964, it included Prince Buster, Jimmy Cliff, and The Blues Busters. But the tour was built around Eric 'Monty' Morris and his two big hits 'Sammy Dead Oh'

and 'Oil in My Lamp'. Yet in a few years Monty Morris had virtually vanished from the Jamaican music scene. Clancy Eccles recorded Monty Morris in 1968 and said this about him: 'Very nice person but a bit too soft, that's why he didn't make any money out of the business. Everybody gyp Monty. He asked me for cash. Monty say "Clancy, I don't want any royalties", so I just give Monty the cash that Monty had asked for. When I went to Monty he was living in a fowl coop.' Monty Morris lives in England now. But for these two songs and a few others like 'Strong Man Samson', the man who might have been Jamaica's first reggae star has been almost forgotten.

'Sammy Dead Oh' is an old Jamaican folk tune and 'Oil In My Lamp' is a traditional gospel song. Morris sang with a broad, rural accent and both songs have a pronounced mento beat, showing how deeply traditional indigenous music influenced the modern Jamaican sound.

Some of the Jamaican performers at the New York World's Fair. Monty Morris is standing on the right, Prince Buster is standing on the left and Jimmy Cliff is crouching on the left.

1964 / **CARRY GO BRING COME**
Justin Hinds and The Dominos

In 1964 Justin Hinds seemed set to become one of Jamaica's music's biggest stars. Needing just one take, a rarity for the perfectionist Duke Reid, 'Carry Go Bring Come' was an instant classic, one of those songs that seem to have sprung directly from the collective unconscious. Number one in Jamaica for over a month, even then it seemed to have been around forever.

Justin Hinds did follow up with moderate hits like 'Botheration', 'Once a Man, Twice a Child' and 'The Stone that the Builder Refused'. But just as suddenly as he had shot to prominence, this man who might have been another Toots Hibbert or Bob Marley vanished from the music scene. According to him: 'I walk away from the music business because the music was getting out of control. It wasn't there with the spiritual vibration. So I stayed off for a while.'

Countryman Justin Hinds

He did have a number one hit in 1970 with 'Drink Milk' and later remade 'Carry Go'. But he never devoted himself full-time to music. Born and raised in Steer Town, Justin Hinds still makes his home in this farming community. His has been a rather unique career, the quintessential example of the artist who refuses to stray from his roots. Emerging every once in a while to release new records, he would steadfastly refuse any offers to change his mode of life, retreating back to country home.

One of his biggest fans was Bob Marley. In a 1975 interview he spontaneously remarked: 'You have another good group in Jamaica what nobody no hear bout neither, you know. Group name Justin Hinds and The Dominos. The little youth there can sing. Them just stay in the country and them voice just fine and strong man. Them come in a studio, them just sing down the whole place.'

Justin Hinds still releases the occasional record and performs now as Justin Hinds and The Revivers, which includes his son Jerome on bass. He has other well-known songs like 'Rub Up Push Up', 'Mother Banner', 'Save A Bread' and 'King Samuel'. But his fame and reputation still rest largely on 'Carry Go Bring Come'.

'Carry Go Bring Come' is famous as one of the earliest protest songs. According to popular legend, the lyrics refer to then Prime Minister Bustamante's wife:

> This carry go bring come my dear, bring misery
> This carry go bring come my dear, bring misery
> You're going from home to home, making disturbances
> It's time you stop doing those things, you old jezebel
> The meek shall inherit the earth, you old jezebel
> The meek don't like to see, wicked disturbances
> It's better to seek our home, in mount zion heights
> Instead of heaping oppression, upon an innocent man
> Time will tell on you, you old jezebel
> How long shall the wicked reign, over my people

Yet there is little tension in the music and 'Carry Go Bring Come' is hardly deemed a protest song today. Indeed it's commonly considered a great party song guaranteed to 'mash up the place' when it's played at oldies sessions – further proof, some say, of the precedent beat takes over lyrics in reggae. (Indeed except for the repeated last line, the song could be easily construed as a warning to gossip-mongers.) What always grabs you is that wonderful, primeval trombone figure. Even though it's repeated over and over again, you still keep wanting to hear it long after the song is finished.

1964 / SIMMER DOWN
The Wailers

An even greater lyricist than Marley once wrote, 'Some are born great, some become great and some have greatness thrust upon them.' 'Simmer Down' is proof that Bob was one of the former. It was only his third record, the first being an amateurish 'Judge Not', the second a catchy cover of a country and western tune 'One Cup Of Coffee'. Cut in late 1963 when he was only eighteen, 'Simmer Down' is a song which rhythmically and melodically, if not lyrically, he would never surpass. According to Leroy Pierson and Roger Steffens: '. . . "Simmer Down", a song Bob wrote some two years before recording it as the first Wailers' song. He had, in fact, won several amateur competitions including the prestigious Opportunity Knocks contest at the Ward Theatre, as a soloist performing "Simmer Down".'

They give this story of The Wailers' first audition with Coxsone Dodd: 'The Wailers faced Coxsone early one December morning. Peter played acoustic guitar and the group sang four songs, "Straight and Narrow Way", "I'm Going Home", "Do You Remember" and "I Don't Need Your Love", Bob's latest composition and the tune he expected would "reach" Coxsone and become a hit. As they finished the last song, Coxsone seemed pleased but not overly impressed. Then Bunny said "Bob, mek we do 'Simmer Down", the song they used as a warm up number in rehearsals. Bob had lost interest in the tune, but before he could protest, Peter was striking out the chords and the group was singing

harmony. Coxsone waved his hand and stopped them after two verses and told them to return the next morning to record the whole set of songs he had just heard, beginning with "Simmer Down", a tune he judged would be a champion in the sound system dances.'

Much of the excellence of 'Simmer Down' was due to the backing of The Skatalites. The tight arrangement of the song's raw energy lend it a driving yet controlled insistency which can still be felt three decades later.

'Simmer Down' was an instant sensation. Pierson and Steffens relate that: 'That evening The Wailers attended a Coxsone dance in western Kingston and were astounded that he was already playing an acetate of "Simmer Down". The crowd loved the song and demanded it be played again and again. When Coxsone released "Simmer Down" for the public sale, he quickly moved seventy thousand copies.'

It's been said that Marley wrote 'Simmer Down' especially for his mother, who wasn't at all pleased that her son had ended up in the violent music business.

'Simmer Down' hit number one in January 1964, the first of many for The Wailers – it's a myth that Bob Marley was rarely popular on Jamaica's

Bunny, Bob and Peter

charts. It's possible The Wailers wrote the song collectively. But none of Bunny Wailer's or Peter Tosh's individual works was ever as good. 'Simmer Down' had the unique Marley touch and its imaginative use of Jamaican proverbs and dialect proved to be one of his hallmarks, as did the burning topicality. Lyrically of course he had a long way to go. There was nothing here to compare with the stark imagery and verbal wordplay of his post-1972 work.

1964 / IT'S YOU
Toots and The Maytals

Toots, as he is the first to admit, was not a great lyricist. But in the art of creating a compelling atmosphere around a pointedly essential phrase, he had no equal. 'It's You' is sheer musical euphoria and a completely convincing portrayal

of ecstasy. This lonely boy has found the love of his life and is experiencing complete joy for the first and perhaps only time in his life. It's impossible to conceive of a happier song. Incidentally the flip side of 'It's You' was the equally celebrated 'Daddy', a slow R&B-like melody which Toots says was inspired by a real dream. 'It's You/Daddy' was probably the biggest two-sided hit in reggae history and likely also the best.

Funnily, when 'Daddy' was laid down for The Maytals' first album with Dynamic Sounds, their manager Ronnie Nasrallah felt it was a weak track. So it was relaid as the flip side of 'It's You'. 'It's You' dutifully became a massive hit, spending several weeks at the top of the charts. One night RJR deejay Tony Verity accidentally played the wrong side, and suddenly 'Daddy' became a song everyone wanted to hear.

COXSONE DODD REMINISCES ABOUT THE YOUNG BOB MARLEY

Coxsone Dodd remembers Bob Marley's early days at Studio One: 'Bob Marley was more or less like an adoption 'cause he used to stay by me, you know. He lived here at Brentford Road for about six years. I had an 'adoption' contract with Bob. It was really keep and care, but they (the Wailers) were really kids then. I used to provide whatever. Let's face it, it's really hard for the artistes. I encouraged them to find a part-time work and not just depend on the recording because it's pretty tough in Jamaica.

'I knew Bob would make it. That's why I took care of the guy so good. We had four rooms at the back and after the lady Bob's mother had left him with couldn't keep him anymore, he came here. The lady even co-signed the contract. I bought him a bed and a stereo and had Ernie Ranglin teach him to play the guitar. His setback was when he joined up with Mortimer Planno who was a Rastafarian. Him just smoke all day and felt like a king. Bob, personally, was good. You could see he had dynamics. I appointed him the leader of the group after Junior Braithwaite (the original leader of the group) left. But he was jealous of the Gaylads. Bob said I had too many artistes and should let some go, including the Gaylads. When they first came the group had the name the Juveniles. They did two songs with that name. Then we wanted a name with more positive action, so I thought of The Wailers because Al Page and The Wailers at that time was swinging in America.

'When they first came to me they had songs that was all do over material so I instructed them to try and do some writing. So that evening we started and we found a topic. And we set up 'It Hurts To Be Alone'. They came in for a rehearsal after that. Then I sent for Ernie Ranglin, got them together. But it took some time for them, because all they had was like their early doo-wop stuff. But I was very impressed with them the first time, because I was open to really get a group with that team feel. Junior Braithwaite definitely had the best voice. After he left for America I demand that Bob do the lead. They needed a lot of polishing but Bob had a gift, you know, he was willing just to get his steps together. He had the makings. When The Techniques came out with "Little Did You Know", man, it was really, really a big struggle for them [The Wailers], because Slim Smith was really a better vocalist than Bob.'

'Broadway Jungle' on the other hand, not only brilliantly evokes the continuous fighting, howling and quarreling of dogs in the Jamaican night (in fact most Jamaicans know it by the title 'Dog War'), but creates a most poignant allegory of the plight of the ghetto slum dweller trying to scratch and claw his way out of the jungle in his search for a better life. As Toots tells the story: '"Dog War" we just go in the studio and feel the riddim. The Skatalites was playing and just think up the words. The words didn't mean anything at first but we make it have meaning after a while. You know, in the jungle, and leaving from Coxsone to Prince Buster.'

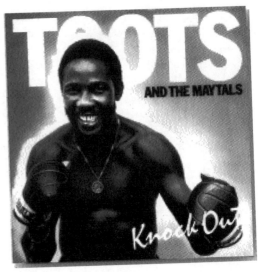

> We were caught in the jungle
> By the hands of a man
> We're out of the jungle
> We're going to broadway
> When we reach out of the jungle
> We're going to jump and shout
> Come on girl, come on boy
> Jump in the line, everybody gonna be alright

There is an unmistakable element of humour and fun in the whole thing – Raleigh and Jerry seem to be having a hell of a time howling in the background and it's hard not to smile while listening to the song. Appropriate of course, because no matter how hard times may get, it's a Jamaican trait to find something in the situation to laugh about, even if only for a minute.

Three things stand out in The Maytals' early work. One is the unashamed dialect speech pattern. While other artists were straining (if not always successfully) to imitate American accents, Toots was holding forth in what Jamaicans call 'the broadest patois' – singing like the common man spoke.

The second quality that leaps out is the call and response interplay of lead and backup singers. This is not unique to Jamaican music, and is usually found in most African derived music forms, but is a trait so pronounced in early reggae that it became almost a signature feature. Toots and The Maytals made it into an unmatchable art form. The razor sharp shout and answer harmonisation is what gives The Maytals'

early work a unique sense of exuberance, with their voices combining almost like multilayered talking drums. Listening to 'It's You', it's hard to believe there are only three men singing, because voices seem to be coming from everywhere.

The third element that makes the music so memorable, is its utter lack of self-consciousness. There's no attitude or posturing – *I want to see my mommy and daddy* – Toots implores in 'Daddy'. And the singers in 'Broadway Jungle' are too caught up in the music and having too much fun to worry about sounding like silly baying hounds. And this is the most attractive part of the whole thing – it sounds so unforced and natural. It's hard to imagine the same atmosphere being created again and such a performance being duplicated. In a sense it captures the lost innocence of the early 1960s which many Jamaicans still yearn for. Thomas Wolfe said you can't go home again, but the guileless gaiety of the young Maytals sometimes makes it seem possible, if only for a while.

1964 / MUSIC IS MY OCCUPATION
1964 / EASTERN STANDARD TIME
Don Drummond and The Skatalites

Genius, they say, is often akin to madness. Don Drummond, the greatest instrumentalist Jamaica ever produced, was a case in point. In 1962,

THE MAYTALS — ORIGINAL YARD-STYLE MUSIC

Today, Jamaicans take reggae's popularity among themselves for granted. Yet as recently as 1960, outside the artificially preserved mento bands of the tourist enclaves, Jamaican music *per se* simply did not exist. The few records made by Jamaican artists were nearly all covers of American R&B.

Even as ska emerged in the early 1960s, there was no reason to believe it would be any more than one of those temporary dance crazes (like the rumba, cha cha, or tango or even calypso) periodically thrown up by southern countries; music which gained a brief popularity in North America and Europe but then just as quickly lost appeal and usually degenerated into a 'vital and to be preciously preserved part of our national heritage (and hence no longer genuinely popular)' native music.

Many of the upper-class openly sneered at ska and its exponents. W. Stanley Moss no doubt expressed the feeling of a lot of 'proper minded' Jamaicans when he wrote in a *Gleaner* review on 27 April 1965: 'Inevitably, it will be the small groups, having retained their names and individuality, which will survive the demise of ska. But the others, having become identified with an ephemeral craze, might come to regret their readiness to jump on the ska bandwagon. What, for example, will the word "Skatalite" mean to the average Jamaican in a few years time?'

If reggae's greatest achievement was to win the unmitigated loyalty of its own people, no man was more responsible for this than Frederick 'Toots' Hibbert. For during the crucial formative years, from 1963 to 1966, Toots and The Maytals stood head and shoulders above all others as the best and most popular vocal group Jamaica had ever seen.

Toots is often given official recognition as the inventor of reggae (as a musical form differing from rocksteady or ska) because he was the first to use the word in song. (Ironically that song, 'Do The Reggay', is one of his lesser efforts). While it seems rather nitpicking to assign the beginnings of a musical form to the use of a word, there is some justification in the assertion. It can be argued that, before The Maytals, Jamaican music was just a regional version of American (or more dismissively, New Orleans) R&B. 'My Boy Lollipop'

may be great dance music, but it's just a cover version of an American original, not that different from faster R&B songs of the time. Even now it's played on American radio as a novelty oldies rock and roll hit with nary a mention of Jamaica.

Even The Skatalites and Don Drummond, for all their indubitable virtuosity and style, were often regarded as mere 'jazz men' playing R&B. The occasional flashes of authenticity like 'Oh Carolina', 'Carry Go Bring Come' and 'Simmer Down' stood out precisely because of their quality. Tunes like 'Sammy Dead Oh', 'Wings of a Dove' and 'Rukumbine' while undoubtedly Jamaican, were in essence modern remakes of old folk songs. And an original musical form cannot be created by simply restyling a limited body of traditional songs.

The Maytals changed all that. True, many early hits like 'Victory', 'Sixth and Seven Books' and 'He is Real' seemed to come straight out of the church – Jamaican versions of American Gospel. But The Maytals found their distinctive voice in 'Never Grow Old', 'Broadway Jungle', 'Pain in My Belly', 'It's You' and 'Never You Change' There was no looking back. From thence flowed a series of brilliant songs which from the very first note proclaimed that here was a music which could only be created by a Jamaican in Jamaica for Jamaicans and there was nothing else like it on earth.

critic George Shearing of *Downbeat* magazine, ranked him as one of the top five trombonists in the world. Yet he was seriously mentally disturbed. According to Coxsone Dodd: 'He was genuinely mad. I used to go to their [the future Skatalites] rehearsals at Homestead Road with Count Ossie's Band, before they move up to Wareika Hills. I think Don smoked ganja too much in those early days. I saw him once at Federal auditioning as a singer. I said, "But you are Don D. You are not a vocalist, you are a musician." He had been playing at Club Havana with Ken Williams, and then gone to Bellevue for a while and now he was imagining he was a vocalist.' Some say his madness was caused by frustration at a lack of recording opportunities. But, says Rico Rodríquez, 'Drummond wasn't doing any re-cording to feel frustration. He used to practice at the time. He had a folio of about 300 selections that he and I used to work on together . . . he was just creating, but he wasn't going into any studios. The frustration that he probably had was from playing in bands before.'

Coxsone Dodd first saw Drummond perform at the Majestic Theatre in 1960. Dodd was still specialising in calypso sessions with performers like Lord Tanamo, but he'd already cut a few singles spotlighting rising jazz musicians – the first being 'Shuffling Jug' by 'Clue J' Johnson. Drummond had a history of mental problems and had just concluded a three-month stay in a mental institution – he'd committed himself – when Dodd caught his live act. Dodd had heard stories about the good-looking mustachioed trombonist's erratic personality, but he was struck by the consistency of his playing. Astonishingly, Drummond didn't possess a trombone of his own but rented or borrowed others. Coxsone expressed his confidence in his new artist by purchasing him a brand new one, naturally charged against royalties. Even while ackowledged as Jamaica's pre-eminent instrumentalist, Drummond's mental problems never went away. Eventually he slipped into complete madness. On January 2, 1965, he stabbed his girlfriend (Maguerita Mahfood, famed rumba dancer) to death, and then gave himself up to the police. He was convicted of murder, but the court judged him insane. He was classified a criminal lunatic and sent to Bellevue Asylum. He died there by his own hand on 6 May 1969.

Maguerita Mahfood (standing rear right)

The Skatalites are the most celebrated band in reggae history, and deservedly so. Apart from making great instrumentals on their own, The Skatalites as a group or as individuals played on almost every ska song of note.

The Skatalites' story began in West Kingston at Alpha Boys Catholic School, a mixture of reform school and repository for wayward boys, which still exists today. Many early Jamaican musicians served their apprenticeship at Alpha – Rico Rodríquez, Herman Marquiz, Tommy McCook, Leroy 'Horsemouth' Wallace, Eric 'Fish' Clarke, Bobby Ellis, Vincent Gordon, Rupert Anderson, Joe Harriot, and Don Drummond.

Many went to Alpha at a very young age. Rico Rodríquez entered when only ten. Before picking up an instrument, the students learnt theory. According to Rodríquez: 'The first thing you learnt at Alpha was the rudiments of music – lines, spaces and scales. Theory was a must. You were asked questions on a blackboard and you gave your answers verbally. You didn't start to play just so – you had to know what you were doing.'

Students were taught European classics and songs like 'Happy Wanderer', 'Sleeping Beauty', Colonel Bogie' and 'Life On The Ocean'. They were discouraged from playing popular tunes they heard on the radio. Members of the senior band, Drummond for example, would stay after school and teach younger students. Rodríquez says: 'Drummond was a quiet person, but a strict teacher. We were friends, but when it came to teaching, it was very serious. If Drummond didn't teach me so well and the bandmaster came along to check on me and I was not that good, that reflected on the teacher. So the standard had to be there at all times.'

Alpha's music teacher was Eric Deans, who led the famous Eric Deans Orchestra in the 1940s and 1950s. According to Deans' daughter Deanna – who later married producer Lloyd 'The Matador' Daley – Brooks, Drummond, Ranglin, Alphonso and McCook all played in this orchestra.

Senior band members played at garden parties and other functions and some became keenly interested in jazz. Joe Harriot, Little Jesus, Roy Harper, Don Drummond and Wilton 'Bogey' Gaynair were some of the outstanding Jamaican jazz musicians of the early 1950s. The primary influences were the big bands like Duke Ellington. Local players, no doubt, found further stimulus in Radio Jamaica's Jazz Hour, which featured leading American artists such as Miles Davis, Thelonius Monk, Art Blakey and Max Roach.

Joe Harriot

The Skatalites were formed in 1963. The band consisted of Tommy McCook and Roland Alphonso (tenor sax), Lester Stirling (alto sax), Don Drummond (trombone), Jah Jerry (guitar), 'Dizzy' Johnny Moore (trumpet), Lloyd Knibbs (drums), Lloyd Brevette (bass), Jackie Mittoo (piano), Lord Tanamo and Tony DaCosta (vocals). They were the cream of the nation's musicians. Most had come through Alpha, and some had gained considerable reputations as jazz players.

There was a certain debate over the idea of such gifted musicians devoting themselves primarily to ska, conservative elements pointing out that ska was a soon to be forgotten fad. But the middle and upper classes began paying more attention to ska. The government invited The Skatalites to play at Bournemouth Gardens, an official spot for garden parties and picnics, on Sundays. The 'uptown' crowd turned out to watch and listen, and responded enthusiastically.

The Skatalites were an acoustic band, sticking to piano and acoustic bass while others picked up the organ. They played from music sheets and charts or the various instrumentalists' parts would be written out. Coxsone was their main source of work, although, like many others, they complained that he did not pay well. They also recorded for Duke Reid and Philip Yap's Top Deck Records. There were rumours of discontent and that Coxsone played Roland Alphonso off against Tommy McCook.

There were also financial and personal problems. Lloyd Brevette got into trouble on several occasions and was somtimes replaced on bass by Jackie Opel, a well-known singer. Members were not earning enough to support their families. Necessity even forced them to manufacture some of their equipment locally. Drummond had a mental problem and was repeatedly admitted to a sanitarium for weeks at a time.

Some say Coxsone felt the band was losing prestige and inveigled Roland Alphonso and Jackie Mittoo to leave, which caused the group's collapse. So after less than two years together, The Skatalites disbanded in 1965. Soul Brothers, headed by Alphonso, came into existence almost immediately. Mittoo became the resident producer/arranger for all Dodd's artists at Studio One from early 1966 until he left the country in 1968. He died in 1990, still only 42.

Yet The Skatalites' story did not end there. The band reformed in various combinations over the years and in the 1990s became a more-or-less set aggregation, comprising many of the original members. In 1996 they were nominated for a Reggae Grammy for their album 'The Skatalites 30-Year Celebration'.

The Skatalites' greatest instrumentals combine a driving beat with Don Drummond's piercing trombone on songs like 'Treasure Isle', 'Man in the Street', 'Dan The Lion', 'Scandal', 'The Rebirth of Marcus Garvey', 'Green Island', 'Schooling The Duke' and especially 'Occupation' and 'Eastern Standard Time'. Reggae afficionados can spend hours arguing over which was the best Skatalites song, but to us there is no doubt that these last two are the best instrumental songs Jamaica has ever produced. And for all the happy go lucky infectiousness of these songs, there is also more than a hint of melancholy. Almost as if Don D could sense the unhappy destiny fate had in store for him.

1964 / JAMAICAN SKA
Byron Lee and The Dragonaires

'Jamaican Ska' is undoubtedly the best reggae record Byron Lee ever made, an infectious, happy go lucky party tune which never fails to get the feet moving. It may be a little mindless – it was once featured in a Frankie Avalon beach party movie – but what's wrong with an occasional dose of good old-fashioned fun? In fact, BLD were also featured in the first James Bond movie, 'Dr No', performing 'Jamaican Ska' in a beach-bar scene.

Byron Lee has been involved in all aspects of Jamaican music from its earliest days, as a band leader, promoter, producer and studio owner. Though few deny his importance, many belittle him for turning the music into pap for uptown consumption. (American pop music critic Robert Christgau derisively called him 'The Lawrence Welk of Reggae'.) In his defence he has this to say: 'Nobody uptown knew what the music [ska] was about, they couldn't relate to it. It can be said that we were responsible for moving the music from West Kingston into the upper- and middle-classes who could afford to buy records and support the music. Then radio picked up the music and it became the order of the day.'

Lee is partly resented because he is of Chinese descent in a mostly black land and grew rich from a music he did nothing to help create while

Byron Lee with Sammy Davis Jr and Ronnie Nasralla.

the true originators ended up poor. He can't help his race, he says. Isn't it enough that he was Jamaican-born and bred? And is it his fault that he was a good businessman and others weren't? Many artists claim that as a producer he never gave proper credits or paid correct royalties. But, except for a few notable exceptions like Duke Reid, Sonia Pottinger and Leslie Kong, they say that of most Jamaican producers.

Hopeton Lewis has this to say: 'I was lead vocalist for Byron Lee's band from about 1971 to 1976. Now people say this and say that. But in my honest opinion Byron Lee was the person who groomed me into a performer and showed me discipline within the music. The money was small, but it was like a school to me. And what I can do today on stage or off stage, how I present myself on stage was because of Byron. So it was definitely a positive thing.'

1964 / MY BOY LOLLIPOP
Millie Small

'My Boy Lollipop', a re-make of the 1957 Barbie Gay R&B hit, came out in London in March

The line *Listen to this one now baby* sounds almost like Sam Cooke. But what makes this song more than just another R&B cover (albeit wonderfully sung) is the driving, insistent, yet laid back ska beat.

The Blues Busters were perhaps the biggest stars of the formative pre-ska years in the late 1950s and early sixties, and made something of a name for themselves overseas. They toured with Byron Lee's band throughout the 1960s and 1970s and are still fondly remembered by many. Both died early and on Phillip's death in 1992, their former managers Byron Lee and Ronnie Nasralla took out a full page memorial ad in *The Gleaner* with the legend 'The Dream is Over'. It must have touched the hearts of everyone connected with the heady, long ago days when a new music was being born.

Millie Small's pals from the Juke Box bar carry her in triumph along Rum Lane.

1964. Millie Small, formerly half of the popular Jamaican duo Roy and Millie and only 15, had been brought to England in early 1964 by Chris Blackwell to cut songs for his Island Records. Ernie Ranglin played on guitar (he would that same year win *The Melody Maker* award for best jazz guitarist) and Rod Stewart (well before his pop superstar days), played harmonica. Leased to Phillips Records worldwide, it made number one in Britain and on 6 June 1964 reached number two in America.

1965 / **SOON YOU'LL BE GONE**
The Blues Busters [Phillip James and Lloyd Campbell]

'Soon You'll Be Gone' shows how derivative much of early Jamaican recorded music was. The phrasing and singing style are so closely patterned after R&B that even throw away slang asides are copied.

> (Ha, ha, listen to this one now baby)
> I guess that's how it's got to be
> I know your little heart is full of misery
> But I still hope and pray
> That you will find another love someday'

THE BLUES BUSTERS

Behold how sweet it is

IN MEMORY OF THE

BLUES BUSTERS

THEIR BEST
SKA & SOUL HITS
1964-1966

HOW SWEET IT IS
WINGS OF A DOVE
YOU'RE NO GOOD
FROM RUSSIA WITH LOVE
THAT'S HEAVEN TO ME
SHAME AND SCANDAL
AND MANY OTHERS

1965 / BLAZING FIRE
Derrick Morgan

Derrick Morgan was one of the biggest stars of early Jamaican music, reportedly at one time having seven records in the Jamaican top ten. He and Prince Buster had a celebrated feud, which apparently began when Buster accused him of stealing a section from one of Buster's songs and putting it in a recording for Leslie Kong. And so Prince cut 'Black Head Chiney Man' in which he accused Morgan of being an 'uncle tom', asking – *Are you a black man or are you a chiney man* – and taunting Morgan with – *Look out black man, you're getting praise without raise.* Morgan retorted with 'Blazing Fire' – *You said it, now its a blazing fire, be still, I am your superior.*

All parties obviously saw the rivalry as a joke. The tongue-in-cheek opening line of 'Blazing Fire' goes *Lutang Moungzhi!*, Chinese for 'You damn fool'. But the back and forth duel sold a lot of records. This was the first of the antagonistic rivalries that were to become a continuing feature of Jamaican music down the years, such as I-Roy and Prince Jazzbo, Ninja Man and Shabba Ranks, Beenie Man and Bounty Killer.

Morgan continued to have hits through the sixties and into the seventies, most notably the celebrated 'Tougher Than Tough' (1967). Ironically he became a sort of icon among the racist but ska loving 'skinheads' in Britain. Born with a serious vision impairment which progressively got worse, he went completely blind about 1985. But Derrick still does shows, and in 1995 he and Prince Buster recreated their famous rivalry on stage. As Prince Buster once sang, time is indeed longer than rope.

Derrick Morgan

1966 / HARD MAN FE DEAD
Prince Buster [Cecil Campbell]

Prince Buster was the most flamboyant character of the early Jamaican music scene, embellishing his matinee idol looks with snazzy suits, flashy cars and a macho swagger. He was also the first all-in-one reggae personality – sound system deejay and operator, record producer, singer and promoter. And there was a lot of substance to his style. Whatever the true story behind 'Oh Carolina', would it have been a definitive classic without Buster's ideas? Arguably the first stirrings of deejay music can be heard in 'Judge Dread', and it was his 'Wash Wash' that broke locally produced ska into Britain. According to Byron Lee, Prince Buster was the 'king' of bluebeat.

Prince Buster was also an early proponent of black consciousness and joined the black Muslim movement. When Peter Tosh was arrested in 1968 for blocking traffic while protesting against the illegal Ian Smith regime in Rhodesia, it was Buster who posted bail.

Perhaps more than any other of the early producers, Buster somehow injected an indefinable but unmistakably Jamaican element into his music. His productions were never subtle, but he had a unique gift for tapping primeval, raw energy as in The Maytals' 'Broadway Jungle' and 'Pain In My Belly'. Buster's own music never reached that same peak, but he did have a knack for catchy lyrics and simple, pungent rhythms. And in this humourous story of a man being buried prematurely, Prince Buster created an enduring metaphor for the resilience of the Jamaican people – *They pick him up / They lick him down / Him bounce right back / What a hard man fe dead.*

1965 / KINGSTON TOWN
Lord Creator

A lot of 'purists' grumble about 'watered down music' when foreign bands cover reggae songs. But reggae artists themselves are usually ecstatic, since it gives them a chance of getting a real return from their songs.

Lord Creator, real name Kenrick Patrick, was one of the biggest stars of the early ska period. But he fell on hard times. At one time he was a street alcoholic living from drink to drink on handouts. Some kind-hearted persons in the music business rounded up enough money to buy him a plane ticket and shipped him back home to his family in Trinidad.

Lord Creator

Lord Creator had long given up music when UB-40 covered 'Kingston Town' in the early 1990s. But the royalties he earned enabled him to come back and live in Jamaica and he even began performing again. To him, having UB-40 cover his song was like winning the lottery.

1965 / DANCE CRASHER
Alton Ellis

From 1965 to 1967 the 'rude boys' captured the nation's imagination and spawned countless songs both celebrating and criticising their 'tough guy' attitude and approach to life. Some say the first 'rudie' song was The Wailers' 'Rude Boy Ska'. The ratchet knife flicking 'rudies' were sometime sentimentalized as 'robin hood' folk heroes. But Alton Ellis had a different view: 'The bad boy business just sprang up in Jamaica and I couldn't appreciate what's happening. Like when I go to a little dance and want to enjoy myself this bad boy thing and them fling bottle bout the place and a lot of stupidness. So I write things like "Dance Crasher":

Oh dance crasher don't break it up
Please don't make a fuss
Don't use a knife and take somebody else life
You'll be sorry cause there's a death sentence
And you won't have a chance
And that will be your last dance.'

'Cause if you kill a man, them go hang you – *You could have been a champion, Like Mr. Bunny Grant.* Bunny Grant was lightweight champion then. I was proud of him because Bunny is a Boys Town boy also and instead of fighting in the dancehall and cause all them fuss they, him be a champion and have a nice successful life. I don't know what him make of it now but then Bunny was very successful and I was pointing at the youth in this direction.

'At one time I think Jamaicans was too subtle a people, too subservient you know. Badly suffering and yet we do nothing about it more than just fold up like cabbage. So maybe that was the time when the revolution business turn over and it start. But I didn't appreciate it from the angle. Because you don't start in the dancehall, that don't really solve any political problem.'

1966 / **BAM BAM**
Toots and The Maytals

'I did "Bam Bam" for Festival. When you wrote for festival you had to write and blot out, write and blot out. First you had to know what a festival song was. The Festival people told that the song must be short and spicy and have good words and as anyone hear it for the first time they must be able to sing it the same time. So it shouldn't have too many words. And it mustn't be a love song like "O baby I love you". "Bam Bam" means I don't trouble no man, but if he trouble me it will be like a fight. You know, stand up for myself. It's sort of a revolutionary song.'

The first and best festival song winner, 'Bam Bam' is an exquisite piece of music. Toots' wordless cry floating over The Maytals' counterpoint chanting and the stop-start bongo drumming constitute one of the high points of Jamaican music. Although it came out in mid-1966 'Bam Bam' certainly wasn't ska, and it really didn't sound like rocksteady either. With its rythmic slowed-down beat and interplay of voice and acoustic drum, 'Bam Bam' has an unmistakably African feel – perhaps the first glimmerings of 'roots' reggae can be heard here. And its themes – *I fight for the right and not the wrong* – and – *This man don't trouble no man / But if you trouble this man / It will bring a bam bam* – would find an echo in countless other Jamaican songs down the years, most notably the Marley/Tosh anthem 'Get Up Stand Up'.

'Bam Bam' is unique in reggae history as the only song to chart in all four decades of the music's existence, starting with The Maytals' original in 1966, the version by Kojak and Liza in the late 1970s, one by Yellowman in the 1980s, and a Pliers cover in the 1990s. Truly a timeless tune.

1966 / **007 SHANTY TOWN**
Desmond Dekker and The Aces

'I write this song because of what was happening at the time. The students had a demonstration and it went all the way around to Four Shore Road and down to Shanty Town (Located in West Kingston, the Shanty Town area consisted of ramshackle dwellings, the majority of them made of cardboard, plywood, corrugated metal or some other discarded material. Hence the name.) You got wild life and thing like that because it down near to the beach. And the higher ones wanted to bulldoze the whole thing

ACES HIGH – REGGAE TAKES WING

'Shanty Town' reached number twelve in the U.K. charts in July 1967 and Desmond Dekker and The Aces went on a short, chaotic tour of England to support the song. Back home they turned out a string of hits during 1967 and 1968 including 'Mother Long Tongue', 'Keep A Cool Head', 'Wise Men' and 'Fu Manchu'. They came second in the 1967 Festival Song Contest with 'Unity', a song many thought better than the winner 'Ba Ba Boom', winning the D&G Sparkling Beverage Award of £100. In 1968 they won the title and £250 with 'Intensified Festival', a tune partly inspired by the 'intensified Tide' detergent ads so frequently heard at the time. Hence lines like – *Music for days, days and extra days.*

Unlike the smooth rocksteady artists like John Holt and The Paragons and Alton Ellis who looked to U.S. soul for inspiration and dealt mainly with love, Dekker's music was firmly rooted in the everyday realities of Jamaican life. His songs are full of local slang and have a strong, rural strain. 'Shanty Town' is a prime example. The call and response interplay between lead and harmony is clearly influenced by traditional Jamaican work songs like 'Hill and Gully Rider'.

In early 1969 Dekker hit big again in England with 'Israelites'. Reggae was fresh – the music had just completed the transformation from rocksteady – and Desmond Dekker and The Aces had behind them a string of original hits excelled only by The Maytals. Desmond Dekker was probably the biggest star in Jamaican music then and the man everyone looked to as reggae's standard bearer abroad. Toots' career had not fully recovered from his imprisonment on ganja charges. Bob Marley was still exploring with Lee Perry, developing the scratchy sound that would later take down and do their own thing and the students said no way. And it just get out of control. And whatsoever you hear on the record, that is what was going down. Man take a stone and throw it through the window, lick after somebody, and you read it as somebody just knock it and gone. Is just a typical riot 'cause I say – *Them a loot, them a shoot, them a wail.*

'It was wild, wild. "007" and "Oceans Eleven" were popular movies at that time. But "Shanty Town" was the one that give me international recognition. It was number one in Jamaica and went to number twelve on the British charts.'

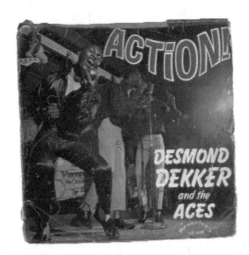

the world by storm. And Jimmy Cliff was in limbo – living mostly abroad, without any recent Jamaican hits.

Despite the constant predictions and wishful thinking, Jamaican music till then had garnered little success abroad. 'My Boy Lollipop' had gone to number two in America and topped the U.K. charts, but although Millie Small made Jamaicans claim it as their own, it was not only a cover of an American original, but was also produced in England. No Jamaican created record had come close to making the American Top 100. There had been sporadic success in Britain, but not enough to give anyone genuine hopes. Perhaps 'Israelites' was the song and Dekker the person to change all that.

So when he went on tour to the U.K. to promote 'Israelites', Desmond Dekker took the musical hopes of an entire nation with him. And to a large extent he satisfied them. 'Israelites' became a worldwide smash, gained gold record status and gave an immeasurable psychological boost to everyone connected with Jamaican music. Before this they lived on theoretical dreams. People kept saying Jamaican music could make it big abroad – but no one had actually 'broken through'. Suppose all the talk about foreign success was just an absurd cabin fever fantasy?

Dekker had to tour without The Aces. It wasn't his fault. One Ace, Winston Samuel, said he was a Rastafarian and 'Rastas did not fly on iron birds'. So he would not tour. The other Ace, Barry Howard, had decided to emigrate to the U.S. and had already booked his passage. He too was adamant in his decision. But even before 'Israelites' there had been friction in the group. According to Leslie Kong, The Aces sometimes refused to appear on stage and The Pioneers often had to back up Dekker. But without The Aces harmonising, especially

Stewart's deep bass vocals which counteracted Dekker's somewhat reedy voice, the impact just wasn't the same.

Still Dekker's career prospered. After 'Israelites' sensational impact, he followed up with 'A It Mek', which made number seven in the U.K. charts, although it failed to chart in the U.S. His version of Jimmy Cliff's 'You Can Get It' went to number two in Britain. He continued to be popular, but not quite equalling his heights of 1968 and 1969. But when Leslie Kong died of a heart attack at 37 in late August 1971, Dekker was devastated: 'His death really cut me up. When Les died, I didn't know what to do or what to say. Once he wasn't there to make decisions for me, I was afraid to make them on my own, for fear that they would be the wrong ones.'

Dekker's and Kong's professional relationship was unique in reggae. From his first song in 1962 to Kong's death, Dekker never recorded for anyone else. His career began to decline. As with virtually every other singer who migrated, his music withered away from its well-watered roots. Jamaicans have short memories, and in a few years Dekker was remembered only for his brilliant hits of 1967-69, his newer material ignored. But he continued to enjoy some success in Britain.

Not even Bob Marley (at least not while alive) sold as many records abroad as Desmond Dekker. Before dancehall's relatively recent chart success, Dekker's international commercial impact was unmatched in reggae. And no one who loves the music will ever forget the irresistible guitar lick, ice cool delivery, and wonderful harmonisations of 'Shanty Town' and the man who brought the sounds of reggae's golden age to the world's attention.

1966 / GIRL I'VE GOT A DATE
Alton Ellis

Alton Ellis has this to say about his biggest hit: 'It was very big, one of the songs that came on just at the time when we needed that change. That, rocksteady feel, we drop it from ska now. "Girl" was one of the songs that come on very strong in the rock-steady sound. The monster bass line, and drop and thing.

'I was always personally inclined to be a more loving type of person. This is something I have come to realise over the years. It's easier for me to sit down and write a song about love than about other situations. I feel it more and express it more. I think it's in my nature. Why? I write things like "Blackman's Pride" and "Cry Tough" but they don't come so fluently. When I sing songs like that, the expression is not as deep as when I sing "Girl", or 'Breaking Up' or 'I'm Still In Love' and things like that. And most of these songs are a story I'm telling about my life – it's personal:

> Girl I've Got a Date / And that just means
> I can't stay late
> All my life / I've been warning you girl
> You just can't be my wife
> Take it from me / I'm as free as the birds in the trees

'About half of my hits were about my first wife Pearl. I did a song called "Pearl" too. This woman, she inspire me a lot and it was unfortunate that we have to separate, but she cause me to make a lot of those songs. "Girl I've Got A Date", yes, and others like "I'm Still in Love", "I'm Just A Guy", "La La". There is a song I'm scared of, I tell you, a song I have on an album called "I'll Never Love Again".

'This is an oath that lived with me psychologically for years. Because of that I'm not so attached to no other woman. Every time I hear that song I remember that deep emotional oath. She was so much in control of my emotions that whenever she hurt me, Coxsone was happy, in the sense that he knew that I have some hit coming out of the situation. He wasn't happy for the problem you understand. The upset just

meant he's certain of a couple of hits. But he is the same one trying to keep us together all the time. She really was a great inspiration to me. But we had to separate, even though we have four kids together.'

1966 / YOU WON'T SEE ME
The Clarendonians

The Clarendonians, a duo consisting of Peter Austin and Ernest Wilson, were one of the biggest acts of the rocksteady era with a string of number one hits like 'Shoobie Doobie', 'Rude Boy Gone A Jail', 'Rudey Bam Bam', 'Tables Gonna Turn' and 'Dancing Forever'. Yet their two biggest hits were covers of The Beatles' 'You Won't See Me' and The Four Tops' 'You Can't Be Happy'.

Peter Austin is glad to have had a life in music, but is not happy with the way he and others have been treated: 'You know we have had no justice. We have been lied to so many times. People have made so many promises to us and then gone back on their word. We have been used, abused and refused. We got a lot of fame, but no fortune at all. We never saw any royalties.

'If it was for the music alone I would have starved. When Ernest went on his own in 1968, I got a job at the airport working with Shell as an aviation supervisor. And it is only through this job that I could buy myself a car and house.

'You know a lot of us artists who helped create this music are bitter. We see all kinds of people making fortunes off of reggae, and we got nothing. Even nowadays you see some hurry-come-up, one-song deejay making more money than we ever did in our entire careers. Somehow it just doesn't seem right.'

1966 / FATTY FATTY
The Heptones

'Fatty Fatty' is not only the best (if that is the word) sexually suggestive song in reggae, it's probably the equal of any 'dirty' song in popular music. The lyrics are wonderfully suggestive – unmistakable in intent but never explicit. And the simple, conversational words are given an almost poetic quality by their uncomplicated, rhythmical spacing. The rhymes in the song are acutely appropriate (mood, food, rude; galore, more, sure), and the throbbing bass line and slightly jerky melody lend a perfectly matched sensual atmosphere. (To show how tastes change, 'Fatty Fatty' was banned when it came out, but is now freely accepted as a 'classic'.)

What really gives 'Fatty Fatty' its unmistakable sense of quality however, is Leroy Sibbles' superb singing. The phrasing is breathtakingly precise, and his sweet tenor hardly disguises the aching feeling of raw desire which comes out most clearly on his moaning 'ahs' – the strained dulcet tones of the would-be seducer who can barely contain his lust. And the beautifully timed harmonisations of The Heptones give the song a dreamlike, flowing quality, not unlike that of a seduction. The manner in which they complete some of Sibbles' lines is almost spine tingling in its delicacy.

Leroy Sibbles tells how he wrote the song: 'I was in the yard playing the guitar. The other Heptones were at work. Most of the time I used to stay home and just write tunes, me alone. When they come home in the evening we just put what I wrote together. So me a fool round and this fat lady name Miss B walk in. She was short and fat, short and round, she walk like a little duck. She was a big woman to me, a

middle-age woman in her thirties. We were only teenagers that time, about 17 or 18. Miss B come in and like a joke I sing, "I need a fat girl". Of course "fat girl" is like a compliment to a woman here in Jamaica. From I sing that, the whole tune come together. After that every day in the bush somebody ask me to sing it. It was a hit before we even recorded it. "Fatty" played twice on the air and then they banned it, say it will spoil the children. But that was good. Because everywhere for months and months it was "Fatty", on the streets, on the jukeboxes. That was when people started knowing The Heptones.'

Sometimes the song is mistakenly regarded as a parody poking fun at fat women. But many Jamaican men have decidedly robust tastes and prefer women of rubenesque proportions, 'solid' as they say. 'Fat gal' is a term of the highest compliment when applied to a woman. (Major Mackerel had a hit in 1987 with 'Anorexol Body' about women trying to put on weight with an appetite enhancing drug designed to combat anorexa nervosa. And one of 1990's biggest sellers was Red Dragon's song taunting skinny women called 'Ku Kun Kun'.) 'Fatty Fatty' may be humourous in its word play but Sibbles sings it with the deadly seriousness of a man who knows what he wants and intends to get it. '*Girl I know you want it, and you're gonna get a lot of it*'. Or as a Jamaican man might otherwise put it – 'Right ya now gal, fun an joke done'.

Jamaica has a long and honoured tradition of (some might call it a pre-occupation with) suggestive, sexually oriented music. Mento, even more than its Trinidadian cousin calypso, was always noted for its earthy themes. Songs such as 'Mary Ann' – *All day all night, Mary Ann / Down by the seaside sifting sand* – and 'Big Bamboo' – *Are you afraid of the big bamboo?* – are still staples on the tourist circuit.

The tradition continued in ska – Prince Buster's 'Wreck a Pum Pum' (sung to the theme of the worshipful Christmas carol 'Little Drummer Boy' no less) being a massive seller in the early sixties. The 'Wreck a Pum Pum' album contained the female answer, 'Wreck a Buddy'. And through all the changing styles of reggae, down through the years the flow of sexually thematic songs has never stopped. The more explicit songs are usually banned from radio but despite, or because of, this, many of the biggest sellers in the history of Jamaican music have been 'pure slackness'.

Songs like 'The One Eyed Giant' – *Baby, have you met the one eyed giant, heh, heh, heh*; 'P-Skank' (or 'Pussy Galore') – *Dark as a dungeon, deep as a well, sweet as honey and it nice no hell. Is what dat?* (by Lee Perry at that, with backup harmonies by The Wailers.); 'Catty' – *Is catty high, is catty low, will catty stand up to any blow? What is catty?* – by the conscious deejay himself, U-Roy; 'Barbed Wire' – *Oh mama, he's got barbed wire in his underpants*; 'Leggo Beast' – *I man no check leggo!* [Jamaican for slut]); all of these and more were banned from radio, and all huge sellers. And there was a classic 'slackness' album called 'Censored' made by Lloydie and The Lowbites (produced by Lloyd Charmers, formerly with The Uniques, using Gladstone Anderson's All Stars). It sold so well that the more explicit 'Censored' Volumes 2 and 3 soon followed. Followed up by the even slacker 'Too Hot To Handle', which featured songs like 'Rum and Pum Pum' and other obscene versions of popular reggae and soul

songs. (Incidentally American R&B had a similar phenomenon around the time with 'Blowfly'.)

The trend has only intensified in the dancehall years with songs like Admiral Bailey's 'Punnany' and 'Punnany Too Sweet' by Lecturer. And these were the mild ones. The increasing coarseness over the years has been unmistakable. Many top selling records of recent times appeared on charts with the legend NFAP or not fit for airplay. And the unmatchably crude (and incredibly funny and inventive) Yellowman made live dancehall 'slackness' a virtual art form.

Those of gentler sensibilities ('decent' people as they style themselves) find 'slackness' an intolerable part of dancehall. But Lloyd Lovindeer puts it thus: 'It is what the crowd demands and expects and as long as no children are around, what is wrong with giving the people what they want?'

For good or bad, slackness is now a signature feature of live deejays, exploring aspects of human sexuality in the most graphic possible manner and to an extent probably unmatched in any other form of music. In the early 1990s there were signs the public demand for slackness was lessening. And then in 1993 came Lady Saw, as if to show that anything men could do women could do better, with selections like 'Stab-up the meat' and 'If him lef me, a no mi pussy fault'. Feminists who had always condemned 'slackness' as yet another brutal expression of deep rooted misogyny were left speechless. The media castigated Lady Saw relentlessly. Some bands refused to back her. The Jamaican Music Awards banned her. And she continued to sell out shows everywhere she went. She gave as good as she got in 'What Is Slackness?', condemning the government for all the poor and hungry children in Jamaica. Her defence of her music is that she will stop doing slackness – as soon as she has made enough money to buy her mother a house.

1966 / **THE TRAIN IS COMING**
1967 / **PUPPET ON A STRING**
Ken Boothe

Ken Boothe

Ken Boothe's unique styling makes him many people's favourite reggae singer. He recalls his first hits: 'In 1966 an English singer won the European Song Contest singing "Puppet On A String". Coxsone was in England then and brought it back. I did a couple more songs the same day, "Train", "Puppet on a String" and some more. Downbeat release "Train" first.

'That was my first big thing, "The Train is Coming". Even when I walk on the street, school children would be singing it. They used it in different ways. Like they sing "the jeep is coming baby". Because the police used to go around and run you off the corner. It was so popular that one time some police and me was in conflict. After that every song I sing was just a hit – "Puppet", "Moving Away", "The Girl I Left Behind".'

1967 / **GOT TO GO BACK HOME**
Bob Andy

Bob Andy admits himself that he is not a great singer. But in this song his reedy, plaintive voice combines with the almost pleading melody and rather scratchy beat (the music was slowly changing from ska but had not quite developed into rocksteady) to create a feeling of . . . well it should be sadness. Yet when the song is played at parties in Jamaica and people sing along to it, they're invariably laughing and smiling. The singer and the song feel sad, but the audience doesn't. Maybe it's because they are finding the land of lost content that Bob Andy is singing about. Aristotle called it catharsis.

1967 / **I'VE GOT TO LEAVE YOU BEHIND**
Ken Boothe (written by Bob Andy)

'I Got To Leave You Behind' is the flip side of Bob Andy's most famous song, 'Got to go Back Home'. While the latter expresses the homesickness of a lonely man in a strange world, the former gives the feelings of the same person reluctantly leaving the world he knows behind.

It's an emotion that many Jamaicans know very well. Few other people have emigrated in such numbers. Hard and fast figures are difficult to come by, but it's reliably estimated that the number of first- and second-generation Jamaicans living abroad, chiefly in U.S., Britain, and Canada, at least equals the two-and-a-half million population of the island. And to a far greater extent than most immigrants, Jamaicans abroad have clung tenaciously to their roots, music being one of their strongest links to the homeland.

Apart from those who emigrate, large numbers of Jamaicans go abroad on contract work for specified periods of time, most prominently farm workers. Interestingly, the upper-classes and intellectuals at home castigate the average Jamaican (at least the average Jamaican male) as lazy layabouts. But Jamaicans abroad, especially in the U.S., have gained a reputation as extremely hard working and enterprising. (Sometimes too enterprising, as the drug posses have shown.)

In any event, the lines

I'm gonna tell you good bye babe
And I don't want to see you cry babe
I'm leaving you behind, but it's just for a time

It's not my wish that we must part
Don't worry baby I won't break your heart
I'm going to a far away land
I'm gonna make life for you and me, please understand

capture exactly the feelings of the vast number of Jamaicans who have been in that position, forced by economic necessity to leave the land of their birth. A land which has never been able to feed its overabundant progeny; a land which many born there speak very ambivalently about; but a land which they never cease to regard as their true home.

Because of its emotional honesty, 'I've Got To Leave You Behind' is more than just another

SEARCHING THE WILDERNESS FOR HOME

At one time 'Got To Go Back Home' was regarded as an anthem for Rastafarians seeking repatriation. The 'Back To Africa', specifically Ethiopia, movement was serious enough in the early 1960s for the Jamaican government to commission a study. Delegations were even sent to Ethiopia to examine the feasibility, and supposedly a few brethren did actually emigrate. But there was unhappiness on both sides. It became obvious to the transplanted Jamaicans that bad as things might have been economically back home, they were considerably worse in Ethiopia. As for Haile Selassie, he reportedly remarked on being briefed on the Rastafarian lifestyle that the last thing his country needed was a bunch of shiftless drug addicts who didn't believe in birth control.

Later on the song became a panacea to homesick Jamaicans abroad, especially in the cold winter months when the warm sunshine of the native land beckoned. Listening to the song and singing along with the packed dance hall while you 'smoked a spliff' or 'drank a white's actually did make you feel for a while that you were going to go back home, even that you were there.

I've got to go back home
This couldn't be my home
It must be somewhere else
Or I would kill myself
There is no gladness
Nothing but sadness
Nothing like a future here
I've got to leave this life
I just can't stand this life I'm living

In the morning of course, soberness and financial reality made you realise that you couldn't go back home, at least not right now. But still, one day, one day . . . And a lot of Jamaicans do return home after they have become financially secure or retired.

But Bob Andy wasn't thinking of either of these things when he wrote the song. For one he had never even been abroad. And he was not a Rastafarian at the time. Even in later years, when he did embrace the religion, he pointed that while proud of his Africanness, he was a Jamaican first and foremost. As he put it, 'This is the only country I know how to relate to.'

True the song speaks to many of the hardships faced by the Jamaican poor: – Cause can't get no clothes to wear / Can't get no food to eat / Can't get a job to get bread. But as he tells the story, the home he was singing about was an imaginary one, the home inside of us all where the cares of the world will vanish and the troubles of this too solid flesh melt: '"I've Got To Go Back Home" was really a very inspirational song. I mean the morning when I wrote that song I was crying and I don't know why I was crying. And it was the first song to be recorded that morning in the studio. And I just heard the thing in my head, it's one of those pieces of material that you don't really take much credit for, it just happens you know. I had recorded before that "Crime Don't Pay" which is also on the "Song Book" album, but it was still in the days of the dancehall hits.

'In those days on Sundays they used to play a lot of dances at a place called Gold Coast past Harbour View Drive-In and go out some more on the sand there. Coxsone used to play out there on a Sunday. People used to keep big dances out there. Those were the days of smoking a lot of herb and drinking hot beer and just go and have some fun on the beach. "One more box of hops, says the man to the bartender". And I was out there one night sitting out with Jackie Mittoo and having a good time with the guys, having a good time on the beach and looking far off at the Harbour View screen.

'And suddenly I heard "I've Got To Go Back Home", and it was played seventeen times in a row . . . Stitt was playing. By the end of about the seventh or eighth time people had started putting hands on shoulders and were marching through the place to this song. And it occurred to me then that something was going to become of this song. You know it's funny, "Got To Go Back Home" was never really a radio hit. It was mainly heard in the dance halls. The radio picked up on it after it came out on the album.'

maudlin tear-jerker. The man in the song is sorry, but mostly for the woman he's leaving behind, because she's going to miss him so much. In fact, how is she going to live without him, poor thing? For the lines

Don't worry about me when I am gone
Just care yourself till I return
Don't fret yourself, don't pine too much
I'll soon be back with that magic touch

are also deadly accurate in expressing the Jamaican male psyche. Jamaican men, seemingly without exception to hear them talk, regard themselves as God's gift to women. The guy in the song isn't boasting , he's just (as far as he is concerned) telling it like it is. And while he promises that – *Don't worry baby, I won't break your heart* – it's not a promise to stay faithful, which, as anyone who has lived here will testify, is an apparently ridiculous concept to Jamaican men. But he is promising to come back home – *I'm leaving you behind / But it's just for a time.* Of course, we don't get to hear the woman's side of the story. But it's probably safe to say that she's a step ahead of him, for Jamaican women are at least a match for the men. 'Bun fi bun', they say.

1966 / **SOUNDS AND PRESSURE**
1967 / **TAKE IT EASY**
Hopeton Lewis

Hopeton Lewis' 'Take It Easy' and 'Sounds and Pressure' are regarded as two seminal records of the rocksteady era. He remembers how they came about: 'Well, I was walking down Half Way Tree after I leave the studio, and I just start to hum this line, "Take It Easy". Basically I'm a laid back person. And I find myself humming, *Take you time, take you time, No need to hurry, No need to worry.* When I got home and sit down, I start writing the song. Everybody just moving and I'm going slower than them.

'"Sounds and Pressure" came after "Take it Easy" but was released earlier. I was on the way to a studio session one morning and didn't have anything ready to record. I just came up with the idea of sounds and pressure and start working it. I start singing it to Gladdy and was basically leaning on the chords he was playing. I would say something, he would give me a chord and then I started singing. It wasn't like "Take It Easy", where I had it in my mind whole before I went into the studio. Leslie Butler played the solo on "Sounds and Pressure", one of the greatest piano solos I've heard.'

1967 / **LOVING PAUPER**
Dobbie Dobson

On the surface 'Loving Pauper' may seem like just another 'I can't give you anything but love baby' lament. But in Dobbie Dobson's almost pleading entreaties, you hear the voice of a thousand penniless Jamaican youths struggling to hold on to their self-respect amidst the petty embarrassments of poverty:

I'm not in a position to maintain you
The way that you're accustomed to
Can't take you out to fancy places
Like other fellows I know can do . . .
Jewelry and things, I can't buy
Or drive you in a GT car
If you're hungry girl, I can't feed you
On my money girl, you won't get far

I got so many patches on my clothes girl
A hole in the bottom of my shoe
But if you prefer love to romance
Then you got to tell me I'm alright

Everyone, especially the deejays, love to laugh at 'boops and boopsies' – those nubile, young girls maintained in style by rich, old men. But the poor young men scorned by their female

Dobbie Dobson

counterparts for sugar daddies with flashy cars and ready cash surely find little humour in the situation. Poverty may be one thing. But humiliation, even if only in one's own mind, is another.

A big hit when it first came out, 'Loving Pauper' has proven to be one of the most covered tunes in reggae history. In fact Ruddy Thomas' version was the number one song of the year on the 1978 RJR Top 100.

1967 / ON THE BEACH
The Paragons

Between 1965 and 1970, The Paragons released some 16 singles, most of which went to number one on the Jamaican charts. 'On The Beach', perhaps a spiritual descendant of The Drifters' 'Sand In My Shoes' and 'Under The Boardwalk', was one of the finest tunes ever produced by Duke Reid, a timeless evocation of a timeless Jamaican tradition.

> Let's go and have some fun
> On the beach where there's a party
> We're gonna have a ball
> Dancing and singing and winding and all
> Holding hands together and laughing and all
> Then we'll dance dance dance dance
>
> One more box of hops / Says the man to the bartender
> One more box of hops / Says the man, I won't surrender'

Go down to Hellshire or Fort Clarence any Sunday and you still see everything John Holt sings so beautifully about. The beat is a little heavier, but the vibes are just as mellow.

THE DUKE OF TREASURE ISLE
•••••••••••••••••••••••••••••••••

While there is disagreement as to who was the greatest producer Jamaican music ever had, there is no dispute that the best three were Coxsone Dodd, Duke Reid and Leslie Kong. Coxsone, by virtue of having outlived his peers, is the most famous. But on a hard record-to-record comparison, a substantial case can be made that Duke Reid was at least his equal.

Reid, a tall, stocky man, was a policeman for ten years before joining his wife Lucille in her liquor business. One way to increase the liquor sales was to provide entertainment to the public and then sell them Red Stripe, rum or stout when they got thirsty. With this in mind, Reid bought speaker boxes and a sound-system in the early fifties, a time when the dancehall scene was booming. Reid more than held his own, and became one of the city's leading sets, challenging Coxsone Dodd's Downbeat and Tom the Great Sebastien.

It was in these days that Reid received his nickname of 'Trojan' (from which Trojan records took its name) and his 'bad man' persona took hold. As a carry over from his police days, Reid always carried a gun, which probably made sense in the rough and ready liquor and music businesses. At any rate, the image of Duke the Trojan, six shooters at his side and bandoleers across his chest, being carried aloft by an adoring crowd after 'mashing down' a rival sound, is one of the cherished icons of reggae mythology.

At first sound systems played hot American jazz and R&B. But as music tastes in the U.S. changed, the supply of records with the driving beat that Jamaicans liked began to dry up. And like his fellow sound system operators, Reid began to look at home for what he could no longer find abroad, cutting local songs in effort to rediscover the dying 'beat'.

After the early days of cutting records at Federal, Reid installed a sound system over his liquor store and called it Treasure Isle. His first recordings were with Derrick Morgan, the musicians being the same ones everyone used, the core of which later became The Skatalites.

Treasure Isle was never as innovative as Dodd's Studio One, and much of the spontaneity and experimentation that made Dodd's ska recordings so exciting was missing in Reid's, which were more measured and careful. But instead there is the virtuosity and confidence of the best musicians in the land playing a style they are completely comfortable with and know is already successful. Some of The Skatalites' best songs were made for Treasure Isle – Baba Brooks' 'River Bank' and 'Guns Fever', Don

Drummond's 'Green Island', 'Musical Storeroom' and 'Eastern Standard Time', Tommy McCook's 'Latin Goes Ska' and 'Yard Broom', and Roland Alphonso's 'Musical Communion'. But perhaps Treasure Isle's biggest hit of the period was Justin Hinds and The Domino's 'Carry Go Bring Come'.

In 1966 The Skatalites split and Tommy McCook went to Treasure Isle forming The Supersonics with Lyn Tait, Ernest Brown, Hugh Malcolm, Hux Brown, Jackie Jackson, Winston Wright, Gladstone Anderson and other great names. Alton Ellis came to Reid, because he paid £50 a side compared to Coxsone's £30, and had a big string of rocksteady hits for Treasure Isle, including 'Rocksteady', 'Breaking Up Is Hard To do', 'Why Birds Follow Spring', 'I'm Just A Guy', 'Cry Tough', 'Willow Tree', 'Aint That Loving You', 'Dance Crasher' and 'What Does It Take'.

But Reid achieved his greatest renown producing harmony groups like The Paragons, Techniques, Melodians, Ethiopians, Sensations, Tennors and Silver Tones. These trios all featured a soulful lead with the back-ups singing elaborate harmonies. Their carefully constructed, harmonically sophisticated sound, with the right chord being sung in just the right place, were the result of Reid's relentless perfectionism. Unlike his rival Dodd, Reid would often demand six, seven or eight takes until he got the result he wanted. The sight of him sitting with his sidearms by his side – and his reputed willingness to shoot out walls and ceilings when he didn't like what he heard – probably, as they say, concentrated his singers' minds wonderfully.

Unlike his contemporaries', Reid's productions were invariably crisp and smooth, professionally recorded and arranged with a commercial sophistication unique at the time. And the attention to detail paid off in a big way. The Paragons, with John Holt as lead singer, reeled off a string of hits destined to become classics of the genre: 'On The Beach', 'The Tide is High', 'Wear You To The Ball', 'Only a Smile', 'The Same Song', 'Talking Love' among others. The Techniques did 'Queen Majesty', 'Oh Babe', 'Run Come Celebrate', 'You Don't Care'.

Tommy Cowan and The Jamaicans hit with 'Things You Say You Love' and then won the Festival Song Competition in 1967 with 'Ba Ba Boom'. Hopeton Lewis did the same in 1970 with 'Boom Shaka Laka'. John Holt recorded 'Ali Baba' and 'Stealing, Stealing' solo. Reid's female singers also did well. Jaya Landis' 'Moonlight Lover' and 'Midnight Confession', Claudette Miller's 'Tonight is The Night' and Phyllis Dillon's 'Perfidia' and 'Don't Stay Away'.

When rocksteady began to change into reggae in 1968, Reid lost some of his edge. Tait and other band members started recording for Leslie Kong, Joe Gibbs and others, thus spreading their magic around. And the new sound of 1969 made some of Reid's music sound dated, belonging to another era. Which, though we are only talking of months, it did. But this only became really apparent later.

In addition Reid was adamantly opposed to the Rastafarian attitudes starting to take hold in the late sixties. It was easy to hold the line in 1966, but in 1969 Burning Spear, The Abyssinians, and The rejuvenated Wailers made their mark – the dykes were bursting. Locks, ganja-smoking and a belief in a divine Haile Selassie could no longer be simply dismissed as hooliganism. Reid's refusal to deal with Rastas and the fresh sounds of the day made him a bit of an anachronism, until 1970.

That was the year of U-Roy, when reggae changed forever. It was over Treasure Isle classics that 'the godfather' chanted, creating the deejay style on record and establishing Reid once again as a pioneer. U-Roy dominated the charts and dancehalls with 'Wear You To The Ball', 'Rule The Nation', 'Tom Drunk', 'Version Galore', 'Wake The Town' and 'Things You Love'. Reid recorded other deejays like Dennis Alcapone, Lizzy and Natural Youth. The formula of classic riddim and hot new chant was irresistible over the next two years, but reggae's cyclical wheel turned once more and Reid's sound faded into the background again. In 1974, after a long illness, Duke Reid died. Gone, but not forgotten. For his music lives on.

John Holt has these memories of Duke Reid: 'He was a good man, because he used to record everybody that comes in, never refuse a talent, and he was the sort of man who encourage you as a youth to do good things with what you were earning now so you could be a man when you get bigger. And he used to pay you to work. Not like most producers. He was a very kind and generous man, bless his soul.'

Duke Reid with Fats Dominoe

1967 / **HOLD THEM**
Roy Shirley

This, according to its creator and singer, is the story of 'Hold Them' as told to Carl Gayle: 'I had the air of the song because I play a little guitar. But I couldn't find the beat. So one night me and a soldier brother stand up at Orange Street and I see some Salvation army people coming down. And when I see them I start humming this tune . . . cause it was some women and men beating drum and cymbals and the way them march, I say this look like it. Because I did want a beat that even when the people walk them feel the music. And the beat just come to me same time. For when the man lick the drum I say "Toom toom ba dum . . . " and the man beat the drum and "Toom toom ba dum toom . . . " Same time I man leave and take up the guitar and form the tune. Believe me, I spend the whole night on the tune.

'The next day I go to Greenwich Farm and a whole crowd a people start dance this music here. A brother borrow a big tenor guitar and sit down with the one tune the whole day. I play the tune till I get scared of the tune because I say, well them going thief it now cause people start hum it now with me. So the next day we do a version for Joe Gibbs. It was Gladdy (Gladstone Anderson) playing piano. At the rehearsal I did carry Slim Smith and Ken Boothe to back it up with me but them couldn't manage it because is a new style. And most people never understand the style. Them say, "Cho!, mek we sing ska." Me say, no man, we have to play this tune just so, man. But when Glady catch it, the man say "But this really a go Bredda Roy, this a go!"'

Coming early in the rocksteady era, 'Hold Them' not only helped to cement the new sound's hold on the public, it created a whole new ethos in Jamaican song. Here ska's frantic exuberance is replaced by a measured tension and nearly expressionless beat. The singer's emotions are held back and controlled, and there is a menacing sense of macho – what would later be known as the 'cool and deadly' feel. Slow and mantric at first, the song gradually builds to a crescendo and there is almost a sense of sexual release in Roy Shirley's cry of 'now now now now now now now now now!' And in a sense the whole song approximates the sexual act, with a tentative beginning, driving mid-rhythm, fevered climax and calm fading way.

Shirley never had many hits and his other big song 'Get On The Ball' sounded a lot like 'Hold Them'. But in his day he was always a stage show staple and his gripping performance of 'Hold Them' never failed to bring the house down.

1967 / **TOUGHER THAN TOUGH**
Derrick Morgan
1967 / **A MESSAGE TO YOU RUDY**
Dandy Livingstone

'Tougher Than Tough' has lyrics as chilling as any 'gun talk' dancehall song ever made.

> Rude boys you are charged with ratchet knifing
> gun shooting and bomb throwing
> What do you have to say for yourselves?
>
> Your honour, rudies don't fear . . .
> Tougher than tough / Rougher than rough
> Strong like lion / We are iron

The rudeboys don't deny the charges and answer with fearless insolence. Yet they still get off:

> Rudies are free, yeah boys, rudies are free

Those who say 'bad man' lyrics only started with deejays are talking nonsense. This song's jagged and measured beat, which helped to establish the rocksteady sound, only adds to the menace.

One of the song's ironies is how different Derrick Morgan's real life persona was from the intimidating protagonist. Born with a severe sight defect and a cheerful soul, Morgan was the last man in reggae to be consciously promoting badmanism. But it is still a disturbing song. Some say that songs like these only reflect society's reality and are not a cause of violence in themselves. An argument with some merit, but one must wonder sometimes if the plethora of reggae songs glorifying lawbreakers, which first came to prominence in the rude boy era, have something to do with the logarithmic increase in Jamaica's murder rate since independence.

'A Message To You Rudy' is a direct response to the 'rude boys', very much in the same vein as The Wailers' 1964 'Simmer Down'. 'Message' was Dandy Livingstone's only big hit. But his cool, unemotional singing and the understated yet powerful rhythm make it a true rocksteady classic.

1967 / **THINGS YOU SAY YOU LOVE**
The Jamaicans

Tommy Cowan remembers: 'I was living at Delacree Road. We were rehearsing and Norris come in weeping and moaning about him and him girl a quarrel and how she treating him bad. And we sat down and through the vibes of that we just write this song. We came up with the words and everything and went to the studio and recorded it. It went to number one in late 1966. Norris was the lead singer on this tune. We used to take turns, but he was mostly the lead. I don't remember ever getting any publishing royalties off it. We didn't know about those things then. In fact we never got anything for any of our other hit songs like "Ba Ba Boom", "Peace and Love" and "Take Warning". I see our songs on a lot of compilations so we're still hoping to get something.'

To Norris Weir, 'Things You Say You Love' turned out to be more than just a song: 'Yes man, I remember exactly how it was. Me and my girl-friend had a real lovers' quarrel. She was just dealing with pure vanity. And the words just came out how I was feeling – *Things you say you love, you're gonna lose / Can't last too long, the way you're gonna feel.* We made up and got married about a month after. We're still married today, all these twenty something years later. I guess that's one love song that really worked!'

1967 / **PRESSURE AND SLIDE**
The Tennors

'Pressure and Slide' and 'Ride Me Donkey' were the The Tennors' only real hits. But their delicate harmonies over the smoothly rocking beat make this a perennial favourite.

1967 / **DON'T STAY AWAY**
Phyllis Dillon

Perhaps the finest female performance in Jamaican music. Phyllis Dillon's delicate phrasing of the innocently naive lyrics – *If you knew how much I love you / How much I need you / You wouldn't stay away* – melds with the effortless rhythm to create reggae's most haunting evocation of girlish first love.

The Jamaicans

MEN ONLY?

Why is reggae such a male dominated music? The significant female artists in reggae history can be counted on one hand, and even these have made their name almost solely as singers. Few have composed their own material. And in the dancehall era, the female element has grown even smaller, although Lady Saw has shown that women can do anything men can do.

Some trot out the old cliches of third world male domination. And Rastafarianss have been especially criticised for their views of women. Though one Rasta who vehemently defended women was Peter Tosh: 'The general shitsem designed to manipulate woman and make it look like a woman is inferior, unintelligent and incompetent. Most people therefore don't realise how important woman is. When men don't realise this, them obviously drop out of some batty-hole. I am no respecter of persons that don't respect woman. I don't say get up and respect every frock tail because is not every frock tail name woman, just like is not every pants name man. Women, generally, within her dignity, must be respected.'

But any Jamaican will laugh at such a concept as female second-class citizenship. Whatever their status, women in Jamaica are not considered inferior either by themselves or men. Businessmen unanimously consider women here to be more intelligent, honest, disciplined and hard-working than the men. Indeed a recent book by Professor Errol Miller, entitled *The Marginalization of the Jamaican Male*, argued that if the current trends in education continue, where females outnumber males in tertiary institutions by a more than two-to-one ratio, the Jamaican male will become redundant.

So why so few women in reggae? Well one reason is the strong divide between sexual roles in Jamaica. Jamaicans on the whole are adamant that certain things are for men and certain things for women. And many times it is the women who insist on such divisions. Men who venture into womanly fields are apt to be castigated as 'Mama Man'. But men can be just as stubborn about such things. Reggae has always been more popular among men than women, who, for whatever reasons, seem to prefer soca and soul music. It's not 100 percent either way, but the difference is there.

Another factor is the propensity of Jamaican women to have babies at a very young age. Jamaica has one of the world's highest incidences of single-parent households, nearly all female. So for Jamaican women a child means responsibility in the extreme. Music has never been a responsible career choice. Coxsone once commented on Hortense Ellis: 'She was one of the best that I had. But she had too many children.' She was probably

every bit as talented as her brother Alton, but unlike him, she was never able to dedicate herself entirely to the music. After raising her family she reactivated her career in the early 1990s and is still performing today.

Desmond Young, President of the Jamaica Federation of Musicians, puts it this way, 'When a female artist gets two hit songs and you sign a deal with her and then she gets pregnant that can jeopardise the contract. It means the company has to repackage her . . . Me not fighting against pregnancy, but them must plan them career.' Then there is the 'battering' that male artists have to undergo just to get recorded. 'The man them have to go dance every night and sleep pon sound box fi bust. Which girl can sleep pon sound box with 96,000 man drunk inna dance? The system that the artists have to travel to reach prominence is rough. You ever go to Arrows (Recording Company Limited)? It look like prison. When you go in there you see 300 man stand ina the yard.'

Entertainment lawyer Lloyd Stanbury puts another spin on things: '. . . the producers prefer to deal with the male artistes because the female ones are more aware of the business . . . you can't trick them. The females are better educated and these producers have difficulty dealing with that since they always want to do business in an informal way.'

1967 / **NICE TIME**
The Wailers

A lot of people think 'Nice Time' is a traditional folk song. It certainly has a timeless feel about it. Bob's daughter Cedella says he wrote the song about her, because she was nicknamed 'nice time'.

1967 / **QUEEN MAJESTY**
The Techniques
1969 / **LOVE I CAN FEEL**
John Holt

Some feel a cover can't be a classic reggae song, because the original inspiration was in another musical form, and the music is generally just a vehicle to carry the words, not generated by them. And certainly the vast majority of covers are reggae in name only, basically second-rate remakes with a metronomic beat added. Nine times out of ten times the song is not improved, but degraded in its reggae version.

'Queen Majesty' and 'Love I Can Feel' are two covers which completely change the feel of the original, invest it with an authentic Jamaican air, and most important of all, make it more musically interesting. And while both are beautifully sung (John Holt and Pat Kelly are two of Jamaica's premier balladeers) it's the rugged, insinuating bass lines that really make them stand out.

Leroy Sibbles gives some insight into the process of doing covers: 'Even when songs are covers, the music is usually different in the reggae version, a totally different bass line and thing. A song like John Holt's "Love I Can Feel" which they used to make

John Holt

"Tempted To Touch" and all those other songs. I think the song itself was a Temptations original. But the music and the bass line and arrangement, we came up with those. And it's very different from any American song'.

'Queen Majesty' is also interesting because it was written by a man, who of all American soul singers, had the greatest influence on the development of reggae. Now Curtis Mayfield is a fine musician, both an excellent singer and songwriter. But he is not usually mentioned in the same breath as say Sam Cooke, or Otis Redding or James Brown. Why did he have such influence here? It's one of those questions no one has an answer for. Just like there's no answer as to why 'Queen Majesty' of all his songs, it certainly wasn't a big hit, was the one that established itself in the reggae pantheon. ('You Don't Care' also did, especially in the version form.) It just goes to show how unpredictable a path reggae travelled in its development.

1968 / **SOLOMON**
Derrick Harriott

1968 / **LONG STORY**
Rudy Mills (produced by Derrick Harriott)

Derrick Harriott was part of one of the earliest of reggae groups, The Jiving Juniors. Later he sang on his own and became a producer and record store owner. Unlike many of his colleagues, he was a shrewd businessman. While many who were much bigger stars now struggle to make a living, he now runs one of the best known record and video stores in Kingston – Derrick Harriott's One Stop. He was best known as a 'soul style' singer and had chart hits into the eighties. Many of his big hits were covers, but 'Solomon' and 'Long Story' were originals which still sound fresh.

Derrick Harriott, then and now

1968 / ABC ROCKSTEADY
The Gaylads

To many 'good old days' reggae lovers, today's music 'not saying anything'. One of their biggest complaints is how ridiculous current song lyrics are. Well no tune in reggae history ever had more nonsensical words than this oldies party favourite (which some say was the first song with an authentic reggae beat). The rhymes come straight from Mother Goose. (Monty Morris' 1961 hit 'Humpty Dumpty' used the same source.)

1968 / IT'S HARD TO CONFESS
The Gaylads

Female reggae artists are rare specimens, and female reggae producers even more so. In fact there has been only one of real note, Sonia Pottinger. Mrs Pottinger ran her Gayfeet and High Note labels out of her Tip-Top Record Shop at 37 Orange Street. She released a few records in the ska era, but came into her own in the rocksteady era with hits like The Gaylads' 'ABC Rocksteady', The Melodians' 'Swing and Dine' and Ken Boothe's 'Lady With The

Starlight'. She continued to have hits in the 1970s with Culture, Marcia Griffiths, Justin Hinds and others before ceasing operations in 1985. Her records don't sound quite like any others in reggae. As she says: 'There is a difference, be-cause of personality, I expect. I did not know the dancehall at the time, so I made the songs for myself. And since I was a normal person, I knew there would be a lot of people who would like my music. I trusted my taste and it worked.'

The Gaylads

1968 / FEEL LIKE JUMPING
Marcia Griffiths

Marcia Griffiths is probably the greatest, and certainly the most durable female singer in reggae history. 'Feel Like Jumping' was her biggest early hit. It may be a little weak lyrically, but Marcia's sweet, young voice combines with the deep, rumbling beat to make irresistible listening.

Marcia Griffiths

1968 / **TOO EXPERIENCED**
Bob Andy

Bob Andy's catalogue has been widely covered in all eras of the music. 'Too Experienced', for example, was as big hit for Barrington Levy in the late 1980s as it was for Andy 20 years before. Not surprising, for its portrayal of uncertain romantic bravado is timeless:

Too experienced to be taken for a stroll
Too experienced to let someone rock and roll
Too experienced to be taken for a ride
I know it's not my foolish pride
But not even the gods can love and be wise.

1968 / **HARD ROAD TO TRAVEL**
Jimmy Cliff

'Hard Road To Travel' was Jimmy Cliff's first great song, and perhaps he never wrote a better one. Although he's remade it a number of times, there's really no more satisfactory version.

They're all either too fast, or too slow, or lack the right beat. But even though no recording does it justice, it's one of those songs which you hear in your head as a classic. And Jimmy Cliff certainly lived the lyrics:

Yes its a hard road to travel
And a rough rough road to go
But I can't give up
My heart is strong
My mind's made up
My faith will carry me through

He remembers the beginning of that long journey: 'I was born in 1948 in Somerton, a hill village about 12 miles from Montego Bay. My father was a tailor. My real name was Chambers but I changed it to Cliff in the early days because it implied the "heights" I aspired to. When I

MARCIA GRIFFITHS RECALLS THE EARLY DAYS

'The first time I sang professionally was at a neighbourhood get together. Phillip James of The Blues Busters heard me singing. There was a concert planned on Easter Monday morning in 1964 with Byron Lee and The Dragonaires and he insisted I should perform on this show because he had never heard anyone like me. I did one song, "No Time To Lose" by Carla Thomas. And boy, from then on it was just green light all the way. It was really fantastic. The house came down that morning! It was really a wonderful experience. I was a young girl, just going on sixteen, And I was very positive. Rather than being afraid or nervous, I wanted to show people what I could do.

'After that their was a fight over me between Ronnie Nasralla, who managed Byron Lee, and Coxsone at Studio One. They both wanted me to sign contracts with them. They were by my house day after day talking to my father. I decided to go with Coxsone because he was really happening then and I liked his vibes. That's where I met everyone: Bob Marley, Rita Marley, Pete Tosh, Bunny Wailer. It was like a reunion for Bunny and me, because we had gone to school together as little children. But that's where I met all the great artists. That's where they all graduated. Studio One was the college. We recorded everyday. Even The Wailers, Bob

and all the artists, would just go and sing everyday. Coxsone would couple me up with all the good male singers. Bob Andy and myself had a big hit in Europe in 1970 "Young, Gifted and Black". My first number one single in Studio One was "Feel Like Jumping".

'Bob and myself released an album called "Young, Gifted and Black". But that was after we left Coxsone to go to Harry J. After that Coxsone released an album because he had enough material on every artist to put out at least two albums. Because all we used to do was just sing and record day after day. That was a wonderful time for me. It was a wonderful learning experience because I was young and had no experience or exposure to the outside world. My first international exposure was when I went to Europe to promote "Young Gifted and Black".

'My first Studio One album was "The Best of Marcia Griffiths". That album has all my hit songs: "Melody Life", "Truly", "Mark My Words", "Tell Me Now", "Feel Like Jumping". Bob Andy wrote all of them.

'I can tell the world that throughout my 24 years in this business, the only time I ever earned from my works is with Bob Marley. As a solo singer I couldn't tell anyone that I have ever received royalties from Tom, Dick, or Harry. Not even the statement.'

finished primary school in 1961 my father decided I should leave Somerton and further my education. So I went to Kingston. I was thirteen-and-a-half. I was all alone, no relatives at all. I didn't know what I was to do and I had no future at all. What was I supposed to do with my life? Cut cane? Work in a banana field? I came to Kingston to go to night school and learn a trade. But my intention was always to sing. I thought, "Yeah, now I get my chance."'

1968 / LET THEM TRY
Alton Ellis

Alton Ellis on his art: 'I was very much into the beat. I could take a song like "Willow Tree" or "Ain't That Loving You" and make it into a Jamaican song. Every young artist do it over today. It's an American song. But I was capable of placing the song so properly within the rocksteady rhythm that you could hear the R&B flavour and feel the rocksteady rhythm at the same time. I put them together properly. And this is one thing I am proud of.

'"Let Them Try" is another song that takes control of me on stage. It's just a song I have deep feelings about, for it wasn't written by me. Is Tony Gregory I first hear sing it one Christmas morning, and Tony blow my mind with it. Tony take it to a stage. And I love it so much that when I hear him sing it, in my mind I just take it to a next stage immediately. Cause him didn't drop on the ground and cut and go on extravagant, him just sing it "Let Them Try". But I get all this heap of vibes out of it and start doing it my way and get more out of it and then I do it in reggae and it's one of the nice ones. But it's basically just a way of expressing a thing the way I feel it separate from the next person.'

1968 / I'M JUST A GUY
Alton Ellis

Alton Ellis expresses a few more thoughts: 'In the earlier days all the guys in the business used to work together. I might have Ken Boothe or Delroy Wilson, John Holt or Pat Kelly or one of

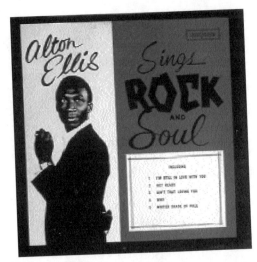

The Heptones on backing vocal. Coxsone used to pay for backing vocals too, so it was extra money, but you also did it for fun and for public recognition more than anything else. You are a guy from the ghetto and you want to be on the radio, the TV, to be on the Christmas morning big concert. It really was the recognition.

'I know guys who were singing in groups in Jamaica from then over 15 years and never collect a penny from the group because he was working otherwise in a good job. But he was getting recognition as a singer all the time. In the later days the business is more spread out and the people branch off. But I still feel very comfortable with these guys when I see them. And you know people only mention guys like us because we are the upfront five or six. But there are a string of other artists who were there at the creation – The Uniques, The Techniques, Delano Stewart.

'Bunny Williams was my drummer on songs like "I'm Still in Love", "I'm Just A Guy", "Aint That Loving You". This was 1967. A couple of the strong riddims that are still alive are due to Bunny's expression as a drummer, the co-ordination of his expression along with mine and Jackie Mittoo's. These are the three people that were able to express this rhythm. That 'one drop' Sly is playing. Listen to "I'm Just a Guy', "I'm Still in Love", "Fatty Fatty", by The Heptones, Ken Boothe's "Puppet On A String" – the 'one drop' that everybody's playing today, that guy Bunny Williams was the one that played it.

'Unlike Calypso that stays with one form over the years with very little changing, reggae is different. I like it because you can name five or six different sounds that are embedded within the sound of reggae music.'

1968 / **54-46**
The Maytals

Ronnie Nasralla remembers: 'When Toots came out of jail, he showed me the songs he had written there. "54-46" just stood out, so we decided to cut it that same day. When Toots recorded the song, it sounded so good that I took the accetate that same night to a party at Garth Moodie's house. When we put it on the crowd just went wild. We had to play it about five times straight. It was a hit even before it was released.

Frankly, I don't think there's a better reggae song than "54-46".'

1969 / **JUST TELL ME**
The Maytals

The question that haunts every man in jail – will my woman wait for me? In '54-46' Toots voiced an innocent prisoner's anger. In 'Just Tell Me' he expresses the lover's uncertainty, does she still love me? – *Just tell me that you love me too / and I will know just what to do / because I love you.* The best part of the song has no words, when Toots shouts, 'Sing that one more time' and breaks loose in wordless elation while the band tears into the rollicking beat, the delight is almost palpable. A song of joy if there ever was one. 'Just Tell Me' and '54-46', while based on the same experience, express completely different emotions and show that like all great artists, Toots

Toots Hibbert

Toots speaks: 'It was really the number I wore while I was in prison, so I have a personal attachment to this song. The reports said I was arrested when I went to bail somebody. The truth is that we (The Maytals) were going to a show in Ocho Rios on our Hondas bikes. Jerry had Raleigh on his bike. I had a suitcase with our clothes on my bike back and was a little way behind them. Then a policeman stopped Jerry and Raleigh and took them to Linstead Police Station to lock Jerry up for carrying an illegal pillion rider.

'I rode with the luggage with our clothes to the station to go bail them. The police tell me to go and get my manager, Ronnie Nasralla. So I ask the gentleman to keep my suitcase since I could ride quicker on the bike without it. And he say "Yeah man. Just put it down over there." So I went to town and come back with Ronnie. And when I come back the police tell me he find herb in my luggage and was going to lock me up for possession. But he's not supposed to search my things behind my back. I'm not so stupid that I would leave ganja there in the police station. They frame me about the herb. I never smoked in those days, you know.

'I spent 18 months in prison at Tamarind Farm. I didn't really have a tough time in jail. I could get my own meals from my home, and I got my own money to spend. I got my guitar, and I was known as a singer. I helped a lot of people there, gave away a lot of money.

'I wrote "54-46" to let people know I was innocent. "Hear what I say. Listen to my story. I am innocent." I wrote that song with all my heart, because that act affected my career seriously. I was about to go on the biggest tour of my career. Chris Blackwell had come down from England and spoken to me and Jackie Edwards and Millie Small. We were supposed to go to England.

'The arrest was a thing that was planned. It was a setup, but I didn't know about it until a policeman told me afterwards. A promoter plan it. I don't want to say who. They didn't want me to go to England and hit first. I don't want to say anything bad or call any name. But I know who it was. It was hard, very hard on me. Not so much physically but mentally, because of the injustice of the whole thing.'

An optimist by nature and a man who does not dwell on the past, Toots relates the incident without bitterness. At the time of his arrest in late 1966, The Maytals were far and away the most popular recording artists Jamaica had ever seen, dominating the charts in an unprecedented manner. Just recently they had won the first ever Festival Song Competition with the wonderfully haunting 'Bam Bam'.

Jamaican music was beginning to establish the first beachheads of popularity abroad, and as its brightest stars, The Maytals were naturally expected to be the biggest draws overseas. Limited in population and resources, Jamaica was never able to compensate its artists with anything like their just rewards. The Maytals, remember, were its biggest stars and yet still they were making their way to a show date on motorcycles. So in 1966 'foreign' really was a promised land to Jamaican musicians.

Toots must have felt on top of the world as he roared along the road to Ocho Rios that afternoon. He had come a long way from singing in the back of the barbershop. A young man of 19, in the prime of his life, happily married (as he had proclaimed to the world only a year before in 'Never You Change') and with a seemingly unlimited musical future in front of him — life doesn't get much sweeter than that. Then suddenly it was all torn from his grasp.

But Toots not only survived the ordeal with his psyche unbroken, he went on to greater artistic heights. '54-46' is not just a song about a man unjustly imprisoned, robbed of his humanity and reduced to a mere number. It's about his capacity not only to endure, but to thrive and grow amidst the hardships of injustice. It's the story of the Jamaican people writ small, a people who endured the unspeakable brutalities of slavery and yet retained their dignity, vitality, sense of self-worth and not least, an astonishing capacity for joy.

'54-46' never fails to ignite Jamaican audiences. This is a piece of music they feel in their bones, a song which has captured the essence of the nation. You can almost hear the ancestral drums of Africa in the hypnotic, throbbing, threatening beat. Ostensibly '54-46' is a song of protest. But for all the suffering and anger it contains, the overall effect is one of ecstasy, the profound satisfaction of a man and people who have faced the worst and yet survived with heart and soul intact.

'There are really three versions of "54-46". It was my number, is my number and that's my number' as Toots jokes: 'The first version was for Leslie Kong. "I say yeah, listen to what I say. I said hear me now." Yes man. That's saying listen to my story. I wasn't afraid to talk about it. If I wasn't innocent I wouldn't want to talk about it. "54-46" was my number. Right now someone else has that number. The whole system was unjust for something like that to happen man. And it happens to other people too you know. It's just not right.

'The second version was for Byron, I think. He and Leslie Kong were very near, very good friends, so it was like working for the same person — *Stick it up mister /*

Put your hands in the air sir / Then you won't get no hurt mister. This is just an idea that came to me. It didn't actually happen to me – *Do you believe I would take something with me / And give it to the policeman* – Yes man, I'm not a fool to leave ganja with the police, that's what this is saying. That was the second version. The third one was with Byron – *Give it to me one time, huh / Give it to me two time, huh huh.* The "Give it to me one time" was an idea from Byron Lee. He always had good vibes in the studio. But I don't have a favourite version. I combine all of them on stage. But it's a natural cultural song, a real true song. Not no make up or pretend something. I put everything into that song because I really feel it.'

The utter conviction and emotional honesty is completely persuasive. You can feel the anguish and anger in Toots' voice. And this is not just any voice – it's the best Jamaica ever produced and one of the finest in modern recorded popular music. As Carl Gayle put it: 'At his best the voice sounds as if it's precariously suspended and you fear that it will break. But you are surprised at how long it remains and you hope it will be there for a long long time.'

At his peak Toots combined Sam Cooke's range, control and melisma with the raw passion of Otis Redding. Here he pushes his voice to its limit. Add to this an utterly compelling rhythm which it's impossible to listen to and not want to dance and – well what more is there to ask for in a piece of music?

The young Maytals

Which is the definitive version? The first probably had the strongest, most gripping bass line and the most passionate vocals. But it lacks the famous 'stick it up mister' and the exhilarating 'give it to me one, two, three, four times' which always sends Jamaican dance patrons wild. So take your choice. It only goes to show that there's no such thing as the perfect reggae song.

Toots wrote great songs both before and after '54-46'. So it's possible that had he not been jailed he might have created a work of comparable quality. But '54-46' is by common consent his, and probably reggae's, finest moment. And without the searing injustice of his imprisonment, it would never have been. Given a devil's bargain, would Toots have willingly traded 18 months of his creative prime for this song? He dismisses such cloud-cuckoo-land questions with a derisive snort. That was then, this is now and what happened, happened. Many music lovers, considering the enjoyment the song has given them over the years, trot out the cliche about 'great art coming out of great suffering'. It's easy for observers to spout such banalities – they did not have to undergo the mental anguish. But does the artist himself feel that the existence of his greatest work is just compensation for being robbed of a vital, perhaps irreplaceable part of his life? Only Toots knows the answer, and he's not telling.

knows and expresses both the sorrows and the happiness of life. As he says 'I sing about reality, things that can happen, real things. Things that happen to me or somebody I know.'

Bob Marley may have written in more depth about certain aspects of the Jamaican experience, but no artist ever painted a broader and truer canvas of daily life in Jamaica than Toots. The physical hunger of 'Pain in My Belly' ('I did that of myself, I had a hernia and was going to get it operated at U.C. hospital. But I guess it has a second meaning for hungry poor people.'); the sheer exuberance of first love in 'It's You'; the happy companionship of 'Never You Change'; the ever present threat of violence described in

'Bam Bam'; the full-blooded celebrations of 'Sweet and Dandy'; the screaming cry against injustice in '54-46'; the harsh strain of ghetto life in 'Pressure Drop' and 'Time Tough'; the inhibition loosening call of 'Pomps and Pride'; the pensive uncertainty of 'In The Dark' and the spiritual questing of 'Rastaman' and 'Never Get Weary'.

It's all there – the injustice, the poverty, the anguish, but also the moments of joy, delight and carefree abandonment. It's easy to dwell on the darker aspects of life in Jamaica. But for all the problems they face, can a people so quick to laugh and smile as Jamaicans be fundamentally unhappy?

1968 / **BABY WHY**
The Cables

Despite all the attention paid to by its 'conscious' lyrics, the most popular topic in reggae is the most popular topic in any kind of music, love. And this is one of the best the genre ever produced. The lyrics are okay – nothing special, but they get the essential idea across. There's the eternal lament of the lovelorn: *Why, baby baby, why oh why / Why did you leave me, for another guy?* And of course the equally eternal hope that she'll live to regret it.

> You wasn't in need of nothing
> Baby when you left me and went your way, girl
> I know that you'll be sorry
> But no use coming and begging me
> Cause I won't hear your plea girl
>
> I was the one who loved you
> But you didn't care till now you've lost me
> You never know the use of a good thing
> Until the day that you've lost it

What really grabs you is the delightful harmonies of lead singer and back-ups, the luscious interplay of guitar and horns, and most of all, the seamless bass of Leroy Sibbles, which plays with the listener's anticipations and never allows you to get bored. The song has the unmistakable signature of all classic tunes – as soon as it's finished, you unconsciously reach for the rewind button.

1968 / **POOR ME ISRAELITE**
Desmond Dekker and The Aces

When first released in Jamaica in 1968, 'Poor Me Israelite' was a moderate hit and hardly caused a sensation. But Graeme Goodall, Leslie Kong's U.K. representative and managing director of Pyramid Record, found it attracting attention: 'When I got "Poor Me, Israelites", I found it did well in the discotheques. The English kids loved it, but it was only played once by the BBC. When I inquired why, they told me it was badly produced. I had Leslie Kong send me the original twin track tapes, remixed them in a British

studio, thinned the bass, brought up the guitar section and compacted Desmond's voice. The English kids only caught on to the word Israelites in the chorus, so I renamed the tune "Israelites".

'When I re-approached the BBC with the new record, they told me they had already tried it. I explained what I had done, so they tried it again and the result was immediate acceptance.'

Dekker toured the U.K., unfortunately alone because of The Aces refusal to travel, doing three shows a night in ballrooms and cabarets. "Israelites" became a hit and in April 1969 was number one and Dekker appeared on British TV's Top of The Pops. "Israelites" also hit number one in Canada, Sweden, West Germany, Holland and South Africa, of all places. It went to number nine on the American charts in July 1969.

THE SESSION MEN

A large part of Baby Why's timeless appeal is the intricate combination of bass, guitar and horns, which make the song sound fresh no matter how many times you hear it. It's a perfect example of how much input session musicians in Jamaica have in a song's creation. As Leroy Sibbles relates: 'The Cables had the words and melody, but I arrange it and create a bass line and thing. You know guys would come to the studio with a song, they would sing it and we create the music for the song.'

Desmond Dekker confirms this is how things worked: 'In those days you just went in with an idea – I always had an idea of what I wanted – and just sing and they find the rhythm and everything, and is you that. I just sing it to Theophilus who play the piano. As long as I give them the melody then everybody just start to play what they feel they should play to make this work.'

Sebastien Clarke elaborates: '. . . Soul Brothers provided musical support for Studio One at the tail-end of ska, but worked right through rocksteady under Jackie Mittoo's direction. Alphonso became responsible for horn arrangements, while Jackie wrote the music . . . Though not credited with co-authorship at the time, Jackie played a seminal roll in the music's development. He would give the bass player his lines, write out the chords for the guitarist, play keyboards himself, arrange and produce the records. Even today [1980] when Jamaican singers enter the studio, all they have to do is sing, and the session leader puts the music to the singers' melodies. Later this haphazard method caused tremendous controversy over the authorship of a number of international hits. The Performing Rights Society, when confronted with a plethora of composers/authors, usually freeze all payments.'

Steven Davis describes a typical session circa 1983: 'Seven musicians, the standard reggae configuration, are on the date. Bass and drums, piano and keyboard, rhythm and lead guitar, percussion . . . Take a typical roots singer who comes in with a tune . . . The singer doesn't play an instrument and usually has no idea what key he sounds good in . . . He'll have no idea of the bass line for his song, no idea of an arrangement. He'll start singing the song to the piano player . . . who will work out chords for the song within three minutes, if the singer has anything worthwhile together at all.

'The piano player will tell the chords to the other musicians and they'll try to thrash out the song. Often [the piano player] will also tell the singer when to sing and will try to keep him in time. Most singers have problems with time because they want to squeeze in so many words. So in reality . . . the piano player or session leader is the co-composer of many of these songs. He usually composes the bridge and writes the words for it too. Sometimes the musicians will insist on doing introductions. Then they'll run down the tune twice, and then record a take. Maybe half-an-hour has elapsed since the singer walked in.

'The drums usually foul the first take. The second take is more often than not the version you hear on record. A great deal of that pure roots reggae feel comes from the musicians not really being familiar with the song . . . If you listen to many reggae singles under headphones, you can usually hear somebody saying 'bridge'. The reason you hear so many wrong notes or missed notes on reggae records is because you're hearing so many first and second takes.'

Byron Lee gave another insight into studio sessions: 'Ninety percent of the genius of reggae musicians happens spontaneously in the studio. The musicians can sit around all day as if they're just stoned and wasting studio time. But they always put out when they have to. Every studio has its quirks, especially this one. You only get hits at Dynamic Sound between one and four in the afternoon. I don't know why. Maybe it just takes that long for the right amount of smoke to build up.'

Coxsone Dodd conducting a session

Eventually it sold over 2 million copies, the first record produced in Jamaica to go gold.

'Israelites' is still one of the most popular reggae songs, and was used in the scores of the movies 'Drugstore Cowboy' in 1989 and 'Miami Blues' in 1990. Yet although it remains Dekker's best known song outside Jamaica, here 'Shanty Town' has always been more popular and is commonly considered a better song.

There is really nothing subtle about 'Israelites'. It's the age-old lament of a man struggling to keep his head above water and stay honest – *Ain't got no job, and my woman done left me. What am I gonna do?*, as the old blues standard puts it. Dekker's deceptively simple lyrics pare the story down to its bare essentials, leaving the listener to answer himself the unstated but obvious challenge of the singer: 'Mister, if you were in my position, what would *you* do?' – *Shirt them a tear up / Pants them a go / I don't want to end up like Bonnie and Clyde / Poor me, Israelite.*

As in almost every great reggae song, there is a kicking beat and a nice blending of voices. But Dekker's mournful voice gives the song lasting power. Since Goodall compacted Dekker's voice in remixing the song, the phrasing sounds very peculiar, as if he is hurrying through the vowels and placing extended emphasis on the consonants. Even Jamaicans have trouble deciphering the lyrics. (Dekker's words in other songs like

'Shanty Town', 'Rudeboy Train', and 'A it Mek' are reasonably clear.)

These hard-to-decipher lyrics have made 'Israelites' notable for the amount of nonsense spoken and written about it. We once heard a disc jockey in Buffalo, New York, assure his audience that Dekker was singing in Swahili! Even informed critics fall into stereotyped assumptions. Stephen Davis and Peter Simon confidently state: 'The first reggae song played on American stations was Desmond Dekker's 'Israelites', with its archetypical reggae theme: Black Africans, the metaphoric lost tribes of Israel, sold into the bondage of a Caribbean Babylon.' Timothy White calls it an 'anti-colonial diatribe'.

Dave Marsh (who incidentally displays first-rate judgment in his choice of reggae songs in his book, *The Heart of Rock and Soul*) shows the understandable confusion Dekker's singing created: 'So far ahead of its time was the first ever American reggae hit, that I actually heard idle speculation that Dekker's then unintelligible lyrics (now easily decipherable after some years experience with hearing Jamaican patois [Marsh's aside]) concealed an anti-semitic tract. Who in the U.S. knew then that Jamaican pop music was dominated by Rastafarians, a religion of liberal biblical construction, in which blacks transported to the Western Hemisphere were considered Ethiopians, but only because the Ethiopians were considered one of the twelve lost tribes. That is, Israelites.'

Some trace the term 'Israelite' to the Rastafarian sect, the 'Twelve Tribes of Israel', which was formed about this time. But Dekker was never a member and was far from being a Rastafarian. The Aces actually broke up because Barry Howard (the other was Winston Samuel, the one with the deep voice) was a Rastafarian who refused to fly on an 'iron bird' and tour overseas with Dekker.

Israelite here is most likely used in a Jamaican folk synonym sense – 'You work like a Trojan; You suffer like an Israelite'. Certainly there is nothing whatsoever in the song about rastafarianism or black African repatriation – where would – *I Don't want to end up like Bonny and Clyde* – fit into this scheme? And substituting another word or phrase for 'Israelite', like say 'things so tight', changes the aural impact, but in no way alters the song's meaning.

In Desmond Dekker's words: 'Until this day people still asking me what the song says. I heard people say, "Well, what do you say, Dekker? Get up in the morning, bake beans for breakfast? Get up in the morning same thing for breakfast?" I just correct them and say it's "slaving for breads" – *Get up in the morning / Slaving for breads sir / So that every mouth can be fed / Poor me Israelite –* breads is money. Get up in the morning, slaving, go out there to get some dough. We call it breads. In America they treated it like a novelty song like "Tie Me Kangaroo Down Sport". But "Israelites" dealt with how you feel and what you are going through. It's still strong today because it is brutal, it's reality.' He must still be marveling at the hidden complexity which critics have found in his basic cry of despair.

1968 / MY CONVERSATION
The Uniques

Slim Smith, The Uniques' lead singer, is universally regarded as one of the greatest singers reggae ever produced. And nowhere were his intricate vocal talents better displayed than in the exquisitely sung 'My Conversation'. Slim was still a big star at the time of his death, so his early and untimely death was a great shock to the entire country. Alton Ellis remembers the sad circumstances: 'I hate to talk about Slim Smith, Keithy. Cause I know the birth of his career and I was there at the end. I was in the middle of it, when he came to England we did some tunes together and it end up in a big company hand. I think what was wrong with Slim was his character. He wasn't a strong type of person with a good head. And he wasn't able to keep the boat steady when it start rocking, and if you can't balance the boat it just turn over.

'It was a night when Bunny Lee was doing some recording and Keithy come to the studio

and wanted to sing. Say stop the studio, him wanted to sing, crazy like, not himself. Bunny Lee make him sing some song, but we can hear that's not Keithy you know, that's not him, but we put it on record. The same night him was acting crazy like, say some guy want to fight him, but Bunny Lee say no, and tell them take him home. And them lock him in a house and him mash-up the place and mash-up the window and him bust this vein punching through the window. And him not being conscious of the danger to shout somebody and say look do something about this, him just stay in there and feel tired and lay down and just bleed to death. Him start shouting when him start to feel the pain but that was too late.'

1968 / STEPPING RAZOR
Peter Tosh (written by Joe Higgs)

'Stepping Razor' may have been best known as Peter Tosh's signature song, but it was Joe Higgs who was its creator: 'I was born in Kingston on June 3, 1940. I started out singing with Roy Wilson. We used to live on the same street and go down to the rehearsals at Bim and Bam. We got together in a contest when we were each qualified in the first ten solo singers. Among them were Wilfred 'Jackie' Owens, Owen Grey, Laurel Aitken. The promoter had a problem – they were supposed to choose eight for the finals,

Joe Higgs

but they couldn't decide which two to eliminate. So he said: "Would you guys sing together? Cause I saw you over in the corner singing and you were very good." And we went into the duo section and we were second. That's where we started singing in 1958 as Higgs and Wilson.

'My first time in the studio was with Mr. Edward Seaga (former Jamaican prime minister and current opposition leader). He was our manager, the first person to put us on record. He was the best manager we ever had – we always got paid! He went into politics after this. He saw us at Ward Theatre. We tore down the place. He had thought of putting some money into building a studio. So he built West Indies Records and we made our first record, "O Manny O". We were his only act. The song jumped from 43 to 3 and then spent a couple weeks at number one. Sold plenty.

'We worked for Coxsone after that. We had a big hit with "There's a Reward" in 1964. I wrote "Stepping Razor" in 1967 for the Festival Song Competition. But it was considered a very

subversive message, so it was disqualified from the top eight because of that. That's when I decided to give it to Tosh. As to who write it, well the give away line is – *Don't watch my size I'm dangerous.* I'm five foot four. How can a six foot something guy like Tosh write a line like that? Anyway, I got his signature saying this is a Joe Higgs composition and I've been collecting royalties since 1979.'

1968 / **EVERYTHING CRASH**
The Ethiopians

Jamaicans today, especially the middle and upper classes, tend to speak of the 1960s as a golden age, when there was no crime, violence, social unrest or political problems. A totally unrealistic view of course. Jamaica has deteriorated in many ways, but improved in others. (The joke is that in the old days the middle class could walk anywhere and feel safe. Now they have to drive through with windows up.)

Jamaicans have little historical perspective and are very good at believing only what they

A bus depot burned out in civil unrest in the late sixties

want to. The songs of the era provide a collective social document which contradict the simple-minded 'everything was better then' assertions. If crime was no problem, why so many 'rudie songs' And what about the riots mentioned in song like 'Shanty Town'? And what about the political unrest so graphically chronicled in 'Everything Crash'?

It *might* be easy to take Jamaica's political stability for granted nowadays. But clearly The Ethiopians repeated chant 'Everything Crash' shows the uncertainty of that era. In the face of such widespread social upheaval, doubts must have gone through many minds. Jamaica was only six years independent. Would it go the way of so many other newly freed ex-colonies and descend into anarchy and chaos? Or suffer a military coup or armed revolution? There were no shortage of salutary reminders of the depths to which a country could fall when the reciprocal bonds of social contracts have all been broken. Haiti and Cuba were only ninety miles away.

Everything crash
Watermen strike
Electric company too
Down to the policeman too
Everything crash
What gone bad a morning
Can't come good a evening, whoa
Every day carry bucket to the well
One day the bottom must drop out
Everything crash

So every time it's played on the radio, The Ethiopians' tune provides a mini-history lesson and reminds us that though all times seem good when they are gone,  Jamaica had plenty of troubles back then too.

1968 / **LONG SHOT KICK THE BUCKET**
The Pioneers

Ranking behind perhaps only football – the sport of the masses, and cricket – the sport of the educated, in popularity, horse racing has a tenacious grip on the common imagination. Indeed more horse racing songs have been made in reggae than about all other sports combined.

Part of the sports' continued prominence is that since time immemorial every race from Caymanas Park, the nation's only racetrack, has been broadcast live on the radio. In the old days there were only two stations and both carried live racing. Which meant no matter where you went, you were bound to hear it. This continual diet of excited 'down the stretch' commentary has influenced DJ music extensively. It takes little imagination to see the inspiration of race announcers' breathless calls of close finishes in the rapid-fire speed-raps of deejays like Papa San. Of course in the inimitable Jamaican way of seeing everything in somehow sexual terms, every male deejay proclaims himself 'champion jockey with an extra long whip, full a stamina and love to ride, and can go the full distance and win the big race every time'. The female deejays on the other hand urge their sisters to 'perform like champion horse and show say you is A-1 class'.

'Long Shot Kick The Bucket' is the most enduring of all racetrack reggae songs. As the song suggests, it comments on the death of a popular racehorse.

> What a weeping and wailing down at Caymanas Park
> Long Shot, him kick the bucket
> It happen, it happen in the first race
> And it cold up the place

Of course, for all his sorrow at Long Shot's death, the singer doesn't forget his personal problems – *All me money gone a hell* (maybe this was the real tragedy that inspired him).

Interestingly 'Long Shot', who had inspired an earlier eponymous Pioneers' hit, was far from a champion. Indeed he raced in the very lowest class. But he had great endurance, and kept on running long after other horses of his age had retired. For a long while he was the oldest horse on the racetrack and ended up running in 202 races, the most in local racing history. There is still an annual race run in his honour, the 'Long Shot' Trophy, which was once won by a horse owned by singer Gregory Isaacs.

Long Shot's tenacity, coupled with his catchy name, somehow caught the public's imagination. And he became one of the most popular horses at Caymanas Park, clapped whenever he came on the track, the object of many sentimental bets. On the rare occasions the game, old campaigner won a race, he would receive a standing ovation, even from those he had cost money. So when he died at age 12, falling during a race, it was like the death of a minor national hero, sadly noted even by those completely uninterested in the sport. Very unimportant in the larger scheme of things perhaps, but an incident which touched many people, however slightly, and was etched in song forever by the Pioneers' tune, which hit the charts only weeks after Long Shot's death.

1968 / **NANNY GOAT**
Larry and Alvin

Although 'Do The Reggay' used the word first, many people consider that 'Nanny Goat' was the first song with a true reggae feel. 'Nanny Goat' is one of the countless reggae songs which quote from old-time Jamaican proverbs. In this case it's – *What sweet nanny goat a go run him belly.* (Bob Marley's 'Simmer Down' also uses the same metaphor.) In other words people don't always know what's good for them. It's no accident that proverbs are common in reggae songs. Jamaica has a large stock of vivid, colourful, and thought-provoking folk sayings which still sprinkle

everyday conversation: 'Sorry fe mawga dog, mawga dog turn round bite you'; 'Coward man keep sound bone'; 'Every empty hoe have him stick a bush'; 'Chicken merry hawk de near'. As they say, proverbs are a people's wisdom.

1968 / **LOVE ME FOREVER**
Carlton and His Shoes

The most uniqely named group in reggae history. Actually it was supposed to be 'Shades', but someone spelt it wrong. 'Love Me Forever' is one of Jamaican music's purest love songs, and its B-side 'Happy Land' is famous as the formative basis for 'Satta Amassagana', one of reggae's most covered anthems.

1969 / **LIQUIDATOR**
Harry J Allstars

Session men are the unsung heroes of reggae. A few like Don Drummond or Sly Dunbar and Robbie Shakespeare become well-known in their own right, but the vast majority labour in obscurity. Yet they are the foundation of the music, creating the beat that is the music's soul. Keyboardist Winnie Wright played on countless reggae classics, yet even the most devoted reggae fans hardly know his name. 'Liquidator' was his biggest moment in the sun, its organ-dominated rhythm track making the British top ten. Even then, producer Harry Johnson stole the session men's thunder by giving them the cheesy name of the Harry J Allstars. As if he had anything to do with playing the instruments.

1969 / **HELLO CAROL**
The Gladiators

Hello Carol / I'm depending on you / Got a fever and fresh cold / I'm depending on you / No more tears on my pillow / Like a flowing river / No bachelor / Without relations

Love in its purest and most unembarassed form, 'Hello Carol' is perhaps reggae's most unabashed recognition of man's need for woman's comfort in times of trouble. The vocals are so earnest and unaffected that for once you believe that this

Jamaican man is sincerely pouring out his heart without any ulterior motives.

Of course the ladies might interpret it differently. For as a Jamaican woman listening to the song remarked cynically to us, she's heard this kind of rubbish many times before and it's probably just another 'sweet mouth lyrics' attempt to get Carol into bed.

1969 / **PRESSURE DROP**
Toots and The Maytals

Wordless vocal segments are a key feature of some of the greatest reggae songs ('Dibbi dibbi dibbi di di' in '54-46', 'Pom pom pom pom pom pom' in 'Book of Rules', 'Whoa, oh, oh, oh' in 'Cherry Oh Baby', the 'Hmmm, hmmm' echo in 'Shanty Town'.). As if to say there are feelings which are too deep for words to convey, and too personal for any musical instrument but the human voice to give expression to. 'Pressure Drop' takes this tendency to its extreme limits – there are some words to give a kind of idea of what Toots is singing about, but not enough to give the song a definite meaning. It consists of wordless moans and sentence fragments repeated in diminishing length until at the end, he repeats one word, 'pressure', again and again as if it has taken on some obsessive meaning.

What kind of pressure is he singing about? – '"Pressure Drop", now I was thinking about the suffering of the people. No politics or anything. Just the things I see. The people under a lot of pressure. From before I born poor people were under pressure. And I figure pressure was going to drop on you, on us. "Is it you" whoever doing the pressure, whoever the cap fit. There have to be someone pressuring the people, somebody causing the people to suffer. And I am singing for the people and telling them my feelings. Maybe they not even looking on the song that way, but that is how the song come out, what I meant.'

In the end, it's not what Toots says, it's how he says it. The words in 'Pressure Drop' might not have any obvious meaning, but the singer's distress is clear, and those 'Hmmm hmmm hmmms' are profoundly satisfying.

Perhaps 'Pressure Drop' defies conventional analysis because it didn't evolve from a deliberate intellectual process and wasn't written with pen and paper. As Toots tells it, the melody and rhythm came first – created by the group of ace studio musicians following his and Kong's directions. And as Toots sang himself into the 'spirit', the words and feeling came out from some deep recess within and a primal scream of anguish was captured on tape.

As Dave Marsh puts it: '. . . I don't know what the hell he's singing about . . . but it sure does sound important.'

1969 / **SWEET AND DANDY**
Toots and The Maytals

People who write about reggae as a music primarily of rebellion and protest nourished mainly in urban ghettos, are missing the point of at least half the music. A good deal of reggae's appeal and staying power comes from it's versatility, its ability to express the feelings and emotions of the entire Jamaican experience. Yes, 'Trenchtown Rock' and 'Shanty Town' were rooted in the realities that many Jamaicans face every day. But so are songs like 'Cherry Oh Baby' and 'Sweet and Dandy'.

Bob Marley, Jimmy Cliff and Toots Hibbert were all born and spent most of their formative

Coxsone gave this insight into his methods in general: 'About sixty per cent of the records I produced were never released. Some of them the voice just couldn't make it. In those days you couldn't put out records which were off key. But now you can put out anything. I am going to put out some of those I couldn't release in the past. I used to act producer and engineer on the sessions. Those days were not like now, when you have a lot of tracks and if there is a mistake you can just patch it. If anybody make a mistake then, everything had to start from scratch.

'In the studio it was more like left over ideas from the night before, because I'm always planning for the next day in the studio. Even tape recorders weren't easy to get in those days – they were very costly. Being handicapped by not being a writer, a musical writer, I've got to find ways of recording my ideas so I can look back and think of what I was thinking at the time.

'I did a lot of experimenting. I used to record the music, put it on a dub plate and go straight to the dancehall and watch the reaction. Many a time we make the record and change it around, watch the reaction and change it around to suit the fans. How they were moving and not so much as what the people say.

'My main contribution was through the arrangement. The main thing was the use of a lot of rehearsal before recording so all the arrangements were done in rehearsal. We were well rehearsed. We have an idea of what the sound would be like, the structure. I used to notice that whenever an artist was giving problems, one look from the musicians and him get it right. Or the musicians might say "bwoy, this no sound right. Mek we turn it into an instrumental." Right away the artist would get it right.'

years in rural or 'country' Jamaica. Even today half the population still resides out of urban areas. And nearly every city dweller has country relatives who they will visit occasionally. Jamaica is a small place after all, and ten minutes from Kingston one can be in 'bush'. So the country wedding described in 'Sweet and Dandy' is as Jamaican as you can get. If someone has never been to one, they've heard one described. Toots says the song is based on an actual story.

'My mommy used to talk about this wedding in her family. I was actually too small those days to remember it. But I would hear the same thing from my bigger sisters and brothers when I got older. And the story inspired me to write "Sweet And Dandy". It seemed like a good theme for a Festival song.'

Lovers of so-called 'conscious' music would have you believe that any reggae devoid of political rhetoric is unimportant and doesn't 'deal with reality'. But reality is what actually happens in people's lives – the good and the bad. Times are often hard in Jamaica, and crime and violence are a part of too many lives. But Jamaicans know happiness too, and few songs anywhere express unbridled joy as well as this one.

What makes 'Sweet and Dandy' more than just another 'jump up' tune is its humanity. In a

few telling phrases Toots captures the nervousness of the about to be bride and groom, the
anxious relatives worrying that the couple will
make fools of themselves and everyone else, and
the general exhilaration that ensues after all is
forgotten in the laughter and celebration.

Ettie in a room a cry
Mama say she must wipe her eye
Papa say she no fe fool is like
She never been to school at all . . .
Johnson in a room a fret
Uncle say him mus hol up im head
Auntie say him no fe fool
Is like is not time for his wedding day . . .
It is no wonder
It's a perfect ponder
Why they were dancing
In that ball room last night

But the ever present practical Jamaican streak
is there too. These are poor people and the cost
of the cake and liquor – *one pound ten for the
wedding cake / twenty bottle of cola wine* – is
enough to be worth mentioning. And the line –
*All de people dress up inna white / fe go eat up
Johnson wedding cake* – displays Toots' sly sense
of humour.

Given his wonderful vocal abilities, Toots'
uncanny ear for rhythm is often overlooked. But
few players in Jamaican music ever conceived
more vital 'riddims' or matched them more
appropriately to words and melody. The beat
here is very mentoish in flavour, being very
evocative of the old 'cripple foot' or 'stamp and
slide' dance. It matches the atmosphere of an
old-time wedding perfectly. And the singing is so
joyous and the feeling so warm that you want the
song to go on forever, especially when Toots
comes in at the end with the title refrain. Sweet
and Dandy for real.

The Sounds of the Seventies

1970 / **DUPPY CONQUEROR**
The Wailers

Bob Marley's unprecedented success overseas did not surprise everyone. Years before his break-through many felt he was the Jamaican performer most likely to make his mark abroad. Witness these comments by Pamela O'Gorman: 'Perhaps the most original mind in Jamaican popular music is Bob Marley. His speech is natural. The bitterness and passion that lie behind so many of his songs are tempered with an ironic detachment and a deliberately limited emotional range, all the more effective because it avoids stridency or self-pity.

'There is nothing harsh in the vocal timbre of his "dread" songs "Screw Face" or "Small Axe" but the message is unmistakable. Above the cunningly distorted, almost convulsive reggae rhythm of "Screw Face" the melodic line weaves a grotesque path, always coloured, underscored and commented upon by The Wailers in the background. New elements creep in: changing textures, changing dynamics and harmonic colour that, however simple, are devastatingly effective.

'There are no sweet songs that Marley sings. His main gift is not a gift of melody; yet his melodies are so closely integrated with the words that they grow on the listener, revealing their true artistry only after several hearings. This is the sign of the true creative mind distinct and different from that of the mere 'tune cobbler' who can turn out a winning product for the Hit Parade at the drop of a fifty dollar note.'

She continues later: '... To me, there seem to be two significant trends which have made

themselves apparent and which, if developed further, point to exciting possibilities. One is the kind of originality shown by Bob Marley, the other is the Rastafarian influence.

'In a JIS radio programme in 1968 Marley was asked about the future of Jamaican popular music. After suggesting that a return to Mento would be too easy, Marley went on to say, "All we want now is the music to the beat . . . the music to carry it . . . better arrangement and thing." Marley went ahead and followed his own prediction– his "Duppy Conqueror", which is probably destined to become a reggae classic, unequivocally showed what could happen when the beat became submissive to the creative demands of the composer.'

This was written in 1972, well before Bob had begun to make his mark overseas. Everyone has 20/20 hindsight. But when someone prophesies an event before it happens, respect due.

1970 / **RIVERS OF BABYLON**
Brent Dowe and The Melodians

As Randall Grass puts it: '"Rivers of Babylon"'s lyrics were based on Psalm 137 of the bible . . . The psalm's somber mood, the droning harmonies and the measured reggae pulse add up to a hypnotic spell that is miles away from rocksteady. There's no sense of beginning, middle or end (nor verse, chorus, bridge) to the song. It seemingly could go on forever, just as the Rasta drummers would play endlessly, obliterating time . . . Leslie Kong, like most Jamaican producers, had little or no musical expertise. But he did have an ear for quality and a willingness to take the time to get the music right. He was not particularly innovative, but stripped the music down to gimmick-free, almost formulaic essentials. And the sessions he oversaw have an identifiable signature – clean production, bright choppy rhythms, and melodic, soulful vocals.'

Was Kong the greatest of Jamaican producers? Such arguments can never be settled, but he did produce more great singles than anyone else. 'Rivers of Babylon' is of course most famous outside of Jamaica in the jazzed up Boney M version, where it comes across as a feel good song. It's obviously technically superior to The Melodians', with a clearer, cleaner and crisper sound. But form is no substitute for substance. Boney M, to some people anyway, may be great party music. The Melodians' song touches the soul, the scratchy guitar and punctuating bass accentuating the singers' despondent pathos.

1975 / **KING TUBBY MEETS THE ROCKERS UPTOWN**
Augustus Pablo

Augustus Pablo is not only the greatest melodica player in reggae history, he's probably the only significant artist in any musical genre to specialize in playing this instrument. The *New York Times* dubbed him 'the greatest melodica player in the world' – although we are left to wonder who is the world's second greatest?

Rebel Rock Reggae

Pablo Moses, innovator

The reedy, vaguely middle eastern sound of his melodica lends Pablo's work an exotic colour which sets it apart from the work of any other reggae artist. Apart from classic singles like 'Java' and 'Pablo In Dub', he has produced a number of collectors' item dub albums – 'Ital Dub', 'King Tubby

Meets The Rockers Uptown' , a masterpiece of texture and space, and 'East Of The River Nile'. He ranks with King Tubby and Lee Perry as one of the three most significant influences dub has ever known. It is hard to imagine the existence of über-producer Tricky without the pioneering work of Pablo and others.

1970 / **SATISFACTION**
Carl Dawkins

1971 / **PICTURE ON A WALL**
Freddie Mckay

Like any kind of music reggae has its one hit wonders. And while it might seem unfair to dub Freddie Mckay and Carl Dawkins as such – because they were both stars in their day – these songs are chiefly what they are remembered for. 'Satisfaction' was reportedly one of the biggest selling records in reggae history, moving over 80,000 copies.

1970 / **YOU CAN GET IT**
Jimmy Cliff

Few songs display their creator's character more accurately than 'You Can Get It'. Perhaps the most disciplined and hard-working of all reggae stars, it is more than mere talent which has made Jimmy Cliff probably the most famous living Jamaican singer

1970 / **WEAR YOU TO THE BALL**
U-Roy and The Paragons

'Wear You To The Ball' was possibly the most influential reggae song of all time and arguably the most important record in popular music since James Brown's 'Papa's Got a Brand New Bag'.

U-Roy was not the first deejay – in the beginning there was Count Matckukie, and then King Stitt, the ugly one. But Matckukie never recorded, and Stitt's records were never more than novelties, mainly instrumentals with a few shouted remarks. It was U-Roy who established the deejay style as a legitimate musical form and not just a passing fad. 'Wear You To The Ball'

give him my guitar and he start to play some of his songs, and he was interesting because he had good artistic feeling. "Sitting In Limbo" wasn't finished then, so I started to sing it and he said "why don't you put that line there!" So it developed in England and finished in South America Argentina with Guilly Bright. The feeling of limbo was from Jamaica. It was 1970 before "Harder They Come". It was at that time I felt that feeling. I'd been in England for four years and come back to Jamaica not making it in England. Like I leave to make it and come back to Jamaica and find I'd lost the popularity I had. People even start thinking I'm a foreigner.

Sitting here in limbo, But I know it won't be long
Sitting here in limbo, Like a bird without a song . . .
Sitting here in limbo, Waiting for the dice to roll
Sitting here in limbo, Got some time to search my soul

'"Sitting In Limbo" is a crying out song, you know. You are in an environment you can hardly

was not his first hit, but it made the greatest impact, and more importantly, continued to hold up over the months and years. Dancehall and rap start with this song.

To many 'Wear You To The Ball' is the best deejay song ever and U-Roy certainly gives a command performance. He makes a pleasant, listenable song superbly exciting by filling in the slow, meandering gaps and playing call and answer with The Paragons. But what U-Roy says doesn't make a lot of sense. It is basically a copy of the usual radio deejay patter – a mixture of exhortation, commentary on the song, bragadoccio and nonsense.

'Oldies lovers', who think dancehall is nonsense yet consider U-Roy the ultimate 'conscious' deejay, should listen again. This does not mean to say 'Wear You To The Ball' isn't a great song. When music is this electrifying, who cares what it means?

1970 / SITTING IN LIMBO
Jimmy Cliff

Jimmy Cliff's words: 'It was in 1970 that I wrote "Sitting In Limbo". I had the idea for the song before I left England and went to South America for the second time. I met this brother from Panama called Guilly [Guillermo] Bright. So he came to his hotel and I was playing him some of my songs. And he says he was a writer too. So I

Jimmy Cliff

see, trying to get ahead. Every man always wants to go ahead. Everybody wants to go ahead. It's the natural thing with the human being to want to achieve and to be. But the system only makes the environment to hold you down or hold you back if you're an unfortunate one. So "Sitting In Limbo" is one of those songs sitting in limbo, but you always have to know within yourself that there's a way out. You always have to have that positive or even optimistic feeling. But you can be optimistic and not positive, you know. Because when you're optimistic, you're waiting, you're hoping. But your hopes don't come through all the time, so you have to be positive and put action with the positiveness to make it happen.'

1971 / **MANY RIVERS TO CROSS**
Jimmy Cliff

Naturally Jamaicans have a great love of gospel music and most reggae stars (like soul music pioneers) learnt to sing in church – Jimmy Cliff among them: 'I sang in church too. It was the Pentecostal denomination and in that church there was no choir. The congregation was the choir. So I always going and singing along and clapping. At first I'd just sing and bang a tambourine, then I started on guitar and piano.'

'Many Rivers To Cross' is not overtly religious in its lyrics. There are a few biblical illusions (*Wandering I am lost*) but the song is ostensibly about a guy losing his girl and feeling lonely – *And if loneliness would leave me alone / It's such a trial to be on your own / My woman left me she didn't say why / Well I guess I have to cry.*

Cliff did say about it: 'I wrote this song in Jamaica. That was the same period of time when I came back to Jamaica after four years, before the movie, dissatisfied with myself for not accomplishing what I went to England to do. And so that's when I wrote "Many Rivers To Cross". Like the white cliffs of Dover, we used to go across with my little van and take the ferry down in Dover and go across to France or Germany and work for nothing. That's "Many Rivers To Cross".'

Yet the whole thing is awash in church organs and the singing so spiritual, that it sounds like a hymn about something more important than just 'I miss you baby'. The effect, and this is why it's often played on Jamaican radio when someone important dies, is of a man searching for spiritual meaning in his life. Whether or not this was his intent, only Jimmy Cliff knows.

In another context, he had this to say on religion (it's quite noticeable that interviews with reggae singers rarely fail to touch on religious matters): 'The human being is made up of the trinity, physical, mental and spiritual. When we're born as a baby, we want physical things. Then as we start to grow, mental things, intellect start to develop. You ask questions about what things are. Then as you grow more you start to realize your spirituality, you realise there's another force out there more than yourself. Having realised these things, I try to put them into perspective and see how I relate to this higher force and then eventually how I relate to everything else.'

Perhaps 'Many Rivers To Cross' describes a part of this quest.

1971 / **CHERRY OH BABY**
Eric Donaldson

'Cherry Oh Baby' is a very simple song, consisting of little more than a stop-start bass-guitar beat, an overdubbed organ and Donaldson's reedy, grainy pleadings. But his pained earnestness is overwhelming, and it's hard not to feel that he really is in love with this girl, and that her hoped-for acceptance (*Yeah yeah yeah yeah*), or dreaded rejection (*woe woe woe woe*) will be the defining event in his life.

> Oh Cherry oh Cherry oh baby
> Don't you know I'm in need of thee
> And if you don't believe it's true
> What have you left for me to do

'Cherry Oh Baby' highlights the transformation reggae has undergone since becoming an 'international' rather than 'hometown' music. The singer with his broad dialect comes across as

THE COUNTRY OF JAH

It's a commonly accepted belief among Jamaicans, one often repeated in the media, that Jamaica has the most churches per square mile of any country in the world. (And, the joke goes, beside every church there's a horse race betting shop and rum bar.) There are no definite statistics to support this statement, but as they say here 'If it no go so, it go close to so'. To anyone familiar with the country, it's difficult to believe there's any place where churches are more common. And the possibility that there are more denominations per capita anyplace else is almost inconceivable. Jamaica has only two-and-a-half million people but it has hundreds of breakaway sects.

Sociologists have posited any number of reasons for this. Two of the most common are that Christianity was drummed into the slaves to keep them docile (It didn't work. Jamaicans remain the most undocile people on earth) and tribal divisions worked to fragment the religion. Whatever the causes, the plethora of sects certainly reflects the basic anarchic tendencies of Jamaicans (rich and poor), who seem to resent any kind of imposed discipline. As to explaining the depth of religious feeling (which no one who has lived in Jamaica can doubt), an old parson's jest comes as close as anything. Jamaica is too beautiful, he argued, to be the result of an accident – there must be a God who created it.

A lot of foreigners mistakenly assume most Jamaicans are Rastafarians, but the cult has never attracted even five per cent of the population. Jamaica is an overwhelmingly Christian country and people's lives are infused by religion. While not attaching much importance to ritual or dogma, the overwhelming majority of Jamaicans find it impossible to conceive of even the possibility of the non-existence of a supreme being of some sort, whether it be Haile Selassie, Jah, or Jesus Christ. The open profession of atheism is considered a crime on par with homosexuality (always preceded here by 'Godless'), evils for which no punishment is too great. Which is not to say there aren't atheists or homosexuals in Jamaica. But if they value their well-being, they learn to keep their perversions (as Jamaicans see it) hidden.

In few countries outside the Islamic world does religion play such a dominant role in people's lives. It

permeates Jamaican life almost completely, and almost no public meeting can begin without blessings from a religious minister. While most national anthems extol a country's virtues, commemorate victories, or laud heroes, Jamaica's is in effect a prayer to God for guidance:

> Eternal father bless our land / Guard us with thy
> mighty hand
> Keep us free from evil power / Be our light through
> countless hours
> Strengthen us the weak to cherish / Give us freedom
> lest we perish

In 1991 there was a huge furore when the churches and the government clashed over the issue of restarting a public lottery, which the churches had succeeded in getting banned in the 1970s. The government finally overrode the church on the issue, but the lottery eventually failed. 'A judgment from God!', exulted the faithful. (Alas for the righteous – the lottery was brought back in a new form in late 1994 and has proved massively successful.)

Although, as ever, religiousness is not a consistent thing in Jamaica. The churches may condemn lotteries and casinos, but race horse betting is a way of life here. And along with being one of the most religious countries on earth, Jamaica has one of the world's highest, if not the highest, rate of illegitimate births. Something like 85 per cent of babies here are out of wedlock.

Dancehall music gives the clearest expression of the unusual Jamaican outlook. For all the obscenity and crudeness found there, stage show artists make frequent and unabashed references to 'the almighty'. The same artists who deal in uncompromising 'slackness' will record songs of praise and veneration. Lady Saw was banned from the 1995 Jamaican Music Awards for 'slackness'. Yet she had a big hit this same year with 'Glory Be To God'. In early 1997 Ninja Man, the original 'hortical don gorgon' of hardcore 'gun talk' deejays, caused a national sensation when he was publicly baptized as a 'born again' Christian. Now dubbed Brother Desmond, he vowed to forsake all badness and perform only for the Lord, because 'Religion sweeter than dancehall'. And Brother Desmond's first appearance drew the biggest gospel concert audience in Montego Bay's history.

a 'country boy' singing unselfconsciously about the abiding concern of his life.

Oh Cherry oh Cherry oh baby
Can't you see I'm in love a with you
And if you don't believe I do
Then why don't you come and try me
I will never ever let you down
I will never make you wear no frown
If you say that you love me madly
Then babe I will accept you gladly

'Cherry oh Baby' came out when the deejay invasion had just started. Looking back, it was clearly a record ahead of its time, pointing out reggae's eventual path of evolution. Despite all the foreign acclaim for Bob Marley's 'conscious music', Toots 'Jamaican soul' and Jimmy Cliff's 'international beat', this was the future. The unessentials are pared away – no horns, no lead guitar, no back-up singers; and what he's singing about is an everyday problem. All you are left with is a rugged, compelling bass and drum rhythm and a man's voice expressing his personal concerns in the language and tone he's used to. Which is essentially what dancehall is today.

During Donaldson's 1971 Festival Finals performance, the press reported, he sang but was not heard because the audience sang louder. The 'oldtimers' danced, the 'youth' went wild. It is still the most popular festival song of all time, and judges complain every year about the 'Cherry Oh Baby' imitations. Two dancehall albums based on its singular jerky beat came out in 1991 and no less than three songs used the riddim. Twenty-four years after its release, 'Cherry Oh Baby' is still acknowledged as the largest selling record in Jamaica's history. Clearly, with his simple, unpretentious song, Eric tapped some unconscious nerve that runs deep in the Jamaican psyche.

1971 / SMALL AXE / BATTLE AXE
The Wailers / Lee Perry and The Upsetters

Lee Perry had a vital impact on Bob Marley and The Wailers. Their partnership from 1969 to 1971 produced a string of classic songs like

'Duppy Conqueror', 'Small Axe', 'Soul Shakedown Party' and 'Mr. Brown' which all bear the trademarks of Perry's production style – mysterious atmosphere, unusual sound effects and jagged rhythms. The albums 'Soul Rebel' and 'African Herbsman' show the high, some say unmatched, level of creativity and inspiration that The Wailers' music reached with Lee Perry. Certainly Perry's influence can be heard on 'Catch A Fire' and all the later albums.

Perry recollects: 'There was a problem between us small operators and the bigger boys. One Sunday morning I get up and think over the whole thing and I got this idea. I said, "well if they are the big three we are the small axe". And I started to write the song. I got stuck at a certain part so I bring it to Bob. Bob read it and start to sing a melody. Bob created the melody for that. We were stuck for about three quarters of an hour and I went for a bible. I don't quite remember if it was a verse of Psalms or Proverbs, but we saw it there, "why boasteth thyself oh evil men". That was when the beat change again. After that we went straight into an album entitled "Soul Rebel". Then we made "Soul Revolution".'

1971 / TRENCHTOWN ROCK

In many ways 'Trenchtown Rock' represents Bob at a crossroads between the extremes of 'Simmer Down' and 'No Woman No Cry'. Genius in full

BOB MARLEY — REGGAE SUPER HERO

Bob Marley is by far the most famous figure Jamaican music has ever produced. Mention Jamaica and foreigners who scarcely know in which hemisphere the country is located will cry in recognition 'Bob Marley!' Millions of people the world over know of reggae only because of Bob Marley and have never heard of another Jamaican musician. It is a truly unique fame covering all corners of the earth, surpassing in universality the adulation accorded to other 'rock martyrs' like Elvis Presley and John Lennon. Musical considerations aside, Marley's global renown has also made him an unmatched cultural icon in Jamaica. No other Jamaican in any field has ever been so lionised.

Naturally, given the hype surrounding his career and the inevitable canonisation granted by his early death, some question the authenticity of his mantle of greatness. Was he really that much better than anyone else? Might there not have been others whose work was of comparable quality but who were never promoted so extensively? Is Marley possibly overrated?

Fame is no guarantor of merit. An artist's renown is not always in proportion to his abilities. Elvis Presley is incomparably more famous than Muddy Waters. There can scarcely be a person on this planet who has not heard of Presley, while Waters is hardly known outside the cult of blues lovers. In countries like Jamaica which are ignorant of the blues, Waters is totally unknown, and even in America it's doubtful one person in ten knows the name.

Presley probably never wrote a song in his life; Waters almost single-handedly transformed the blues from the solitary acoustic guitar player into a co-ordinated electric ensemble called a blues band. Since the blues are the tap root of modern popular music, it's no exaggeration to call Muddy Waters the father of electric pop music. Presley, in the final reckoning, was basically what Sam Phillips prayed for when he said, 'If I could find a white man who could sing like a black man, I could make a billion dollars.' As for their respective bodies of work, well it's like comparing Bing Crosby and Louis Armstrong. But there you are – national debates in the U.S. about Elvis 'The King' Presley stamps, oblivion for Muddy Waters.

So being the most famous doesn't necessarily mean you're the best. Furthermore, Bob Marley was pin-up-poster handsome. For all his black pride, Marley was half-white, with quite Caucasian features. This made it possible for North Americans and Europeans to accept and identify with him (a la Jimi Hendrix) in a way they couldn't with someone like, say, Peter Tosh. Leroy Sibbles is quite frank about the subject: 'As great as Bob Marley was, I think Peter Tosh was just as good. But he couldn't make it as big as Bob, because Bob had a lighter complexion, and the record companies were able to promote him more because he was accepted easier. Look at Toots. There's no one better than Toots – black, white, blue or pink, but he never reached the level of Bob Marley, because of the same reason.'

Add to this Marley's disconcerting resemblance to a dreadlocked Christ, continue the doubters, and you go a long way in explaining his continuing popularity and the esteem, almost reverence in which he is held.

Some of Marley's fervent admirers definitely get carried away; the man was a singer and songwriter (who like all musicians, did produce the occasional lousy tune) after all, not some latter day biblical prophet – he

certainly never claimed such a role for himself. So one can understand why certain skeptics, exasperated by the woolly headed ramblings of some Marley devotees, see his post-1972 persona as essentially a product of corporate hype.

In 1975, when Marley was in the process of becoming a big star but not yet an untouchable icon, Carl Gayle made these observations: 'Ever since the first Island LP "Catch a Fire", there's been a growing interest in the Wailers among rock music lovers, spurred on by Island's promotion campaign and the music news media. It became obvious to Island pretty soon, that Marley was the one on whom to pin the genius tag. Bob, with his rebel Rasta image, was projected as the key figure to the exclusion somewhat of Peter Tosh and Bunny Livingston who have been as important to the Wailers sound as Bob Marley himself since 1964.

'The music media quickly realised that Bob, with his uncompromising lifestyle and cultural roots, his hairstyle and his religion makes a very attractive figure for a rock music public. And they've lapped it up. Island Records have always had that progressive/cult image and Marley fitted in neatly. As the heroes of rock music gradually grew out of fashion, so Bob became more attractive.'

Bob Marley is more than a 'Jamaican Elvis Presley'. He was able to create great songs in all eras of Jamaican music. 'Simmer Down', 'Trenchtown Rock' and 'No Woman No Cry' are all very different, yet each is the equal of any reggae song produced in its time. Collectively, they illustrate the single quality that separates Marley from his compatriots, the ability to grow with the music and adapt his art to changing times.

Toots Hibbert is the only person whose *oeuvre* bears comparison with Marley's. It is not difficult to argue that before 1973, Toots had produced a superior body of music. The difference between the two men, and between Marley and other reggae artists, was shown in the following years. While Toots never adapted to reggae's internationalisation with the new demands the wider non-Jamaican audience made on the artists, Bob literally thrived on the changed circumstances, expanding the music's horizons as no reggae artist before or since.

Tommy Cowan once gave a fascinating insight into Marley's creative process: 'Sometimes when Bob was writing a song, he would call some youth on Hope Road, like those who sold newspapers, put them in a ring and ask each one to come up with a line for the song. Even other people he knew, he would call them and say: "You come wid a line and if you can't come wid a line you drop out-a-the-ring." When he was finished, he had a whole song using the thoughts of many people who some others would have considered insignificant. I remember him doing "Zion Train" and "Redemption Song" like that.'

In another conversation Tommy gave a totally different side to the multi-faceted Marley personality: 'I went to visit Bob and he was playing a Bee Gees album. I laughed at him and said, "Why you listening to foolishness like that?" He answered, "Look, these guys sold ten million records last year. They must be doing something right and I'm trying to figure out what it is."'

Bob Marley was also a ruthless musical perfectionist. Former band member Tyrone Downie has this memory: 'When on tour just rehearsing, Bob was so obsessed. You wake up in the morning and all you're supposed to think of is . . . rehearse 'til you're tired and it's too dark. And if a Wailer make a mistake, especially during a show, Bob would mark it. He just wanted it to be like we all know it's supposed to be. And whoever wasn't doing it right, he told them either to listen to the record, ask somebody who knows, try to do it, or don't play.'

Since his death, Bob Marley's estate has been embroiled in bitter legal disputes, which have caused dark mutterings in many corners. 'Half the story has

never been told', he once sang, and the skyrocketing value of the Marley brand name probably means it never will be. But so what. Ian McCann wrote: 'Marley may or may not have been the saint some have portrayed him to be. Marley may have been a shrewd businessman, a sharp dealer. He may have been the most honest man in music. He may have been a womaniser, or he may just have had a lot of love to give. He may have been a prophet, or just another minstrel with a knack for a deep sounding song. It really doesn't matter any more. What does matter is the music. That music speaks for itself.'

cry before the onset of self-awareness? His greatest piece of street poetry uses the language of the people to create a philosophy at once authentic and profound – *One good thing about music / When it hits you / You feel no pain.*

The Wailers themselves realised the song's importance. According to Bunny Wailer, 'Trenchtown Rock' was the tune that made them really start to search.'

The phrasing is only partly in Jamaican patois, but the sharply rising and falling cadences leave no doubt about where this music was created. And Bob never wrote a sweeter or lovelier melody. The youthful vitality of 'Simmer Down' has been tempered, but the man singing is still full of genuine emotion.

As Dave Marsh says: 'Bob went on to arguably greater, certainly far bigger things, but not truer or more powerful ones, because there are none.'

1971 (1966) / **MAWGA DOG**
Peter Tosh

It is interesting to compare the original ska 'Mawga Dog' with its better known reggae version. Both are brilliant songs, but evoke very different sensibilities. The 1965 song is almost an innocent calypso with playful horns. In 1971, the pared down rhythm matches the harsh words and the threats are no longer veiled – *gal leggo me hand, go hold on to some other man* – becomes *gal, go way from me, me no want to see you round me.*

The music is no longer frolicsome, but sharp and cutting. Tosh's clear and assertive singing toughens the biting lyrics. What makes the cut Tosh's most enduring song is the lightness of the beat. The hard edge is there but the song never bogs down as so many of his later pieces do.

'Mawga Dog's hard, unsentimental lyrics reveal the fatalistic bitterness which was a central part of Tosh's character. The song's theme of inevitable betrayal by those you nurture, was sadly prescient. For Tosh's murderer, Dennis Lobban, was an aspiring dub poet who Tosh had taken under his wing – *Sorry fe Mawga dog, Mawga dog tun round bite you / Put hog inna white shirt, Him bound fe wallow inna mud mud . . . .*

PETER TOSH – REBEL WARRIOR
....

The most outspoken reggae artist of all time was born Winston Hubert McIntosh in Church Lincoln, Westmoreland, October 9th, 1944, the only son of Alvera Coke and one of many children fathered by James McIntosh. Tosh would later bitterly recall that his father, the pastor of the church his mother attended in Savanna-la-Mar, would not acknowledge him.

'I have no mother here. I have a bearer. Jah mother is my mother, and Jah is my father. My earthly parents don't know my potential or my divine qualities. They weren't taught how to diagnose or know or to be aware of such things. They were looking at skin quality, skin complexion, and because me born so rass-claat-black, me know seh mi was a curse, according to the shitsem them time they. I born come learn say if you brown you can come around, if you white, you perfectly alright and if you black you in the back. Me never come pon the earth under no wedlock. Me is what them call illegitimate – that mean say me is a criminal (laugh) . . . bombo-rass-claat! That's why me a go write a song called "Illegitimate Children". It took me years to know that I was one.

'My father, James McIntosh, is a bad boy, a rascal. That's what him do for a living. He just go around and have a million-and-one children! Right now me have many brothers that me don't know. I was the only child me mother have.'

He played musical instruments as a child, although the only formal training he received was six months of piano lessons in grade five. He later went to live with his aunt in Savanna-la-Mar, moving to Denham Town in Kingston in 1960.

'I got myself an old guitar when I was a youth in the country – it was Wailer's first guitar, you know. The first tune I ever recorded was "I'm The Toughest". I did that around 1964-5 for Clement Dodd. I did some other tunes like "Mawga Dog", "Arise Black Man", "Leave My Business", "400 Years", "Stop That Train", "Soon Come", "Go Tell It On The Mountain" and many others that I don't remember. We [The lers] all group up in Trenchtown as youths. I used to live up on West Road, Bob and Bunny live down on Second Street. Second Street was off West Road, only a coupla blocks down the way. I was way down in my teens at the time, maybe 17. It was about '62 that we started, and Wailing Wailers was about '64-'65. I was playing an instrument – see, I was the beginning. I teach Bob to play guitar. Yeah, mon! Before I played guitar, I played piano and organ. I played piano as a youth, because my mother – her name is Alvera – said I'm gonna learn that. My mother and father didn't know anything 'bout instruments.

'Me just one time see a man in the country play guitar and say "My, that man play guitar nice". It just attract me so much that me just sat there taking it in for about half-day and when him done – he was playing one tune for the whole half-day – he had hypnotized me so much that my eyes extracted everything he had done with his fingers. I picked up the guitar and played the tune he had just played with him showing me a thing. And when he asked me who taught him I tell him it was him!

'Joe Higgs was a brother amongst The Wailers for years. He was encouragement, and he inspired us and kept us together. I also looked up at Horace Andy, and admired Delroy Wilson and Ken Boothe, but them rather sing commercially about "I love you darling" and all of that. Now me like Max Romeo, because him sing about reality. Me really like to sing about reality and life and not only the love of your girl, but the love of your brother too.'

Tosh was a radical from the beginning. His first recorded run in with the law came in March, 1968 when he participated in a demonstration protesting the hanging of blacks by the illegal Rhodesian regime of Ian Smith. He was arrested for obstructing traffic in Spanish Town when he and another man refused to move when ordered to do so. Prince Buster raised his bail.

Tosh had a habit of offending people, even from the early days. In one incident at Studio One, he ordered records and refused to pay for them. He went on to curse and intimidate the sales staff, and when confronted by Dodd, said The Wailers were owed and he didn't have to pay for the records because they were as much theirs as Studio One's. Dodd stopped just short of exchanging blows with Tosh but banned Peter from coming back to Studio One to do business, although other members of The Wailers family were allowed to do so.

The tendency grew extreme as he grew older. He would be disrespectful to persons undeserving of such treatment and use profanities anytime and anywhere, cursing stewardesses, policemen, hotel workers, waiters, even record company executives – one reason, allegedly, for CBS's failure to renew his contract in the 1980s. He also called Chris Blackwell 'Whiteworst', blaming him for The Wailers breakup. Tosh began alienating even close, life-long friends. And the cause of his altercations with his Matthews

Lane brethren often seemed to be his lady Marlene.

A lot of people weren't shocked when he was murdered – saddened and hurt, yes – but not surprised. The murder on Friday, 11 September 1987, was reportedly the result of a robbery attempt gone wrong, instigated by Dennis 'Leppo' Lobban. Lobban was a long-time associate of Tosh's, and a man with a long list of gun-related jail terms, including a 15-year term for two attempted homicides. He had just come out of jail eight months before the murder. Tosh was reportedly shot while hurling obscenities at the hold-up men. Some rumours claimed Lobban had taken the rap for Tosh over a gun charge and was not being 'taken care of'. Others traced the ill-feelings to Tosh's girlfriend's abrasive attitude towards his friends and acquaintances. And as usual, people whispered about drugs.

But for all Tosh's personal unpredictability, the greatness of his music was never in question. He was aggressively fierce in his delivery and acknowledged as a superb stage performer, excelling even his former partner Bob Marley. Many people believe Marley's music lost the threatening edge Tosh provided when The Wailers broke up.

Tosh was the first act signed by the Rolling Stones when they formed their own label, and the 'Bush Doctor' album was the first release on the Rolling Stone Records. He and Mick Jagger cut 'Walk and Don't Look Back' as a duo. Perhaps the Stones' guitarist and long-time rock 'bad boy' Keith Richards, who was instrumental in signing him, saw a kindred spirit in Peter.

1971 / MY JAMAICAN GIRL
The Gaylads

B. B. Seaton is one of the forgotten men of reggae. As lead singer with The Gaylads he had hits from the earliest ska days, like 'Rub It Down' and 'Lady with the Red Dress', right through rocksteady and into reggae.

'My Jamaican Girl' is a perfect example of how the vibes in certain aspects of reggae have changed over the years. Before the deejay era, women seemed almost revered in Jamaican song. No song made this more clear than this sweetly sung paeon of praise to Jamaican womanhood:

> African girls are nice, French girls too
> But when it comes to loving
> I've got to give the credit to you
> Cause you're my Jamaican Girl

How different from what Admiral Bailey would be chanting twenty years later – *Gimme punaany / want punaany / cooly punaany / chiney punaany / whitey punaany / blacky punaany / any punaany is the same punaany.*

Yet although they might be expressing themselves differently, any Jamaican woman will tell you that both Mr Seaton and Mr Bailey have similar intentions. And in a certain sense one cannot help admiring dancehall's frank, if often brutal, attitude to sexual relationships – at least the Admiral is being honest about what he wants. But perhaps music should be able to express ideals as well as reality. It's difficult not to mourn reggae's loss of chivalry, which some say began unintentionally with U-Roy. Many words can be used to describe deejay music, but romantic is not one of them.

B. B. Seaton today

1971 / SATTA MASSAGANA
The Abyssinians

Donald Manning of The Abyssinians relates the story of Satta Massagana: 'That was the first song I do. At that time I was the only Rastaman in the group and in this song I talk about God, The King of Kings and The Lord of Lords, because I had been reading about those things. We did it on our own Clinch label and it cost us £91. On the song I play bongo and bass drum, Bongo Herman play repeater drum, Bongo Les play funde drum, Leroy Sibbles play bass, Richard Ace play piano, Fay play the drums, and Don D junior was on trombone. Bernard Collins sing lead and me and my brother Linford sang harmony. We recorded "Satta" in 1969, but it didn't start selling until 1971.'

'Satta' became one of the most influential reggae records ever. Partly sung in the ancient Ethiopian Amharic language, its militant lyrics, cool harmonies and understated rhythm had an enormous impact. In many ways it is the first really African oriented roots reggae song. And the bass line that Leroy Sibbles created for the song is one of the most versioned of all 'riddims'.

1971 / BETTER MUST COME
1974 / HAVE SOME MERCY
Delroy Wilson

'Better Must Come' is indelibly stamped in many Jamaican's minds as Michael Manley's campaign slogan in the 1972 general elections. Manley's People's National Party used the 1971 hit as their theme song and won easily. Yet as Delroy Wilson told it, the song had nothing to do with politics. Rather it expressed his personal despair at seeing so many other reggae singers gaining financial and international success while he, the first person from Trenchtown to make a record and one of the music's earliest stars, was still struggling.

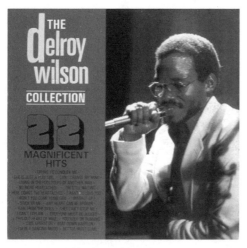

I've been trying a long long time / Still I can't make it

Everything I do / Seems to go wrong

It seems I done something wrong

Who God bless no man curse

Thank God I'm not the worst

Better must come, better must come

Better must come some day

Although 'Have Some Mercy' is ostensibly a love song, it seems almost to have the same theme, of Delroy pleading with fate for success.

Alas, Delroy never did have an international hit, although he was always a revered singer in Jamaica. He died in 1995 from a liver problem exacerbated by heavy drinking. His funeral was estimated to be the biggest for any Jamaican entertainer since Peter Tosh.

1971 / DRAW YOUR BRAKES
Scotty

Stop that train, I want to get on

My baby's leaving me behind

I tell you that girl has really left I to cry

When she wave bye bye

Scotty is not really a great 'riddim rider', but in 'Draw Your Brakes' he manages to express the anguish of the deserted lover (he sounds as if he's on the verge of crying) utterly convincingly. He fills in the gaps in the original so compellingly

that a decently listenable mellow tune with a nice back beat becomes a cry of despair. (But he'll probably find a new girl next week. This is a Jamaican man after all. In fact, the girl probably left him because he was cheating on her.)

1972 / ROD OF CORRECTION
Clancy Eccles

Another song made famous by politics. A reminder of how playful and almost innocent Jamaican elections once were. In 1972, Michael Manley, hailed by his supporters as a 'Joshua' leading his people into the promised land, brandished his 'rod of correction' at rallies to ecstatic applause. Then Prime Minister Hugh Shearer and his deputy Edward Seaga once claimed to have stolen the 'rod', but 'Joshua' retorted that theirs was a fake, he still had the real thing. How distant such days seemed in the 1980 elections when Jamaica was in the throes of a civil war (in all but name) and over 800 people were murdered.

1972 / JOHNNY TOO BAD
The Slickers

A universal anthem of disenchanted ghetto youth if there ever was one, 'Johnny Too Bad' is in many respects the quintessential reggae song. Until Leroy Pierson's article, few people outside the Trenchtown music scene knew anything about the identity of its composer. The label composer credit, 'The Slicker', was obviously another in the long line of fraudulent pseudonyms created by Jamaican producers.

Through interviews with some of the principles actually involved in making the record and others who lived in Trenchtown at the time, Pierson more or less established the song's author, or perhaps more aptly its originator, as Trevor Wilson, younger brother of the late Delroy Wilson. There are never any certainties in Jamaica, but a number of people, including Bunny Wailer, Winston 'Pipe' Matthews and Lloyd 'Bread' McDonald of The Wailing Souls, Niney the Observer of The Destroyers and Messiahs, and Winston Bailey and Derrick

Crooks of The Slickers, generally corroborate each other in singling out Trevor Wilson, not only as the man who wrote 'Johnny Too Bad', but the man who *was* 'Johnny Too Bad'.

According to these men, Wilson, nick-named Batman because 'him can do acrobatics good', actually did walk around with a pistol in his waist and rob and shoot and loot. And apparently, as he lived so he died, shot dead in an ambush by the friends of a man he had beaten up: *One of these days, when you hear a voice say come / Where you gonna run to / You gonna run to the rock for rescue / There will be no rock.*

The story as these men tell it is more than the standard 'poor ghetto kid with no option.' Because the consensus is that Trevor was more talented than his brother Delroy. He could play guitar, play drums, sing and was a good enough songwriter to compose not only 'Johnny Too Bad' but at least two Delroy Wilson hits, the ironically named, given their creator's ultimate fate, 'Badness No Pay' and 'Run For Your Life.'

But as Bunny Wailer puts it: 'Well he was a good singer, but him never have the will like Delroy.'

Lloyd McDonald put a finer point on it: 'A very good singer and songwriter, but one of them man dem who love the gun, and him go pon the wrong side of it. Him can sing an thing, but he couldn't take the frustration, like how Delroy would a sing and get no money and still a sing. You know, the reward is small. He couldn't take that. Him prefer the gun business . . . Him almost was in our group too, that's why I can tell you bout him. Yeah, him talented, write a whole heap of tune. When Wailing Souls was forming, it was just me and Pipe. We want a third man, and Trevor was one of the first man we went to. Even start to rehearse. But bwoy the badness, we couldn't take it. Just badness him deal with, so him just go nowhere.'

Walking down the road with a pistol in your waist / Johnny you're too bad / Walking down the road with a ratchet in your waist / Johnny you're too bad / You're just robbing and stabbing and looting and shooting / Now you're too bad.

While there is no dispute that the song originated with Trevor Wilson, there is some disagreement as to how much of its final form was his creation. According to Bunny Wailer: 'Trenchtown is a place where there is 'nough talent. People searching. Well, Slickers was like one of the groups searching. They come round and they heard this song that Trevor was singing, so they just go ahead and recorded it without him knowing. They didn't get the whole of the song, so they did the part they knew.'

According to Derrick Crooks of The Slickers, when the song hit the charts, Trevor demanded that the group buy him a pair of Clark's Booties. Niney the Observer remembers Wilson saying that 'Byron Lee them' were going to buy him an S-90 bike off his royalties.

But for all the unsophisticated transparency of the lyrics, what does it mean? It certainly is not a song of 'poor ghetto boy' self-pity. Indeed given Trevor Wilson's background, it is almost a song of self-condemnation. Over and over we hear 'you're too bad.' And eerily, he predicts his subsequent fate. Or seems to. For who or where is this voice saying come coming from. And who or what is the rock he's going to run to for rescue and which will not be there?

Only Trevor Wilson knew, and he died in 1975 – too young, and too bad. Bunny Wailer summed it all up – 'It is a serious thing, could make a movie.'

1972 / HAIL THE MAN
Ken Lazarus (Written by Ernie Smith)

Ken Lazarus

In its first ten years of independence from Britain, Jamaica experienced strong economic growth, greatly expanded its infrastructure and markedly improved social services.

Yet the people were dissatisfied. For that decade of JLP government also witnessed rising unemployment in the face of an obvious, sometimes flaunted, wealth – a wealth which never seemed to 'trickle down' to the poor as promised by the authorities.

Michael Manley, an articulate and charismatic leader and scion of Jamaica's first family of politics, was seen by many as the 'Joshua' who would lead the people into a new promised land of equality. Campaigning to the rhythms of 'Better Must Come', Manley and the PNP danced to a landslide victory in the 1972 general elections.

Jamaica was full of optimism and to many a limitless future beckoned. An idealist in the best and worse sense, Manley promised a future where no one was poor and announced grand social programmes to eliminate poverty. Free education for all was decreed, and even opposing JLP ministers joined in praising the leader's vision of universal literacy. Those who asked where the money to pay for all this was to come from were derided as neo-colonial imperialists.

Ernie Smith's 'Hail The Man' summed up the country's mood perfectly (Smith penned the song and released it on an album, though Ken Lazarus had the hit single): *What could you say / To the coming of a brand new day / When the shadows are falling away . . . / You'll say Hail The Man . . .*

At the time Smith was perhaps the most popular musician in Jamaica, especially among the bourgeoisie. He had first come to prominence in 1970 with 'Ride On Sammy' and 'One Dream'. Then he won the 1972 Tokyo Song Festival with 'Life is Just For Living', originally written as, and later turned into, a beer commercial. 'Pitta Patta' was number one for five straight weeks in 1972, and 'Duppy Gunman', maybe his best song, was on everyone's lips in 1973. In 1974, many seriously considered him the nation's most talented musician, bar none, a man on the verge of international acclaim.

The future of both Manley's Jamaica and Ernie Smith is painful to recount. The themes of

universal brotherhood were as tissue in the face of economic reality. Jamaica's productivity would have had to soar to pay for Manley's socialist* programmes, but it stagnated as the work-ethic weakened. The PNP got further and further entangled in theoretical doctrines and even flirted with mildly communist ones. Castro's Cuba became a model of inspiration.

Doctrinal fanaticism began to creep into politics of all stripes, and both the PNP and JLP armed political henchmen in ever increasing numbers. A Pandora's box had been opened and soon no one controlled these vicious gangs walking the streets with M-16s. Gun crime soared. Frightened by the growing political instability and violence, many of those able to afford it shipped away money, wife and children. When things got worse, they too left. Investment dried up and the economy faltered.

In 1979 and 1980, violence reached civil war levels and Jamaica seemed on the verge of chaos and self-destruction. But somehow the abyss was avoided and British-instilled parliamentary tradition held. Manley resisted the temptation to abrogate the constitution and called elections. The campaign was marred by unprecedented violence for which each side blamed the other. But to Manley's lasting credit, he allowed the people to speak, accepted their verdict, and graciously handed over the reins of government to Edward Seaga's JLP.

Poor Ernie Smith was one of those who had been forced to abandon his country. In the mid-seventies, concerned about what he saw in Jamaica, he released 'Jah Kingdom Go To Waste' – *While them fight for the power and the glory / Jah Kingdom go to waste.*

In the ever-increasingly irrational and overheated world of Jamaican politics at that time, this was construed

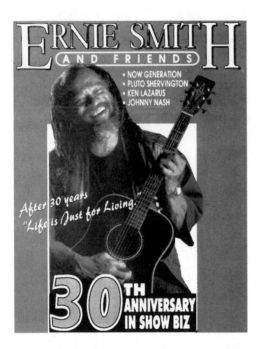

ERNIE SMITH
(AND FRIENDS)
- NOW GENERATION
- PLUTO SHERVINGTON
- KEN LAZARUS
- JOHNNY NASH

After 30 years
"Life is Just for Living."

30TH ANNIVERSARY IN SHOW BIZ

1972 / **THE HARDER THEY COME**
Jimmy Cliff

They tell me bout pie up in the sky
Waiting for me when I die
But between the day you're born and when you die
No one seems to hear even your cry
But as sure as the sun will shine
I'm gonna get my share what's mine
And then the harder they come, the harder they fall
One and all

'The Harder They Come' tells an age-old story – innocent country boy comes to the city, is embittered by perceived injustice, turns to a life of crime and, after brief notoriety, dies violently at the hands of the law. Excellently directed and acted, the film transcends its stereotypical origins for two reasons – it's set in Jamaica and revolves around music. Few films evoke the urban realities of the late 20th century so powerfully. The circumstances the film captures are as real today as they were 30 years ago, but it's the music that makes 'The Harder They Come' one of the most popular films to come out of the third world. Even without its soundtrack, it would be an important and eminently watchable social document – Toots, Jimmy Cliff and the rest make it a riveting, emotional experience.

Ivanhoe Martin, the movie's protagonist, was based on the real life Vincent 'Rhygin' Martin, a notorious criminal in the late 1940s. Myth-makers have tried to venerate him as a sort of Robin Hood, but he was just a vicious, common criminal who drove fear into the hearts of the poor. Most breathed a sigh of relief when he was cut down in a hail of police bullets. Louise Bennett's poem 'Dead Man' summed up the national reaction to his life and death:

Memba dem days wen big fraid
Hole we every weh we tun?
Ef dem hear a car back-fire
People sey a Rhygin gun!
Koo dem fus picture him pose fah,
Gun dem ready blazing lead!
Koo de las picture him pose fah
Eena dead house, lidung dead!

as an anti-government tract. Continuing threats, whether officially inspired or not, left him with no option to emigrate if he valued his life. (Pluto Shervington's case was even more ironic. He cut a number one tune called 'I Man Born Ya' in which he asserted patriotically: – *I man born ya / I naw leave ya / Go America / Go a Canada / Oh no sah / Pot a cook ya / Belly full ya / Sweet Jamaica* – it was still a big hit when he too was forced to migrate.)

Smith had begun to embrace Rastafarianism in Jamaica, and like so many of his exiled country-men, turned to it for solace and comfort. He continued to perform abroad, but his muse seemed to have vanished. When he returned to Jamaica in the late eighties, he was reduced to purveying nostalgia. Singing his lilting melodies of the past, he's a popular performer on the hotel and restaurant circuit. Still possessed of a rich, melodious baritone, and a fine guitar player, he no longer churns out tuneful and topical songs. The once smiling, effusive entertainer now seems an introverted, almost melancholy performer, as if ruing the lost dreams of those hopeful years. Those who remember the promise of long ago can only shake their heads.

A lot of the actual movie material came from Jimmy Cliff's own experiences: 'In West Kingston we had political violence and they tear gas my house all the time and tear gas Back O' Wall too . . . When they bulldozed Back O' Wall people had to move into the cemetery. Soon I got to know about ganja and other things that pass through the area. I never needed a gun because I was penetrating the music you know. But I grew up in an environment that I could have gone either way, but I chose the music.'

Music aside, the basic story is one that has repeated itself too often in Jamaica. Sandokhan (named from a European B-movie, 'Sandokhan the Magnificent') and 'Natty' Morgan, killed in the early 1980s and 1991 respectively, achieved every bit of the fame that the real and fictional Martins did.

Natty monopolised the newspaper headlines for months. He kidnapped two people who were never found again. Every shooting incident was attributed to him. Rumours that Natty was in an area – and he was everywhere at once – made residents fearful to go out at night. When he was killed after months of speculation that he had fled the island, huge crowds gathered at the morgue, unwilling to believe it was true until they had seen it with their own eyes. Even after death, Natty's funeral caused a sensation. His girlfriend put a funeral wreath in the shape of an M-16 on his casket, with 'Natty The Hero' written on it. The priest threw it out of the church.

Plus ca change, plus c'est la meme chose, (the more things change, the more they are the same).

1972 / **S-90 SKANK**
Big Youth

The greatest ever Jamaican motorcycle tribute song, S-90, after the then popular Honda S-90 bike, has very few words and in many ways is a piece of reggae scatting. Which is not surprising. Big Youth has always maintained his love for jazz and lists John Coltrane as one of his main influences: 'My first big hit was "S-90 Skank". Then there was "Screaming Target", "The Killer", "Tea For Two", "Rocking", "Cool Breeze", "Dock of The Bay", "Chi Chi Run", "Ah So We Stay", "Streets of Africa", "Joe Frazier". That time I had five in the top ten and the other two 29 and 30. I had one, two, four, five, six in the two charts.

'Through all these times I was number one man. Only Dennis Brown could stand with Big Youth. But all that fame and fancy producers didn't make me nothing. Some of this music make me famous in England even though I never been there. But I will not fight for money. These producers are not so-called thieves, they are direct thieves who rape and rob you.

'When I do a version of a song in

those days I come up with my very own lyrics, right away it's an original, creation I come in with. We have a familiar rhythm that can create a certain impact. Maybe some of the rhythms we do may be American songs somebody do over, singing about "baby love" and not really coming with a philosophy or a teaching that bring mankind together. Me only know about suffering. So when me sing its out of the depths of desolation and God really hear. You've got people out there in the world who really need inspiration. The youths today not dealing with consciousness.

'With jazz, and rhythm and blues, when you build your reggae that way, it's like you have every combination. That is how reggae heartbeat music come about. If you follow jazz and you don't have a good head, you can't take it. So we would pick from those kind of things to make great music. I don't think reggae is any different from any other music. I think it's the same as jazz, with the same feeling as jazz. Some of these lyrics related to a people and their environment, but that does not mean people living in other environments won't understand them.'

1972 / OFFICIALLY
Lloyd Parkes

Lloyd Parkes was a former backup singer with The Techniques, and 'Officially' was his only real hit as a solo singer. But he plays a more prominent role in Jamaican music today than any other singer from his era. His instrumental group Lloyd Parkes and We The People, for which he plays bass, is probably the most popular backing band in the country.

1972 / SKYLARKING
Horace Andy

Horace Andy's reedy tenor played off a churning bass line and punctuating horn line to poign-

Horace Andy

antly capture the frustrations of the unemployed young men that are an eternal feature of Kingston's streets: *Begging you a five cent sir / Begging you a ten cent sir.*

Prince Jazzbo shrewdly recognised a wicked rhythm and by adding his nonsensical exhortations and playing studio tricks with the instrumental track, versioned 'Skylarking' into the maniacal 'Crabtalking'. Released in the midst of the burgeoning deejay music phenomenon, it was almost as huge a hit as the original, and definitely more popular at dances.

1973 / SCHOOL
Prince Jazzbo

Anyone who doubts that deejay music was rap's precursor need listen no further. Jazzbo's rhyming couplets were put on record before Kool Herc, who invented rap, had even set up his sound system in New York. Not that the words are the central part of the song. It's the creative studio engineering, wicked riddim and Jazzbo's manic energy that make this one of the most exciting deejay tunes ever made.

1973 / **EVERYTHING I OWN**
Ken Boothe

'I did "Everything I Own" at the end of 73 into 74. Boy, the day the post man came to my house and I got this telegram and I see "Everything I Own" at 58 in the British chart, I start run up and down round the yard and tell everybody. Ha, ha, ha! But I can tell any artist this. When you have a song in the international charts, if you can't perform good to keep up that song, it doesn't make sense. When I went up to England, the people around me explain how the business go internationally. You have to work to keep the song in the chart.

'I did the first show in the Top of The Pops, the BBC TV programme. If you don't do the first one good, the song drop. So you can imagine I pray that when I go on stage . . . Cause I've never been in the international scene before. In the BBC you have a lot of stage in different places, and you have this big act, that big act and I'm looking at all of them everybody getting ready. Is mime you do, the record playing and you miming. So if one little mistake make, and they see is like a flaw, it can make the tune.

'When my segment come, I pray to the Lord. It came through good, man. The week after I did the show it went up in the Top 10. And I did so many Top of The Pops shows. After about 3 weeks when they counting down all the Jamaicans in England was at the radio listening to hear where 'Everything I Own' was. And when them hear it is number one, the amount of phone call I got from Jamaica, all over the world, congratulating me . . . and thanks to the people who really love that song and make it reach where it reach.

'"Everything I Own"' was number one in a lot of European countries. I don't regret much, because I'm still earning out of that song, even performing. But during that time the company got bankrupt and everything went down the drain. A lot of companies, when they get two million seller, or three million seller, they just bankrupt. But I really love the exposure I get from it.

'Financially it wasn't a help. Up till now I don't get a statement from that song from the company. I don't get the gold and the silver records I'm entitled to. And is two songs, the follow up "Crying Over You" went to number ten. All now I haven't seen anything out of these. And you know I don't feel no way over it. As long as there's God, I don't let material things bother me.'

1973 / **WESTBOUND TRAIN**
Dennis Brown

Dennis Brown is best known nowadays as the king of lover's rock. But the then 'boy wonder' is full of energy in 'Westbound Train', pushing his youthfull voice full force over Niney the Observer's raw rhythms, creating a pulsating crowd rocker.

1973 / **BOOK OF RULES**
The Heptones

'Book of Rules' is celebrated among music writers for its lyrics. According to Dave Marsh: 'The lyrics are a straight paraphrase of the Bible, the potential of human lives interpreted in a way peculiar to Jamaicans, living as they do in a trap between the squalid beauties of a preindustrial culture and the disintegrating splendors of an imperial one. In other words, it's the kind of song Bob Dylan and the self-help oriented singer-songwriters who travel in his wake would be proud (and lucky) to write or sing.' He quotes the first verse:

Isn't it strange how princesses and kings
Cut clown clad capers in sawdust rings
That's why common people like you and me
Will be builders for eternity
Each is given a bag of tools
A shapeless mass, and a book of rules

Stephen Davis writes: 'Their best song . . . captures the Heptones' lyric power, among the most complex and most direct in reggae,' and he also quotes the first verse.

How disappointing alas, to find the words come from an inspirational book whose author had probably never heard of Jamaica. As Leroy Sibbles remembers it: 'Barry wrote "Book of Rules". I arranged the song and play bass on it.

DENNIS BROWN — THE CROWN PRINCE

'My father was a dramatist. He wrote plays. I feel that is where the performing side of me comes from. I got started by accident. My brother was a comedian and was having a show one night. He invited me to come and I ended up singing with the band. While playing one night with the band, Coxsone Dodd passed through the club and heard me. That was about a year after I started. He invited me down to the studio. I was about 12 or 13. My first record was "No Man Is An Island".

'I had a lot of confidence recording for Coxsone in the early days. Mainly because I was established as a boy wonder then, and a lot of people loved to hear me sing. Not only the musicians, but other artists like Ken Boothe and Delroy Wilson and all the others, we just groove. Went right in and recorded songs and listened them. If there were any mistakes, we would correct them on one or two takes.

'I wasn't thinking of competing with any artist. I was more thinking of being among them and sharing thoughts with them; sharing views, ideas, etc. To be with them was so much . . . you find that most artists who come in the business and try to compete against other artists never last long, because they exalt themselves too much.

'Growing up in a band, I used to enjoy singing with the bands. It was like exercise for my voice, but it was bleaching doing so many gigs. I didn't get enough rest going out weekends and sometimes I not reach home till breakfast next morning. Make me pale and tired, just like bleaching your clothes. See I was still in school them. I did well at school but I don't know how, it was so rough. Like we'd have a tour round the island, every night doing a show with around a dozen acts, and I would often come in from the country and still have to go to school, wasted. So it was heavy. I don't know how I cope with all that at all. And sometimes I'd skip a whole term just keep on singing. I was 16 coming up 17 and my parents wanted me to forget this nonsense, further my education and become an accountant, a doctor, something they could look up to. But I didn't

see that road, my road was just to deal with music, strictly music.

'When I write a song I try to follow Joseph's way – deliverance through vision from all – true vibration. I want to be a shepherd in my work, teaching and learning, really singing so much. I have to get that feel that I can see something and say yes, I must write about this. But to just sit down and churn out a song, no. Confusion. Can't pick up the lyrics, like dog-ends in the street. That would be an everyday thing and you don't want such. You want something new, something the people can relate to and hopefully, profit from. I don't want to just sing it and not live it. I must live it. If I can sing songs that people can watch me living, then they can take my work.'

The words came from some book. This dread came and brought the idea to Barry – *Isn't it strange how princesses and kings / Cut clown clad capers in sawdust rings* – you know we Jamaicans don't really talk like that. Then Barry continued the idea – he added the part about the *sun will be only missing for a while* – and we helped too.'

But even if the lyrics aren't original, 'Book of Rules' is still a wonderful piece of music. And a good deal of this has to do with the singing. Randall Grass says: 'The Heptones took the smoothness of The Gaylads to new heights on both romantic material ("Pretty Looks", "Why Must I") and message songs ("Equal Rights", "Heptones Gonna Fight") penned mainly by Sibbles, but sometimes by others. Sibbles' singing had a mellow edge that contrasted sharply with many other singers of the era, thus adding another dimension to the vocal group tradition. Morgan and Llewellyn sailed above, often in falsetto harmony, as Sibbles relentlessly poured out anguish, passion or determination as the song demanded, between the punctuating response of the harmonised lines. With The Heptones, a rough call-and-response merges with a smoother romantic style. Their classic "Book of Rules" is probably the most tuneful piece of philosophy ever recorded, combining raw feelings and precise harmonies.'

Dave Marsh describes it as: ' . . . sinuous

harmonies that took language already rendered as much rhythmically as cognitively and elevated it to a form of sound poetry.'

Leroy Sibbles is superlative on bass – tying voices and backbeat into a seamless whole, punctuating each phrase with a precision which makes every word feel important, and so insinuating that it's impossible to keep still while listening to the song. As he points out in another context (although 'Book of Rules' is perhaps the consummate example of what he says):

'It's not easy to play reggae bass line and sing at the same time. Reggae bass line is different than other types of bass. It provides more rhythm than just the bottom line. It's not just holding beat. It's playing a rhythm there.'

Jamaican or not, the lyrics are still lovely. And what is for our money the most beautiful couplet in reggae, perhaps in popular music, is certainly entirely appropriate to Jamaica and its people's outlook – *Look friends, the rain that's falling from the sky / I know the sun will be only missing for a while.*

1973 / IN THE DARK
Toots and The Maytals

'In The Dark' is a superb song, with a haunting melody, an irresistible beat, and thought-provoking lyrics. The singing is exquisite. Toots' smoky tenor blends marvellously with the lightly sugared back-up harmony. Excellently produced and full of subtle nuances, 'In The Dark' is one of the finest blends of passion and craftsmanship in reggae:

> Riddle me this, riddle me this, riddle me, riddle me that
> I'll bet you don't know just where I'm at
> In the dark, you live your life
> In the dark, you want cheat and lie
> In the dark, you want to fuss and fight
> In the dark, you will get no light

According to Toots: '"In The Dark" is a natural truth, a moral cultural music. Teach people that you must reach for the truth, the light. If you stay in the dark you won't get no understanding, you will stay foolish. You must try come out of the dark and improve yourself

Why did Toots Hibbert never become a major international artist? It certainly wasn't for a lack of talent. He had as much sheer musical ability as any Jamaican artist who ever lived. In the vivid words of fellow reggae artist Leroy Sibbles: 'There's no one better than Toots – black, white, pink or blue.'

International music critics have never stopped singing his praises. In his book *The Heart of Rock and Soul*, Dave Marsh accorded him the top two reggae songs of all time and placed '54-46' in his top 100 popular songs of the rock era.

The best of Toots' work bears comparison with anyone's over the same period – 'It's You', 'Broadway Jungle', 'Never You Change', 'Pain in My Belly', 'Bam Bam', '54-46', 'Just Tell Me', 'Pressure Drop', 'Sweet and Dandy', 'Time Tough', 'In The Dark' and 'Just Like That'. Poor production may mar some of the earlier works, but they do not hide their musical quality. If these songs do not last, nothing else in Jamaican popular music will.

Toots' best songs have a rare ability to drag even indifferent listeners into the music and keep them engrossed. (Incidentally he tests whether a song is working by observing casual onlookers. If only the head is nodding, something is wrong. A good song, he says, must get the feet tapping and the body rocking.) While a master of the pointed phrase, he generally eschews ornate verbosity, and some downgrade his work because of this. But those who believe music to be a unique language of the soul which touches people on a

higher than merely verbal level find little in reggae, or popular music anywhere, to equal Toots. His songs are always masterpieces of layered rhythm, never becoming boringly metronomic, and have an unmatched textural richness. After five years of repeatedly listening to every reggae song of note (in preparing this book), it's the music of Toots Hibbert that we find ourselves returning to with the greatest anticipation.

When reggae first began gaining popularity abroad, Toots and The Maytals was the band that caught everyone's eye and ear. Legend has it that Chris Blackwell only signed The Wailers because he was unable to obtain The Maytals' signature.'

The exhilarating studio performance of 'Sweet and Dandy' in 'The Harder They Come' in 1972 whetted the world's appetite and their tours of the U.K. and the U.S. over the next few years were sell-outs. The 'Funky Kingston' album appeared on many international critics' ten best albums in 1975. Their 1976 album 'Reggae Got Soul" put them on the U.K. charts. *Rolling Stone* voted Toots and The Maytals the group to watch in 1976 in their year-end awards. They toured with the rock group The Who throughout the U.S. There seemed no reason that Toots shouldn't become a star of the magnitude of Bob Marley or even Jimmy Cliff.

But something went wrong and he seemed to hit a plateau. One problem was his refusal to go dread. The startling 'angry dreadlock' image became so imprinted abroad that foreign audiences would only accept reggae

artists who fit the role visually. But adamant that rasta was in the heart and not on the head, Toots refused to 'locks up' as a marketing tool. He remembers: 'I was doing shows abroad and thing. But then everybody started growing locks. But I myself say I never see the prophet Marcus Garvey or the emperor grow locks. So why should I have to grow locks to show I am a true rasta? And people all start to believe if you don't have locks you can't sing reggae, and if you don't have dreadlocks you can't be rasta. Nothing wrong with locks, but that don't make you a rasta.' Apart from that Toots' ever-present broad smile didn't go well with the cool, brooding anger Marley and Tosh projected so well. Toots always was and remains one of the common people, a man uncomfortable outside of his native milieu. In the end the inability or unwillingness to adopt certain mannerisms and attitudes was probably the limiting factor on his overseas success. As he says: 'I started getting discouraged with the music business. I wasn't getting any proper pay from the recording company, never got proper pay from *any* recording company. When Bob got sick and died I really was upset, because we were always close from the young days. And I wrote a song for him which they hardly play, "Tribute To Bob". It's funny you know. I wrote a "Redemption Song" and a "Get Up Stand Up" before Bob.'

The 1980 'Toots Live' album, which put him in the *Guinness Book of World Records* for fastest album to be made (it was processed, pressed and in the shops 24 hours later), brought him into prominence again. But he didn't release another album until 1992, the R&B oriented 'Toots in Memphis'. It was a decent enough effort but he was very far from his roots and it came through in the music.

Since he does only the occasional show in Jamaica and has released only the one album in 15 years, a lot of people think Toots has semi-retired from the music business. Yet the opposite is the case. Few musicians spend more time in the studio, and when he's not in the studio, he's usually on tour abroad. But somewhere along the line Toots became a musical perfectionist.

Anything deviating even slightly from his exacting standards is ruthlessly wiped off the tape. Furthermore he is a proud man, loath to simply do over his old songs, and very reluctant to do covers. As his wife once remarked to a producer pleading for Toots to an album of reggae oldies 'Frederick doesn't like to sing other people's songs, you know'. But his current works in progress show the gifts of melody and rhythm have not vanished and that there is still great music in the man. True music lovers can only hope Toots will break free of his 'art for art sake' monomania and once more begin producing with the public in mind.

Toots does not fit easily into the Jamaican 'oldies' scene, for those trapped in a rocksteady time warp find his music too unsettling for their comfortable, nostalgic sensibilities. And he is ignored by the simplistic two-chord world of dancehall which often equates 'consciousness' with incoherent, incomprehensible, mannered lyrics. But hype is hype, fads are fads, and class is class. Those who judge songs strictly on musical worth know that no other reggae artist alive has produced music of comparable quality, and realise that Toots Hibbert is a living legend.

and try to do the things that are better. People tell me say, *Yes Bwoy – Yes Nyah – Yes Bra Toots – Love you.* And when you kind to them everyday, they do bad things to you afterwards. They tell me love, what good things love can do, they tell me love endlessly up to the last moment when they turn their back: *I'm so lonely I'm so blue, I keep on loving no one but you,* that's a personal thing right there. So it's a mixture like. But "In The Dark" is one of my favourite songs.'

1974 / TIME TOUGH
Toots and The Maytals

I go to bed, but sleep won't come
I wake up in the night, and can't stand my feelings
Early in the morning, it's just the same situation
Then comes the landlord knocking on my door, knocking on my door
I've got four hundred years rent to pay, and I can't find no job

Reggae has produced a thousand 'suffarah' songs, but none more vividly expresses the stark reality of a man struggling to keep his head above water than 'Time Tough'. Its spare, direct lyrics and edgy, unsettling rhythms give a riveting 'engagee' view of what poverty really means to the common man, and even adds a touch of social commentary. As Toots says: 'Four hundred years rent to pay means you'll never stop paying rent. Four hundred years we black people are here in Jamaica, but most of us hardly own anything.'

But he doesn't wallow in melodramatic hysterics or mount any self-righteous hobby horse, and the result is a plain song of convincing honesty. Compared to the repetitive, rhetoric spouting, musically-cliched, sleep inducing bombast that so often passes for 'reality' music, 'Time Tough' is a jolting splash of cold water in the face.

1974 / **FIRE BURNING**
Bob Andy

Many feel Bob Andy was the best pure songwriter in reggae history. Certainly he wrote more hits for other people than anyone else in Jamaican music. And his knack for addressing ageless issues means his songs are continually revived. 'Fire Burning' is a prime example – *I can see the fire is burning, it's getting hotter and hot / And the haves will want to be in the shoes of the have not*s – are lyrics still potentially applicable to Jamaica's woefully imbalanced social structure.

Bob Andy with Marcia Griffiths

'Fire Burning' would later highlight another kind of injustice. When Marcia Griffiths released a version of 'Fire Burning' in 1991, not only did it prove to be one of the year's biggest selling songs, but Cutty Ranks deejay combination with Griffiths called 'Half Idiot' was also a hit. In 1995 Andy sued Donovan Germaine, Marcia Griffiths and Cutty Ranks over these versions of 'Fire Burning'. He won substantial damages.

1974 / **LOVE IS OVERDUE**
Gregory Isaacs

Loneliness is a constant thread running through Isaac's songs, and none are more evocative than 'Love Is Overdue'. In one of popular music's great verses he captures the bitter-sweet paradox of unrequited devotion: *And whose voice is gonna tell me good night / Now that you're gone out of my sight / Who's gonna tell me lies and let me think they're true / Now that your love is overdue.*

1974 / **MOVE OUT A BABYLON**
Johnny Clarke

Johnny Clarke has not released much in Jamaica recently, but is reportedly a very big star in Africa. But there was a time in the mid seventies when he rivalled Dennis Brown in popularity. His best song was this earnest, guileless tune which lyrically and musically captures the essential innocence at the heart of Rastafarianism – the belief that the pure-of-heart shall flourish, while evildoers shall suffer, in this world and the next – *Move out a babylon, Rastaman / And leave all the wicked men / Only righteous men shall prosper / In the kingdom of Jah the Almighty.*

RASTAFARIAN REBELLION

Not having lived in Jamaica for extended periods, many who write copiously about reggae consistently overestimate the importance of the Rastafarian religion in Jamaica. It's understandable, since most non-Jamaicans first became aware of reggae through the dreadlocked Bob Marley. Observers of alien cultures tend to focus on

those aspects which are most foreign from their own familiar worlds. But non-Jamaican reggae writers often give the impression that a large portion of Jamaicans are practising Rastafarians. 'Noted Rasta poet-politician Samuel Brown recently asserted that six out of every ten Jamaicans are Rastas', wrote Timothy White unquestioningly.

Yet as anyone who lives here can attest, not five in a hundred Jamaicans are 'rastas' in word or deed. Even in the movement's heyday, it's doubtful that one in ten persons were 'dreads'. The proportion of reggae musicians wearing 'locks' is much greater than in the general population. But before say 1972, nearly all reggae artists were 'baldheads.' Then Bob Marley became an international dreadlock superstar. Suddenly foreigners expected

every Jamaican musician, if not every Jamaican, to be a Rastafarian. Local musicians quickly realised that locks added to overseas appeal, and many formerly clean-cut crooners became dreads almost overnight. (And people like Toots Hibbert who refused to pretend to be something they were not, found some promoters less than willing to book them.)

To be sure most Rastafarian musicians are sincere believers. Many musicians, including Dennis Brown, Freddie McGregor and Judy Mowatt, in time joined the Twelve Tribes of Israel, a sect founded in Trenchtown in 1968 by Vernon Carrington. The Twelve Tribes had a highly organised pyramidical structure, and gained many prominent uptown and downtown adherents. Not that other Rastafarian sects were any less convinced in their beliefs.

There is no doubt that Rastafarianism has played a major role in defining Jamaica's idea of

itself. Almost everything which makes Jamaica so different from the host of sea and sun and beach islands scattered around the world can be traced back to Rastafarianism and reggae. Many tourists think Jamaica's national colours are red, green and gold (they are black, green and yellow).

Until very recently, say 1993, there was a marked dichotomy in reggae artists' appearances. Those with a primarily overseas audience still tend to be 'locksmen'. While the singers and deejays who catered to the 'massives' generally sport conventional hairstyles. There were exceptions though, like Tony Rebel, Charlie Chaplin, Cocoa Tea and Half Pint. Still, Rastas were considered old-fashioned and out of place in the dancehall, regarded by many as relics of the past, much as Americans view 1990's hippies.

But, surprisingly, in 1993 there was an upsurge of interest in Rastafarianism. Deejays like Capleton and Buju Banton began to grow locks and espouse the faith. Cultural singers like Garnett Silk and Luciano began talking of Africa as the homeland once again. Perhaps it was a reaction against the nihilism of 'gun and gal pickney talk' that lead to a search for something of spiritual depth. Not that this conversion was universal. A controversial song and dance called 'Mock The Dead' which made fun of Rastafarian's mannerisms became popular in the dance halls. Only time will tell what the future role of Rastafarianism in Jamaican music will be, but it's likely to be a perpetual and continuing influence.

One of the original tenets of Rastafarianism was the rejection of 'Babylon' – established society and all it stood for. But Marley's protest songs are now tourist resort staples. And the strongest critics of dancehall hearken back to the 'Bob and Peter' era as reggae's golden 'conscious' age condemning today's songs as 'pure slackness'. So the symbols of revolution have become icons of tradition – the rebel is turned guardian. As the American writer Will Durant put it, 'there's no humourist like history.'

1974 / **HOLD MY HAND**
Stanley and The Starlights

Even in today's hard-core dancehall Jamaica, mento influenced 'country' reggae retains a fair-sized following, especially in rural areas. Nowadays 'mento-reggae' is most commonly heard during the annual Festival Song Contest (or Popular Song Contest as bureaucrats have re-titled it). Although festival music quality has fallen dramatically from its glory days of the 1960s and early 1970s, it still garners a certain amount of support every year.

Stanley Beckford, whose back-up group is now called The Turbines, was and is the most popular of these 'mento-reggae' artists. His 'Soldering' was a massive hit in the 1970s, and he won the Festival Song Competition as recently as 1994 with 'Dem A Pollute' (although 'Chiquita' was far more popular with the populace).

'Hold My Hand', whose melody is strongly reminiscent of Gogie Grant's 1956 U.S. pop-country hit, is perhaps Stanley's best song. *When the moon is out / and stars are shining / well come on girl / let me hold your hand.* A haunting evocation of pastoral love, it transports you momentarily back to more innocent and uncomplicated times.

1975 / **NO WOMAN NO CRY**
Bob Marley

Bob Marley is best known throughout the world for the music he made while at Island Records – 'No Woman No Cry', 'Redemption Song', 'War' and so forth. But many in Jamaica feel his best work was done before he was 'discovered' by Chris Blackwell and marketed worldwide. Some maintain Marley never surpassed songs like 'Simmer Down', 'Nice Time', 'Bend Down Low', 'Duppy Conqueror', 'Trenchtown Rock' and 'Small Axe' and that his music lost something when The Wailers broke up. Even Chris Blackwell is on record as saying that Bob's best tracks are the ones that Lee Perry produced.

Quit a few famous Island songs were remakes of earlier Wailers' hits – among them 'One Love', 'Kaya', 'Lively Up Yourself', 'Stir It Up',

'Bend Down Low', 'Small Axe', and 'Put It On'. The Island works were far superior in production values, but in his efforts to appeal to foreign audiences, some argue, Marley's music lost in vitality what it undoubtedly gained in sophistication. No one knocks Bob for 'selling out', if that is what he did. When you consider the state of penury in which he and The Wailers existed before Island, versus the fame and fortune he gained in a few years, he would have been a fool to do otherwise.

But his music did change. Dub poet Linton Kwesi Johnson described 'Catch A Fire' as 'International Reggae', incorporating rock, soul, blues and funk. It had a lighter, 'toppy' mix and moved away from the bottom heavy 'drum and bass' sound. And the guitar was emphasised in a clear attempt to appeal to rock audiences.

In 1979 Dave Marsh had this to say about Bob Marley's music: 'Under his direction the group continued to make some of the most exciting music of the Seventies, climaxing with the 1976 London concert captured on "Live". But thereafter as Marley became more prominent among rock listeners, he took the band in the direction of superstar guitar ... his compositions are meandering, his lyrics exploit the usual Rastafarian political/religious imagery less effectively than they did when he was aided by Tosh and Livingston ... The group's best songs remain exciting, but the more recent work is tame in comparison to the Marley-Tosh-Livingston collaborations.'

'No Woman No Cry' is a case in point. It is a wonderful ballad but, as the guitar solo in the 'Live' version shows, not fundamentally reggae. The beat is hardly pronounced and is far from being an integral part of the song. It's undoubtedly great music – very moving and thought-provoking, with a warm, delicious melody. But it is laden with self-consciousness. Witness this conversation between Carl Gayle and Marley in 1976:

Gayle: Is your music different now from say ten years ago?
Marley: . . . The message always been the

same you know, but is a different way of putting it . . .

Gayle: But you wasn't conscious of what you were doing like now?

Marley: No. Them time dey we young man. We sixteen, seventeen. God just give we the inspiration. The difference is you understand what you a do now. Ten years ago you never really understand it.

The singer in 'No Woman No Cry' is no longer an ordinary man talking to his equals, but a philosopher-king lecturing his audience. At points the lyrics become mannered, wavering between heartfelt experience and contrived emotion. Compare the unforced vernacular Jamaican country proverbs of 'Simmer Down'

> Long time people them used to say, What sweet nanny
>   goat a go run him belly . . .
> Chicken merry, hawk de near
> And when him de near, you must beware

to the clearly pronounced, nearly formal English of 'No Woman No Cry'.

> And then Georgie would make the fire light
> And it was logwood burning through the night
> And we would cook cornmeal porridge
> Of which I'll share with you

There are two sides to every story, especially in anything concerning Jamaican music. But 'Simmer Down' shows the 'pre-Islanders' have a

'No Woman No Cry' is arguably Bob Marley's most famous record, yet the credits list V. Ford as the song's writer. Who was he? According to Marley: 'Vincent Ford is a bredda from Trenchtown. Me and him used to sing long time. Me and him used to live in the kitchen together long long time. Him good, but him sick now.'

Vincent 'Tartar' Ford, who is a paraplegic diabetic confined to a wheelchair, still hangs out sometimes at the Bob Marley Museum in Kingston. Was Ford's credit a lawyer's way of circumventing contract obligations. In discussing the album 'Rastaman Vibration', Stephen Davis says: 'Bob took credit for only three of the album's songs, the rest being divided between other Wailers and friends. While Bob probably wrote all the songs, he was still signed to Danny Sims as a songwriter and he wanted to avoid paying Cayman Music the major portion of his composer's royalty. The album's opening tracks, "Rastaman Vibration" and "Roots, Rock, Reggae" are also credited to Vincent Ford.'

One-time Marley manager Don Taylor gives presumably first-hand details: 'Bob and I decided to put some of the new songs under fictitious writers' names so as to escape Danny Sims' ownership . . . I myself placed such names as Allan Cole, Carlton Barrett, Family Man Barrett and Rita Marley on the songs we had recorded for the "Rastaman Vibration" album . . . The arrangement was further perfected by frequently putting on the album "R. Marley, writer" . . . which could be interpreted either as Robert Marley or Rita Marley.'

People forget Bob was not some 'wandering barefoot minstrel oblivious o' the world's weary cares'. He was a shrewd businessman – he could scarcely have left a multi-million dollar fortune otherwise. He might have lacked formal education but he was street-sharp and smart enough to take advice on what he didn't know. Still, none of this proves that Vincent Ford is not the real author of 'No Woman No Cry'. Many Marley fans insist that it sounds like a Bob song. And, they ask, how is it that V. Ford wrote a classic like this and yet made so few other contributions to reggae? But Ford and his son are adamant that the song is as credited – why shouldn't he have written it?

---

point. Because it has something which the Island recordings lack – not only youthful energy but spontaneous emotion. The man, or boy, truly believes what he is saying and is so much at one with his milieu that the words flow as naturally as a conversation. It may not be a profound message but it's genuine, and you don't stop to wonder if the singer really believes what he says.

1975 / **NATTY SINGS HIT SONGS**
Roman Stewart

The words need no interpretation:

I get up every day, and look into the world
I see big cars, I see pretty girls
I'd be a better man if I get money in my hand
Help me O Jah, I want to sing a hit song

I want to sing a hit song
Don't keep me down
I want to sing a hit song

Being a ghetto child it seems my life is not worth while
What's come over me, I'd love to change my style
But everything I do, old neggah fight I down
That's why I want to mash up the town

Roman Stewart's repeated pleadings have an edge of heartfelt desperation. No song ever gave more graphic expression to what music really means to an unemployed ghetto youth without any other possible means of escape.

1975 / **MARCUS GARVEY**
Burning Spear

Burning Spear began as a group in 1969 when lead singer Winston Rodney and bass singer Rupert Willington began recording as a duo for Sir Coxsone. 'I was in the hills of St Ann's and run into Bob Marley going to his farm with a donkey. I say I would like to get involved in music. Bob say to check Studio One.

'You remember Kenyatta? (Jomo Kenyatta, freedom fighter and first president of independent Kenya.) He was a burning spear and I took his name. After I find myself in the business, I realize that it was Jah's wish to have I carry the message through the music.

'People really go for the words in "Marcus Garvey". They like heroism and Garvey is one of our national heroes. He was born in St Ann's

Burning Spear

Bay. I'm from there too. As a child I used to hear big people talk of him. I read about him and they were right. Garvey said certain things would happen and right now it happen. Can't get no food to eat, can't get no money to spend, it's reality. I see myself can't get those things so I know the younger youth feel it more than me. So the song says *come little ones, come, let me do what I can for you and you alone.* Then I say – *he who knows the right and do it not shall be spanked with many strifes.* So it going to cause weeping and wailing. And I remembered a man named Bag O Wire who communicated with Marcus Garvey. He was a give away man, a betrayer – *Where is Bag O Wire . . . He's nowhere around . . . He can't be found.* Garvey had many opposers. The words are all natural words.

'I work out everything for the musicians and tell them how to play it. Me have all the vibes within myself . . . if a guy not singing message, he's not in it, for it's what people deal with. And if you go out there and talk it, it going cause trouble. But if you sing it, it can't cause no trouble . . . The people will feel the message because of the gimmick, which is the message.

'When I write, the lyrics come first, then the melody. We pick up the arrangement in the studio, at the time we're recording the album. As to location, inspiration is international. Anywhere you are, inspiration can be there. You don't have to be in Jamaica to create or have inspiration. As long as your mind and thoughts are functioning properly any kind of inspiration or vibes can come to you.'

1975 / **SOLDERING**
Stanley and The Starlights

Soldering a wha de young girl want, soldering

Styles and fashions may come and go, but in reggae certain themes are undying. Even in the midst of the African oriented, revolutionary themed roots reggae surge of the mid 1970s, this paean to young girls' favourite activity was a massive sensation. A song very much in the tradition of the mento classic 'Big Bamboo', 'Soldering' inspired a flood of copycat versions – including Welding, Watering, Hammering, Torturing, Learning, Natty Dread A Wha The Young Girl Want. The authorities did not believe that Stanley was referring to a female teenager's propensity for rewiring stereo sets, and promptly banned the song from radio play. Which, of course, made it even more popular.

In the liner notes to 'The Starlights: Soldering', Stanley related the song's inspiration: 'Well, on Wednesday evening I went out to the Browns Town Market with my grandmother. I saw a higgler who just come off a market truck, and then overheard her telling her companions,

"Me soon come . . . me a go solder." When she returned, a Rasta who was standing nearby called out to her, telling her that he had loved her since a long time ago. She blushed and told him that she had no use for him because he smoked too much weed. I turned to her and asked her if she wanted to love me since I was a young man. She told me that young fellows drank too much rum and that some of them were criminals. As far as I was concerned, she wanted loving, but she did not want it from any man at all. I remember an old calypso song and so I wrote the lyrics for "Soldering" and collaborated it with that melody and air. The song took two weeks to complete.'

1976 / STOP YOUR FUSSIN N FIGHTING
Culture

This Rastafarain vocal harmony trio led by Joe Hill tends to fall under the shadow of Burning Spear and even Black Uhuru. This is perhaps an injustice. On a song-by-song basis, their body of work – which included 'Two Sevens Clash', 'Holy Mount Zion', 'This Train', 'Behold', 'Down In Jamaica' and 'Stop Your Fussing And Fighting' – compares favourably with any from the roots period. 'Stop Your Fighting' shows Culture at their best, setting typically militant lyrics against raw roots rhythms. Burning Spear's Winston Rodney and Culture's lead singer Joe Hill were perhaps the two definitive roots singers. Yet they were wholly dissimilar on stage.

Spear had a cool, almost cerebral stance. On the other hand, the tall, lanky Joe Hill's performances were energetic, gravity-defying and nothing short of electrifying. Both men exuded raw passion. But while Spear evinced the concentrated energy of a focused laser beam, Joe Hill brought to mind a crackling cane fire.

1976 / YA HO
The Jays

'Ya Ho' was perhaps the first disco-45 hit. The lyrics are based on the famous pirate song from Treasure Island – *Sixteen men on a dead man's chest / Yo ho ho and a bottle of rum.* This roots classic is a perfect example of reggae's occasional ability to transform the banal and cliched into something quite magical.

1976 / TENEMENT YARD
Jacob Miller and Inner Circle

Jacob Miller was perhaps the greatest 'What might have been' in reggae. An exuberant, amply proportioned man, he was possessed of a fine tenor which often employed a trademark stutter. A better live performer than vinyl artist, Miller's

Tommy Cowan has done it all in reggae — sang, written, produced, promoted, emceed: 'I've been all over the world with reggae shows in one capacity or another. It's funny how the response differs even in America for instance. In the mountains of Arizona you have the Hopi Indians. The entire village comes out for the concerts. They find reggae very spiritual, especially roots reggae with a message. And there are some other Indians in Phoenix. We did a show there and when we were leaving they line up and cry.

'In places like California is like a white yuppie crowd, white middle-class. That's reggae's following in most of America. But in some areas there's a heavy black following. Like in Richmond and Norfolk Virginia, the audience is like 99 percent black. Dancehall hasn't really caught on with these crowds. They really don't understand it. The deejays are surprised sometimes at this, and more than once I've seen a deejay draw a Bob Marley tune because this is the crowd's vibes. But guys like U-Roy, Papa San and Tiger and Shinehead went over well.

In Africa now Reggae is a serious thing. In Zimbabwe, Kenya, Nigeria, Liberia. It's popular everywhere. It's enormous in Nigeria. But the reaction. Some of the people really get wild. I've seen people bang their heads against the wall till blood comes when

U-Roy come on with "Wear You To The Ball". They just get so excited, so far out of themselves. U-Roy is really a big name in Africa. Marcia Griffiths used to be big. Shabba now. Bob Marley, of course. I haven't been to Africa in a little while. I was invited there this year. It's always difficult over there. But Africa is a two fold thing. You might get a little money. But you always reserve the thought that things might not go exactly right. But if you look on it as you're making a contribution then it feels better.

In Europe now, reggae popular all over, even Greenland one time wanted a show there. In 1980 Bob Marley broke attendance records all over Europe. Sold out everywhere. In Milan Stadium there was 100,000 people. In Japan now, it's the latest and the greatest. They really love reggae there. Dancehall, everything.'

most enduring song is probably 'Tenement Yard' (produced by Tommy Cowan), a lament against poor people's lack of privacy. His biggest hits came as lead singer for Inner Circle during the second half of the 1970s, when his explosive stage act made them maybe the biggest draw in Jamaica — Inner Circle was billed above Bob Marley at the legendary Peace Concert in 1978. When Miller died in a car crash on 23 March 1980, he was only 25.

1976 / THREE LITTLE BIRDS
Bob Marley

Is 'Three Little Birds' a joyful cry of the eternally optimistic human spirit? Or is it a cloyingly sentimental and irritatingly repetitive ditty? It's a matter of taste. Some say Bob saw the three little birds picking through herb seeds on his doorstep and addressed the lyrics to then Miss World Cindy Breakespeare. According to others it's a

The I-Threes, Judy Mowatt, Rita Marley and Marcia Griffiths

tribute to the I-Threes. Marcia Griffiths remembers how they began: 'The I-Threes started when I was doing cabaret shows at House of Chen in New Kingston and I invited Rita and Judy to come and give some harmony. After my performance the audience insisted that we do something together and we did a couple of Sweet Inspiration songs and it went down so nice that ideas came to everybody and we say, "Let's form a group." Bob heard that we're working the following night and came to listen to us and was impressed. We decided seriously now that we'd really get together as a group. I suggested the name and nobody could understand. I explained, as if you say we three, it would be I three. So we decided on the name. Then Bob invited us to do "Natty Dread" and it was a hit song. And every other song that Bob asked us to do was a hit. And Bob said "I notice that everything I-Threes do with me is just a hit." So we just became like a package. Three of us became like one – mentally, spiritually, emotionally. We shared a lot of things together as sisters and we found that we "grooved" beautifully. Even in tours and recordings each of us was inspired by each other and we get ideas from each other, not to speak of Bob. Bob inspired us so much, even some things that

he would do and say, we created from that.

'Working with Bob was a beautiful experience. Words can't explain it. Bob brought out the best in you, because even though you know you're giving your best, he would never tell you that it's good. So him always keep you wondering, but he knows that you really doing good. The things that Bob would bring out of us, sometimes we just laugh, because they're so unusual . . . unique . . . different sounds and things like that. We get carried away sometimes just from the things that Bob did musically, because I've never seen another person like that. He's just different. Very, very unique. One of the reasons that I was inspired to write this song "He's a Legend" was from all the experiences I've had working with Bob over the years. It just came out of me. Bob wrote "Three Little Birds" about us you know!'

1976 / DREAMLAND
Bunny Wailer

Bunny Wailer always was overshadowed by the strong personalities of Marley and Tosh, but on his own has proven to be a great singer and composer. 'Blackheart Man' is considered one of reggae's most important albums. Though Marcia

Griffiths sang the big hit version, 'Dreamland' is Wailer's signature tune. And a great song it is. As Bunny tells it, he was always a dreamer: 'As a youth, I always asked myself "What will I really be?" There were seven brothers between parents and about nine sisters – but there was no game, no plan, for any of us. Like some child says he would like to be a doctor, but I couldn't even imagine telling myself a lie like that. As my hobby I took the rubber off some electric wire, used the fine copper wires for strings, and nail a large sardine can onto a piece of bamboo wood and make a guitar! I did this long before I imagined I would be a singer of any sort.'

1976 – NEVER YOU CHANGE
Toots and The Maytals

Keep heart, darling
Bear in mind, all the time
Love will come, stop fretting
It's very hard to find
But when you find one
That is good and kind
Never you change

People who believe love songs have to be slow, syrupy and sentimental might disagree, but 'Never You Change' is arguably the best love song Jamaica has produced. Certainly none defines more honestly what the word should mean, or what everyone hopes it will. The wonderful melody and engrossing beat make it an indisputably great song, both in the ebullient ska original and the reflective ballad-like remake on the 1976 'Reggae Got Soul' album. It is touching to note that Toots wrote both 'It's You' and 'Never You Change' for his wife Doreen when she was only 18. Toots is no saint – he is a Jamaican man after all – but over 30 years later he and 'D' are still happily married.

Toots Hibbert is not a rich man, but he is not a poor one either. And in the truly important things in life that no amount of money can buy, he is blessed, especially in his warm close knit family. Even though they are now adults, he is still the strict father to his son and daughters and the usual indulgent grandpa to his grandchildren. Hopeton, his son, is a bass player who tours often with his father and the Skool band. His daughters Melanie, Leeba and Genevieve formed a singing group called 54-46 and had a number one song in Jamaica in 1990 and a U.K. Top 40 hit. But Genevieve turned Christian and with husband Robert now has one of the island's top gospel acts. Unfortunately, in 1993 Melanie tragically died of heart failure when only 29.

Bob Marley sang – *in this great future you can't forget the past*, and Toots has certainly lived these words. (Interestingly, Toots' house has a large 'One Love' on the front, and this is its mailing address.) He's very generous to old acquaintances. Even when Raleigh Gordon, who died in December 1994, was no longer involved in the music business, he would often visit Toots to play ludo (parcheesi) and reminisce about the old days. Long after Raleigh retired and the cheques stopped coming in, Toots often helped out his old compatriot. And Toots still speaks with wistful fondness of the other Maytal, Jerry Mathias, wishing he was still around. (Jerry retired from the group and emigrated to the U.S. at the insistence of his wife, who was tired of the lack of financial reward in the music business.)

In 1991 a 'Studio One Reunion Concert' was held at the National Arena, and Toots was asked to perform. Toots never had a really big hit for Coxsone, and does not have a lot of good to say about their brief association, nor did he have much confidence in the show's organisers and their abilities and willingness to pay him. It also promised to be a somewhat melancholy affair, since many of the one-time stars had fallen on hard times. Most of those who had managed to hold on to success ignored the event. But after visiting some of the forgotten 'originators', Toots felt obliged to perform 'for old-times sake'. He got the night's biggest applause and and ended his set declaring 'Coxsone and Studio One will always be number one!' Backstage there were heartwarming renewals of the old friendships of the early days. 'Never You Change' Toots sang. And he certainly hasn't.

1976 / POLICE AND THIEVES
Junior Murvin

'Police and Thieves' was not only a massive local seller in 1976, it crossed over to the U.K. to become the anthem for the violence-troubled Notting Hill Carnival that year. The Clash later covered it on their first album. Part of the song's appeal is undoubtedly Lee Perry's imaginative production.

Junior Murvin

1976 / BALLISTIC AFFAIR
Leroy Smart
1976 / WAR INNA BABYLON
Max Romeo
1976 / RUN FOR YOUR LIFE
Jackie Parris

In the late 1970s violence in Jamaica threatened to tear apart the very fabric of society. A lot of it was political and at times there seemed to be an almost undeclared civil war between supporters of the two parties. The level of 'common' criminal violence also soared to unprecedented levels. In time the two became inextricably entangled.

These three songs give differing perspectives on the matter. 'War Inna Babylon' shows the Rastafarian viewpoint – Babylon is self-destructing, and that may be no bad thing:

> Marcus Garvey prophecy say
> In these times one must live ten miles away
> I man satta pon the mountain top
> Watching babylon burning red hot
> War inna babylon, Tribal war inna babylon

Lee Perry's rhythms are slow, complicated and

THE UPSETTER

Apart from having been a major influence on Bob Marley, Lee Perry is one of reggae's most important producers and a significant artist in his own right. Junior Byles 'Curly Locks', Max Romeo's 'War Inna Babylon' and 'Police and Thieves' are only a few of the great reggae songs he helped create. He has released a huge number of dub albums and is probably second in importance in this field only to dub's inventor, King Tubby.

In recent years 'Scratch' has become very erratic and unpredictable. But Carl Gayle's interview with him in 1975 gave some good insights into his creative process: 'At first I was a follower of Sir Coxsone Downbeat sound system. They called me "Little". There was a dance called "Chicken Scratch" and I cut a tune for it and they started calling me Scratch. Then I was audition manager for Coxsone. I would hold auditions and I select the ones that I feel are good enough. He says fine. We call a rehearsal and cut the tune. Coxsone used the sound system to promote his records. I never operated it. I went round and dealt with the pressings and distribution, the shops.

'I split with Coxsone in 1968. "The Upsetter", that tune has a meaning – *You'll never get away from me / I am the upsetter / Suffer you bound to suffer. You take people for fool yeah / Then use them as a tool yeah / But I am the avenger.* After spending that time with Coxsone and the amount of work that I did and the pay that I got . . . I was hurt about the whole deal. After that I worked for West Indies Studios and Joe Gibbs. I who really taught Clancy Eccles recording. We had a good thing going there, then he started his own thing.

'I prefer instrumental tunes. There are only a few singers that could really sing the type of tunes that I really appreciate. Guys like Bob Marley could sing what I want. But most artists in Jamaica don't sing as a feeling, they sing for money. When I arrange something the instrumental has got to be there because I won't stop until I get it.'

'Producing is not a thing you learn, it's born in you. You have a feeling toward the music. Once you know the artist has a good melody line and the voice is good, you can think of the type of rhythm to fit that melody. It's a thing you have to feel.'

On his work with the original Wailers: 'Bob and me used to know each other from Coxsone days, but the first thing we ever did together was "Try Me" in 1969. Bob was absent from the recording scene for a long time between 1968 and 1969. He had some bad management and things like that so he got fed up and

kind of cooled off for a while. Or what he wanted to portray, he couldn't find the right sort of people to work with.

'Bob mentioned that he wanted me and him to work together and I said fine. One Saturday I was doing some recording at a little shop in Orange Street. I said to him, "look Bob I want to write a tune with 'yes me friend, we on the street again' in it." He gave me the third line, I gave him the fourth line and so on. We started to work together and the ideas started to flow 'till we made the tune "Duppy Conqueror". Then he came up with the idea "I'm a rebel, soul rebel" and I arranged the music for that song "Soul Rebel". He wrote the lyrics.

'"Trench Town Rock" I had nothing to do with. When me and Bob split, he did that for himself. As far as I'm concerned, every song that Bob Marley sing is good. That is the only artist in Jamaica that I really admire and nothing Bob can do can be wrong as far as I'm concerned. I just like the way he's professional. I think he's the best. I and him even quarrel 'cause there are certain things between me and Bob that no one can understand. We work together, we have ideas and in Jamaica, professionally and musically we are blood brothers man so there's nothing he can do wrong for me. You see I believe in originality and Bob is an original.

He don't muck about, honestly. If you say "Bob, I want us to sit down and write a tune about this bamboo cup", he will just take up the guitar until he finds a melody. Most of the time I have a pen writing and he's singing. I write and he sings it. I don't tell no lie, Bob Marley was a great man!

'Peter Tosh is another good writer. He writes how he feels. Any time Peter writes a tune, he writes it for a reason. He doesn't do it because he wants to sing a song. He does it because it means something to him or he's saying something about somebody or something. He doesn't do things for a quick price. He does it because he wants to send a message.

'I like Bunny's voice very much. The message that Bunny writes is not so easy to understand like Bob and Peter. Bunny is a man who believes in Rastafari so much he gives himself less time to think. He would do great if he gave himself more time to think. He did a song for me called "Dreamland" which can't get stale. It's a beauty. He's a guy that don't like you to rough him. If you cool with Bunny you can get anything out of Bunny. They all play a great part in the Wailers. There's no harmony section in Jamaica can sound as good as Wailers' harmony.'

Max Romeo, left, and Leroy Smart

detached while Max Romeo's singing is observational, uninvolved and almost derisive. It's almost as it's happening somewhere other than where he lives.

'Ballistic Affair' is a heartfelt plea for the violence to stop.

> We used to lick chalice and cook ital stew together
> We used to play football and cricket as one brother
> Not through you rest a Jungle
> Or you a block a Rema
> You a go fight gainst you brother
> That no right me sister
>
> Let us all live as one
> Throw way you gun
> Throw way you knife
> Let us all unite
> Everyone is living in fear
> Just through this ballistic affair

(Jungle, in Arnett Gardens, and Rema, in Wilton Gardens, are two politically-tribalised Kingston housing projects referred to in Jamaican parlance as 'garrison communities'.)

Who could disagree with Leroy Smart's clear-headed assessment and sensible solution? And the straightforward, measured beat adds to his uncomplicated logic. It is insanity for former close friends and brothers to kill each other over a few words or dollars. Yet we know his preaching will be in vain. For human reason is a feeble irrelevance when the dogs of war are let loose. 'Run For Your Life' shows the common man outlook on all of this:

> Run for your life he's behind you with a knife
> Run, run, run
> Don't try to stop or he might take your life
> Run, run, run
> If you should stop he will stab you in your back
> Keep on running
> Don't look behind
> Find somewhere to hide
> Run for your life he's behind you with a gun
> Run, run, run'

The insistent, unselfconscious vocals and driving rhythm – punctuated by drum bursts which sound like bullet shots – give a vivid representation of a frantic and frightened society. What concerns is not so much the origins of the violence, but the sheer terror of daily existence. Who is right or wrong matters very little when life has become nasty, brutish and short.

1976 / **WAR**
Bob Marley

'War', a speech by Haile Selassie calling for racial harmony set to music, became a rallying cry for Zimbabwean Freedom Fighters in the Rhodesian civil war. Tommy Cowan relates this story: 'I was

SALISBURY CELEBRATES INDEPENDENT ZIMBABWE 18th APRIL, 1980

BOB MARLEY AND THE WAILERS RUFARO STADIUM SALISBURY 18TH/19TH APRIL 1980

stage manager with Bob Marley when he played the Zimbabwe independence celebration in 1980. Bob Marley is very highly regarded there. When we went there we learnt from people that in Rhodesia you could have gotten two years in jail for having a copy of "Kaya" because it had a spliff on the cover. And they told us you could have gotten one year for having any other Bob Marley album. People told us they had to hide and buy it. So it became a very expensive commodity. You had to buy bootleg from England so it cost like 25 pounds. And families would go hungry for a week to buy a Bob Marley album.

'In Zimbabwe the power of Bob Marley was so great, that when he was performing at that independence ceremony, when he was on stage playing, the prisoners broke jail in hundreds and tear down the fences of the stadium and come in. The concert had to be stopped, there was tear gas everywhere in front of Prince Charles and everything. And these prisoners walk through the tear gas to see Bob Marley. Heavy thing. And afterwards they went back to jail peacefully. They broke out just to see Bob Marley.'

1976 / ONE LOVE
Bob Marley and The Wailers

In one sense Jamaica is a lucky country. The last war here (excluding the maroons) was fought between the Spanish and British over 300 years ago, and the biggest battle in the island's history, The Battle of the Rio Nuevo, saw about 300 casualties. One only has to go 90 miles in either direction to Haiti, Cuba or the Dominican Republic, where tens of thousands have died in wars, massacres and revolutions in this century alone, to realise the island's good fortune.

Yet Jamaica has one of the world's highest murder rates. Excitable, volatile and ultra aggressive in defending whatever they view as their rights, Jamaicans have a reputation for belligerence even among their cousins in Guyana, Trinidad and Barbados. This innate aggression coupled with a general physical fearlessness, make Jamaican criminals some of the most violent and ruthless in the world, not only at home but abroad. Jamaican posses are among the most feared criminal gangs in both the U.S. and in the U.K.

For all its pleas for peace and love, reggae's history is the bloodiest of any music, except maybe for the blues. The list of prominent artists who have died violently is appallingly long including stars like Peter Tosh, Carlton Barrett, Tenor Saw and Garnett Silk. Bob Marley himself barely survived an assassination attempt in 1976. Nor were he and his entourage always on the receiving end. His best friend, Alan 'Skill' Cole, admits to using naked force to get Bob's music on radio in the hard days before Marley became a superstar. Listen to Cole's testimony in court: 'It was a difficult time. We had to put out lot of strength, what you call muscle, to get played by the various disc jockeys. So it was my duty to see that these things happened . . . sometimes we had to go there and beat disc jockeys and deal with programme directors . . . We had to send guys to smash their cars or things like that. Threaten them . . . if you don't play the records you better leave the station . . . quite a few people left the station during that year. Disc jockeys, programme directors . . . Some went out to leave the country . . . Well, that was the period he got most of his number one songs in Jamaica.'

In the same trial Marley's former manager, Don Taylor, testified that Marley twice beat him up in Africa: 'He (Marley) beat me up. Every time he hit me, Alan had that submachine gun. I couldn't believe Alan holding the gun at me. We were supposed to be alright. Finally, Bob's kids, Ziggy and all of them, come through the door, and that's how it stopped. Ziggy said: "Don is so good to you. He take six gun shots for you just a year ago (during the assassination attempt) . . . I got real mad. I went to the police, bought a gun and decided I was going to kill somebody. I couldn't believe he did that to me. That's the second time. All this time, in the next breath, "Don, you are a good man. I still want you to manage me." I said, "What's up with this man?"'

In early 1994 Taylor wrote a book purportedly telling the true story of his relationship with Marley. Before publication he received a letter from an attorney-at-law which included the following: 'We act for Mrs Rita Marley, Mr Chris Blackwell, Mr Neville Garrick and other members of the Marley family . . . We wish to warn you that if . . . the book does libel any of our clients, our instructions are to file an action you without further notice seeking both damages and injunctive relief.'

The excerpt was printed on the back cover of the book. None of the persons named come off too well in the book, but nobody sued. (When Roger Steffens asked Bunny Wailer about Taylor's book, Bunny laconically replied, 'Well, it's probably mostly true.')

On the other hand, it's alleged that Taylor ripped off Marley for years. Marley supposedly beat him up on discovering this and subsequently fired him.

How ironic then that 'One Love' has become the Jamaica Tourist Board's unofficial anthem. One of the sweetest melodies Bob ever wrote, it has the timeless feel of a folk song and will probably enter the pantheon of tunes, like 'Linstead Market' or 'Evening Time', which are simply accepted as part of the nation's indigenous culture. Certainly it's a song Jamaicans, and the whole world, should take to heart:

> Let's get together and feel alright
> Hear the children crying, (One love)
> Hear the children crying, (One heart)
> Saying give thanks and praise to the Lord
> And I will feel alright
> Saying let's get together and feel alright . . .
>
> Let's get together to fight this holy Armagedeon
>   (One Love)
> So when the man come there will be no due (One song)
> Have pity on those who transgress, gross sinners
> There ain't no hiding place, from the father of creation

It's also one of those rare songs which an artist improves on the second go. The Wailers' first cut of 'One Love' as a ska tune back in 1966, without the interpolated Curtis Mayfield lyrics, where they sung 'holy war' instead of 'holy Armagedeon'. The new version is slower and more drawn out, has a much greater feeling of depth, and there's that delicious 'tinkling' hook. Even Wailers' fans admit that the soft boices of the I-Threes fit the song's theme and melody beautifully.

'One Love' is perhaps the most universally popular of all Marley tunes. There are still a sizable number of Christian fundamentalists in Jamaica who view Bob Marley as just another blasphemous Rastaman. But even they sing along when 'One Love' is played. And every time another senseless 'tribal war' breaks out in the ghettos of West Kingston, you can almost hear Bob Marley's voice – 'Hear the children crying!'

1977 / **THREE PIECE SUIT**
Trinity
1977 / **UPTOWN TOP RANKING**
Althea and Donna

Both these big hits were cut on the same 'Just Another Girl' riddim. Trinity was one of the biggest stars of the second wave of deejays ushered in by Big Youth who in their day dominated stage shows and charts. Yet 'Three Piece Suit' is one of the very few deejay hits of the era which still bears listening.

Althea and Donna were mere schoolgirls when they cut 'Uptown Top Ranking'. But they managed to capture a certain vibe which not only took it to the top of the local charts, but made it a number one song in the U.K. Althea is still singing, and in 1994 had a local hit in combination with deejay Papa San on a cover of The Wailers' 'Simmer Down'.

Althea and Donna

1977 / **FADE AWAY**
Junior Byles

Jo Jo Hookim tells the story of 'Fade Away's creation: 'It was really Chinna Smith who produce "Fade Away". We were there on a Sunday, and this fellow Snapping (Theophilus Beckford), for some reason he usually come there on a Sunday and row that we must use him. So Chinna decide to use him and make that song. It's just Chinna, Sly, and him make that song. Nobody else. It is the only song Snapping has

ever played for us. Junior Byles was okay. I was a little bit scared when he would come for royalties because he was always staring up at the sky and what not. Yes, because sometimes when he would come is just pure bones he would throw down in front of you. Where he get them from, Heaven knows.'

Junior Byles created other reggae classics like 'Beat Down Babylon' and 'Curly Locks'. But he was genuinely mentally unstable. For a period he was actually living on the streets eating from garbage cans. There are rumours that he is now in a mental institution.

1977 / **96 DEGREES IN THE SHADE**
Third World

An eclectic, self-contained musical aggregation, Third World has always combined a middle-class rock and R&B sensibility with a love for roots reggae and African music. Some see them as a sort of Jamaican version of Earth, Wind and Fire.

Despite their prolific output, more than fourteen albums to date, Third World's forte is powerful live performances. A band always unafraid to experiment, their 'Explanations', a thematically linked show comprising songs from their first two albums, was perhaps the most ambitious musical concept ever staged in Jamaica. A sort of reggae opera, it was as close as Jamaican popular music ever came to creating a 'Tommy' (*a la* The Who). Songs became long instrumental jams

featuring Santana-style guitar licks, African drumming, long solos and even on occasion, Cat Coore playing the cello. Debuting in 1977, the show ran for weeks to sold out houses.

Their canon would come to include everything from the roots reggae of The Abyssinians' 'Satta Massaganna' and Burning Spear's 'Slavery Days' to a disco version of The O'Jays' 'Now That We've Found Love' and a Stevie Wonder collaboration, 'Try Jah Love'. '96 Degrees In The Shade', from their eponymous 1977 second album, represents perhaps their finest artistic moment.

Based on the bloody 1865 Morant Bay Uprising, which was brutally suppressed by the colonial authorities, this song captured all of the band's strengths and avoided most of their weaknesses. Playing well within their considerable musical talents and eschewing the instrumental excesses which worked so well in live shows, Third World created their masterpiece – a simple, unembellished protest against injustice.

1977 / **HAVE MERCY**
Mighty Diamonds

Often reflecting the revolutionary ethos of the era by dressing in green army uniforms for their rousing live performances, The Diamonds' sweet, soulful singing combined military lyrics and evocative harmonies. One of the biggest acts of roots reggae's heyday in the late 1970s, they

had a string of hits like 'Right Time', 'Bodyguard', 'I Neeed A Roof', 'Pass The Kutchie' and perhaps their best song, 'Have Mercy'.

So-called 'conscious' reggae often seems to consist of little but repetitive, self-righteous, 'Rasta better than Babylon' cliches. But devoid of attitudinal posing, the open vulnerability of this song's biblical inspired lyrics is a heartfelt plea on behalf of all mankind.

Have mercy on a good man, and help him, we pray Jah man
Have mercy on a good girl, and help her, we pray Jah man
Man was made to suffer, and women made to feel the pain
Stay by our side, and guide us, we pray Jah man
Give us all your blessings, and help us, we pray Jah man

Soaring above the swirling back beat, The Mighty Diamonds' plaintive harmonies attain an almost ethereal quality and reveal the genuinely spiritual dimension of roots reggae at its best.

1977 / **NATTY REBEL**
U-Roy and Bob Marley

'Natty Rebel' is an excellent example of how a good deejay can make a good song even better. 'Soul Rebel' by itself is a nice, catchy tune, but U-Roy's perfectly timed commentaries transform it into a punctuating statement of defiance.

1977 / **FORTY LEG DREAD**
Prince Mohammed

1978 / **TRIBAL WAR**
George Nooks

George Nooks, aka Prince Mohammed, was one of the few artists in Jamaican history ever to have hits both as a deejay and singer. His 'Tribal War' is a roots classic and 'Forty Leg Dread', based on a newspaper story about caterpillars infesting uncombed dreadlocks, was a massive hit. Nooks also pulled off one of the great comebacks in reggae history, where successful returns to the limelight are as rare as in boxing: nearly 20 years after his last hit, he hit the top ten in 1996 with a cover of 'Homely Girl'.

1978 / **NUMBER ONE**
Gregory Isaacs

In both his songs and personal life, Gregory Isaacs often seems to wear his heart on his sleeve. In the tenderly caressed verses of 'Number One' his vulnerability is almost completely laid bare, ending with the nearly whispered plea of a man who has obviously known many travails of the heart – *If you want to be my number one / Please don't ever hurt this man.*

THE COOL RULER

The 'cool ruler' emerged in the mid-1970s and developed a unique style – cool, almost detached, hypnotic and seldom boring. He has been called the 'Marvin Gaye of Reggae'. Although no-one else sounds quite like him, there is a vague similarity to Burning Spear. He is to lover's rock what Burning Spear is to roots reggae. His singing is a combination of fire and ice. There is measured passion, an urgent longing tempered with cool control. He is a classicist

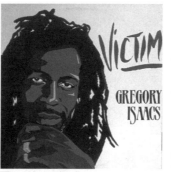

hearkening back to the days of Frank Sinatra. Every word is clear and he is a master of phrasing, caressing every note. Gregory is a skilled songwriter with excellent word play.

He has an uncanny feel for a crowd, switching songs and mood. He is one of the small band of singers who can hold their own in the dancehall even in the age of deejays. His popularity remains unflagged and only Dennis Brown can compare for constant durability. In the movie 'Rockers' he virtually steals the show by being himself, despite a stellar musical caste.

Most dancehall singers work in combination and do short sets. Gregory can do a long show and hold the audience drawing on his vast range of hits like 'My Number One', 'Top Ten', 'Night Nurse', 'Rumours', 'No Speech No Language', and 'Border'. He works a crowd uncannily, building up a climax and shifting into another song before they orgasm, in the manner of a skilled seducer. His charms travel well and he is a massive star in Africa.

He shares some of his thoughts: 'I represent John Public. Making the people happy is what make me happy. But people assume more time I'm not happy, through most time I keep to myself and concentrate a lot, read a lot, meditate. Read up my Bible. All kind of

books, fact and fiction, history. But I was self-taught. I read a lot to uplift my mind. I love reasoning with people, too. One word a man can tell from him mouth and that give me inspiration. What keeps me going? Religion, food, willpower. God keep me alive and I take the best care of myself. Food. My lifestyle too, and my levity amongst people, cause I live good amongst people, cause I assist people who God can't assist.

'My biggest regret in life is when I start deal with drugs. Four times I go to prison as a tenant, but low sentence. One time I was sentenced to three years, for guns but I didn't do the sentence because there was a fine instead. A man give me them to keep. One of the guns was my own and I plead guilty because, as you have seen on the records, I'm no snake in the grass nor no hypocrite. Anything I do, I'm big enough to own up to it, cause it can be hurtful too.

'Prison is like a college, actually. You learn how to live with all different nations – convicts. Because there's all different kind of people in prison . . . You know a lot about astrology, studying enough mankind, cause I learn a lot. Because at the time I'm in isolation, time to look into my life, and you can just study, and you have to know how to survive to live. I wrote songs like "Days of Penitentiary", "Out Deh" and "Condemned" in jail.

'Loneliness is when you're alone and you don't want to be alone. You need somebody in your life and you don't have somebody. Nuff of my time I lived in loneliness. Lonely yet so happy, because is only an individual can make themself happy. If you're lonely, is only you can make yourself happy, right? Because you can be around people and still don't be happy. You have to make yourself happy, condition the mind.'

1978 / **THIS TRAIN**
Culture

The strong millenarian bent which has always been present in the Jamaican religious outlook was even more pronounced in the beliefs of Rastafarians. 'This Train' is a traditional spiritual of probable American origin, gives a vivid expression to this perspective on life. Culture's version of the song was a massive hit in 1978. But way back in 1966 Peter Tosh and Bunny Wailer had cut a version for Coxsone Dodd. And Bunny Wailer used the song to close his seminal 'Blackheart Man' album.

1978 / **THE SAME SONG**
Israel Vibration

The story of Israel Vibration is one of the most heart-warming in Jamaican music. For surely no reggae singer ever dreamed harder than Apple Craig, Skelly Spence and Wiss Bulgin, three physically disabled men who began singing together while living at the Mona Polio Rehabilitation Centre. Even though they sometimes need their crutches for support when performing, their music is all anyone notices when they sing on stage. If reggae is a triumph of the human spirit, this is undoubtedly its greatest victory.

Israel Vibration

1978 / **RUB A DUB STYLE**
Michigan and Smiley (produced by Coxsone Dodd)

Coxsone had perhaps the finest ear in reggae history. He kept producing classics well into the dancehall era: 'The original track for "Rub-A-

Dub Style" was Alton Ellis' "Just A Guy". This track was so popular. Only the mix is different . . . in and out music . . . the echo and so forth was different.' With a fresh-on–the–scene Michigan and Smiley just tearing the riddim apart with their staccato back-and-forth wordplay, 'Rub A Dub Style' is one of the few deejay tunes that never seems to grow old.

1979 / **NICE UP THE DANCE**
Michigan and Smiley

No one ever gave a better description of the sound-system atmosphere than Michigan and Smiley.

> Say long time I no deejay inna dance
> Long time I no chant inna dance
> Me come to nice up the area
> Me come to nice up Jamaica . . .
> Started to talk and the dance really cork
> Gate man a laugh and the cashier a laugh
> Can't find a bottle with a cork
> Me say me can't get no place to walk
> I want a food before the food done sell off
> The cane man an him idren a laugh
> Promoter and his idren have to laugh
> How them laugh

Chanted over the quintessential 'Real Rock' riddim, the duo's unaffected call and response style captures the good-natured spirit of a street dance. 'Nice Up The Dance' is not only a riveting piece of music, it's urban folk poetry.

SOUND-SYSTEM CULTURE

It's hard to conceive of a country where music plays a larger role in people's lives than Jamaica. 'Music drenched' one might call it, because it's almost impossible to escape. Radios blare everywhere during the day. And at night, the tropical, open windowed style of life means almost every breeze carries the distant strains of some sound system through your house, no matter where you live.

Jamaica is a small ex-colonial country and there is nothing here that has not been copied from Africa, Europe, America or Asia. Yet something in the Jamaican psyche manages to change everything it adopts into something which, in the end, bears little resemblance to the original. Reggae music is the prime example.

Reggae not only sounds different from music anywhere else, it's largely listened to in a different way. Sound systems, an almost unique Jamaican phenomenon, are still the primary mode of musical dissemination. At the beginning they were essentially large, mobile record players which enabled the large segment of the population who could not afford their own players to hear the latest music.

But instead of vanishing as the populace became wealthier and able to afford individual equipment, the sound systems took on new life. The intermix of large crowds and music apparently created an atmosphere which made listening at home pale in comparison. More money meant bigger and better sound systems. And far from disappearing, they multiplied rapidly. Today even the smallest hamlet will boast at least two 'champion sounds'. (Never one of course – what's the use of having a 'set' if you can't have a clash?)

Sound systems are the number one form of away from home entertainment in Jamaica. With the coming of dancehall, their role in the music industry has only grown stronger. Because any worthwhile 'clash' must have popular deejays and singers around to hot up the scene. There are periodical outcries against the 'noise pollution' sound systems create. No doubt complaints often are justified, as anyone who has tried to sleep while thunderous bass shakes the roof rafters can testify. Noise pollution laws are sometimes enforced by police. But these attempts at reducing the volumes are sporadic. Almost as if the government recognises that sound systems are the poor's one guaranteed form of entertainment – the musical opium of the masses, so to speak which keeps an unruly segment of the populace fairly manageable. As one dancehall song proclaimed – *If you no want shot fe bust, make the sound turn up!* Bob Marley himself sang in 'Bad Card' – *Turn the speakers up, I want to disturb my neighbour.*

In 1997 legislation was passed in parliament stating that between the period from 2am to 6am music must be played below a certain volume. The law appeared to have teeth. But the big question, as with so many other laws in Jamaica, was whether it would be rigorously and consistently enforced. If it is, it will mark the beginning of a social revolution in Jamaica.

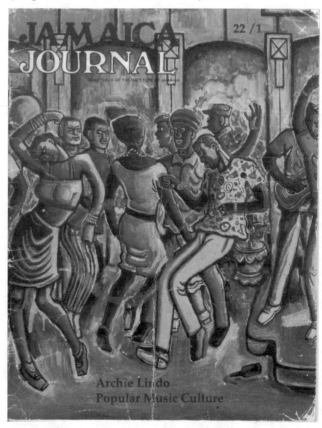

Archie Lindo
Popular Music Culture

1979 / **STEPPING OUT OF BABYLON**
Marcia Griffiths

Marcia Griffiths recalls a friend having given her the master rhythm of 'Stepping Out Of Babylon' to her. They molded it a bit, then she took it home on a cassette to muse over melody and words. Finally, thinking the rhythm 'too political, too militant' for a woman's delivery, she took it to another songwriter – Bob Marley: 'Well he liked the rhythm, and he danced to it . . . but, maybe the time was too short for him to come up with lyrics. But in the end, I felt that it was purposely left up to me. The melody and lyrics came almost all of a piece one day after I had been reasoning with a sister, telling her about many of the problems I had been through and was still having. It was she who suggested that I had expressed these things so well, that I should put them on paper and to music.

'I was saying that even though I've suffered so many injustices, it really doesn't bother me because I know there is another world for me. The chorus, "steppin' out of Babylon", is not necessarily a movement in the physical sense. It means rather that you are moving out of corruption and into a state of greater purity than what you might be experiencing in daily life. Babylon can be either a situation or a system, but it is hell to anyone who knows of love, and light and warmth. So we want to step from a lower life into a higher one, and it's not just a physical step, but an inner evolution.'

1979 / **OH MR D.C.**
Sugar Minott

Ganja is usually associated in the popular mind with rhetoric spouting, dreadlocked Rastas and tough talking, flashy drug dealers. But in this touching tale, whose rhythm and melody are based on the rocksteady classic 'Pressure And Slide', Sugar Minott shows another reality. (D.C. stands for district constable. Ishen and collie are terms for ganja.) The lyrics speak for themselves:

Time so rough and time so tough
Coming from the country / With my bag of collie
I buck up on a D.C. / Him want to come hold me
Don't you run now youthman / You won't get away
If you slip you will die / And if you run you can't hide
Cause I've got my dick / Stuck right in my hip

Oh oh D.C., don't you take my ishen
Oh oh D.C., don't you touch my collie

The children dying for hunger / And I man a suffer
So you've got to see / It's this collie that feeds me
Fifty cents a stick / And a dollar a quarter
That's what keeps me alive / Me and two kids and wife
So give me a chance sir / And let me go little faster
Just let me pass through / And Jah will bless you

The Sounds of the Eighties

1980 / **ONE LOVE JAM DOWN**
Michigan and Smiley

1980 was perhaps the most important year for the Jamaican nation since gaining independence in 1962, not so much for what happened as for what did not. Politics had so degenerated that a civil war in all but name was being fought in the streets. The island's homicide rate that year was estimated to be the highest in the world for countries not at war, and worse than many places like Ireland, where so-called 'active guerrilla wars' were being fought. The prospect might seem far-fetched now, but it seemed a real possibility then that in this heated atmosphere both parties might head for the hills with their guns and plunge the country into chaos. One need only look at countries like Liberia and Sierra Leone to see the fate Jamaica possibly escaped.

In the midst of the tribal war, Michigan and Smiley's 'One Love Jamdown' was a clarion call for unity.

> No more uptown, downtown
> We all rock together on one ground
> Whether you black, white, yellow or brown
> We all rock together in reggae Jamdown
> Whether you roots branch leaf or stem
> We all rock together as Jah Jah children

So popular was the song that the follow-up, 'We Need A One Love', recorded live at Reggae Sunsplash, also became a hit.

It's hard to say how much of a role this song and others like it played in cooling antagonisms enough to allow elections to be held and their results respected. But even today, Michigan and Smiley's hypnotic, call and answer chanting, set against the heavy, repetitive, punctuating bass line, elicits an impulsive feeling of brotherly love.

Incidentally, to anyone who has seen both groups, Michigan and Smiley's vocal style, stage manner and physical appearance undoubtedly prefigured that of Run DMC – the first 'superstar' rappers and seminal contributors to hip-hop music. 'One Love Jamdown' is one of the clearest examples of reggae deejay music's direct influence on rap.

1980 / **REDEMPTION SONG**
Bob Marley

Many think 'Redemption Song' is the master's greatest moment. It is achingly beautiful, and its introspective, acoustic simplicity almost seems to prophesy Bob's premature death. It has become something of a 'standard' all over the world, sung by everyone from schoolchildren to anti-nuclear protesters.

1981 / **ONE DRAW**
Rita Marley

Bob Marley attracted musical talent like no artist in reggae. One thing that made The Wailers special from the very beginning was that Marley, Peter Tosh and Bunny Wailer were each talented artists in their own right. None of the backup singers with other great reggae groups went on to have significant careers of their own – Toots and The Maytals, John Holt and The Paragons, Leroy Sibbles and The Heptones, Desmond Dekker and The Aces, even Burning Spear.

Rita Marley too is unique. No other reggae performer's wife ever came close to having the kind of musical success that she did. 'One Draw' is her best known song, and deservedly so. It's one of the best message and party song combinations in reggae and Rita sings it with a wonderful ebullience that extracts every ounce of excitement from the bouncy tune.

After The Wailers broke up, Bob Marley continued to be surrounded by musical excellence. For the I-Threes' Marcia Griffiths, Rita Marley, and Judy Mowatt are arguably the three best female singers in reggae history. And Judy Mowatt's 1980 'Black Woman' album is generally acclaimed the best reggae album ever made by a woman.

It continued even after Bob's death. Ziggy Marley is certainly the most talented offspring any reggae singer ever produced, although some feel his brother Stephen is just as good. Even Bob's baby-mother, Cindy Breakespeare, and her son Damien, have started to carve out musical careers of their own.

Whichever way you look at it – genes, osmosis or merely coincidence – the magical Marley musical touch is certainly a remarkable phenomenon.

1981 / **OLD BROOM**
Wailing Souls

One of roots reggae's finest groups, The Wailing Souls may not be heard much in Jamaica anymore, but many of their songs like 'Old Broom' still remain popular. Indeed Tony Rebel used its catchy hook in his big 1992 hit 'Sweet Jamdown'.

The early Wailing Souls foursome have become a twosome but they are still going strong, but mainly abroad from Jamdown

1981 / **NEVER GET WEARY**
Toots and The Maytals

To those who see reggae as protest music, Peter Tosh and Bob Marley's 'Get Up, Stand Up' is perhaps the most famous of all Jamaican songs. Indeed, the 1994 version of the *Concise Oxford Dictionary of Quotations* quotes the lines: *Get up, Stand Up / Stand Up For your Rights / Get Up, Stand Up / Don't give up the fight.* (The book's cover includes a picture of Bob Marley, who incidentally is the only non-Caucasian and non-Western figure shown – two tokens with one stone, so to speak. The other deathless Marley quote is – *I shot the sheriff / but I swear it was in self defence / I shot the sheriff / And they say it is a capital offence.*)

But truth to tell, 'Get Up, Stand Up' apart from its big, bandwagon chorus, is a rather ordinary song showing little thematic development or imagination. It might be a great crowd singalong for one verse, but it makes for tediously repetitive listening at home. (The Bob Marley 'Live' version is somewhat redeemed by the album's overall excitement, but is nowhere close to being the best song on the LP.) Furthermore the verses:

Most people think great God will come from the sky
Take away everything and make everybody feel high
But if you know what life is worth
You will look to yours on earth . . .

We sick and tired of the ism schism
Say we die and go to heaven in Jesus name
We know what we understand
Almighty God is a living man'

are almost a direct contradiction of each other. In one breath, Marley and Tosh seem to be espousing militant atheistic materialism, yet in the next they say, 'No it's only Christianity that's rubbish. What we believe in, Rastafarianism, is true.' (One hates to criticise anyone's religion, but considering the song's fatuous humbug, the lines – *You can fool some people some of the time / But you can't fool all people all of the time* – are especially ironic in light of Haile Selassie's reputation in Ethiopia.)

'Never Get Weary', while not nearly as well-known as 'Get Up Stand Up', is in every way a superior work. It's as musically innovative and interesting as anything in the roots catalogue, and there are no more powerful lyrics in reggae.

I was walking on the shore and they took me in the
  ship
And they throw me overboard
And I swam right out of the belly of the whale
And I never get weary yet
They put me in jail and I did not do no wrong
And I never get weary yet
Say they put me in jail and
  I didn't get no bail
And I never get weary yet

It just goes to show that in reggae, as in anything else, hype and reality are two different things.

1982 / MAD OVER ME
Yellowman

No music on earth gives a more catholic reflection of its society than dancehall. Everything and anything is grist for the deejay mill. The inspiration for this particular dancehall smash was a tomato-ketchup ad.

1982 / PASS THE KUTCHIE
The Mighty Diamonds

'Pass The Kutchie', which had its genesis in the 1968 instrumental 'Full Up', was a big Jamaican number one for The Mighty Diamonds. In 1982 the group Musical Youth covered 'Pass The Kutchie' in pop style. The new version was called 'Pass The Dutchie' and was a worldwide smash selling into the millions. In a radio interview, a member of Musical Youth admitted that the group had made enough off the song to retire if they so chose. (There is some dispute here, though, others claim managers ripped off the group, although no one denies the song made millions for someone.)

Yet Leroy Sibbles, who created 'Full Up' got very little from 'Pass The Dutchie' and is still

making a struggling-singer's living. 'Pass The Dutchie' was not a unique case. Sibbles has created many rhythms which underlaid hits for which he never got proper credit. The bass line of John Holt's 'Love I Can Feel' was another Sibbles creation that underlaid a big international success, in this case Inner Circle's 'Sweat'.

1982 / SWEETIE COME BRUSH ME
John Holt

John Holt is perhaps the longest-lasting reggae star of them all. Not only did he record some of rocksteady's greatest hits with The Paragons, he remained a big star when he went solo in the 1970s. Holt had hits well into the eighties, the charming 'Sweetie Come Brush Me' being one of 1982's biggest songs, and had another number one with his cover of 'Carpenter' in 1990. Many still feel that John Holt and Dennis Brown are the two greatest ballad singers Jamaica has produced.

John Holt knows how to wear a suit, with or without locks.

LEROY SIBBLES — REGGAE'S UNSUNG HERO

When discussing the outstanding figures in reggae history, commentators inevitably roll out the names Jimmy Cliff, Toots Hibbert and Bob Marley – the Bach, Mozart and Beethoven of the form, so to speak. There can be no disputing their importance of course – Toots almost single-handedly established the music in its homeland; without Marley reggae might never have gained worldwide prominence; and as the star of 'The Harder They Come', the single most important vehicle in the music's dissemination abroad, Cliff's significance cannot be argued.

Yet strictly in terms of musical influence, Leroy Sibbles' contributions to Jamaican music remain unsurpassed. He is the greatest all-round talent in reggae history – a superb tenor and lead singer on some of its greatest songs; the main creative force on The Heptones' string of hits, having written all but three or four; and one of the finest bass players reggae has known.

And on bass and as the leader of Coxsone Dodd's house rhythm section in the late 1960s, he was the genius behind some of Studio One's greatest numbers. Perhaps no other artist in Jamaican music was associated with more classic tunes. Apart from The Heptones' hits, songs like 'Baby Why', 'Satta Massagana', 'Pass The Kutchie', and 'I'm Just A Guy', to name only a few, owe their existence as much to Sibbles as anyone else. It's no accident that the chief attraction in these songs are their expressive bass lines.

Sibbles' unique contributions to Jamaican music continue well into the 1990s. Twenty years after their creation, his unmatchable Studio One riddims form the core of dancehall music – without Sibbles, dancehall as we know it would not exist. It is in combination with his timeless riddims that so many deejays create their blistering vocal broadsides.

Marley and, to a lesser extent, Cliff, both attained international stardom. Toots, though not as well promoted, has achieved international acclaim from critics and fans. Leroy Sibbles is almost virtually unknown abroad, and for a time, almost forgotten in Jamaica. Even those in the music business are sometimes unaware of his contributions to the music.

Winston Barnes witnessed a classic example of this ignorance: 'Leroy Sibbles, on the stage at the Mahi Temple, Miami, got little or no respect from the dancehall massive in the house. Until that is, guitar in hand, he proved to the audience that he not only sang on the original to a recent big dancehall hit (the rhythm of 'Fatty Fatty'), but also played the bass line on the original.'

Unfortunately this tendency of Jamaicans to consign one-time musical heroes to oblivion even as the music they created is celebrated, is all too common. When Pliers' version of The Maytals' 'Bam Bam' went to number one in 1992, many young people thought it was an original! Had Bob Marley not been acclaimed abroad and died young, even he might have suffered a similar fate.

1983 / **IT MUST BE LOVE**
Carlene Davis

Carlene Davis' versions of 'Like Old Friends Do' was the number one song on the RJR 1982 Top 100, and 'It Must Be Love' was number five in 1983. Next to Marcia Griffiths, Carlene (who is married to singer-producer-promoter Tommy Cowan) is probably the most consistent female voice in reggae over the last 15 or so years. A lover of country music, she gives her thoughts on its popularity here: 'Jamaicans tend to relate to sad songs. And they like slower music, since the pace of life is slower here. In cold countries you have to move faster to keep warm. Here you can just go with the flow. Plus Jamaicans are a very spiritual people and a lot of country music is gospel. Jamaicans like melodies they can sing along to. And when we find something we like, we just keep liking it. That's why even today you have guys like Sanchez singing Skeeter Davis songs in the dancehall.'

COUNTRY MUSIC — A JAMAICAN FAVOURITE

One curious aspect of Jamaican musical tastes is the huge popularity of country and western music, especially the traditional, sentimental type. Ray Charles is a great favourite here mainly for 'tearjerkers' like 'I Can't Stop Loving You', 'Crying Time' and 'Seven Spanish Angels'. Songs like Freddie Fender's 'Before The Next Tear Drop Falls', Sami Jo's 'Tell Me A Lie', and even an old chestnut like Patti Page's 'Tennessee Waltz', remain perennial favourites. Even today Patsy Cline, Charley Pride, Marty Robbins, Skeeter Davis and especially Jim Reeves sell a considerable quantity of records.

Journalist Winston Barnes, who was a local radio deejay in the sixties, jokes that if music charts in Jamaica then were based on telephone requests, Jim Reeves' 'Guilty' would have topped the charts permanently. When he returned for a short guest stint at JBC in the early 1990s, Barnes was amazed to find that 'Guilty' was still one of the most requested songs. In 1992 we heard a radio host introduce a show saying – and these were his exact words – 'Ladies and gentlemen, I now present a man who is

Skeeter Davis – Jamaican crowd pleaser

in my estimation the greatest singer and entertainer of all times and one of the greatest human beings that ever lived, the late, great Jim Reeves.'

In 1982, the Bob Marley Entertainment Centre in Montego Bay was opened with a World Music Festival, which featured an eclectic mix of performers including Aretha Franklin, Gladys Knight and The Pips, Joe Jackson, The Beach Boys and The Grateful Dead. But for Jamai-cans the star of the show was the early 1960s country and western hit maker, Skeeter Davis. All but ignoring the other performers, bus loads of Jamaicans from all over the island, especially the country parts, converged to see in person this voice they had grown up with. Observers remember Skeeter weeping tears of joy as throngs of ecstatic fans sang along with her word for word – they knew every one of her songs by heart.

No one who listens to the radio here on Sundays, when almost nothing but old favourites are played, could have been surprised. Skeeter is still a perennial favourite here, and did a series of concerts in 1995.

Funnily, Jamaicans appear not to care for the new 'rock-country' breed of artists like Billy Ray Cyrus and stick with their 'good-old country' favourites. Stringy, syrupy and mushy – that's what we like. It is doubtful any foreign artist has sold more albums in Jamaica in the last fifteen years than Kenny Rogers.

It is difficult to point out any direct influence of all this on reggae's development. But you do hear definite echoes in a lot of Jamaican gospel music, and quite a number of country and western covers have been big hits here.

1983 / REVOLUTION
Dennis Brown

Arguably the finest 'pure' singer Jamaica has produced, and reputedly Bob Marley's favourite reggae artist, Dennis Brown has remained a bona fide star ever since he burst into prominence in 1972. Yet, while he has had more chart hits than perhaps anyone else in reggae, many feel he has been over prolific and done too many covers. Of course, that is a minority view, and his countless fans obviously feel that there is no such thing as too much of the 'crown prince'.

Picking the best of his massive catalogue is a difficult task, but 'Revolution', a churning spiritual call to arms, is possibly his most popular hit.

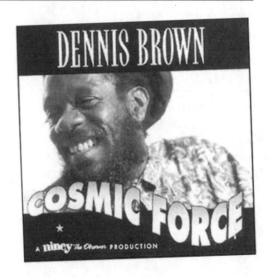

1983 / **UNMETERED TAXI**
Sly and Robbie

Sly and Robbie are probably the most important instrumentalists in Jamaican music since Don Drummond and The Skatalites. They have played on and produced countless reggae hits. In the drum and bass instrumental, 'Unmetered Taxi', they decided to highlight their own talents and the result was one of the greatest 'in the groove' records in reggae.

1984 / **PRINCESS BLACK**
Eddie Fitzroy

It's a common complaint from older women that dancehall constantly degrades women. (For

Eddie Fitzroy

whatever reasons young girls seem not to share these feelings and by all accounts are the biggest buyers of 'gal pickney music' and 'slackness'.) And Eddie Fitzroy is a man who agrees that the deejays sometimes go too far. Which is why he did a song like 'Princess Black' – 'Them did say culture dead when I did it'. At that time women were so down-trodden and demoralised. The songs coming out then were calling them all sorts of names, like 'credel' and 'concubine'.

'Princess Black' was like an anthem for black women. Fitzroy's biggest hit, the song was a tribute to his mother, and took him all of five minutes to write. It created such an impact that its title was used for a series of stage shows across the island.

1984 / **FOREIGN MIND**
Junior Reid

As a group, Black Uhuru has had very little success since the early 1980s, but former lead singer Junior Reid has consistently turned out good songs as a solo artist. 'Foreign Mind' was one of his best, a satirical take-off of those 'foreign minded' persons who find fault with everything Jamaican and praise only what comes from abroad

SLY AND ROBBIE — RIDDIM TWINS

Sly and Robbie share some thoughts.

Robbie: 'When I started to play bass my hero was Family Man [Aston Barrett] of the Wailers. He was the first to play really strong, simple, melodic lines with a deep feeling. When I started searching to find my own style, and what I came up with was to play as simple and direct as I can, so that the people, the real audience, can relate to my sound. From early sessions me and Sly were already thinking about producing. I never liked the bass sound on older reggae records and Sly never liked the drum sounds.

'The musicians would play some nice things, but because the records weren't very well-produced, you couldn't hear the true sounds of the players. We began to just build everything from the bass and drums, first getting our own sounds just right as the foundation, then adding the other instruments and voices. Basically we work the same way on everything we produce constructing the groove.

If a musician want to say that they are a reggae musician and play only reggae, or they want to say they are a country musician and only play country – that's their business. I don't feel it's right. I feel if you're a musician, you should be a musician. Whatever music come up, no matter what form, colour, size or shape, you should be able to tackle it. A fisherman not gonna go out there and say, "Today I'm gonna only catch trout." I learned that music, no matter where it might be, is just the same as anywhere else. No matter what the name, it's still music. Whether it be reggae or disco, soul, funk, jazz or boogaloo, it's music.'

'Now, in Jamaica people like to dance, and they will accept any music that makes the foot move, whether it's calypso, boogalu, funky, disco, moon-rock, stars-rock, sun-rock, anything. Everything have a different time and phase to go through. Reggae's going through a phase now, which is just deejays, that's happening now, like in the U.S. rap music is happening. Some of them write some pretty good stuff. Most of it is really comical, catchy, something that'll make you laugh. Sometimes people need to laugh instead of going out and listening to serious stuff. Everything have its phases and stages.'

Sly: 'Al Jackson, Jr. – of Booker T and the MG's – was my first hero on drums, along with Roger Hawkins of Muscle Shoals, who played on those Atlantic Aretha Franklin records, and Benny Benjamin on early Motown sides. I especially like Al Jackson, because he kept it tight and simple and didn't roll around the tom-toms unless it was necessary   but he was always locked into the groove. In Jamaican music my earliest influence was Lloyd Nibbs of the Skatalites. I learned and listened as a boy during the ska and rocksteady eras. One of my first actual recording dates was on an Ansell Collins record, when the style was already reggae with the 'one drop' on the backbeat. I listen to R&B, reggae, pop, new wave – a lot of sounds. My favourite drummers today are Steve Gadd, Earl Young, Charlie Watts, Aynsely Dunbar, all kinds of different stylists.

'Another example of how I mix up styles a little bit is the version of the old Temptations hit, "Don't Look Back", with Peter Tosh and Mick Jagger. I used a rhythm on the drums that comes out of the Pocomania church services in Jamaica. It's a gospel thing that's particular to that church, and I used a similar beat on the tune "Youth of Eglinton" with Black Uhuru.

'One of the changes I think we made on Jamaican music was in the late 1970s, when everybody was doing four beats to the bar on bass drum, working around that kind of disco-fied pattern. On a couple of very popular Dennis Brown albums during that period, and especially 'Love and Devotion' by Jimmy Riley, we did like a slowed-down Motown/Stax kind of beat, but still keeping the backbeat happening on the guitar chord. That shook things up down in Jamaica a bit. I learned to be very disciplined. Know when to play and when not to play. There might be a lot of musicians around when you're playing, so you have to leave space for everybody. I learn a lot from these musical experiences. We know exactly when to play and when not to play.'

On what makes Sly and Robbie unique

Sly: 'I don't know. We're just playing what we feel. That's natural. People ask us all the time. We go inside a studio and start playing something. We don't know what we're gonna play. I start playing and it sounds great and we say "Record it!". Some other guy might say it's too simple, but the best music, I think, is when it's simple and not so difficult that people can't understand.'

Robbie: 'Coming together as a unit putting that force out, that's something natural. We don't really practice, we both really good players, right? The chain's as strong as its weakest link, so we try to stay together. A lot of duos never realize that have a good thing going and break up. They never know what they had until they lose it. It's like everything else. Everyday you can get up and find a dollar or two in your pocket and you never really get hungry. But as soon as you don't have any money in your pocket, you start feeling hungry. You must understand when you have something and don't try to abuse it. We show respect for one another. We know we have a good thing going.'

Sly: 'Each of us can go out and do individual work, but it wouldn't be the same. We're better as a team, much stronger. Teamwork is always the best in anything. You should not fly a plane alone without a co pilot or navigator. A lot of people say that we're really big, but we don't think so. We don't call ourselves big or superstars. We just the same young Sly and Robbie., not the old Robbie and Sly.'

1984 / JAMAICA JAMAICA
Brigadier Jerry

While he never recorded prolifically, Brigadier Jerry is considered one of the key formative influences of the modern dancehall style, credited by a lot of deejays as having invented stylistic flourishes such as the speed rap, and the stop and go. All of which he shows to fine advantage in 'Jamaica Jamaica'

1986 / WHAT THE HELL THE POLICE CAN DO
Echo Minott

Many consider Papa Levi's 'My God My King' as perhaps the most 'conscious' deejay song ever done. Produced in 1984, it is as verbally elaborate and clearly enunciated as any dancehall tune ever made. On the other hand, Echo Minott's tale of a man threatening his woman and telling her there's nothing the police can do, is often considered just another example of dancehall's violently misogynistic tendencies. Yet this very catchy song was the number one song for 1986 on the RJR Top 100.

And truth to tell, to our ears at any rate, 'What The Hell' is a far more enjoyable piece of music than 'My God My King'. For all its social commentary, 'My God My King' bogs down somewhere in the middle when Papa Levi forgets he's chanting to rhythm and just keeps chatting in pretty much unvaried monotone. Long before the song is finished our minds have drifted elsewhere.

'What The Hell' may be unpolished and almost crude, but Echo Minott does what a deejay is supposed to do, play counterpoint with the rhythm and keep our interest musically with change of pace and tone. And if the slice of life lyrics are not especially attractive, they have the convincing ring of reality. The story Echo Minott tells may not be pretty, but it is those aspects of Jamaican society that condone such behaviour that are to blame, not a song telling it like it is. Does shooting the messenger ever solve anything?

1985 / **RING THE ALARM**
Tenor Saw

One of the brightest stars of the early 'computer riddim' days, Tenor Saw is one of reggae's most tragic figures. Barely two years after creating this undisputed dancehall classic, he was found dead from gunshots, reportedly a victim of mysterious drug 'runnings'. The song's chorus hints at profundity - *Ring the alarm, another sound is dying* - and Tenor Saw's portentous tone invests it with a feeling of importance. But if you listen closely and think about it, it's just another sound clash song – *Four big sounds inna one big lawn / all of then think them a champion*. Proving again that over analysis can not only lead to paralysis, sometimes it takes all the fun out of music.

Tenor Saw

1985 / **HERE I AM**
Barrington Levy

One of reggae's most underrated singers, Barrington Levy produced a string of big songs in the 1980s including 'My Woman', 'Here I Am', 'Under Mi Sensi' and 'She's Mine'. Levy possesses an effortlessly buoyant voice, and his ability to capture dancehall's raw energy with his sharp phrasing is heard to excellent effect in the vigorous 'Here I Am'. He didn't have much chart success in the early 1990s, but his talent never went away. In 1996 he and deejay Bounty Killa combined on the huge hit 'Living Dangerously'.

1985 / **WHAT ONE DANCE CAN DO**
Beres Hammond.

Beres Hammond joined the 'proggresive reggae' band Zap Pow in 1975, while still a teenager.

But he really burst onto the music scene in the late 1970s with 'One Step Ahead', a b-grade Jamaican 'Philly Soul' imitation. He continued in the same vein until the 1-2 punch of 'What One Dance Can Do' and 'She Loves Me Now' which, although similar to what had preceded, somehow managed to get it right. He has often struck gold over the years, but has tended to be too prolific, and his large volume of mediocre work has tended to drown the gems which he occasionally produces. Yet even if Beres has never quite achieved the fame of a Dennis Brown or Gregory Isaacs, over the past 15 years or so, no reggae artist has had more consistent chart success.

1985 / **SOLIDARITY**
Black Uhuru

During their years at Island Records from 1980-1983, Black Uhuru cut a series of ground breaking albums – 'Sinsemilla', 'Red', 'Tear It Up', 'The Dub Factor' and 'Anthem'. 'Anthem' earned the group the very first reggae Grammy, but it was 'Red' which critics acclaimed as a masterpiece. Black Uhuru (Uhuru is Swahili for freedom) was founded by Derrick 'Duckie' Simpson in the mid 1970s. The group went through various aggregations but it was Simpson, Michael Rose and Sandra 'Puma' Jones who made Black Uhuru a household name in music.

Rose left the group in 1983 and Jones died a few years later. And although the group still exists in name, the sound of the late seventies and early eighties has never been recaptured. Indeed, there are now two aggregations touring under the name 'Black Uhuru'. How ironic that perhaps the best single from this fractious group was a grand espousal of unity entitled 'Solidarity'

1985 / **GIRLIE GIRLIE**
Sophia George

One of those rare occasions when we get to hear the Jamaican woman's side of the story: *Young man you too girlie girlie / You just a flash it round the worldy / You have one up east and one up west / One up north and one down south.* 'Girlie Girlie' was a huge smash at home and abroad. Needless to say, very few men bought copies.

1985 / **EVERY POSSE GET FLAT**
Blood Fire Posse

Reggae is dance music and new styles emerge with the consistency of April showers, or in Jamaica, October rains. Old-timers remember things like 'Rent A Tile and 'Pop A Top from the 1960s, the 'S-90 Skank, 'John Crow Skank' and 'Rub-a-Dub' from the 1970s, while the dancehall eighties and nineties saw moves like the 'Cool and Deadly', 'One-Foot Skank', 'The Bogle', 'Butterfly', 'Tatie', 'Go Go Wine' and the 'Erkle'.

Every once in a while a dance craze seizes the comon imagination and sweeps the nation. Such was the case in 1985, when every posse in the land was getting flat with an infectious enthusiasm that occassionally resembled mass hysteria.

1986 / **GREETINGS**
Half Pint

The example *par excellance* of how music never really grows old in Jamaica. This 1986 hit was a recut of the 1967 Studio One instrumental 'Heavenless', which itself was a remake of the Don Drummond original. Ten years after its release, and 30 years after 'Don D' created the

rhythm, 'Greetings' is still guaranteed to 'mash up' any dance. It might be well be the most crowd pleasing dancehall tune ever made.

1989 / POCOMANIA DAY
Chalice and Lovindeer

One of the most appealing things about dancehall music is how unashamedly it reaches back to its roots for inspiration. Pocomania has always been recognised as one of reggae's key formative influences. But there were certain periods, especially the middle-to-late seventies and early eighties, when it was scorned as 'old time, backwards, country bumpkin, quashie foolishness'. Dancehall however has not only embraced it as a musical influence but on occasion laughs affectionately at the sheer outlandishness and unaffected exuberance of 'poco'. 'Pocomania Day' was a big hit, as were the poco-influenced

'Revival Time' by Chalice in 1986, and 'Chaka On The Move' by Chaka Demus in 1990. Surely it's a sign of cultural confidence and emotional health when people are unembarrassed by their past.

1986 / BOOPS
Super Cat

1988 / YOUNG GAL BUSINESS
Chaka Demus

1990 / TWICE MY AGE
Shabba Ranks

As anyone who has eyes can see, in Jamaica, 'May-December' relationships between the sexes are probably as common here as anywhere in the world. Most of these 'old man young girl' couplings are definitely based on the 'money-honey' basis, the men providing the money and the girls the honey. Deejays have never ceased to make fun of this aspect of life. Super Cat's 'Boops' was one of the first and most famous songs on the theme and inspired a whole slew of songs like 'Government Boops' and 'Babylon Boops'. Variations on the subject have multiplied – 'Young Gal Business', 'Count Out', 'Brinks' and others.

Chaka Demus advises an admirer about 'young gal business'.

Newcomers to Jamaica, witnessing all these 'May-December' relationships, might feel sorry for the young girls apparently seduced by older men. But the deejays view things rather differently. They tend to see it as Chaka Demus does – *Young gal business control Jamaica / Gal a rule man drive Benz and Mazda / Gal a rule man drive BM and Jaguar.*

Super Cat puts it more graphically – *See Boops de, watch gal a nyam him out.*

And in their duet, Shabba Ranks and Crystal give the girls' side of things – *She no want no idle jubie / She want her man to have compense / For her man pocket must have strength / Because she have to pay light bill and rent.*

The tender-hearted might feel queasy with relationships described in such mercenary terms. But just as dancehall stripped reggae down to drum and bass, a lot of Jamaican men and women have apparently peeled sexual matters down to the bare essentials and are content to deal with matters on that level.

1987 / **PUNAANY**
Admiral Bailey

Admiral Bailey was the hottest dancehall star of the late eighties, and it's amusing to see how he has transformed himself into a 'clean' deejay in the 1990s, teaming with Byron Lee on some of his big soca hits and starring in television ads for banks. Despite his jovial personality, Mr Bailey certainly wouldn't have been any advertising agency's idea of a good corporate spokesman back in 1987. For although he had three of the years top ten songs – 'Two Year Old', 'Big Belly Man' and 'Punaany' – all were dubbed NFAP, or not fit for airplay, and banned from radio.

One can see why. Because in 'Punaany', the Admiral practically drools over the mike as he reads the menu. And in the process he gives a perfect summation of the Jamaican male psyche – *Gimme punaany / Want punaany / Any punaany is the same punaany.* It may not be the most socially redeeming song, but as they say, the truth always hurts.

Presumably the new clean-cut Admiral Bailey would not appreciate this regular feature that appears in the weelky publication, Hardcore..

There is a special place reserved for ladies who are endowed by nature with that special feature that makes them highly desirable and attractive. We call that place...

THE BUFFER ZONE

Do you belong in the buffer zone? Give us a call and we will put you there!

Warning!! No artificial enhancement allowed!!
(We check for authenticity)

1987 / JAMAICAN WOMAN
Fabulous Five

Fab Five's gift for catchy and witty tunes often gets lost in their party-hearty, touring machine image. It's often forgotten that their resident musical genius Grub Cooper has produced the majority of commercial jingles on Jamaican radio and television.

This may not seem significant at first glance. Yet the 'stream of consciousness' and 'found object' approach that Jamaican dancehall artists take to song composition means that many of these jingles have crept into the dancehall canon, both melodically and lyrically. Yellowman had more than one hit taking off Fab Five composed ads. And Ninja Man has been known to do the same thing at stage shows. So while few of their songs may stand alone as 'art', it's undeniable that many of the catchiest hooks in Jamaican music have originated in the fertile minds of the Fab Five crew.

And incidentally 'Jamaican Woman' does show that at least some Jamaican men respect their women as more than just sex objects.

1987 – WEAR YU SIZE
Lt Stichie

Having attended teacher's college, Stichie is the only deejay, other than Lovindeer, with a tertiary-level education. Perhaps this is what has enabled him to continually re-invent himself and so carve out what is, for a deejay, an exceptionally long-lasting career. He first came to prominence in 1987 and yet eight years later was still popular enough to be the RJR 1994 TOP 100 deejay of the year.

Stitchie tells a funny story of why he decided to become a full-time musician: 'I was a very fast runner and, in fact, because I got a track scholarship I was able to attend teacher's college. One year I was training hard to go to the Olympics, and everyone told me I had a very good chance of making the Jamaican team, but then I pulled a muscle and there went all my chances. So I say to myself "Bwoy, I know my tongue can't strain.

So maybe a music career is a better deal than track and field." And so I began to devote myself to music.'

1987 / INNA DE BUS
Professor Nuts

Many people would have us believe that deejay music consists of nothing but 'gal-pickney music' and 'gun talk'. But humour has always been a staple of the dancehall. Not only is Professor Nuts perhaps the most consistently funny of all deejays, but his humour is always highly topical. 'Inna de Bus' makes a joke of Jamaica's atrociously overcrowded public transportation system. His 1991 hit 'Tansoback' ridiculed the ultra-aggressive macho attitude of many Jamaican men that so often leads to unnecessary violence, and sometimes tragedy. Some say 'him taking serious thing, mek joke', but as long as we can laugh about our problems, there's hope for the future.

1987 / HOL A FRESH
Red Dragon

They say nothing is off limits in the dancehall and this song makes you believe it. Could a song urging various people to bathe more frequently – 'hol a fresh' means to take a bath – become such a huge hit in any other musical arena?

1987 / **LEVEL THE VIBES**
Half Pint

Half Pint manages to impart a rough, almost 'deejayish' tone to his songs and is one of the most exciting of all dancehall singers, as his string of big hits like 'Winsome', 'Greetings' and 'Level The Vibes' testify.

1987 / **PUSH COME TO SHOVE**
Freddie McGregor

Freddie McGregor, 'the man with the beautiful teeth', is the closest thing reggae has to a matinee idol today and is also a popular figure in local advertising. He has an excellent voice, but many feel he's too content with being a 'ladies' pet' and has not made the most of his undoubted natural ability.

1988 / **WILD GILBERT**
Lloyd Lovindeer

Two things about 'Wild Gilbert' are strikingly reflective of Jamaican society. Its strongly humourous bent, despite its topic – the greatest natural disaster of Jamaica's 20th century – mirrors the Jamaican tendency to see life as a comedy of the absurd.

> Natty dread locks sit down inside
> A look how Gilbert a go on outside
> When breeze lick down Mr. Chin Restaurant
> Natty dread jump up and chant
> Lick them Jah, gwan go do it
> Is them did give the dread pork to eat

While giving a broad overview of various 'Hurricane' experiences, the song does not dwell on these in the detail. Jamaicans are a people, fortunately in many ways (as with slavery for example), with a very limited interest in the past, remembering only what they choose to. 'Wild Gilbert' lists merely what one might call discomforts, which are easily and plausibly turned into jokes.

Lloyd Lovindeer

THE DEEJAY AS ORAL HISTORIAN

On September 12, 1988, Hurricane Gilbert, the greatest natural disaster Jamaica has suffered in the 20th century, swept across the island leaving some 30 people dead and damage to the sad tune of billions of U.S. dollars. Jamaica made an astonishingly quick recovery and within three months life was back to normal for most people. In six months Gilbert had almost been forgotten. One of the few permanent reminders of the cataclysm was the torrent of songs inspired by the event. There were probably hundreds, naturally most of pitiful quality. But as Pamela O'Gorman says in her 1995 article 'Gilbert Songs': ' . . . a new dimension has been added to historical record keeping in societies such as ours. One can foresee the day when many of today's songs assume a new kind of value and significance as essential source material for better understanding our past history. Today, six years after the event, "Wild Gilbert" is the only hurricane song remembered, the only one still heard on the radio. Mostly because it was a far better song than the others.

' . . . The Lovindeer "Wild Gilbert" was in DJ style, but it had far more musical variety than most of the other DJ examples. The chorus, with words based on a familiar English nursery rhyme, was catchy and singable and it was matched by the second melody of "oono see mi dish" where words and music caught the imagination. Thereafter Lovindeer gave us a DJ chant, changing his rhythmic step and his pitch when necessary, adding a call and response pattern at one of the high points ("You see mi fridge – a Gilbert gi mi", etc.: words which struck a response from the whole population). He then proceeded to tell the story of Natty Dread, which contained an element of tension eventually resolved on a humourous note. Both verbally and musically, he captured the attention of the listener from beginning to end.

'Lovindeer's situation is unique in two ways. He is the only popular deejay over 40 and is one of only two whose education goes past a high school level (the other is Lt Stitchie), being a former English Teacher at Kingston College High School. Many do not consider Lovindeer, who also sings occasionally, a real DJ. His habit of stealing other's musical motifs have made him unpopular in some circles. It must be said in his defence that he usually improves, lyrically anyway, the material he re-works. He has an excellent feel for everyday Jamaican vernacular, and his songs do have a much longer shelf life than average. Plus, he has a definite gift for topical social commentary, as in his 1990 hit "Find Your Way", a take off a famous speech by former prime minister and current opposition leader, Edward Seaga.

'In the final analysis, Lovindeer lacks the gritty edge of reality one finds in the work of the best, young, ghetto DJs. Still, he plays the vital role of bringing literacy and perspective to dancehall music, preventing it from becoming completely pre-literate and totally inward looking. If his songs sometimes lack authentic feeling, they at least broaden dancehall's usually limited repertoire of themes and vocabulary and give hope that the music may one day be able to appeal to the mind as well as the body and heart.'

Full of bully beef, full of bully beef
Me can't get to cook so me full of bully beef . . .
Water wet up me shoes and a wet up me hat
Wet up me dog and a wet up me cat
Wet up the bed, wet up me parrot
Water wet up me whats-it-not . . .
Jook them Jah with storm and thunder
Tear off them roof and break them window.
Two sheet of zinc blow off a Joe house
Dread flash him locks and start to shout
'Selassie I Jah, King of Kings
Show them how we run things
Blow away them house, but make them survive
So when them see I them will realize
Is true I merciful why them alive!
Little after that Gilbert turn back
Lick off the roof off of Natty Dread Shack
Him say 'Blouse and skirt, Jah must be never know
Say I and I live right here so!

Truly harrowing experiences, deaths and economic ruin are ignored. Jamaica has always preferred humour to history.

The other characteristically Jamaican element is the strong evocation of God – *Sellasie I Jah, King of Kings / Show them say how we run things* – was indeed a common reaction among many religious people, who almost seemed glad to see the Almighty demonstrate his might to the heathen unbelievers, rationalising any disaster that might strike God-fearing folk like themselves in the same way Natty does. It's interesting to note that the most popular of the 1993 earthquake songs (only a minor hit) was called 'God Moves Inna Mysterious Ways'.

The direct social impact of 'Wild Gilbert' is often overlooked. There was a time when rich uptowners scorned deejay music as 'dibbi dibbi' rubbish, completely ignoring dancehall in favour of soca, Bob Marley and North American pop. Hurricane Gilbert, however, was an experience every Jamaican – rich or poor, white, black, yellow or brown – went through. So 'Wild Gilbert' was a song with which everyone could identify. Indeed it was the first deejay song many of the upper-class had ever bothered to listen to.

Nowadays, not even the poshest uptown sessions can ignore dancehall. Mirage Night Club, the 'stooshest' club in Kingston in the early 1990s, was originally designed with an exclusive upscale market in mind and opened with a 'minimal dancehall' policy. But when the market speaks, business must listen. Patrons demanded and were given deejay music and Mirage now gets some of its biggest crowds on dancehall night. Of course, 'Wild Gilbert' was not solely responsible for changes like this, but it did more than any single song to establish dancehall as the universal sound of Jamaica today.

Hurricane Gilbert was indirectly responsible for blowing the dancehall scene uptown and upmarket. The wonderful painting on the opposite page was done by Joel Robb of Kellits Secondary School, for the 1989 National Arts Exhibition for Schools.

Steely and Cleevie had a huge hit with the riddim of J. C. Lodge's 'Telephone Love'.

1988 / TELEPHONE LOVE
J. C. Lodge

The 'Rumours' rhythm was by far the most popular of 1988. 'Rumours' and 'Telephone Love' were only two of the big hits it spawned. The men responsible for it, and many others of the late 1980s and 1990s were Wycliffe Johnson and Cleveland Brown, popularly known as Steely and Clevie. Here they share some of their thoughts on music:

Clevie: Because I play real drums and percussions, I add a human feel to drum programming. That is what I attribute our success to. A lot of people are programming drum rhythms but the drum beat sounds mechanical – because they probably don't have any formal drum experience. Although we are criticized for playing two-chord rhythms, we are not limited. By simplifying the rhythms and using our extensive knowledge of music to program, Steely and I have been able to make rhythms which we can tell from day-one are going to be chart-toppers. A lot of the rhythm patterns and styles in dancehall come from

Africa. You can hear them in Jamaican folk music and gospel music. And a lot of Steely and Clevie rhythm tracks derive from Pocomania. I actually program to sound realistic and I don't intend to give up either.

Steely: I started recording with Clevie when I was 12. He was 15 at the time and we played on Hugh Mundell's 'Africa Must Be Free' and a few recordings for Augustus Pablo. Then we started recording. My playing is influenced by greats like Ernie Ranglin, Lloyd Brevitt and Jackie Mittoo. When for instance, we know that a tune calls for an Ernest Ranglin type of guitar, we try and tone the keyboard with the feel. We are not just making sounds on the equipment by chance. What is funny though, is that it was just by accident that we found a bass sound when the machine we had fell and broke. A circuit was soldered and there was an error in that job which turned out to be like a blessing. We took out that circuit and put in a new frame to keep the sound. It's just God's plan for what you have inside you to come out in your music though.

1989 / COME BACK TO ME
Tiger

Tiger had an unparalleled sense of timing and a unique style, incorporating groans, growls and grunts into stream of consciousness vocal improvisation that verged on scatting. More than any other performer, he embodied the oft-quoted definition of dancehall as vocal drumming.

Along with Ninja Man, Tiger was perhaps the most naturally talented deejay of the modern dancehall era, both taking a similar unplanned and uncontemplative approach to their music and frequently achieving a genuine emotional intensity. But this completely intuitive approach resulted in a very inconsistent body of work. They produced moments of sonic exhilaration when they hit, but when they missed, their songs were almost unlistenable.

Both seemed to pour their whole soul into their art. Possibly it was their need to sustain this passion in the day-to-day grind of the dancehall that led them to experiment with mind enhancing drugs. Amidst the distractions of girls, cargo and motorbikes, perhaps only drugs could supply the adrenalin rush they craved. Both were at one stage confessed cocaine addicts.

Tiger first burst on the scene in 1987 and polls that year showed him to be the island's most popular entertainer. But a year later he was down and out on the streets, having sold all his possessions to buy drugs. But the jungle man managed to overcome his chemical dependencies and roared back to the top of the charts in 1989 with one of the great dancehall love songs, 'Come Back To Me'. He continued to have chart success into the nineties, but in 1994 disaster struck when he was involved in a near fatal motorcycle crash. Some radio stations reported that he had died. He survived, but apparently suffered some brain damage. He has tried to make a musical comeback, but seems not to have regained full control of his faculties. Every dancehall fan hopes that he will in time return to full strength and once again thrill stage shows with his inimitable vocal skills.

1989 / ONE BLOOD
Junior Reid

You could a be an African or an Englishman
You could a be an Irishman or whether Pakistan
One Blood, one blood, one blood

A massive hit in reggae circles both home and abroad, Junior Reid's anthem of unity addresses the racial problem with typical Jamaican directness – whatever the nationality or colour, it's the same red blood in the veins. Now a song like this has a special resonance here. For some Jamaicans like to think their 'blessed isle' is a shining example of racial brotherhood. But does the national motto, 'Out of Many, One People', reflect actual reality or wishful thinking?

By rights, race relations in Jamaica should be no better or worse than anywhere else. The globe is littered with countries having a similar colonial past. Yet somehow, in a typically haphazard and unreflective manner, Jamaicans have produced an exceptionally racially tolerant society. Few racially mixed countries have remained so free of ethnic strife. There have been class and work related disturbances like the Frome riots of 1938, but never physical persecution of minorities. The closest instance, the anti-Chinese riot in 1965, was essentially rooted in economics, not race, although it's hard to define the line of distinction between these categories.

The racial indifference Jamaicans demonstrate at the polls is certainly remarkable. In the rest of the world, deliberately or not, whites elect whites, and blacks elect blacks, but 'a no so it go a yard.' Voters are mainly of African descent, but race has never been an overriding factor in elections here. The country's leaders since adult suffrage have been of all shades.

Some claim it's not racial indifference, but a 'black inferiority complex' where, as Peter Tosh bitterly puts it, 'White is right, and brown can stay around, but black must stay back.' It's thought-provoking that Bob Marley, reggae's biggest ever star, and still a worldwide symbol of black consciousness, had a white father and rather caucasian features.

In some circles a black skin, as opposed to an easily assimilated light-brown, is still a barrier to social and professional advancement. Class and race are inextricably intertwined here. While the rich and middle class can vary in colour, the poor are all black. Often this leads to the equation of black equals poor and white equals rich – where all white persons are treated as if they are well off while a black man will be considered poor unless he can prove otherwise. Since the rich here, as everywhere else, are given privileged treatment, the lighter skinned still seem to be granted preferential status.

Understandably, all this causes many black persons to regard the nation's official 'out of many' policy as camouflage for continued white domination – 'Jampartheid'. But the basis for such attitudes is largely class, not race. Rich black people are treated little differently than rich white people in Jamaica. And there is one big difference between class and race discrimination – a man can change his social status over time, but not his skin colour. To be sure, some naked prejudices still exist, but indisputably there has been a gradual improvement in racial attitudes over the years. All white bank tellers, army officers and West Indies cricket captains were realities only three decades ago.

The island has its shortcomings, but the lack of self-doubt Jamaicans display abroad is surely developed at home. Few in Jamaica today are prevented by skin colour from attaining positions they deserve on merit. Change might have come slowly, but it has come, and without the catastrophes that have accompanied it in so many other places. It's been a hard road to travel and there's a rough, rough way to go. But few countries been more successful in eliminating purely racial barriers than One Love Jam Down.

1990 / **BORDER CLASH**
Ninja Man

In the classic folk tradition of songs like 'Linstead Market' and 'Dog War a Matches Lane', 'Border Clash' takes a fairly unimportant event (Border Clash was only one of the innumerable stage shows taking place in 1990) and stamps it on the popular imagination with a vivid recreation of incident and atmosphere.

> Cause remember when St. Catherine and the Kingstonian
>   them clash
> You know say what a deejay business dey 'pon that
> Over Coney Island where the place it block
> You know from Ferry highway you couldn't find no
>   where fe stop
> Me tell oono the border clash, border clash

And the way Ninja plays off and with the riddim (one of dancehall's most famous, the 'punnany' riddim) and changes verbal tone, texture and pace, adds compelling musical virility. (A university English professor who finds dancehall interesting remarked, on hearing the song for the first time, 'This is deconstructionist!' It's hardly likely Ninja Man knows the meaning of the term, but the comment is quite understandable.)

'Border Clash' unmistakably illustrates that deejaying is an art form. Dancehall haters scoff that 'Anyone can deejay. It doesn't take talent like singing'. Well, deejaying and singing may use different skills – Ninja Man for example is a terrible singer, with little range or tonal sense. (Is it accurate to say that singing is primarily a melodic art whose instrumental counterparts are the violin, piano or guitar, while deejaying is a rhythmic one whose foil is the drum?) But the ability to do what Ninja does here is not something to be scoffed at. It certainly cannot be convincingly imitated.

It's difficult to judge a recent song's quality – what sounds good after two or even five years, often seems dated in ten or twenty. But 'Border Clash's' riveting visceral appeal and rhythmic variety make you wonder if it might not in time become one of those popular tunes which define Jamaica's musical heritage.

1991 / **BANDALERO**
Pinchers

Despite the inconsistent quality of his material, Pinchers has always stood out among dancehall singers because he brings an almost deejayish energy to his better songs like 'Don is Don', 'Return of the Don' and 'Bandalero'. 'Bandalero' displays the fascination which cowboy movies and songs have always held for Jamaicans. Pinchers throws a whole bunch of western names and references together – El Paso, Zorro, Gringoes, Passero, Al Pacino (Al Pacino doesn't really belong there but it rhymes) – in a rather

THE BORDER CLASH SYNDROME — VIOLENCE IN THE DANCEHALL

The lyrics of 'Border Clash' say a lot about the Jamaican psyche, especially displaying the penchant for extremes. Other audiences might be content to show disapproval in merely vocal terms. But not Jamaican stage show audiences. What Ninja Man talks about, the stone and bottle throwing is not hyperbole, it is actual fact. The practice has cooled down a bit (nowadays restless audiences merely wave empty bottles dangling from the little finger and the artists get the idea), but in 1990 and 1991 it was widespread.

The most famous incident was Bunny Wailer at Sting in 1990, when he refused to change his material as the audience was demanding. 'Shandying' it came to be called after the 'shandy' bottles supposedly used. It was probably because 'Border Clash' preserved the incident in song that the practice attracted such widespread attention.

> You see if you go 'pon stage and you no singing well hot
> You know say a shandy bottle lick you and make you drop 'pon you back
> You think a one time me see Cedric run off a that
> Him have fe run with him guitar when a singer go on like idiot
> Inna the border clash, border clash' . . .
> You see when the St Catherine deejay jump 'pon the mike and chat
> And when the people them kick up and make the place get block
> You see if them move and go on like them no know what fe chat
> You know say a pure stone and bottle and one of dem bound have fe drop

(Incidentally, it's not only dancehall audiences who sometimes go to extremes. Back in the mid-1980s an unpopular contestant was chosen Miss Jamaica. The uptown audience booed loudly and, when she made her victory walk, she was greeted by a hail of cups and oranges, one of which hit her right on the nose, sending her scurrying offstage.)

Yet stage-show audiences are just as extreme in showing approval. A few years back the real mark of approval of a good performance was the gun salute, real live ammunition fired into the air. Inevitably, a few accidental deaths occurred (one by a policeman), leading to a police crackdown

on the practice. So audiences could only then point fingers in the air going 'pram pram' or 'buuy buuy'. Then there were firecrackers to simulate guns. At one time the fire salute was popular — spraying an aerosol can and setting the fumes afire, leading to a brief burst of fire shooting in the air. A toned down version is the flashing of lighters.

Clearly dancehall treads close to the dangerous fringes of violence. 'One World a Bomb', 'New Gun fe Bust', 'Ten Gun fe Bust' are all titles of songs Ninja Man performed, as he assures us, to the unanimous approval of the audience:

> Me bawl one house a gun, one house a gun
> And when me draw that they one you know the place tear down
> Me draw one world a bomb, one world a bomb
> And is like say the whole a inna the place is like is an invasion
> Me bawl ten gun fe bust, ten gun fe bust
> And you want to hear the people them say this ya one dangerous
> Me bawl move from here, move from here
> And you see gal pickney and man them start jump inna the air

It's this bloodthirsty streak that many condemn in dancehall, and rightly so. Unchecked, it would eventually lead to unpopular performers being shot dead on stage. In fact deejay Super Cat threatened to draw a gun after being 'bottled' at Sting 91.

Dancehall is as emotionally expressive as any music in the world today, both in terms of performers and audience. And that is mostly for the good. Perhaps one of the reasons Jamaica has escaped violent social upheaval is the unique 'letting off of steam' which the dance halls allow to the most volatile elements in the populace. As a dancehall song put it— *If you no want shot fe bust, make the music turn up.* (Jamaican audiences apparently cannot enjoy music not at full volume).

Even the biggest dancehall fans realise there must be limits. Mass social outcry must be heeded by the entire music industry. So far this self-censorship has seemed to work. Although there are still occasional eruptions, extreme slackness (sexually explicit songs) and gunmanism have been toned down. Because although emotional release is one thing, social anarchy is entirely another.

confused hodgepodge of bragadoccio and creates a great song. The lyrics might be nonsense but the swaggering attitude and breathless singing makes this one of the most exciting dancehall tunes ever made.

1991 / **TRAILER LOAD OF GIRLS**
Shabba Ranks

1991 was a vintage year for dancehall, producing a slew of memorable songs. 'Trailer Load' was one of the best. Remarkably well produced for a dancehall tune, it remains one of the most danceable songs in reggae. Shabba gives voice to every Jamaican man's dream

> Girls girls every day / From London, Canada and USA
> Girls girls every day / But the best girls come from Ja
> Me have a trailer load a girl / A wharf fe clear off

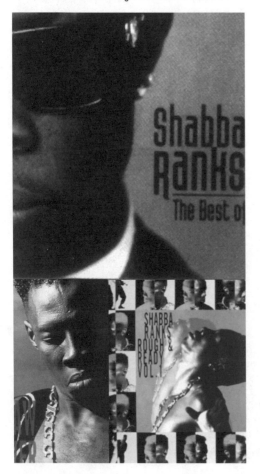

THE DEEJAY AS FOLK HERO

All who have heard Ninja Man at his best agree that his unmatched verbal dexterity make him potentially the greatest dancehall deejay ever. Producers marvel at his ability to come up with spur of the moment lyrics. And his extemporaneous ability has vanquished all comers on stage. His sheer unpredictability always enthralls fans - he's as likely to croon a set of country and western hits or gospel songs as perform his big hits. He is rarely less than entertaining and has an uncanny ability to read a crowd.

Few of Ninja Man's records charted after 'Border Clash', yet he remained immensely popular live. Ninja, always capricious, was said to have become almost unmanageable. While in New York for a show, a loaded gun was found in his possession. He was convicted on illegal possession and imprisoned for a year in the U.S. Rumour ran wild that he was actually in prison on murder charges and had been given a life sentence. But one year later, Ninja was back home. A series of homecoming shows made him a big star again. But then word went around that Ninja was on crack. There were continuing rumours of drug problems, then an open confession on stage, then another public vow that he was cleaned up. The public fascination with him continued even though it seemed his talents were being wasted. But Ninja tore up Sting 1995, outperforming every big deejay in the land. It seemed the Don Gorgon of yore was back. But drug problems continued to haunt him and he slipped out of the limelight.

Then in early 1997 while attending a gospel tent, Ninja Man was publicly baptized as a born-again Christian, adopted the name Brother Desmond, and swore not only to deejay for God but to convert his former dancehall brethren. For a solid week the daily afternoon paper 'The Star' featured an aspect of Ninja Man's conversion on its front page. Videos of his conversion sold like hot cakes. Newspaper editorials debated whether his conversion was real or a way of gaining public sympathy and rekindling his flagging career. What the future holds for Ninja, only the one above can know. But the extraordinary interest the Jamaican common man seems to take in his trials and tribulations (and remember there are no press agents and spin doctors involved here, it's all spontaneously generated) looks certain to continue for a long while.

What do the women think about a song like this? Judging by how they fill the dance floors when it comes on and sing along to every line, they must love it.

While not perhaps the most talented deejay Jamaica has produced, Shabba is certainly one of the most disciplined. Almost every dancehall fan will tell you that Shabba can't hold a candle to Buju or Ninja on stage. But by listening to management and channelling his not inconsiderable abilities into well produced and packaged songs, Shabba managed to become the first dancehall star to have an international impact, and won back-to-back Reggae Grammys in 1992 and 1993.

1991 / **STRIVE**
Shinehead

1991 / **BIG AND BROAD**
Heavy D / Super Cat / Frankie Paul

Shinehead and Heavy D are both Jamaicans who emigrated to the U.S. as youngsters and seem equally at home with dancehall and rap. Heavy D of course is a genuine rap superstar with a number of platinum and gold albums. In the early 1990s he was named president of Uptown Records. It couldn't have been the money why he started dabbling in dancehall in 1991. But something in the music attracted him, and he was quoted as saying, 'Dancehall is way ahead of rap.'

Frankie Paul, who was born blind, was one of the biggest dancehall singers of the eighties, but has not released that much lately. Super Cat, whose self-appointed 'apache' nickname comes from his half-Indian ancestry, is one of the shrewder minds in dancehall and cunningly releases only one or two well produced tunes a year. He thus avoids the fate of so many deejays who get hot, let go a slew of underproduced tunes, see their novelty fade and hear the public cry – 'Him done'.

Heavy D, dancehall dabbler and above, Super Cat

1991 / **HALF IDIOT**
Cutty Ranks and Marcia Griffiths

Cutty Ranks' combination version with Marcia Griffiths of Bob Andy's original 'Fire Burning' was a huge hit in 1991. This is how Andy feels about deejay versions of his songs: 'If they think it enhances it and it helps sales, it's all right by me. It's heartening to know that your work can trigger that kind of inspiration. I respect and have appreciation for the things that are done in the singjay and deejay style, but it's difficult to compare them to singing done to an arrangement or rhythmic structure. But I see deejaying as poetry to some extent.'

And it must be admitted that Cutty Ranks, gruff, staight ahead bulldozer chanting lends a menacing force to this song. When Bob Andy or even Marcia Griffiths sings it alone, 'Fire Burning' is a warning. Cutty Ranks makes it a threat.

1991 / **STRANGE**
Papa San

One of the more unusual reggae tunes cut in the 1990s, 'Strange' reminds you of a country and western 'spoken ballad', but has a definite dancehall feel. It highlights the versatility of Papa San, who is as talented a deejay as there is and certainly the most inventive tongue twister of them all. 'I Will Survive', 'Style and Fashion', 'Strange', 'Maddy Maddy Cry', and 'Acid' are all

Papa San, and Chaka Demus, right.

totally different songs, but each was a big dancehall hit.

1992 / **HOT THIS YEAR**
Dirtsman

Dirtsman, the brother of top deejay Papa San, was a mostly second-rank deejay before 'busting out' with 'Hot This Year', a gritty chant of 'watch out world, here I come' defiance. Not that he had much time to enjoy his success. Barely a year later he was gunned down in circumstances still unexplained.

1992 / **MURDER SHE WROTE**
Chaka Demus & Pliers

A star in Jamaica since 1987, Chaka Demus broke into the big time in combination with the smooth voiced Pliers, scoring several top five UK hits and actually topping the charts with 'Twist and Shout' in 1993. While Pliers is a good singer it is definitely Chaka who gives the duo their magic. Vocally he is perhaps the most viscerally exciting of all deejays, and his cutting, sharp edged bass sends a thrilling surge of energy through his material.

WHY DON'T I HATE DANCEHALL?

In bad moods it's not difficult to dislike Jamaicans or their music. Loud, crude and irritating are the words that spring to mind as some idiot minibus driver cuts you off, blowing his horn and swearing at the top of his voice, while the damned repetitive, pounding bass and guttural shouting of what seems like a million radios (and you can't get away from it because it's everywhere) hammers your brain cells dead.

Yet at other times Jamaicans seem so exuberant, so ready to argue their convictions, so quick to laugh at life, so totally at ease with themselves and the world, that it's hard not to think of them as the most enjoyable people on earth. And dancehall, which reflects all these qualities, feels like the most invigourating music the times have to offer.

Sometimes primitive, repetitious and obscene, dancehall can also be utterly compelling. Unsophisticated it may be, but dancehall has genuine energy. It's a spontaneous expression of a people's emotions, not some plastic, soulless Madison Avenue creation about as meaningful to its audience as a stick of chewing gum.

Music obviously reflects a peoples' character, perhaps it is the most profound reflection. And music's primary role will always be to give convincing expressions of emotions, to express what people feel but cannot themselves describe. What we like most in dancehall is its utter emotional honesty, the fearlessness with which it dis-cusses almost any issue and situation, and the willingness to laugh at any and everything – the same reasons we like Jamaican people.

No one at all in touch with Jamaica as it is (as opposed to how they wish it to be) can doubt that today dancehall is the music of the masses; the music that moves them, that expresses their feelings, that mirrors their social reality. The deejays talk about what they see and experience. Some bleat about 'sexism' and 'racism', and the 'punnany' and gun business may be unpleasant. But reality is reality. No sensible person advocates slackness and gun talk, especially on radio. But there must be a good reason why it's popular in the dancehalls.

According to deejay Super Cat 'It's from people coming out of the street. Out of the ghetto. And these are not people that live soft. They live hard. Suffer hard. So what they got to sing about is nothing too soft. They singing about everyday living. Sufferation. What's going on in the ghetto. Guns. Drugs . . . It's not glorifying it [violence]. The youths are saying, the guns are here. Don't think we live in a bed of roses in this world. Because the people who manufacture gun is never going to stop. The gun was never made in the ghetto. If you look at a gun you see "Made in Japan" or "Made in Germany or America". None of the gun ever say "Made in Jamaica". But they all come here.'

They say talking never solves anything, but by speaking about national problems and concerns via music, Jamaica has surely avoided some of the social explosions that pent up frustrations have caused in other countries. Rap artists in America who talked about race problems were accused of fostering racism. But after the 1992 riots in Los Angeles, they seemed more like prophets. Sweeping dust under a carpet doesn't mean the dust disappears.

1993 / **ACTION**
Terror Fabulous and Nadine Sutherland

1993 / **SWEAT**
Inner Circle

Jamaican men, to hear them talk at any rate, are extremely confident of their sexual abilities and consider themselves indisputably the world's best lovers. The lyrics from these songs say it all: *Action, not a bag a mouth / Action make the gal them bust out / Sweet loving like the falling rain /* *Sweet loving to mix up her brain* – and – *Girl I'm gonna make you sweat / Sweat till you can't sweat no more / And if you cry out / I'm gonna push it, push it some more.*

They say it's not boasting if you can back-up your promises. Yet a survey of Caribbean women, in which a large number of respondents were Jamaican, reported that they considered their male counterparts poor lovers. To quote one: 'Men are stupid. They want us to make plenty noise. So we make plenty noise so that

JAMAICAN HOMOPHOBIA

Buju Banton is possibly as good a deejay as Jamaica has produced. When 'Boom Bye Bye' became a hit in 1992, Buju was cementing his status as Jamaica's most popular artist and just beginning to tour abroad. Shabba Ranks had won the first of his Reggae Grammys and had become an almost international star. Buju, some said, might be even bigger. Then 'Boom Bye Bye's lyrics caught the attention of homosexual groups in America and Britain.

majority in favour of jailing homosexuals. Indeed a 1996 poll indicated that 96 per cent of Jamaicans were against homosexual relationships being legalised. The dancehall is full of songs condemning homosexuality and no stage show goes by without at least one ringing condemnation which inevitably draws a huge chorus of approval from the crowd.

Apparently advocating the killing of homosexuals, the song understandably became embroiled in controversy. *Newsweek* condemned the song as 'hatefilled'. (Ironically it's a pretty lousy song. Apart from the notorious chorus – *Boom Bye Bye inna batty boy head / Rude boy haffi know say nasty man fe dead* – it's just monotonous chatter over a rather boring rhythm)

Sporadic protests began at Buju's concerts, often led by ACT UP. Then Shabba Ranks was asked his opinion of the song by a U.K. journalist. He volunteered that he agreed with the song because, in his words: 'God created Adam and Eve, not Adam and Steve'.

Suddenly Shabba's concerts started drawing large-scale 'gay' protests and pressure from these organisations forced the cancellation of a number of his shows. Shabba at first was unrepentant. But management deemed it prudent for him to apologise and he not only retracted his statements, but agreed to work with gay groups in promoting homosexual tolerance. His concerts were now able to proceed in peace. Buju's reaction was the opposite. He continued to condemn homosexuality. His culture did not accept such behaviour, he said. Unlike Shabba, his shows continued to be dogged by protests.

The reaction in Jamaica to these events was straightforward. Shabba Ranks lost credibility in the eyes of the dancehall massive. 'Shabba bow' was the common view. He had given in to foreign and economic pressure and betrayed his beliefs. Buju on the other hand became an even greater idol of the masses – a man who put his money where his mouth was.

The militantly anti-homosexual attitude of Jamaicans, men and women alike, is startling. Few subjects arouse such strong emotions here and polls have shown a strong

A newspaper report in early 1993 that the government was thinking of legalising same sex relationships was met with such overwhelming and vocal public disapproval that the prime minister's office quickly made a statement disavowing any such plan. For weeks radio talk show lines were jammed with callers denouncing the government for even considering such a proposal. Rumours of a planned 'Gay Pride' march drew a large crowd of stick-wielding protesters, although no gays actually turned up.

In January 1996 a concert was held in aid of the Jamaican Council of Human Rights which was, and remains, in danger of closing for lack of funding. To quote from a newspaper review (and any irony is clearly unintentional): 'It was not just another reggae concert, but a medium to expound on society's double standards, prevailing inhumane circumstances and social injustice . . . Most of the night's performances could be felt from the soul. Each word uttered spoke to the suffering of the downtrodden, and each message concurred to touch the inner conscience . . . The Exterminator Crew kicked off the night's proceedings with the highly religious Jesse Jenda'u . . . [who] launched into his sermon pronouncing damnation on homosexuals and the wrongdoings of Babylon. He read scriptures

from the Bible to substantiate his declaration that all homosexuals should be put to death.'

What accounts for this virulent strain of homophobia? Some psychologists, accurately or not, attribute this to a lack of real male self-confidence in a society where 85 per cent of children are born out of wedlock, and the vast majority of boys lack full-time male role models while growing up. Perhaps the Jamaican male penchant for rambunctious displays of exaggerated machismo is an overcompensation for deep-rooted uncertainties.

But a line in 'Boom Bye Bye' touches on another aspect of Jamaican antihomosexuality: *Woman a the most beautiful thing God ever put pon the land / Me love her from her head down to her foot bottom.* For despite a certain misogynistic streak, the accepted creed of the dancehall is that for good or bad, women must be the most important thing in any man's life. Any other attitude is contrary to the father's plan. This is why 'slackness' in the dancehall finds favour with many young female patrons, who reportedly are the biggest fans of 'slackness' and buy the most records of this type. (What women do hate is 'gun talk' lyrics.)

Indeed there is almost a flaunting of female sexuality in dancehall fashion. One of Jamaica's biggest celebrities throughout the nineties has been Carlene, 'the dancehall queen', whose main claim to fame was a superbly rounded shape, a flair for skimpy 'dancehall' designs, and outstanding 'whining' (dancing) ability. The 'Butterfly' dance craze of 1993 and 1994 was almost solely restricted to females. Some expressed amazement that women should so willingly degrade themselves. But the girls and women who thrust out their posterioral charms while rhythmically closing and opening their legs obviously felt otherwise, seeming to revel in the lustful stares of transfixed male onlookers. Apparently sex to Jamaican women is not vulnerability, but a source of female power. They hate homosexuality perhaps even more than the men do, possibly seeing it as a threat to female sexual sovereignty.

Of course non-Jamaicans can get a wrong impression about Jamaica's attitude towards homosexuals from songs like 'Boom Bye Bye'. What such songs are condemning is not so much homosexuality as open homosexuality. Some very prominent personalities and politicians are strongly suspected to be gay and yet are accorded respect and voted for by the public. Jamaicans are not exactly gunning down known gays in the street or fire bombing their homes. The public seems prepared to accept homosexuality as long as it's not made an open issue. The common feeling seems to be that 'Maybe them people can't help it. But them must hold them little corner. Why them want to push it down people's throats when God almighty condemn it?'

The whole topic would certainly provide extremely interesting material for a very brave psychology doctoral student.

Dancehall Queen turned media celebrity, Carlene

they can finish fast because it is painful and all they want to do is bang, bang.' (Perhaps this is why Lady Saw does songs like 'If You Can't Do the Work, Then Make A Next Man Try'.)

The male reaction to the study was predictable. (Not that a lot paid attention to it.) 'Men tend to resent the notion that they are not the wonderful lovers they think they are.' But one has to ask, if Jamaican women really feel their men are lousy lovers, where did Jamaican men get this exalted impression of their libidinal skills? Well, as a frank Jamaican lady told us: 'Look, men's brains are in their pants. To get anything from them you have to full their belly. And believe me, food alone is not going to fill these guys' belly! But when you finish and tell them "Oh darling, you are the only man who can satisfy me," and you see them smile to themselves, you know things ready to let off.'

On the other hand, the flocks of female tourists in Negril seem to confirm Jamaican men's high opinions of themselves. Maybe Jamaican women are just hard to please?

Terror Fabulous and Nadine Sutherland

THE DEEJAY AS FOLK POET — TONY REBEL

Those who claim the music has only gone backwards since the golden era of Bob, Toots and Jimmy should compare 'One Day' to Jimmy Cliff's 'You Can Get It', popularly regarded as a reggae classic. The messages are similar, endurance in the face of hardship. Yet the two songs are in the same class. And 'One Day' has much more lyrical depth. It's interesting too to compare the language ofboth. Cliff's song is framed in 'text book' English and grammatically correct throughout.

> Persecution you must fear / Win and lose you've got
> to get your share
> Put your mind set on a dream / You can get it as
> hard as it seems . . .
> Rome was not built in a day / Opposition will come
> your way
> But the harder the battle you see / The sweeter the
> victory

Tony Rebels' song incorporates the language of everyday Jamaican conversation:

> You must always be optimistic / Inna you thought
> Check the future a go better than the past
> Anything you do you do it / Straight from the heart
> And tek weh you get / Till you get what you want . . .
> You might get up every day / And see things a run
> And question yourself say / How you no get none
> But, humble daughter, patient son / Soon and very soon
> Fi you slice a go come . . .

at the same time sounding highly literate:

> Mi say you must have aspirations and dreams
> And if so be the case / Well you better make haste
> Find the ways and means . . .
> Cause the wickedest thing / Is when you don't
> have hope
> And you full of despair / And you receive and
> get deceive
> And you just don't believe / That you can reach
> somewhere

In its creative use of Jamaican vernacular 'One Day' ranks with anything Louise Bennett or Bob Marley ever did. And Tony Rebel gets his messages across because he accepts that tastes change and that a musician's first job is to please his audience: 'Right now the people's heart is in the computer riddim. After this get old too, maybe they're going to combine this one now with that old one, and a different sound will come forward . . . Everything is just a whole evolution of the music, just like how we used to have ska and rocksteady, and now it's dancehall. This deejay thing evolve from everything and maybe down the road something else. The change is all around and the change is rapid.

'The most important thing in the music is what you're saying, so to get what you're saying across, put it to the kind of music that people like . . . People want to hear the words, but they want to hear the kind of music they like, and we have to listen to them.

'People accept the beat and the melodious sound you bring across on the beat. So whether a cultural song, or a slackness song, or whatever, once you get it across on the riddim that people can dance to, they will accept it. Why put it on a riddim that nobody going to dance to? When people hear a nice riddim that keep them going, that's the one they're going to buy, because when people go to a party, they want to hear something lively. I'm in the style just like any deejay, and on the same riddim, but I'm sending a message.'

Tony Rebel is a man of firm convictions. He was a practicing and preaching Rastafarian long before deejays like Capleton and Buju Banton began espousing spirituality and celebrating Jah and Haille Sellasie in the dancehall. As he says in his 1994 hit 'Nazerite Vow' — *Say we no bow, we no gow, ras then, ras now / Long time me tek fi me Nazarine Vow.*

His songs draw vivid and accessible portraits of the ghetto view on life, forcefully conveying its wants, problems and pleasures in the language it speaks. 'Reggae Pon Top', 'Sweet Jamaica', 'Nazerite Vow', 'Fresh Vegetable', 'Chatty Chatty', 'Vibes of The Time', 'Teach The Children' and 'Jah by My Side' all display a biting, witty and incisive intelligence. No one has addressed the broad concerns of poor Jamaicans in the 1990s more profoundly.

As he says: 'Dancehall artists need to know their responsibility. They need to realize the power of words. They need to realize how influential music is, how music can give people strength and how it can weaken them too. They are like the watchmen of the city and they are supposed to sound the trumpet and if they don't, the guilt will be on their shoulders.'

1993 / **ONE DAY**
Tony Rebel

Everybody bawling one day one day
Everybody hoping somehow some day

The theme song of every Jamaican musician who ever clawed his way out of the ghetto. Lots of would be singers have talent. But the one who made it have something more; they had the determination to be a success and the will to never give up.

1993 / **HELLO MAMA AFRICA**
Garnett Silk

1995 / **IT'S ME AGAIN JAH**
Luciano

A few years ago reggae singers seemed an endangered species in Jamaica, especially 'conscious' singers singing about spiritual realities. But in the last few years there has been a remarkable flowering of 'roots' artists. Garnett Silk was one of the brightest stars in years, and more than a few people saw traces of Bob Marley in him. Alas he died tragically in December 1994 in an accidental fire.

Luciano seems to have taken up where Garnett left off. As he says: 'Garnett was more like a brother, a father, a tutor, and a forerunner.

That's why I took the forty day break this summer. It was a kind of fuel I needed to energise myself. When he moved on I knew the work for me became harder still.'

Luciano has released a number of excellent songs which manage to combine spiritual messages and good music – not a very common combination in reggae today. His lovely 'It's Me Again Jah' would not be out of place in any church and easily holds its own against any 'roots' classic. His 'Where There Is Life' was one of 1995's best local albums, and Luciano is certainly reggae's most promising singer.

Garnett Silk

Blues and reggae seem to manifest almost opposite sensibilities. One is inward looking, pessimistic, unhopeful of change; the other assertive, sometimes aggressive, and essentially optimistic. But they share certain similarities. Both were created by the poorest strata of former plantation slaves. Blues and reggae artists sing primarily about personal ordeals – things seen or experienced, matters that affect them directly. And a startling number of major artists in both genres have died in violent circumstances – from Pinetop 'Boogie Woogie' Smith, Sonny Boy Williamson and Little Walter to Peter Tosh, Tenor Saw and Dirtsman.

The resemblances between dancehall deejays and blues singers are even more striking. One marked common heritage is the artist as literal outlaw – Lead Belly being jailed, more than once, for murder; Super Cat allegedly gunning down fellow deejay Nitty Gritty in supposed self-defence. Another is the common adoption of unconventional stage names. (In this respect there is a curious difference between deejays and reggae singers, who usually use their given names. And the aliases they do adopt are 'regular', like Jimmy Cliff or Bob Andy.) Compare Bounty Killer, Admiral Bailey and Yellowman to Muddy Waters, Howling Wolf and Lead Belly. A third is the insistence on self-written material – blues singers, at least until the 1950s, nearly always wrote their own material, or at least reworked it into an original form; while no deejay worthy of the name copies anyman's lyrics. (Yet reggae singers do covers, perhaps too regularly.)

Like some of the greatest blues singers, many deejays cannot read and write. Which may account for the emotional directness and total lack of self-consciousness of both musics – feelings pass straight from artist's brain to his audience without being filtered through pen and paper. Of course there is probably some trade off between subtlety and emotional force.

Blues singers as a whole, even when hugely popular with their native working-class audiences, never quite gained respectability and were never embraced by middle-class black America. And so it is with the deejays, who are almost folk heroes with the masses, their numerous brushes with the law constantly drawing front page coverage. But 'decent' people have little good to say about deejays, unless of course the foreign media embrace them, as with Shabba Ranks.

Interestingly, the 'one of us' identification deejays elicit from the ghetto massives seems to be lost with uptown and foreign acceptance. Shabba Ranks has won two reggae Grammys and became almost an international celebrity, appearing in *Time* and *Newsweek*, but has been rejected by the masses on stage (though partly because he is not a good live performer). In 1990 he was literally 'bottled' off stage. He appeared at Reggae Sumfest in 1994, but hardly caused a sensation. Ninja Man on the other hand has never come close to having a foreign hit, and the biggest news he ever made abroad was to get jailed for a year on gun charges in the U.S. Yet Ninja remains an idol of the masses, the 'Don Gorgon' champion of live stage shows.

It might seem difficult to discern a musical similarity between the blues' melancholy brooding and dancehall's almost arrogant exuberance. Yet there is a common thread of complete emotional honesty and openness. There are no taboos – nothing is too commonplace, too ridiculous or too obscene to be commented on. More than any other musical forms, the blues and dancehall express the Roman poet Terrence's philosophy – *Homo sum: humani nila me alienum puto* – I am a man: nothing human is alien to me.

1994 / **GOOD LIFE**
Coco Tea

There is a curious dichotomy in dancehall music. At any given moment in time, the biggest stars of the day are always deejays. And it is definitely the deejays who the common man identifies with. Every fan will have his favourite – you hear people saying 'Ninja a me deejay! or 'A Buju me rate!' And nothing draws a bigger stage show crowd than the promise of a 'clash' between two top deejays.

Yet although singers seem not to arouse the same fervour, they tend to have a far longer shelf life. Coco Tea is a prime example. While he has never been a 'superstar' in terms of chart hits or stage show drawing power, he has managed for some 15 years to produce consistently good tunes that keep him in demand both on the radio and the live circuit. Yet deejays who were hot when he first started out – like Lui Lepke, Lone Ranger, Nigger Kojak, Eeka Mouse – have been almost totally forgotten. Eeka Mouse is an particularly instructive case in point. In 1981 he

Capleton

was one of the hottest deejays in the country with one of the year's biggest hits in 'Wa Do Dem'. Yet at Sting 1995, when he tried to gain entrance into the V.I.P. section, he was ignored by media and promoters and turned away by security asking, 'Who you think you is?' It must be tough being an 'old' deejay.

1994 / TOUR
Capleton

Capleton is one of the most popular of 'conscious' deejays, and 'Tour' was a big hit both here and abroad. Some say that if Buju Banton is dancehall's Bob Marley, then Capleton is its Peter Tosh

1994 / CAN'T EVEN WALK
The Grace Thrillers

Early gospel music in Jamaica was essentially an American bequest. But over the years gospel music has both grown in popularity and become more Jamaican. According to author Peter Manuel: 'Often associated with Pentecostal congregations, gospel in Jamaica has assimilated both black and rural white gospel styles from the United States and blended them with various other foreign and local influences. Stylistically speaking, much of this music is quite close to reggae, but with certain distinguishing features,

such as differently accentuated drum patterns, a busy tambourine, and prominent clapping. Many top reggae session musicians are heard on these Revivalist-influenced Christian recordings.'

Many people, including a lot of non-believers, consider that local gospel music today is of a higher musical standard and at least as creative as dancehall. The nation's best known gospel aggregation is The Grace Thrillers, founded by Noel Willis in 1971. A group consisting of four musicians and six singers, Grace Thrillers might well be the most popular and original band in the country. Certainly the excitement they create at their shows puts those of Third World, Chalice and Mystic Revealers to shame.

The Grace Thrillers

'Can't Even Walk' is a hymn written by Americans and has no reggae beat. Yet there is something unmistakably Jamaican in The Grace Thrillers' unhurried styling and slightly hesitating rhythms. It's become virtually the national anthem of gospel in Jamaica and is arguably the most widely popular song produced here in the last decade. You certainly don't have to be a Christian to find it extremely moving.

DANCEHALL SOCA — WEST INDIAN MUSICAL FUSION

Byron Lee is a musical survivor. While the other bands of the early 1960s have long since disbanded, the one bearing his name is the most popular in Jamaica. But now it plays mostly soca, the calypso derived music of the pre-Lenten Trinidad Carnival which has made such a big impression on Jamaica in the past five years.

Byron Lee virtually created carnival in Jamaica. He began playing soca here years before most Jamaicans knew anything about it. (In the conscious 1970s, calypso was despised here as too frivolous and light-hearted, irrelevant to the people's struggles. But times have changed.) And it was he who organised the carnival road march here.

A lot of people maintained that while carnival might work for the peaceful Trinidadians, Jamaicans were too aggressive for such a mass spectacle and fights would break out all over the place. Byron Lee had faith in the common Jamaican man and every carnival has gone without a hitch. It's now the biggest musical event of the year, more universally enjoyed than Festival, Sunsplash or Sting. The ironic thing about all this is how Lee's role has been reversed. While in the early days of ska he was mainly responsible for taking it from downtown to uptown, with soca he has done the opposite.

Because for a long time soca was popular only with the Jamaican upper-classes. With that snobbishness so prevalent among the rich everywhere, they sneered at dancehall and adopted soca as 'their' music. Dancehall was all slackness, they sniffed, while gyrating and 'winding' with wild abandon to suggestive soca rhythms. The small carnivals held here, apart from the student carnival at the University of the West Indies, were completely upper-class events. Their road marches were almost comical, confining themselves to the upper-class residential areas – true 'white and light brown' affairs.

In 1990 Byron Lee organised his carnival on Constant Spring Road, a thoroughfare frequented by all classes. Jamaica Carnival was attended not by hundreds of the well to do, but by hundreds of thousands of people from every walk of life. The detractors and naysayers were proven wrong as the entire city of Kingston partied in unison. Police called it the biggest mass gathering in the country's history as a quarter million spectators lined the entire route twenty deep.

Soca has become so popular that some musical chauvinists fret about it supplanting reggae in the popular esteem. Which is nonsense to any sane observer. Jamaicans gladly embrace soca during their carnival, just after Easter. But since new soca songs come out only once a year, they grow tired of them after a month and turn back to their staple diet of dancehall, where new releases never stop coming.

At any rate Byron Lee had once again played a decisive social role in uniting the musical tastes of differing classes, this time going top down instead of bottom up. But the story doesn't end there. As with everything they touch, Jamaicans began altering soca to suit their own preferences. And little by little dancehall rhythms began creeping into soca. (Of course in Trinidad dancehall is the most popular music outside of carnival time, so they too had dancehall influenced soca songs.)

Byron Lee's live shows always incorporate snatches of current dancehall hits into his soca repertoire. And in 1993, the biggest soca hit in Jamaica was 'Dancehall Soca Bogle', based on the dancehall craze, The Bogle. In 1994 it was 'Soca Butterfly', after another exceptionally suggestive dance. 'Soca Tatty' followed suite in 1995. All three combined dancehall chanting and a rugged soca beat. Red Plastic Bag's 'Ragga Ragga' did the same thing while making good-natured fun of 'ragga' (as dancehall is called in England and some parts of the English Caribbean) and was a smash hit all across the West Indies in 1994.

Some people think it's a wonderful combination. Dancehall's raw authenticity lends a visceral substance to what is essentially a good time music, while soca's more carefully crafted melodies and harmonies, especially its brilliant use of horns, gives a bright exuberance to dancehall. Who knows, the combination might be the sound of the future. And if it is, we will have Byron Lee to thank.

1994 / **MURDERER**
Buju Banton

Author Lorna Gunst titled her investigation into Jamaican criminal gangs *Born Fi Dead* after a poem written by a poet she knew only as Wayne. Now one of the authors knows this poet very well, indeed they are closer even than brothers. So in tribute to this ghetto bard, we enclose here the poem in its entirety. (Certainly no song captures the poem's spirit more accurately than 'Murderer'.)

> Nihilist?
> Lumpen?
> Uptown bullshit!
>
> Respeck I ah deal wid.
> respeck mi area,
> repeck mi don,
> repseck mi bredren,
> repeck mi woman.
>
> Dis mi,
> an yuh mamam papa granny pickney a go feel it.
>
> Dis mi, boom bullet fire!
> It no matter, I have a dog heart.
>
> If mi dead, ah so!
> Man born fi dead.
>
> Accepting the offering,
> Papa Ogun sits on his hilltop,
> wondering when his own mortality
> will be tested.
>
> And in history's dustbin,
> Marx bides his time

1995 / **CELLULAR PHONE**
Bounty Killer

Remarkably, Jamaican artists today earn most of their money performing live. Records basically serve only as advertisements. Even a number one song probably won't make any money unless it 'bust a foreign'. But a hit does serve notice that the artist is hot and therefore can command large fees at sound clashes and stage shows. And of course singers and especially deejays also earn money with 'dubplate specials', versions of their hit songs recorded for specific sound system sets.

The declining Jamaican dollar (which went from J$5.50 to US$1 in 1989 to 40:1 at the end of 1995, then down a touch to 35:1 at the end of 1996) has so pushed up costs that producers of 45s rarely even cover expenses. Declining sales have made matters worse. Apparently Jamaicans prefer hearing their favourite songs at dances and shows. The only two songs in the last ten years to sell more than 30,000 copies have been Sophia George's 'Girlie Girlie' in '85 and Lovindeer's 'Wild Gilbert' in '88. The biggest selling record of 1995 was 'Anything For You' by Snow and friends with 22,299 copies. When you consider that over 22,000 attended Sting 95, it's clear that even Bounty Killer, the top-selling deejay of 1995, probably earned more in that one night than with his biggest hit of the year, 'Cellular Phone', which only sold about 14,000 copies.

1995 / **SLAM**
Beenie Man

Gimme the gal with the wickedest slam
The kind a gal who know how to love up she man
And if you want to get the medal
You haffi get the slam from a real ghetto gal
If you want to get the pedal and wheel
If you want to get you banana peel
If you want know how good loving feel
You haffi get a gal who live a Maxfield

Beenie Man

The most popular song for many a year, 'Slam' was so hot that Beenie Man – the fashionable deejay of the moment – cut a 'Slam Part 2' which also hit the charts. In one week in early 1995 each of the three major newspapers carried columns analysing the song's implications. It was generally seen as an acknowledgement that in Jamaica, sexual power and mystique are potent substitutes for economic power.

In any other country 'Slam' would probably be considered racist, sexist and elitist. And there might be a few Jamaicans who think this is so. But whenever the song is played at a party or dance women – young, old, black, white, rich, poor, uptown, downtown – squeal with delight and begin 'winding' to its suggestive rhythms. The men, well we stand up and watch. It's not a song a man can dance to without feeling rather silly. We once tried telling a group of young women that this song denigrates all Jamaican females, but our argument tended to dissolve amidst the peals of high-pitched laughter.

1995 / BOOMBASTIC
Shaggy
1995 / UNTOLD STORIES
Buju Banton

In 1995 Shaggy and Buju Banton were the two biggest names in reggae. Yet both made their

names in contrasting manner. Shaggy has concentrated on the international market and succeeded in coupling an authentic dancehall feel and accent with commercial pop showmanship. At one time it seemed he might well become dancehall's first legitimate international superstar.

On the other hand, Buju Banton was the voice of Jamaica. His ground breaking 1995 album 'Til Shiloh' caused many to acclaim 'the Gargaumel' as the Bob Marley of dancehall, and certainly he has acquired something of the prophet's mantle. Ironically, 'Til Shiloh', which Jamaican critics unanimously considered the best reggae album in years, was not even nominated for the Reggae Grammy. Many suspect that Buju's unrepentant attitude concerning the 'Boom Bye Bye' affair in 1992 has not been forgotten in international entertainment circles.

'Boombastic' and 'Untold Stories' capture Shaggy and Buju's contrasting personas. A good-natured 'champion lover' boast, 'Boombastic' couched its lewdity in harmless sounding metaphors – *You are the bun and me a the cheese* and *Just like a turtle crawling out of my shell*. Prepubescent girls the world over sang along to the catchy beat, probably thinking that 'Mr boombastic, Mr fantastic' likely referred to the deejay's dancing abilities. Shaggy laughed all the way to the bank.

'Untold Stories' on the other hand was a hard-core 'suffarah' song with acoustic guitar under-tones reminiscent of Marley's 'Redemption Song'. Some prominent Jamaican businessmen were so taken with it that they acclaimed Buju a prophet. But does it really take a seer to realise that there are a lot of poor people in Jamaica having a hard time of it? Is this news? It will be interesting to see how both songs sound a few years down the road. A nonsense song it may be, but 'Mr Boombastic' has a certain musical wit. Although it's undoubtedly and earnestly socially relevant, 'Untold Stories' is a bit stagnant melod-ically and limited in tonal variety. When the message comes before the music, a song rarely ages well

1995 / **GLORY BE TO GOD**
Lady Saw

The most popular female deejay in reggae history, Lady Saw created a sensation when she burst on the scene in 1993. Not necessarily because she was talented, but because her material was extremely salacious. The press condemned her roundly and some bands refused to back her. Frankly there seemed to have been some sort of double standard at work, because many male deejays have done songs just as coarse without arousing such an outcry. Regardless, the

Lady Saw

public lapped her up, and continues to be a big draw. It's unfortunate that Lady Saw made her name as 'the queen of slackness' and has been almost typecast as such. Because she is a dynamic stage performer, a top-notch riddim-rider and her lyrics demonstrate excellent word play. There is probably no better deejay in Jamaica right now, male or female.

Unusually for a deejay, she also has a pretty good voice. Indeed she had her biggest hit in 1996 as a singer with 'Give Me A Reason', which won her a number of awards as vocalist of the year. And for all her fame as the dirty lyrics lady, perhaps Lady Saw's most creative work was 'Glory Be To God', which works both on the secular and sacred level. It's a stirring praise song which also makes you want to bounce and sing. A joyful noise onto the Lord indeed.

1996 / NUFF GAL
Beenie Man

It's no secret that there is a double standard for men and women in Jamaica when it comes to sex. But never is it more blatantly revealed than in songs like 'Nuff Gal'. A 1995 dancehall hit 'Sketel Boom', threw scorn on women who have more than one man at a time. Yet 'Nuff Gal' positively celebrates male promiscuity. The astonishing thing is that these songs were just as popular with the women as with the men, perhaps even more so.

Polygamy seems to be unofficially accepted in Jamaica. The 'wifey' and 'matey' phenomenon is all but institutionalised. 'Wifey' is the main woman, to whom the man may or may not be legally wed. 'Matey' is the number two girl. Of course, a lot of men have more than one 'matey', and it has become such a part of the Jamaican vernacular, that anything second best is likely to be described by the adjective 'matey'. So 'matey' shoes means a type of cheap footwear. Enlightened, liberal, forward-thinking men and women naturally condemn such neanderthal attitudes. In civilised socities, surely men should be ruled by the large head, not the small one. But when women sing-a-long lustily to lyrics like – *Man fe*

have nuff gal and Gal inna bungle / gal from Rema and gal from Jungle / nuff gal and none a them mustn't grumble / all ghetto youth come take me example – and – *one-burner businesss can't run things again / Man fe have bout fifty gal friend –* what kind of message are they are sending to their male counterparts?

On the other hand, as a world-weary friend commented, maybe outsiders have no business trying to teach old dogs new tricks. If both male and female denizens of the dancehall are comfortable with the philosophies expressed in songs like 'Nuff Gal', who is to tell them they are wrong?

1996 / LIVING DANGEROUSLY
Barrington Levy and Bounty Killer

'Living Dangerously' was the biggest selling record in 1996 and voted song of the year in most awards. Yet the critics gave it mixed reviews. Many thought it a pretty good song – nice beat, strongly sung and exciting deejaying. But others saw it as a somewhat crude cover of an American original and were inclined to wonder if Bounty Killer's rather toneless deejaying added anything musically. But these things are always hard to judge so close up. Who knows, ten years hence 'Living Dangerously' might be deemed a classic. Maybe the naysayers are just getting on in years. As some wag once remarked, something

Barrington Levy

Everton Blender

horrible always seems to happen to popular music when you reach 35 or so.

1996 / WHY BE AFRAID (JAH BY MY SIDE)
Tony Rebel

1996 / GHETTO PEOPLE SING
Everton Blender

Somehow reggae artists consistently manage to create completely different-sounding songs using exactly the same riddim. 'Why Be Afraid' and 'Ghetto People Sing' are two excellent cases in point. Both are top-notch tunes likely to be enjoyed years from now. As long as dancehall keeps producing such tuneful, thought-provoking songs, the doomsayers anxious to perfrom reggae's last rights are in for a very long wait.

1996 / FIRE PON ROME
Anthony B

As befits a people who seem to count animated, hand-waving, on-top-of-the-voice conversation as one of their two favourite pastimes, the press in Jamaica is probably as free as any in the world. Occasionally, thin-skinned politicians attempt to bridle abrasive journalists in court, but such cases never amount to much. Certain quarters see the supposed sexual obsession of newspapers like *X-News* and *Hardcore* as evidence of excessive freedom, but that is surely for the public to decide.

Jamaica's attachment to freedom of speech is most clearly seen in its music. No forum could

Anthony B

conceivably address a broader range of societal concerns than dancehall, where songs addressing current incidents and issues are cut on an almost daily basis. The government attempts to set limits on the parameters of debate by occasionally banning from radio airplay songs deemed potential disturbances to the social order. These

'not fit for airplay' songs generally fall into two categories, sexually explicit or socially disturbing. There is no controversy about the first type. What is acceptable for mature, consenting adult ears can not always be suitable for a public medium listened to by all ages.

But certain songs are banned from the radio

DANCEHALL QUEEN

'The Harder They Come', 1972, was the first fully Jamaican-produced movie. An exciting and engrossing film blessed with a superb sound track, it became a minor cult classic, one of the most famous movies to come out of the third world. Jamaican film has not reached such heights again. 'Smile Orange', 'Countryman' and 'Rockers' were all passable low budget efforts. But the highly hyped 'The Lunatic' in 1990 was a disappointment. 1995's 'Klash' featured big name foreign stars, but proved an unwatchable disaster.

So when 'Dancehall Queen' was screened in 1997, few held their breath. The producers reportedly made only three prints, expecting the film to go almost straight to video release. Yet 'Dancehall Queen' surprised everyone by becoming the most popular local film since 'The Harder They Come', and deservedly so. Despite certain plot flaws and less than big budget production effects, this excellently acted movie managed to portray life in the Kingston of 1997 as vividly as 'Harder' did life in 1972. The names and faces and dress styles were different, but the underlying realities of the ghetto seemed hardly to have changed at all.

Strictly as film, there is not much to choose between the two. Both are emotionally compelling social documents but neither is a cinematic masterpiece. But what lifts 'Harder' to another plane and makes it a riveting and memorable experience is its soundtrack, which includes some of the best popular music produced anywhere. Every song is a reggae classic and for sheer consistent quality no other Jamaican album comes close. Sad to say the 'Dancehall Queen' soundtrack is not in the same league. It is pretty representative of the current dancehall scene and does capture some moments of raw energy, but most of the songs are forgettable.

In a sense the comparison is unfair. 'The Harder They Come' collected some of the cream of reggae's golden years from 1967 to 1971 with only the title track being a new song. 'Dancehall Queen' mixed some recent hits with songs created for the movie. Furthermore, in 1972 relatively few persons controlled reggae

production and it was easy to get the rights to a collection of big hits. Indeed Dynamic Sounds controlled all the songs on 'The Harder They Come' (which is probably why there are no Treasure Isle or Studio One of Tuff Gong tunes). In 1997, however, no one company would have the rights to so many big hits over a five-year period.

With all these caveats in mind, a comparison of the two soundtracks still gives a fair idea of how far reggae has travelled in the ensuing 25 years and provides food for thought about where it's going. Yes, the beat has changed and instruments are different and deejays are now more popular than singers. But when all is said and done, listening to both albums leads to the inescapable conclusion that the music in the earlier movie is simply better – more varied rhythmically, more captivating melodically, more interesting lyrically and more distinctively Jamaican. The two title songs are cases in point. The song 'The Harder They Come' was not the best in the movie, but it was and is a reggae classic. The title track 'Dancehall Queen' is full of energy but lacks imagination and its original beat is more disco-funk than dancehall-reggae.

not for obscenity but seemingly because station managers or politicians do not agree with the views expressed. Extreme libertarians argue that such constraints are blows against the concept of freedom of speech. But the authorities' fear that such songs might disturb Jamaica's fragile social structure is quite understandable. In any event,

it's highly doubtful such strictures have much effect, since forbidden songs usually become massive hits at the countless dances and sound clashes held nightly all over the island. By allowing anger to be vented in an emotionally charged yet non-physical manner, such vocal statements of defiance act as steam valves which prevent a pressure cooker from exploding. As such they probably help rather than hinder the cause of non-violent change.

One 'not fit for airplay' hit which gained a great deal of notoriety was 'Fire Pon Rome', the song which thrust deejay Anthony B into the limelight. He has not had a great deal of chart success, but is hugely popular on the live circuit and has dominated many major stage shows, outperforming some pretty big names.

1997 / **YOU NO READY FI DIS YET**
Tanya Stephens

Jamaica has a lot of attractions - beautiful beaches, stunning scenery and a vibrant folk culture. But most Jamaican men will tell you that the greatest thing about this country is its women. We might jeer them in private and castigate them in song, but Jamaican men readily admit that we can't live without them. Even if we could, what would be the point?

Jamaican women are in our view wonderfully unique. They certainly are as independent as any

---

> Still 'Dancehall Queen' was the biggest song of 1997, heading the *Star* Top 40 for nine weeks, and Beenie Man once again was deejay of the year. Over the past few years he has dominated the charts to an unprecedented degree. He had two of the year's top ten hits in 1994, three in 1995 and three in 1996. In 1997 as of September 26, he has had five number one hits and has topped the charts for 15 out of a possible 40 weeks. He has probably chalked up more number one tunes than any other artist in the history of Jamaican music. Now Beenie Man is creative, adventurous and always looking for new ideas, even venturing to Nashville to cut a country tune. But it's hardly likely that he has become more successful, in relative terms, than Toots Hibbert, Bob Marley, John Holt, Jimmy Cliff, Gregory Isaacs or Dennis Brown because he is a greater artist than any of these – his chart achievements may rather be an indication of an increasingly limited artistic base.
>
> Since deejays began to rule a new dancehall headliner has emerged almost annually. Yellowman, Josey Wales, Super Cat, Admiral Bailey, Tiger, Lt Stitchie, Ninja Man, Papa San and Shabba Ranks were each in their time 'guaranteed to cork any session'. But since 1994, when Beenie Man and Bounty Killa emerged to contest deejaying supremacy with Buju Banton, no local marquee stars have come forth. (Lady Saw is a possible exception, but a woman does not elicit the hardcore identification of the predominantly male dancehall massive. Shaggy tends to concentrate on foreign markets. And while Luciano is probably the most popular reggae singer since Gregory Isaacs, only a deejay can really 'rule dancehall'.)
>
> The popular new domestic artists like Goofy, Red Rat, Anthony B and Sizzla have all been of the supporting cast variety and Beenie and Bounty continue to virtually monopolise the charts. Is this domination a temporary aberration? Or is it a sign of stagnation? Dancehall's current popularity at home is certainly not in doubt. But a ceaseless ferment of new ideas firing a constant changing of the musical guard has always been a reggae hallmark. If the music begins to stand still, will it begin to die?

Tanya Stephens

females on earth – whoever heard of a subjugated Jamaican woman? Yet they never lose sight of their femininity, considering it and rightly so, God's greatest gift to the human race. As we see it, they are simply the most spirited and delightful creatures on the planet.

But of course there's no good without a bad. As intriguing and adorable as they may be, Jamaican women are not what one would call undemanding. Nor are they exactly famous for vows of unconditional and undying fidelity. Tanya Stephens makes this pretty clear in her big number one hit:

Josey Wales

> You never stop to think say a woman must come
> You have to satisfy her before you say you done
> You can't say a thing if you end up a get bun
>   *[bun = burn = cockolded]*
> You no ready for this yet boy
> You never stop to wonder that woman have mood
> You have to know how to handle it when gal a
>   feel rude
> That's why so much man a nyam out oonoo food
>   *[eat out your food]*
> You no ready for this yet boy.

Like they say, if you can't stand the heat, stay out of the kitchen.

1997 / **WHO SHOT THE COLONEL**
Colonel Josey Wales

In early 1997 the hard-core deejay Colonel Josey Wales was shot in the back and nearly died. On recovering, he released a song about the experience – a steel-string twanging, foot-pedal thumping, shit-kicker yodelling, country-and-western hoedown that sounded as if it was recorded in Nashville about 30 years ago. It promptly rocketed to the top of the dancehall charts. Yeehaw! Boring predictability is not one of Jamaica's major problems.

CHANGING CULTURAL CHANNELS

Similarity of language, geographical proximity, and disparities of size and wealth have all contributed to the habits and mores of the U.S. being widely copied here. Considering the country's size, Jamaica's indigenous culture has proven to be remarkably resilient, even proving a catalyst in the creation of one of the world's few net exporting music industries. But anyone observing Jamaica today must wonder if its indigenous culture will eventually be marginalised.

Until about 1991 Jamaica had only one television station, and television sets were affordable only to the fairly well-heeled. So the influence of American television, while certainly not negligible, was limited in extent. However, in the past few years this situation has changed dramatically. Not only have television sets dropped steadily in relative price, but most people now have access to cable. Dozens of channels are instantly available, all pumping out American pop culture 24 hours a day. This must inevitably have widespread social repercussions, and already there are signs of extensive cultural shifts. A few years ago for instance, basketball was very much a minority sport here. Now, thanks to being seen on TV almost every night, it is challenging cricket's status as the second most popular sport in the country behind football (soccer). And, as in the U.S., everyday conversation is becoming increasingly television oriented.

The video cultural penetration has been most marked in the cities, but this has always been the case with outside influences. When radio and sound systems first made inroads here 50 years ago and the Kingston masses began listening almost exclusively to American rhythm & blues, rural Jamaica was still immersed in mento and gospel. Reggae's three great founding fathers Toots Hibbert, Bob Marley and Jimmy Cliff came to the city only as teenagers. Toots, for example, knew nothing about rhythm & blues before coming to Kingston. His musical universe before this consisted almost entirely of church hymns and mento. It is the experiences and mindset men like him brought to rhythm & blues that created ska. Reggae has been an almost entirely urban phenomenon, but it can be very persuasively argued

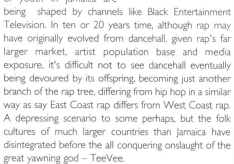

that it is the slower-paced, reflective countryside which has nurtured the habits and traditions that give 'yard' music, and Jamaican culture as a whole, its distinctive flavour. How can these be maintained, not

only in face of television's advancing tide, but also the relentless demographical shift from country to town?

Ineluctably, the mores of youth in Jamaica are being shaped by channels like Black Entertainment Television. In ten or 20 years time, although rap may have originally evolved from dancehall, given rap's far larger market, artist population base and media exposure, it's difficult not to see dancehall eventually being devoured by its offspring, becoming just another branch of the rap tree, differing from hip hop in a similar way as say East Coast rap differs from West Coast rap. A depressing scenario to some perhaps, but the folk cultures of much larger countries than Jamaica have disintegrated before the all conquering onslaught of the great yawning god – TeeVee.

For Jamaica's music to have survived intact so long as it has is exceptional, a tribute to those distinctive transmitters of culture who have reflected on Jamaica's own unique experiences. Many of us will mourn its passing, regretting the loss of its unpredictable feistiness We will fondly remember the dogged attempts to create its own heroes and stubborn refusal to have its tastes dictated by bloodless, grey-suited accountants thousands of miles away. Unsophisticated, and often lacking intellectual depth, this nevertheless was and is an unapologetically engagee music and culture of a people who despise passive spectatorship. You're supposed to sing and dance along to reggae, not sit and listen.

If and when the world becomes one big plastic Disneyland, as predictably bland as a McDonald's hamburger, and we measure out our politically-correct passions in vapid, meagre measures, perhaps the occasional spark of spontaneous emotion will enable us to slip the bonds of internet ennui and switch off the damned boob-tube. Then we will lick on some Maytals or Paragons, or Michigan and Smiley, or Lady Saw, and remember what it was like to feel glad to be alive and celebrate life, not merely existing to fulfill the bored dictates of international consumer marketing campaigns. Not everyone feels that way about reggae. But on behalf of all who do, we say thank you to those who created the music of Jah.

Appendices

The charts up to 1973 were supplied by Frankie Campbell. He took weekly charts from JBC Radio and compiled the top songs for each year. The charts from 1978 are from RJR's annual survey. No radio charts exist for the years 1974 to 1977. There has always been controversy about the accuracy of music charts in Jamaica, but no other method of judging a song's popularity exists. So while the charts may not always be correct, they are all we have. In the land of the blind, the one-eyed man is king.

1960

1 **LITTLE SHEILA**
LAUREL AITKEN

2 **WORRIED OVER YOU**
KEITH AND ENID

3 **TELL ME DARLING**
WILFRED 'JACKIE' EDWARDS

4 **MANNY OH**
HIGGS AND WILSON

5 **PLEASE LET ME GO**
OWEN GREY

6 **EASY SNAPPIN**
THEOPHILUS BECKFORD

7 **WE'RE GONNA LOVE**
WILFRED 'JACKIE' EDWARDS

8 **LITTLE VILMA**
BLUES BUSTERS

9 **LOLLIPOP GIRL**
JIVING JUNIORS

10 **BOOGIE IN MY BONES**
LAUREL AITKEN

11 **HEAVEN JUST KNOWS**
WILFRED 'JACKIE' EDWARDS

12 **DUMPLINGS**
BYRON LEE

13 **COME BACK JEANNIE**
LAUREL AITKEN

14 **FOR LOVE**
OWEN GREY

15 **I LONG FOR THE DAY**
HIGGS AND WILSON

16 **CHERRY**
BONNIE AND SKITTER

17 **MY BABY**
JACKIE ESTIC

18 **FAT MAN**
DERRICK MORGAN

19 **IT IS A DAY**
HIGGS AND WILSON

20 **MY HEART'S DESIRE**
JIVING JUNIORS

21 **SHUFFLING JUG**
CLUE J AND THE BLUES BLASTERS

22 **JENNY LEE**
OWEN GREY

23 **THE WICKED**
BONNIE AND SKITTER

24 **DRAGON'S PARADISE**
BYRON LEE

25 **DOG IT**
MONTY AND THE CYCLONES

26 **YOUR EYES ARE DREAMING**
WILFRED 'JACKIE' EDWARDS

27 **HONEY GIRL**
LAUREL AITKEN

1961

1 **TIME TO PRAY**
THE MELLOW LARKS

2 **OH CAROLINA**
FOLKES BROTHERS

3 **MURIEL**
ALTON AND EDDIE

4 **TIMES ARE A GOING**
MARTIN AND DERRICK

5 **VERONA**
JIMMY SINCLAIR

6 **IT'S ONLY A PITY**
KEITH AND ENID

7 **BA BA BLACK SHEEP**
C. BYRD

8 **IN AND OUT THE WINDOW**
MONTY AND ROY

9 **OVER THE RIVER**
JIVING JUNIORS

10 **THERE'S ALWAYS SUNSHINE**
BLUES BUSTERS

11 **WHENEVER THERE IS MOONLIGHT**
WILFRED 'JACKIE' EDWARDS

12 **HUMPTY DUMPTY**
ERIC 'MONTY' MORRIS

13 **SEND ME**
KEITH AND ENID

14 **ROCK A MAN'S SOUL**
MELLO CATS

15 **FEEL SO FINE**
DERRICK AND PATSY

16 **A THOUSAND TEARDROPS**
RHYTHM ACES

17 **RIVER JORDAN**
CLANCY ECCLES

18 **JUDGEMENT DAY**
LAUREL AITKEN

19 **SINNER WEEP**
OWEN GREY

20 **COME ON HOME**
HIGGS AND WILSON

21 **LAST NIGHT**
BYRON LEE

22 **JOY RIDE**
BYRON LEE

23 **MARY LEE**
LAUREL AITKEN

24 **SHA BA DA**
HIGGS AND WILSON

25 **OH MA OH PA**
MELODY ENCHANTERS

26 **REFERENDUM CALYPSO**
LORD LARU

1962

1 **INDEPENDENT JAMAICA**
LORD CREATOR

2 **BEHOLD**
BLUES BUSTERS

3 **FORWARD MARCH**
DERRICK MORGAN

4 **DARLING TOGETHER**
GIRL SATCHMO

5 **BE STILL**
DERRICK MORGAN

6 **INDEPENDENCE IS HERE**
A. C. T. JOE

7 **HURRICANE HATTIE**
JIMMY CLIFF

8 **MONEY CAN'T BUY LOVE**
ERIC 'MONTY' MORRIS

9 **WE'LL MEET**
ROY AND MILLIE

10 **BEWILDERED AND BLUE**
JIMMY JAMES

11 **THEY GOT TO COME**
PRINCE BUSTER

12 **IN MY HEART**
DERRICK MORGAN

13 **ARE YOU MINE**
THE ECHOES

14 **I CARE**
DERRICK MORGAN

15 **NEVER NEVER**
BOBBY ATKIN

16 **LITTLE SCHOOL GIRL**
RUDDY AND SKEETER

17 **HOUSEWIVE'S CHOICE**
DERRICK AND PATSY

18 **PACK UP YOUR TROUBLES**
ERIC 'MONTY' MORRIS

19 **WHAT HAVE I DONE**
KEITH AND ENID

20 **SUGAR DANDY**
JIVING JUNIORS

21 **THE HOP**
DERRICK MORGAN

22 **ONE DESIRE**
OWEN GREY

23 **BROTHER DAVID**
LAUREL AITKEN

24 **SCHOOLING THE DUKE**
DON DRUMMOND

25 **MEEKLY WAIT**
DERRICK AND EYVONNE

26 **THEY GOT TO GO**
PRINCE BUSTER

27 **ONE HAND WASH THE OTHER**
PRINCE BUSTER

1963

1 **THE END**
LORD CREATOR

2 **EMPTY CHAIR**
BYRON LEE

3 **COME TO ME SOFTLY**
JIMMY JAMES

4 **ROUGH AND TOUGH**
STRANGER COLE

5 **WE WILL BE LOVERS**
LORD CREATOR AND NORMA

6 **RUKUMBINE**
CARLOS MALCOLM

7 **HONOUR YOUR MOTHER AND FATHER**
DESMOND DEKKER AND THE ACES

8 **MUSICAL COMMUNION**
BABA BROOKS

9 **COME DOWN**
LORD TANAMO

10 **RIVER BANK**
BABA BROOKS

11 **DON'T STAY OUT LATE**
LORD CREATOR

12 **MAN TO MAN**
LORD CREATOR

13 **WHEN YOU CALL MY NAME**
STRANGER AND PATSY

14 **YOU ARE THE ONE**
WINSTON SAMUELS

15 **WATERMELON MAN**
BABA BROOKS

16 **ON THE TRAIL**
BYRON LEE

17 **FATSO**
AL T JOE

18 **RELOAD**
SKATALITES AND DON DRUMMOND

19 **OH SHIRLEY**
ROY AND SHIRLEY

20 **ONE MORE TIME**
LLOYD BREVETT

21 **TEARS IN MY EYES**
ROY AND PAULETTE

22 **SINCE YOU'VE BEEN GONE**
ROY AND MILLIE

23 **MY DARLING**
TONY GREGORY

24 **PORTRAIT OF MY LOVE**
BYRON LEE

25 **LITTLE SCHOOL GIRL**
LLOYD WILLIAMS

1964

1 **BONANZA SKA**
CARLOS MALCOLM

2 **CARRY GO BRING COME**
JUSTIN HINDS AND THE DOMINOS

3 **JAMAICAN SKA**
BYRON LEE

4 **MY BOY LOLLIPOP**
MILLIE SMALL

5 **WASH WASH**
PRINCE BUSTER

6 **SAMMY DEAD**
ERIC 'MONTY' MORRIS

7 **TEAR UP**
SKATALITES AND ROLAND ALPHONSO

8 **DADDY**
MAYTALS

9 **SIMMER DOWN**
WAILERS

10 **BE PREPARED**
WINSTON SAMUELS

11 **JESERENE**
DESMOND DEKKER AND THE ACES

12 **TONGUE WILL TELL**
PRINCE BUSTER

13 **PORTRAIT OF MY LOVE**
BYRON LEE

14 **I GOT A PAIN**
MAYTALS

15 **JOHN TOM**
DERRICK HARRIOT

16 **CRY ME A RIVER**
JACKIE OPEL

17 **YEAH YEAH BABY**
STRANGER AND PATSY

18 **OIL IN MY LAMP**
ERIC 'MONTY' MORRIS

19 **EASTERN STANDARD TIME**
SKATALITES AND DON DRUMMOND

20 **DOG WAR**
MAYTALS

21 **THE FIT IS ON ME NOW**
OWEN AND LEON

22 **SWEET WILLIAM**
MILLIE SMALL

23 **YOU'RE WONDERING NOW**
ANDY AND JOEY

24 **HANGING UP MY HEART**
BYRON LEE

25 **WINGS OF A DOVE**
PRINCE BUSTER

1965

1 **WIDE AWAKE IN A DREAM**
BLUES BUSTERS

2 **EVERY NIGHT**
JOE WHITE

3 **IT HURTS TO BE ALONE**
WAILERS

4 **SNAKE IN THE GRASS**
PAUL MARTIN

5 **DANCE CRASHER**
ALTON AND THE FLAMES

6 **BABY COME ON HOME**
TONY GREGORY

7 **BROWN EYES**
SAINTS

8 **GUNS OF NAVARONE**
SKATALITES

9 **BALL OF FIRE**
SKATALITES

10 **SLOOPY**
BYRON LEE

11 **LONESOME FEELING**
WAILERS

12 **A PLACE CALL LOVE**
TECHNIQUES

13 **CONTACT**
ROY RICHARDS

14 **BURKE'S LAW**
PRINCE BUSTER

15 **I'M ONLY HUMAN**
DERRICK HARRIOT

16 **I REMEMBER**
LAUREL AITKEN

17 **EL PUSSYCAT**
SKATALITES AND ROLAND ALPHONSO

18 **LITTLE DID YOU KNOW**
TECHNIQUES

19 **LOVE AT LAST**
PARAGONS

20 **AND I LOVE HER**
BYRON LEE

21 **NEVER YOU CHANGE**
MAYTALS

22 **SOMETHING SPECIAL**
SKATALITES AND ROLAND ALPHONSO

23 **GOT TO LEARN TO LOVE AGAIN**
WILFRED 'JACKIE' EDWARDS

24 **WHEN I LAUGH**
MAYTALS

25 **BABY HOW I LOVE YOU**
DOBBY DOBSON

1966

1. **KEEP ON RUNNING**
WILFRED 'JACKIE' EDWARDS
2. **THE TRAIN IS COMING**
KEN BOOTHE
3. **MY LOVE FOR YOU**
JOE WHITE
4. **GIRL I'VE GOT A DATE**
ALTON AND THE FLAMES
5. **BAM BAM**
MAYTALS
6. **RUDE BOY SKA**
WAILERS
7. **007**
DESMOND DEKKER AND THE ACES
8. **PUT IT ON**
WAILERS
9. **SUNSHINE WITH MY GIRL**
PRINCE BUSTER
10. **DANCING MOOD**
DELROY WILSON
11. **RUDE BOY GONE A JAIL**
CLARENDONIANS
12. **SHOOK SHIMMY SHAKE**
OWEN GREY
13. **SOUNDS AND PRESSURE**
HOPETON LEWIS
14. **THIS IS THUNDER**
BABA BROOKS
15. **CAN'T BELIEVE THAT YOU'RE GONE**
BLUES BUSTERS
16. **SKA BOSTELLA**
SKATALITES AND ROLAND ALPHONSO
17. **YOU WON'T SEE ME**
CLARENDONIANS
18. **RUDY BAM BAM**
CLARENDONIANS
19. **I WILL**
PAMELA BLYTH
20. **DO RE ME**
MIGHTY VIKINGS
21. **SHOO BE DAH**
CLARENDONIANS
22. **TRY ME**
JUSTIN HINDS AND THE DOMINOS
23. **GREEN MOON**
SKATALITES AND ROLAND ALPHONSO
24. **HARD MAN FE DEAD**
PRINCE BUSTER
25. **SAD SAD WORLD**
LLOYD WILLIAMS

1967

1. **PUPPET ON A STRING**
KEN BOOTHE
2. **HOLD THEM**
ROY SHIRLEY
3. **TAKE IT EASY**
HOPETON LEWIS
4. **YOU DON'T CARE FOR ME**
TECHNIQUES
5. **DO IT RIGHT**
DION AND THE TREETOPS
6. **HAPPY GO LUCKY GIRL**
PARAGONS
7. **YOU HAVE CAUGHT ME BABE**
MELODIANS
8. **MOTHER YOUNG GAL**
DESMOND DEKKER AND THE ACES
9. **ON THE BEACH**
PARAGONS
10. **THINGS YOU SAY**
JAMAICANS
11. **ROCK STEADY**
ALTON AND THE FLAMES
12. **YOU AND YOUR SMILING FACE**
PARAGONS
13. **WALK THE STREETS**
DERRICK HARRIOTT
14. **GET ON THE BALL**
ROY SHIRLEY
15. **DOWN BY THE TRAIN LINE**
STRANGER AND PATSY
16. **BA BA BOOM**
JAMAICANS
17. **PRESSURE AND SLIDE**
TENORS
18. **JOHNNY COOL**
PRINCE BUSTER
19. **WINEY WINEY**
KINGSTONIANS
20. **I DON'T WANT TO SEE YOU CRY**
KEN BOOTHE
21. **THE LOSER**
DERRICK HARRIOTT
22. **UNITY**
DESMOND DEKKER AND THE ACES
23. **NICE TIME**
WAILERS
24. **LET ME GO GIRL**
UNIQUES
25. **RELEASE ME**
BYRON LEE

1968

1. **54-46**
MAYTALS
2. **NANNY GOAT**
LARRY AND ALVIN
3. **EVERYTHING CRASH**
ETHIOPIANS
4. **BABY WHY**
CABLES
5. **EASY COME EASY GO**
PIONEERS
6. **LET THEM SAY**
BOB ANDY
7. **NO MORE HEARTACHES**
BELTONES
8. **LADY WITH THE STARLIGHT**
KEN BOOTHE
9. **AH IT MEK**
DESMOND DEKKER AND THE ACES
10. **PENNY FOR YOUR SONG**
FEDERALS
11. **WHY DID YOU LEAVE**
HEPTONES
12. **LITTLE NUT TREE**
MELODIANS
13. **WATCH THIS SOUND**
UNIQUES
14. **BANG A RANG**
STRANGER COLE
15. **INTENSIFIED 68**
DESMOND DEKKER AND THE ACES
16. **BABY**
HEPTONES
17. **LONGSHOT**
PIONEERS
18. **IT COMES AND GOES**
MELODIANS
19. **JUST LIKE A RIVER**
STRANGER AND GLADDY
20. **DON'T LOOK BACK**
KEITH AND TEX

21. **SILENT RIVER**
GAYLADS
22. **BIM TODAY BAM TOMORROW**
MAYTALS
23. **JULIE**
LYN TAITT AND THE COMETS
24. **LONG STORY**
RUDY MILLS
25. **DANCE WITH ME**
DELANO STEWART

1969

1. **SWEET SENSATION**
   MELODIANS
2. **MUSICAL SCORCHER**
   SOUND DIMENSION
3. **DR NO GO**
   HIPPY BOYS
4. **GAMES PEOPLE PLAY**
   BOB ANDY
5. **MORE SCORCHER**
   SOUND DIMENSION
6. **FIRE CORNER**
   KING STITT
7. **1000 TONS OF MEGATON**
   ROLAND ALPHONSO
8. **BONGO NYAH**
   LITTLE BOYS
9. **NICE TO BE WITH YOU**
   BORIS GARDNER
10. **ZILON**
    LLOYD CHARMERS
11. **MONKEY MAN**
    MAYTALS
12. **PUT YOURSELF IN MY PLACE**
    DELROY WILSON
13. **CLINT EASTWOOD**
    UPSETTERS ALLSTARS
14. **LIQUIDATOR**
    JAYBOYS
15. **HOW LONG**
    PAT KELLY
16. **HAVING A HARD TIME**
    KEITH LYN
17. **EVERYBODY NEEDS LOVE**
    SLIM SMITH
18. **WHO DONE IT**
    SOUND DIMENSION
19. **SAMFIE MAN**
    PIONEERS
20. **HIJACK**
    JACKIE MITTOO
21. **FIRE TO FIRE**
    LLOYD CHALMERS
22. **ALIDINAH**
    MAYTALS
23. **SWEET TALKING**
    HEPTONES
24. **SCARE HIM**
    MAYTALS
25. **COME BACK DARLING**
    JOHNNY OSBOURNE

1970

1. **WEAR YOU TO THE BALL**
   U-ROY
2. **RIDE ON SAMMY**
   ERNIE SMITH
3. **DYNAMIC PRESSURE**
   MUSICAL SPECIALISTS
4. **FREEDOM STREET**
   KEN BOOTHE
5. **DUPPY CONQUEROR**
   WAILERS
6. **SATISFACTION**
   CARL DAWKINS
7. **DRINK MILK**
   JUSTIN HINDS
8. **YOU'LL NEVER GET AWAY**
   U-ROY
9. **MONEY MAKER**
   JIM AND DAVE
10. **FUNNY MAN**
    MAYTONES
11. **CECILIA**
    KEN LAZARUS
12. **MY HEART IS GONE**
    JOHN HOLT
13. **RIVERS OF BABYLON**
    MELODIANS
14. **PSYCHEDELIC TRAIN**
    DERRICK HARRIOT
15. **WAKE THE TOWN**
    U-ROY
16. **HOLLY HOLY**
    FABULOUS FLAMES
17. **THAT WONDERFUL SOUND**
    DOBBY DOBSON
18. **POISON IVY**
    SOUND DIMENSION
19. **BEND DOWN**
    ERNIE SMITH
20. **GET TOGETHER**
    CARL DAWKINS
21. **RULE THE NATION**
    U-ROY
22. **STAY A LITTLE BIT LONGER**
    DELANO STEWART
23. **YOU MAKE ME SO HAPPY**
    ALTON ELLIS
24. **RAINY NIGHT IN GEORGIA**
    LORD TANAMO
25. **PEEPING TOM**
    MAYTALS

1971

1. **TRENCHTOWN ROCK**
   WAILERS
2. **PICTURE ON THE WALL**
   FREDDIE MCKAY
3. **MAWGA DOG**
   PETER TOSH
4. **SMALL AXE**
   WAILERS
5. **STICK BY ME**
   JOHN HOLT
6. **TEACH THE CHILDREN**
   DENNIS ALCAPONE
7. **ONE DREAM**
   ERNIE SMITH
8. **LET THE POWER FALL ON I**
   MAX ROMEO
9. **BETTER MUST COME**
   DELROY WILSON
10. **GROOVIN OUT ON LIFE**
    HOPETON LEWIS
11. **MY JAMAICAN GIRL**
    GAYLADS
12. **CHERRY OH BABY**
    ERIC DONALDSON
13. **SHAFT**
    CHOSEN FEW
14. **COME ON BACK AND STAY**
    FABULOUS FIVE
15. **STRANGE THINGS**
    JOHN HOLT
16. **A LITTLE LOVE**
    JIMMY LONDON
17. **RIDDLE I THIS**
    SCOTTY
18. **COOL OPERATOR**
    DELROY WILSON
19. **MULE TRAIN**
    COUNT PRINCE MILLER
20. **ONE LIFE TO LIVE**
    PHYLLIS DILLON
21. **TALK ABOUT LOVE**
    PAT KELLY
22. **6 IN I**
    KEN BOOTHE
23. **DELIVER US**
    ALTON ELLIS
24. **LOVE OF THE COMMON PEOPLE**
    ERIC DONALDSON
25. **OH WHAT A MINI**
    WILLIE FRANCIS

1972

1 **PITTA PATTA**
ERNIE SMITH

2 **OFFICIALLY**
LLOYD PARKES

3 **BREAKFAST IN BED**
LORNA BENNETT

4 **MERRY UP**
GODSONS

5 **JIMMY BROWN**
KEN PARKER

6 **BEAT DOWN BABYLON**
JUNIOR BYLES

7 **S-90 SKANK**
BIG YOUTH

8 **DON'T FORGET TO REMEMBER**
ADINA EDWARDS

9 **THE HARDER THEY COME**
JIMMY CLIFF

10 **I AM INDEBTED TO YOU**
ERIC DONALDSON

11 **BUTTERCUP**
WINSTON SCOTLAND

12 **DARLING OH**
ERIC DUNKLEY

13 **BLACK CINDERELLA**
ERIC DUNKLEY

14 **HAVE A LITTLE FAITH**
NIKKI THOMAS

15 **SKYLARKING**
HORACE ANDY

16 **LEAN ON ME**
B. B. SEATON

17 **ONE NIGHT OF SIN**
JACKIE BROWN

18 **BABY DON'T DO IT**
DENNIS BROWN

19 **POWER VERSION**
DENNIS ALCAPONE

20 **NIGHT OWL**
LEE AND THE CLARENDONIANS

21 **BIG BAD BOY**
ALTON ELLIS

22 **HELP ME MAKE IT THROUGH THE NIGHT**
KEN PARKER

23 **HAIL THE MAN**
KEN LAZARUS

24 **SCREWFACE**
WAILERS

25 **HAVE YOU SEEN HER**
DERRICK HARRIOTT

1973

1 **WESTBOUND TRAIN**
DENNIS BROWN

2 **SILVER WORDS**
KEN BOOTHE

3 **COUNTRY ROAD**
MAYTALS

4 **MELLOW MOOD**
JUDY MOWATT

5 **BUILD ME UP**
BRENT DOWE

6 **CHI CHI RUN**
BIG YOUTH

7 **I SEE YOU**
FUNKY BROWN

8 **YAMAHA SKANK**
SHORTY THE PRESIDENT

9 **IN THE DARK**
MAYTALS

10 **FEEL NO PAIN**
JACKIE BROWN

11 **BOOK OF RULES**
HEPTONES

12 **I'M ALONE**
JUDY MOWATT

13 **ALL I HAVE IS LOVE**
GREGORY ISAACS

14 **AH SO WE STAY**
BIG YOUTH

15 **SINNER**
FATHER HOLUNG AND FRIENDS

16 **GREEN GUAVA JELLY**
THE TILLERS

17 **RASTA NO BORN YA**
SANG HUGH AND THE LIONAIRES

18 **NOBODY'S CHILD**
MAX ROMEO

19 **SCREAMING TARGET**
BIG YOUTH

20 **COOL BREEZE**
BIG YOUTH

21 **DARK SHADOWS**
CHARLEY HANNA AND GRADUATES

22 **PABLO IN DUB**
AUGUSTUS PABLO

23 **CLOSE TO YOU**
BRENT DOWE

24 **CHILDREN OF ISRAEL**
HORACE ANDY

25 **SCHOOL**
PRINCE JAZZBO

1978

1 **LOVING PAUPER**
RUDDY THOMAS

2 **BOOK OF LIFE**
PAM AND WOODY

3 **SOUL SISTER**
DERRICK HARRIOTT

4 **RUNNING UP AND DOWN**
DENNIS BROWN AND BIG YOUTH

5 **ONE STEP AHEAD**
BERES HAMMOND

6 **A JAH JAH**
RITA MARLEY

7 **ZION GATE**
CULTURE

8 **DEATH IN THE ARENA**
THE REVOLUTIONARIES

9 **STARKY AND HUTCH**
TRINITY

10 **HOW CAN I LEAVE YOU**
DENNIS BROWN

11 **PEACE TREATY SPECIAL**
JACOB MILLER

12 **THINGS YOU SAY YOU LOVE**
BRENT DOWE

13 **LOOK INTO YOUR HEART**
JUNIOR TUCKER

14 **TRIBAL WAR**
GEORGE KNOOKS

15 **MISS HARD TO GET**
JACKIE BROWN

16 **JAH JAH GIVE US LIFE**
WALING SOULS

17 **NATTY NEVER GET WEARY**
CULTURE

18 **THE WAR IS OVER**
DILLINGER

19 **NATTY DREAD TAKING OVER**
CULTURE

20 **YOU HAVE FE DREAD**
LORD LARO

21 **ALMIGHTY I**
DENNIS WALKS

22 **WEATHERMAN SKANK**
RAY I

23 **OH LORD**
TAPPA ZUKIE

24 **MONEY WORRIES**
ENOS MCLEOD

25 **BLACKMAN REDEMPTION**
BOB MARLEY AND THE WAILERS

1979	1980	1981

1979

1 **PLEASE MR. DOCTOR**
U BROWN

2 **STEPPING OUT OF BABYLON**
MARCIA GRIFFITHS

3 **I'M IN LOVE WITH YOU**
BERES HAMMOND

4 **AIN'T THAT LOVIN YOU**
DENNIS BROWN

5 **IDENTITY**
MIGHTY DIAMONDS

6 **MOTHER IN LAW**
LEVI WILLIAMS

7 **RUB A DUB STYLE**
MICHIGAN AND SMILEY

8 **JUST LIKE A SEA**
DAVID ISAACS

9 **KEEP ON KNOCKING**
JACOB MILLER

10 **BARNABAS COLLINS**
LONE RANGER

11 **COOL OUT SON**
JUNIOR MURVIN

12 **SUGAR SUGAR**
DORIS SCHAFFER

13 **OH MR. D.C.**
SUGAR MINOTT

14 **MR. BROWN**
GREGORY ISAACS

15 **MANY ARE CALLED**
I-THREES

16 **LIFT UP YOUR CONSCIENCE**
ISRAEL VIBRATION

17 **LOVE DON'T LIVE HERE ANYMORE**
SHARON FORRESTER

18 **FIST TO FIST RUB A DUB**
NIGGER KOJAK AND LIZA

19 **NICE UP THE DANCE**
MICHIGAN AND SMILEY

20 **MAN NEXT DOOR**
DENNIS BROWN

21 **GIRL I'VE GOT A DATE**
DENNIS BROWN

22 **PUT IT ON**
JUDY MOWATT

23 **INTERNATIONAL YEAR OF THE CHILD**
GENERAL ECHO

24 **AMBUSH**
BOB MARLEY AND THE WAILERS

25 **TRICKSTER**
JUNIOR DELGADO

1980

1 **RUB A DUB EVENING**
JOE TEX AND U BLACK

2 **ARLEEN**
GENERAL ECHO

3 **JAMMIN' SO**
MADOO

4 **ONE DROP**
BOB MARLEY AND THE WAILERS

5 **SKY JUICE**
NIGGER KOJAK AND LIZA

6 **LOVE AND DEVOTION**
JIMMY RILEY

7 **LAYING BESIDE YOU**
TAMLINS

8 **ONE OF THE POOREST PEOPLE**
JUNIOR TUCKER

9 **LET'S HOLD ON**
CASUAL T

10 **BOBBY BABYLON**
FREDDIE MCGREGOR

11 **ONCE UPON A TIME**
JACOB MILLER

12 **BALTIMORE**
TAMLINS

13 **DELILAH**
INNER CIRCLE

14 **SITTING AND WATCHING**
DENNIS BROWN

15 **MERRY GO ROUND**
JUNIOR DELGADO

16 **GIVE ME YOUR LOVE**
JIMMY RILEY

17 **DRUNKEN MASTER**
GENERAL ECHO

18 **REGGAE MUSIC**
BARRINGTON LEVY

19 **ONE LOVE JAM DOWN**
MICHIGAN AND SMILEY

20 **JOE GRINE**
MADOO JOE GIBBS AND THE PROFESSIONALS

21 **LET ME LOVE YOU**
DENNIS BROWN

22 **HAMMER**
PETER TOSH

23 **BAD CARD**
BOB MARLEY AND THE WAILERS

1981

1 **LOVE BUMP**
LONE RANGER

2 **SOMEONE LOVES YOU HONEY**
J. C. LODGE

3 **FRONT DOOR**
GREGORY ISAACS

4 **HAVE YOU EVER BEEN IN LOVE**
DENNIS BROWN

5 **MY WORLD IS FALLING DOWN**
TAMLINS

6 **I'LL HAVE TO GET YOU**
TONY TUFF

7 **I STILL LOVE YOU**
CHALICE

8 **CHECK FOR YOU ONCE GIRL**
EDDIE FITZROY

9 **IF ONLY I KNEW**
BERES HAMMOND

10 **ICE CREAM LOVE**
JOHNNY OSBOURNE

11 **WA DO DEM**
EEK A MOUSE

12 **COOL RUNNINGS**
BUNNY WAILER

13 **GOOD TO BE THERE**
CHALICE

14 **OLD BROOM**
WAILING SOUL

15 **BAD CARD**
BOB MARLEY AND THE WAILERS

16 **MY WOMAN**
BARRINGTON LEVY

17 **MIND YOU MOUTH**
BARRINGTON LEVY

18 **LOVE LIGHT**
TAMLINS

19 **21 GIRLS SALUTE**
BARRINGTON LEVY

20 **CRUCIAL**
BUNNY WAILER

21 **PAPA DEE**
TOOTS AND THE MAYTALS

22 **IF THERE'S A SONG**
BERES HAMMOND

23 **THE FOUNDATION**
DENNIS BROWN

1982

1 **LIKE OLD FRIENDS DO**
CARLENE DAVIS

2 **SURROUND ME WITH LOVE**
CYNTHIA SCHLOSS

3 **YO YO**
JOHNNY OSBOURNE

4 **I'M GETTING MARRIED**
YELLOWMAN

5 **SWEETIE COME BRUSH ME**
JOHN HOLT

6 **DISEASES**
MICHIGAN AND SMILEY

7 **MR. CHIN**
YELLOWMAN

8 **GYPSY GIRL**
TONY GREGORY

9 **TREAT THE YOUTH RIGHT**
JIMMY CLIFF

10 **PASS THE KUTCHIE**
MIGHTY DIAMONDS

11 **ARMY LIFE**
WELTON IRIE

12 **TOP TEN**
GREGORY ISAACS

13 **PAIN**
BRIGADIER JERRY

14 **SOLDIER TAKE OVER**
YELLOWMAN

15 **A LITTLE BIT MORE**
DENNIS BROWN

16 **ENTERTAINMENT**
TRISTAN PALMER

17 **ON MY MIND**
AINSLEY MORRIS

18 **HAVE YOU EVER BEEN IN LOVE**
DENNIS BROWN

19 **BIG SHIP**
FREDDIE MCGREGOR

20 **BOXING AROUND**
CORNEL CAMPBELL

21 **PRETTY WOMAN**
MIGHTY DIAMONDS

22 **LOVE HAS FOUND ITS WAY**
DENNIS BROWN

23 **RUB-A-DUB PARTNER**
JIMMY CLIFF

24 **YOUTHMAN PENITENTIARY**
EDDIE FITZROY

25 **JOHNNY DOLLAR**
ROLAND BURREL

1983

1 **YOUR LOVE'S GOT A HOLD ON ME**
DENNIS BROWN

2 **REVOLUTION**
DENNIS BROWN

3 **UNMETERED TAXI**
SLY AND ROBBIE

4 **NIGHT NURSE**
GREGORY ISAACS

5 **IT MUST BE LOVE**
CARLENE DAVIS

6 **ELECTRIC BOOGIE**
MARCIA GRIFFITHS

7 **BUFFALO SOLDIER**
BOB MARLEY AND THE WAILERS

8 **INFORMER**
LADY ANN

9 **LEGGO MI HAND**
JOSEY WALES

10 **BABY COME TO JOSEPH**
JOSEY WALES

11 **COME WE COME FI MASH IT**
TONY TUFF

12 **WATER PUMPEE**
TONY TUFF

13 **LOVER'S RACE**
SUGAR MINOTT

14 **SHOULDER MOVE**
JAH THOMAS

15 **ZUNGUZUNGGUZUNGZENG**
YELLOWMAN

16 **FAT SHE FAT**
JOHN HOLT

17 **MAKE IT UP TO YOU**
J. C. LODGE

18 **YOU LOOK LIKE LOVE**
CYNTHIA SCHLOSS

19 **WATER PUMPING**
JOHNNY OSBOURNE

20 **REBEL TOUR**
BARE ESSENTIALS

21 **SENSEMILLA**
YELLOWMAN

22 **BELLY MOVE**
YELLOWMAN

23 **TRUE CONFESSION**
LITTLE JOHN

24 **RESERVATION FOR TWO**
LLOYD PARKES

25 **DEDICATED TO YOU**
PETER METRO

1984

1 **LICK SHOT**
MICHAEL PALMER

2 **THU-SHUNG-PENG**
FRANKIE PAUL

3 **BELLY MOVE**
YELLOWMAN

4 **MY GOD MY KING**
PAPA LEVI

5 **MAKE IT UP TO YOU**
J. C. LODGE

6 **REGGAE NIGHTS**
JIMMY CLIFF

7 **AS IF I DIDN'T KNOW**
CYNTHIA SCHLOSS

8 **I CAN'T STAND IT**
DENNIS BROWN

9 **WINSOME**
HALF PINT

10 **THE BOMB**
THOROUGHBRED AND UTON DOWE

11 **FOREIGN MIND**
JUNIOR REID

12 **PRISON OVAL ROCK**
BARRINGTON LEVY

13 **ZUNGUZUNGGUZUNGZENG**
YELLOWMAN

14 **RUB A DUB SOLDIER**
PAUL BLAKE AND BLOODFIRE

15 **ON THE TELEPHONE**
BARRINGTON LEVY

16 **PRINCESS BLACK**
EDDIE FITZROY

17 **WORLD A MUSIC**
INI KAMOZE

18 **THE GUN**
EDDIE FITZROY

19 **SHE JUST A DRAW CARD**
LEROY SMART

20 **READY ME READY**
MICHAEL PALMER

21 **HAUL AND PULL UP**
NEVILLE BROWN

22 **BUY OFF THE BAR**
SUGAR MINOTT

23 **TROUBLE IN THE DANCE**
AL CAMPBELL

24 **LIVE GOOD**
LEROY SMART

1985

1 **GIRLIE GIRLIE**
SOPHIA GEORGE

2 **WHAT ONE DANCE CAN DO**
BERES HAMMOND

3 **SHOCK WE A SHOCK**
HORACE MARTIN

4 **GROOVY LITTLE THING**
BERES HAMMOND

5 **TINEY WINEY**
BYRON LEE & THE DRAGONAIRES

6 **BUDY BYE**
JOHNNY OSBOURNE

7 **CHECKING OUT**
DERRICK HARRIOTT

8 **RING THE ALARM**
TENOR SAW

9 **UNDER MI SLENG TENG**
WAYNE SMITH

10 **YOU SAFE**
FABULOUS FIVE

11 **GHOSTRIDER**
GENERAL TREES

12 **SOLIDARITY**
BLACK UHURU

13 **WHEELY WHEELY**
EARLY B

14 **POCOMANIA JUMP**
SASSA FRASS

15 **EVERY POSSE GET FLAT**
PAUL BLAKE AND BLOODFIRE

16 **SUNDAY DISH**
EARLY B

17 **TEMPO**
ANTHONY RED ROSE

18 **HERE I AM**
BARRINGTON LEVY

19 **UPON THE LEVEL**
SUGAR MINOTT

20 **HARD TIME ROCK**
SUGAR MINOTT

21 **SENSE OF PURPOSE**
THIRD WORLD

22 **ALL THE WAY IN**
CYNTHIA SCHLOSS

23 **PUMPKIN BELLY**
TENOR SAW

24 **UNDER MI SENSI**
BARRINGTON LEVY

25 **HERBMAN HUSTLING**
SUGAR MINOTT

1986

1 **WHAT THE HELL**
ECHO MINOTT

2 **GREETINGS**
HALF PINT

3 **MINI BUS**
GENERAL TREES

4 **BOOPS**
SUPER CAT

5 **REVIVAL TIME**
CHALICE

6 **SHE BOOM**
MALLORY WILLIAMS

7 **COST OF LIVING**
HALF PINT

8 **I WANNA WAKE UP WITH YOU**
BORIS GARDNER

9 **SHE LOVES ME NOW**
BERES HAMMOND

10 **GOVERNMENT BOOPS**
LOVINDEER

11 **PUSH COME TO SHOVE**
FREDDIE MCGREGOR

12 **JAH SEND ME COME**
DIGNITARY STYLISH

13 **PROPHECY A GO HOLD THEM**
LEROY SMART

14 **BABYLON BOOPS**
LOVINDEER

15 **ONE SCOTCH**
ADMIRAL BAILEY AND CHAKA DEMUS

16 **POLICE IN A ENGLAND**
PETER METRO

17 **NENGEH NENGEH**
BROTHER DEE

18 **MEMBERS ONLY**
TYRONE TAYLOR

19 **RING ROAD JAM**
FABULOUS FIVE

20 **TENEMENT YARD**
SOPHIA GEORGE

21 **SKIN TO SKIN**
DERRICK HARRIOTT

22 **GIMME RHYHM**
MELLO AND JELLO

23 **GIMME SOCA**
BYRON LEE & THE DRAGONAIRES

24 **WHAT ONE DANCE CAN DO**
BERES HAMMOND

25 **UNDER COVER LOVER**
JOSEY WALES

1987

1 **PUNANY**
ADMIRAL BAILEY

2 **NO WANGA GUT**
TIGER

3 **BIG BELLY MAN**
ADMIRAL BAILEY

4 **TWO YEAR OLD**
ADMIRAL BAILEY

5 **DON'T HURT MY FEELINGS**
FREDDIE MCGREGOR

6 **WEAR YU SIZE**
LT STITCHIE

7 **LOVE TONIGHT**
LEROY SMART

8 **NO MAMA**
SCREWDRIVER

9 **BLUEBERRY HILL**
YELLOWMAN

10 **TALK OF THE TOWN**
LEROY SMART

11 **HOL A FRESH**
RED DRAGON

12 **AGONY**
PINCHERS

13 **PUSH COME TO SHOVE**
FREDDIE MCGREGOR

14 **JAMAICAN WOMAN**
FABULOUS FIVE

15 **NICE GIRL**
LT STITCHIE

16 **LEVEL THE VIBES**
HALF PINT

17 **HEALTHY BODY**
ADMIRAL BAILEY

18 **DEH WID YOU**
SUPER BLACK

19 **BIGGER BOSS**
SHIRLEY MCLEAN/BROTHER DEE

20 **I NEED YOU**
CHOCK TURNER

21 **GONE A NEGRIL**
GENERAL TREES

22 **COME SEE ABOUT ME**
MARCIA GRIFFITHS

23 **CAN'T TAN YA**
TIGER

24 **THE OIL**
LOVINDEER

25 **DON IS DON**
TIGER

1988

1. **LONELINESS WON'T LEAVE ME ALONE**
   SANCHEZ
2. **JUGGLING**
   THRILLER U
3. **NINJA MI NINJA**
   COURTNEY MELODY
4. **KINGSTON 13**
   PINCHERS
5. **SHE'S MINE**
   BARRINGTON LEVY
6. **PROTECTION**
   NINJA MAN/COURTNEY MELODY
7. **MODERN GIRL**
   COURTNEY MELODY
8. **OLD FRIEND**
   SANCHEZ
9. **SARAH**
   FRANKIE PAUL
10. **CASSANOVA**
    FRANKIE PAUL
11. **YOUNG GAL BUSINESS**
    CHAKA DEMUS
12. **SPECIAL**
    KING EVERAL
13. **NATTY DREAD**
    LT STITCHIE
14. **SIZE**
    RED DRAGON
15. **INVASION SOUTH AFRICA**
    BRIGADIER JERRY
16. **DE MUSIC HOT MAMA**
    BYRON LEE & THE DRAGONAIRES
17. **DUCK**
    RED DRAGON
18. **DEDICATE MY LOVE**
    LEROY SMART
19. **RUMOURS**
    GREGORY ISAACS
20. **LOVE ZONE**
    LEROY SMART
21. **PRETTY LOOKS DONE**
    MAJOR MACKEREL
22. **THIS MAGIC MOMENT**
    LEROY GIBBON
23. **NO TROUBLE WE**
    RAPPA ROBERT/TIPPA LEE
24. **TAKE TIME TO KNOW HER**
    TINGA STEWART/NINJA MAN

1989

1. **COME BACK TO ME**
   TIGER AND MALVO
2. **GIRL YOU LOVE ME**
   PAPA SAN
3. **YOUNG AND SHE GREEN**
   THRILLER U AND JOHNNY P
4. **ONE BLOOD**
   JUNIOR REID
5. **LEGAL RIGHTS**
   PAPA SAN AND LADY G
6. **BABY CAN I HOLD YOU**
   FOXY BROWN
7. **SUPER WOMAN**
   KAREN WHITE
8. **WHO SHE LOVE**
   SHABBA RANKS/HOME T/COCO TEA
9. **EYE NO SEE**
   GENERAL TREES
10. **I WILL SURVIVE**
    PAPA SAN
11. **COUNT OUT**
    FLOURGON
12. **SWEETS FOR MY SWEETS**
    SUPER CAT
13. **HEALTHY BODY**
    LITTLE LENNY
14. **STYLE AND FASHION**
    PAPA SAN
15. **WINEY WINEY**
    ADMIRAL BAILEY
16. **POCOMANIA DAY**
    LOVINDEER AND CHALICE
17. **I DO**
    GREGORY ISAACS
18. **ARDENT FAN**
    PINCHERS
19. **ONE BIG FAMILY**
    HALF PINT
20. **SHE**
    HENKEL IRIE
21. **SLOW DOWN**
    FRANKIE PAUL
22. **SAMFIE LOVE**
    JOHNNY P AND DERRICK PARKER
23. **SATISFACTION**
    ROCABESSA
24. **RETURN OF THE DON**
    PINCHERS
25. **STUCK**
    EARLY BLACK

1990

1. **TWICE MY AGE**
   SHABBA RANKS
2. **WORKIE WORKIE**
   BYRON LEE & THE DRAGONAIRES
3. **YOU'LL NEVER GET TO HEAVEN**
   54-46
4. **HERE I AM**
   CHEVELLE FRANKLIN
5. **CARELESS WHISPER**
   THRILLER U
6. **BEEN AROUND THE WORLD**
   ECHO MINOTT
7. **CARPENTER**
   JOHN HOLT
8. **I WANT TO ROCK**
   FRANKIE PAUL
9. **THIS IS WE**
   ADMIRAL BAILEY AND CHAKA DEMUS
10. **HOW AM I SUPPOSED TO LIVE WITHOUT YOU**
    PLIERS
11. **PEOPLE MAKE THE WORLD GO ROUND**
    RUDDY THOMAS
12. **WHO COLT THE GAME**
    RITA MARLEY
13. **BACCHANAL IN THE CITY**
    BYRON LEE & THE DRAGONAIRES
14. **GUILTY**
    GREGORY ISAACS
15. **JUMP UP (WORKIE WORKIE)**
    CHAKA DEMUS
16. **WOULD YOU LIKE**
    KING SOUNDS
17. **BIKE BACK**
    JOHNNY P
18. **STOP LOVING YOU**
    FREDDIE MCGREGOR
19. **OH ME OH MY**
    KAREN SMITH
20. **FIND YOUR WAY**
    LOVINDEER
21. **LIFE GOES ON**
    SPANNER BANNER
22. **ROUND TABLE TALK**
    PAPA SAN AND LADY G
23. **HOT STEPPER**
    INI KAMOZE

1991

1. **TRAILER LOAD OF GIRLS**
   SHABBA RANKS

2. **BANDALERO**
   PINCHERS

3. **STRANGE**
   PAPA SAN

4. **MY FIRST REAL LOVE**
   D. WISDOM

5. **STEP ASIDE**
   BERES HAMMOND

6. **FIRE BURNING**
   MARCIA GRIFFITHS

7. **TEMPTED TO TOUCH**
   BERES HAMMOND

8. **BEST CUSTOM OFFICER**
   LOVINDEER

9. **STRIVE**
   SHINEHEAD

10. **A YU SHAPE**
    ADMIRAL BAILEY

11. **GIVE IT A CHANCE**
    SANCHEZ

12. **FRESH VEGETABLE**
    TONY REBEL

13. **BIG AND BROAD**
    SUPER CAT/HEAVY D/FRANKIE PAUL

14. **POISON**
    DENNIS BROWN/BRIAN AND TONY GOLD

15. **BY SIDE**
    RICHIE STEPHENS

16. **TEASER**
    BYRON LEE & THE DRAGONAIRES

17. **NIGHT AND DAY**
    LT STITCHIE

18. **CROWNING OF THE BROWNING**
    FRANKIE PAUL

19. **EMPTINESS**
    BERES HAMMOND

20. **SERIOUS TIME**
    TIBET/SHABBA/NINJA

21. **BAGDAD CAFE**
    SLY AND ROBBIE

22. **IF BY CHANCE**
    GREGORY ISAACS

23. **HOUSECALL**
    SHABBA RANKS/MAXI PRIEST

24. **CLOSE TO YOU**
    MAXI PRIEST

25. **DIAL MY NUMBER**
    CARLENE DAVIS

1992

1. **MURDER SHE WROTE**
   CHAKA DEMUS AND PLIERS

2. **TING-A-LING**
   SHABBA RANKS

3. **BOGLE**
   BUJU BANTON

4. **BAM BAM**
   PLIERS

5. **LOVE MI BROWNING**
   BUJU BANTON

6. **LOVE ME**
   LEROY SMART

7. **PUTTING UP RESISTANCE**
   BERES HAMMOND

8. **THEM A BLEACH**
   NARDO RANKS

9. **THE GRUDGE**
   BUJU BANTON

10. **FULL ATTENTION**
    BERES HAMMOND

11. **WINE DOWN**
    BYRON LEE & THE DRAGONAIRES

12. **TALK ABOUT FRIENDS**
    LEROY SMART

13. **YU DEAD NOW**
    TIGER

14. **STOP IN THE NAME OF LOVE**
    JUDY MOWATT

15. **ARMSHOUSE**
    CAPLETON

16. **MAMA**
    BABY WAYNE

17. **GRANNY**
    GENERAL DEGREE

18. **SYLVIA**
    COLIN ROACH/BUNNY GENERAL

19. **BUMPER BOTTOM**
    ADMIRAL BAILEY

20. **GOLD SPOON**
    BUJU BANTON

21. **BEEP BEEP**
    TIGER

22. **COCA COLA SHAPE**
    SIMPLETON

23. **TEK HIM**
    COBRA

24. **ALL FRUITS RIPE**
    JUNIOR REID

25. **FALL IN LOVE**
    SANCHEZ

1993

1. **DEPORTEE**
   BUJU BANTON

2. **ACTION**
   TERROR FABULOUS/NADINE SUTHERLAND

3. **SOUND BOY KILLING**
   MEGA BANTON

4. **GOOD LOOKING GAL**
   BUJU BANTON

5. **BOOM BOOM BYE**
   RED ROSE/ROUNDHEAD

6. **GLAMOROUS**
   TERROR FABULOUS

7. **DANCE HALL SOCA**
   BYRON LEE & THE DRAGONAIRES

8. **SWEAT**
   INNER CIRCLE

9. **YOUR BODY IS HERE WITH ME**
   LEROY SMART

10. **LOVE OF A LIFETIME**
    JUNIOR TUCKER

11. **GUN COURT**
    JUNIOR REID

12. **THE PRESCRIPTION**
    LT STITCHIE

13. **LOVE MEANS NEVER TO SAY**
    BERES HAMMOND

14. **GIVE IT UP**
    JUNIOR TUCKER

15. **IF I EVER FALL IN LOVE**
    ANTHONY MALVO

16. **FIND A GOOD MAN**
    LADY SAW

17. **HELLO MAMA AFRICA**
    GARNETT SILK

18. **OPERATION ARDENT**
    BUJU BANTON

19. **MISS GOODY GOODY**
    COLIN ROACH/GALAXY

20. **MONEY FRIEND**
    LEROY SMART/BABY WAYNE

21. **POP STYLE**
    TERROR FABULOUS

22. **IF I EVER FALL**
    SANCHEZ

23. **MERLENE**
    SNAGGA PUSS

24. **TROUBLE FREE**
    KASHIEF LINDO

25. **BUTTERFLY**
    JIGSY KING/TONY CURTIS

1994

1. **MURDERER**
   BUJU BANTON
2. **FOREVER**
   RICHIE STEPHENS
3. **WORLD DANCE**
   BEENIE MAN
4. **TOUR**
   CAPLETON
5. **MATIE**
   BEENIE MAN
6. **ONE WAY TICKET**
   LUCIANO
7. **LISTEN TO THE VOICES**
   JUNIOR REID
8. **MOVE ALONG**
   JUNIOR TUCKER
9. **FLIP UP**
   LT STITCHIE
10. **MICHELLE**
    SPANNER BANNER
11. **JOE BLINDS**
    JUNIOR TUCKER
12. **TEACH THE CHILDREN**
    TONY REBEL
13. **BROWN EYE GIRL**
    SANCHEZ
14. **KUNG FU**
    FUTURE TROUBLES
15. **HELLO CAROL**
    LT STITCHIE
16. **I'M IN LOVE**
    CARLENE DAVIS
17. **GOD OF MY SALVATION**
    BUJU BANTON
18. **GANGA LEE**
    LOUIE CULTURE
19. **WAP THEM**
    LT STITCHIE
20. **SIMMER DOWN**
    ALTHEA AND PAPA SAN
21. **MAN A LOOK YU**
    BUJU BANTON
22. **LOCK ME UP**
    JUNIOR TUCKER
23. **FOWL AFFAIR**
    SILVER CAT
24. **NAH EASE THE FIRE**
    LT STITCHIE
25. **HOT LADY**
    RICHIE STEPHENS

1995

1. **SLAM**
   BEENIE MAN
2. **CELLULAR PHONE**
   BOUNTY KILLER
3. **DONE WIFE**
   COBRA
4. **BOOMBASTIC**
   SHAGGY
5. **ANYTHING FOR YOU**
   SNOW AND FRIENDS
6. **UNTOLD STORIES**
   BUJU BANTON
7. **STOP LIVING IN THE PAST**
   BEENIE MAN
8. **IT'S ME AGAIN JAH**
   LUCIANO
9. **HOW LONG**
   CAPLETON
10. **TEAR OFF ME GARMENT**
    BEENIE MAN
11. **I WANNA KNOW**
    FREDDIE MCGREGOR
12. **DEFEND APACHE**
    BEENIE MAN
13. **MR. HEARTBEAT**
    BOUNTY KILLER
14. **BIG UP AND TRUST**
    BEENIE MAN
15. **MAVIS**
    MERCILESS
16. **NICKY**
    GENERAL B
17. **LORD WATCH OVER OUR SHOULDER**
    GARNETT SILK
18. **DENGUE FEVER**
    BEENIE MAN
19. **BOOK, BOOK, BOOK**
    BOUNTY KILLER
20. **SOCA TATIE**
    BYRON LEE & THE DRAGONAIRES
21. **SHY GUY**
    DIANA KING
22. **HERE COMES THE HOT STEPPER**
    INI KAMOZE
23. **QUARTER TO TWELVE**
    SIMPLETON
24. **GAL**
    BOUNTY KILLER
25. **WILDFLOWER**
    RICHIE STEPHENS

1996

1. **LIVING DANGEROUSLY**
   BOUNTY KILLER/BARRINGTON LEVY
2. **FED UP**
   BOUNTY KILLER
3. **OLD DAWG**
   BEENIE MAN
4. **GO GO WINE**
   CAPTAIN BARKEY
5. **NUFF GAL**
   BEENIE MAN
6. **WHEN I HOLD YOU TONIGHT**
   GENERAL DEGREE
7. **MAESTRO**
   BEENIE MAN
8. **HOTTY HOTTY CREW**
   MONSTER SHACK
9. **BENZ & BIMMA**
   BOUNTY KILLER
10. **UNTOLD STORIES**
    BUJU BANTON
11. **LOVE SOMEBODY**
    JUNIOR TUCKER
12. **BLACKBOARD**
    BEENIE MAN
13. **BAD MIND**
    CAPLETON
14. **LITTLE & CUTE**
    FRISCO KID
15. **GO NOW**
    BOUNTY KILLER
16. **GIRL DEM NATURE**
    BOUNTY KILLER
17. **OLE GALLIS**
    MERCILESS
18. **STOP THE FUSSING & FIGHTING**
    JUNIOR REID
19. **MACARENA DANCE**
    NIGGA MIKEY
20. **FUDGIE**
    GOOFY
21. **I CAN'T SLEEP BABY**
    SANCHEZ
22. **HOTTY HOTTY**
    DELLI RANKS
23. **LIFT UP YOUR HEAD**
    EVERTON BLENDER
24. **BAN MI FI THE TRUTH**
    BEENIE MAN
25. **TELL ME WHY**
    RICHIE STEPHENS

Artist Rankings

These rankings are based strictly on chart successes from 1960 to 1996. We gave points based on annual chart rankings. So a number one song gets 25 points, number two gets 24 points and so forth down to number 25 getting one point. Adding these up gives an artist's total score. Byron Lee and The Dragonaires top position is based primarily on longevity. (The fact that he and his brother own Jamaica's two largest record distribution companies may also have something to do with it.) Had there been charts from 1974 to 1977, Dennis Brown, Beres Hammond and Bob Marley would undoubtedly have higher scores. Based on his current chart hits, Beenie Man will probably move into the top spot after 1997. It's noticeable that in the past five years the charts have become less varied, with a relative handful of artists dominating. Does this mean Jamaican music is becoming stagnant? Time alone will tell.

	ARTIST	POINTS	CHARTERS
1	BYRON LEE & THE DRAGONAIRES	241	22
2	DENNIS BROWN	237	18
3	BERES HAMMOND	225	14
4	BOB MARLEY & THE WAILERS	223	16
5	BEENIE MAN	217	13
6	BUJU BANTON	197	12
7	TOOTS & THE MAYTALS	155	14
8	JOHN HOLT & THE PARAGONS	152	10
9	DERRICK HARRIOTT & THE JIVING JUNIORS	146	13
10	ADMIRAL BAILEY	139	9
11	BOUNTY KILLER	133	10
12	DERRICK MORGAN (INCLUDING DUETS)	126	10
13	LEROY SMART	124	11
14	KEN BOOTHE	123	7
15	YELLOWMAN	120	9
16	BRENT DOWE & THE MELODIANS	117	8
17	GREGORY ISAACS	112	9
18	JUNIOR TUCKER	110	8
19	PAPA SAN	104	7
20	DESMOND DEKKER AND THE ACES	103	7
21	LT STITCHIE	102	9
22	BARRINGTON LEVY	100	9
23	LORD CREATOR	100	5
24	WILFRED 'JACKIE' EDWARDS	100	6

OUR REGGAE TOP 100: 1960-1980

1	1968	54-46	Toots and The Maytals
2	1971	TRENCHTOWN ROCK	Bob Marley and The Wailers
3	1966	007/SHANTY TOWN	Desmond Dekker and The Aces
4	1967	HOLD THEM	Roy Shirley
5	1967	ON THE BEACH	The Paragons
6	1968	BABY WHY	The Cables
7	1966	BAM BAM	Toots and The Maytals
8	1964	CARRY GO BRING COME	Justin Hinds and The Dominos
9	1974	LOVE IS OVERDUE	Gregory Isaacs
10	1971	MANY RIVERS TO CROSS	Jimmy Cliff
11	1961	OH CAROLINA	The Folkes Brothers
12	1977	HAVE MERCY	Mighty Diamonds
13	1965	MAWGA DOG	Peter Tosh
14	1974	BOOK OF RULES	The Heptones
15	1976	NEVER YOU CHANGE	Toots and The Maytals

16	1970	RIVERS OF BABYLON	Brent Dowe and The Melodians
17	1975	ONE LOVE	Bob Marley and The Wailers
18	1964	IT'S YOU	Toots and The Maytals
19	1963	WHEN YOU CALL MY NAME	Stranger and Patsy
20	1970	WEAR YOU TO THE BALL	U-Roy and The Paragons
21	1976	WAR	Bob Marley and The Wailers
22	1964	EASTERN STANDARD TIME	Don Drummond and The Skatalites
23	1971	CHERRY OH BABY	Eric Donaldson
24	1978	RUN FOR YOUR LIFE	Jackie Parris
25	1965	DANCE CRASHER	Alton Ellis
26	1967	DON'T STAY AWAY	Phyllis Dillon
27	1973	SCHOOL	Prince Jazzbo
28	1979	OH MR. D.C.	Sugar Minott
29	1964	SIMMER DOWN	Bob Marley and The Wailers
30	1967	GOT TO GO BACK HOME	Bob Andy
31	1971	SATTA MASSAGANA	The Abyssinians
32	1975	NO WOMAN NO CRY	Bob Marley and The Wailers
33	1964	MY BOY LOLLIPOP	Millie Small
34	1966	FATTY FATTY	The Heptones
35	1974	IN THE DARK	Toots and The Maytals
36	1978	REDEMPTION SONG	Bob Marley and The Wailers
37	1965	SOON YOU'LL BE GONE	The Blues Busters
38	1966	I'VE GOT TO LEAVE YOU BEHIND	Ken Boothe
39	1972	JOHNNY TOO BAD	The Slickers
40	1975	MARCUS GARVEY	Burning Spear
41	1964	SAMMY DEAD	Monty Morris
42	1966	GIRL I'VE GOT A DATE	Alton Ellis
43	1968	TOO EXPERIENCED	Bob Andy
44	1976	POLICE AND THIEVES	Junior Murvin
45	1964	JAMAICAN SKA	Byron Lee and The Dragonaires
46	1967	NICE TIME	Bob Marley and The Wailers
47	1968	SWEET AND DANDY	Toots and The Maytals
48	1979	NICE UP THE DANCE	Michigan and Smiley
49	1964	MUSIC IS MY OCCUPATION	Don Drummond and The Skatalites
50	1967	THINGS YOU SAY YOU LOVE	The Jamaicans
51	1969	PRESSURE DROP	Toots and The Maytals
52	1976	YA HO	The Jays
53	1964	OIL IN MY LAMP	Monty Morris
54	1967	QUEEN MAJESTY	The Techniques
55	1969	SMALL AXE/BATTLE AXE	Bob Marley and The Wailers
56	1983	REVOLUTION	Dennis Brown
57	1964	RUDE BOY SKA	Bob Marley and The Wailers
58	1967	TOUGHER THAN TOUGH	Derrick Morgan
59	1972	S-90 SKANK	Big Youth
60	1976	DREAMLAND	Bunny Wailer
61	1966	EASY SNAPPIN	Theophilus Beckford
62	1967	A MESSAGE TO YOU RUDY	Dandy Livingstone
63	1974	HAVE SOME MERCY	Delroy Wilson
64	1978	NUMBER ONE	Gregory Isaacs
65	1963	ROUGH AND TOUGH	Stranger Cole
66	1968	HARD ROAD TO TRAVEL	Jimmy Cliff
67	1974	MOVE OUT OF BABYLON	Johnny Clarke
68	1978	RUB A DUB STYLE	Michigan and Smiley
69	1962	HOUSEWIVE'S CHOICE	Derrick and Patsy
70	1967	PRESSURE AND SLIDE	The Tennors
71	1972	SKYLARKING/CRABTALKING	Horace Andy
72	1981	ONE DRAW	Rita Marley
73	1960	TELL ME DARLING	Wilfred 'Jackie' Edwards
74	1968	MY CONVERSATION	The Uniques
75	1970	SITTING IN LIMBO	Jimmy Cliff
76	1977	FADE AWAY	Junior Byles
77	1960	DON'T STAY OUT LATE	Kenrick Patrick

78	1968	TAKE IT EASY	Hopeton Lewis
79	1972	OFFICIALLY	Lloyd Parkes
80	1977	STOP FUSSIN AND FIGHTING	Culture
81	1965	HARD MAN FE DEAD	Prince Buster
82	1968	IT'S HARD TO CONFESS	The Gaylads
83	1968	POOR ME ISRAELITE	Desmond Dekker and The Aces
84	1976	BALLISTIC AFFAIR	Leroy Smart
85	1963	KING OF KINGS	Jimmy Cliff
86	1968	MY JAMAICAN GIRL	BB Seaton
87	1970	SATISFACTION	Carl Dawkins
88	1981	NEVER GET WEARY	Toots and The Maytals
89	1963	RUKUMBINE	Carlos Malcolm and The Afro-Jamaican Rhythms
90	1968	I'M JUST A GUY	Alton Ellis
91	1974	TIME TOUGH	Toots and The Maytals
92	1977	NATTY REBEL	U-Roy and Bob Marley
93	1961	OVER THE RIVER	Jiving Juniors
94	1967	PUPPET ON A STRING	Ken Boothe
95	1969	HELLO CAROL	The Gladiators
96	1977	96 DEGREES IN THE SHADE	Third World
97	1968	FEEL LIKE JUMPING	Marcia Griffiths
98	1969	LOVE I CAN FEEL	John Holt
99	1970	KING TUBBY MEETS THE ROCKERS UPTOWN	Augustus Pablo
100	1965	BLAZING FIRE	Derrick Morgan

OUR DANCEHALL TOP 30: 1983-1995

1	1990	BORDER CLASH	Ninja Man
2	1985	RING THE ALARM	Tenor Saw
3	1994	IT'S ME AGAIN JAH	Luciano
4	1991	BANDALERO	Pinchers
5	1991	HOT THIS YEAR	Dirtsman
6	1991	STRANGE	Papa San
7	1986	GREETINGS	Half Pint
8	1986	WHAT THE HELL	Echo Minott
9	1996	JAH BY MY SIDE	Tony Rebel
10	1986	BOOPS	Super Cat
11	1995	BOOMBASTIC	Shaggy
12	1994	TOUR	Capleton
13	1985	GIRLIE GIRLIE	Sophia George
14	1994	MURDERER	Buju Banton
15	1989	COME BACK TO ME	Tiger
16	1991	TRAILER LOAD	Shabba Ranks
17	1989	ONE BLOOD	Junior Reid
18	1992	DANCEHALL SOCA	Byron Lee
19	1992	MURDER SHE WROTE	Chaka Demus
20	1995	SLAM	Beenie Man
21	1993	ONE DAY	Tony Rebel
22	1987	PUNANY	Admiral Bailey
23	1989	POCOMANIA DAY	Chalice and Lovindeer
24	1987	INNA DE BUS	Professor Nuts
25	1994	CAN'T EVEN WALK	The Grace Thrillers
26	1996	NUFF GAL	Beenie Man
27	1995	GLORY BE TO GOD	Lady Saw
28	1993	ACTION	Terror Fabulous and Nadine Sutherland
29	1995	UNTOLD STORIES	Buju Banton
30	1985	WHAT ONE DANCE CAN DO	Beres Hammond

INTRODUCTION

1. The phrase has been widely attributed, including to Duke Ellington and Fats Waller.
2. 'The Universal Appeal of Marley', *The Sunday Herald*, February 26, 1995
3. 'From Field to Platform: Jamaican Folk Music in Concert', *Jamaica Journal* (1987)
4. Peter Manuel, *Caribbean Currents: Caribbean Music from Rhumba to Reggae* (Philadelphia: Temple University Press, 1995) p. 144
5. Barry Floyd, *An Island Microcosm* (London: Macmillan, 1979) p. 38

THE HEARTBEAT OF A PEOPLE

1. Interview
2. *Reggae Report* 7:8 (1989) p. 17
3. Stephen Davis, *Bob Marley: Conquering Lion of Reggae* (London: Plexus, 1988) p. 123
4. Liner notes – Muddy Water: The Real Folk Blues

ROOTS MUSIC – KUMINA, QUADRILLE, MENTO, BLUES AND JAZZ

1. Rex Nettleford, 'Caribbean Perspectives: The Creative Potential and the Quality of Life' in *Caribbean Rhythms – The Emerging English Literature of the West Indies* ed. by Jones T. Livingston (New York: Washington Square Press, 1974)
2. 'From Field to Platform: Jamaican Folk Music in Concert', *Jamaica Journal* (1987)
3. Stephen Davis and Peter Simon, *Reggae International* (London: Thames and Hudson, 1983) p. 26
4. Ibid.
5. Bruno Nettl, *Folk and Traditional music of the Western Continents* (Englewood Cliffs: N. J.: Prentice Hall, 1965)
6. 'An Approach to the Study of Jamaican Popular Music', *Jamaica Journal* 6:4 (1972)
7. 'African Retentions: Yoruba and Kikongo Songs in Jamaica', *Jamaica Journal* (1983)
8. Stephen Davis and Peter Simon, *Reggae International*
9. *Revival Cults in Jamaica* (Kingston: Institute of Jamaica, 1982)
10. Joseph Owens, *Dread – The Rastafarians of Jamaica* (Kingston: Sangsters Bookstores, 1976) p. 17
11. Barry Chevannes, *Rastafari: Roots and Ideology* (Syracuse University Press, 1995) p. 20
12. Joseph Owens, *Dread – The Rastafarians of Jamaica* (Kingston: Sangsters Bookstore, 1976) p. 22
13. 'Kumina: The Most African of Jamaica's Cultural Heritage', *The Sunday Herald*, February 19, 1995
14. Ibid. p. 7

15. Peter Manuel, *Caribbean Currents: Caribbean Music from Rumba to Reggae*, p. 149
16. Suzanne Francis Brown, 'Roots and Rhythm', *Sky Writings* 100 (1995)
17. Ibid.
18. Stephen Davis and Peter Simon, *Reggae Bloodlines: In Search of the Music and Culture of Jamaica* (USA: Anchor Books, 1977) pp. 9-10
19. Sebastien Clarke, *Jah Music: The Evolution of the Popular Jamaican Song* (London: Heinemann Educational Books Ltd, 1980), pp. 12-14; Stephen Davis and Peter Simon, *Reggae Bloodlines: In Search of the Music and Culture of Jamaica*, p. 10
20. Rex Nettleford, *Caribbean Cultural Identity: The Case for Jamaica* (Kingston: Institute of Jamaica, 1978)
21. Stephen Davis and Peter Simon, *Reggae International*, p. 28
22. Stephen Davis, *Bob Marley: Conquering Lion of Reggae*, p. 8
23. Ibid.
24. S. H. Fernando Jr, *The New Beats: Exploring the Music, Culture and Attitudes of Hip Hop* (New York: Anchor Books, 1994) p. 43
25. Barry Chevannes, *Rastafari Roots and Ideology*, p. 15
26. Colin Larkin, ed. *The Guinness Who's Who of Reggae* (London: Guinness Publishing, 1994) p. 8
27. *Africa O-Ye*, pp. 26-27
28. Mickey Hart, *Drumming On The Edge Of Magic*
29. Peter Manuel, *Caribbean Currents: Caribbean Music from Rumba to Reggae*, p. 11
30. Suzanne Francis Brown, 'Roots and Rhythm', *Sky Writings*
31. Justin Whyte, 'Mento Music: Our Indigenous Orchestra', *The Gleaner*, September 15, 1995, p. 1C
32. Ibid.
33. Louis Marriot, *Who's Who & What's What in Jamaican Arts and Entertainment* (Kingston: Talawa, 1996) p. 310
34. Stephen Davis and Peter Simon, *Reggae International*, p. 38
35. Peter Manuel, *Caribbean Currents: Caribbean Music from Rumba to Music*, p. 155
36. 'Kingston's Popular Music Culture', *Jamaica Journal* 22:1 (1989)
37. Sir Philip Sherlock, 'Foundations of Nationhood – From Peasantry to Proletariat', *Jamaica Observer*, December 28, 1995
38. *Jamaica Journal* (1983) Reprint of article originally published in *The Jamaica Standard*, June 2, 1939
39. 'Kingston's Popular Music Culture', *Jamaica Journal*
40. Liner notes – Matador Records, Heartbeat Records
41. Peter Manuel, *Caribbean Currents: Caribbean Music from Rumba to Reggae*, p. 154

42. 'Kingston's Popular Music Culture', *Jamaica Journal*
43. Ibid.
44. Ibid.
45. Ibid.
46. Sebastien Clarke, *Jah Music: The Evolution of the Popular Jamaican Song* (London: Heinemann Educational Books, 1980) p. 62
47. Stephen Davis and Peter Simon, *Reggae International*, p. 135

SOUND SYSTEM DAYS AND NIGHTS

1. 'Kingston's Popular Music Culture', *Jamaica Journal*
2. Interview with Andrew Clunis, *The Star*, December 2, 1994
3. Balford Henry, *The Sunday Gleaner*, September 17, 1995
4. Interview
5. Liner notes – 'Tougher Than Tough'
6. Sebastien Clarke, *Jah Music: The Evolution of the Popular Jamaican Song*, pp. 57-97
7. 8. Ibid.; Liner notes – 'Tougher Than Tough'
9. S. H. Fernando Jr, *The New Beats: Exploring the Music, Culture and Attitudes of Hip Hop*, p. 39
10. Stephen Davis and Peter Simon, *Reggae International*, p. 39
11. Liner notes – 'Ska Bonanza', Heartbeat Records
12. Interview
13. Interview
14. Interview
15. Stephen Davis and Peter Simon, *Reggae International*, pp. 38-39
16. *The Beat* 5:5 (1986)
17. Liner notes: 'Tougher Than Tough'
18. Interview
19. Frankie Campbell, charts
20. Colin Larkin, ed. *The Guinness Who's Who of Reggae*, p. 8
21. Sebastien Clarke, *Jah Music: The Evolution of the Popular Jamaican Song*, p. 75
22. Stephen Davis and Peter Simon, *Reggae International*, p. 39
23. Essay, Jamaica Institute of Music
24. 'An Approach to the Study of Jamaican Popular Music', *Jamaica Journal* 6:4 (1972)
25. Interview

RHYTHM AND BLUES: RASTA AND OH CAROLINA

1. 'Kingston's Popular Music Culture', *Jamaica Journal*
2. 'Some Reflections on the Rastafari Movement in Jamaica: West Kingston in the early 1950s', *Jamaica Journal* 25:2 (1995)
3. Joseph Owens, *Dread – The Rastafarians of Jamaica* (Kingston: Sangsters Bookstores, 1976) p. 121
4. Kenneth Bilby and Elliott Leib, 'Kumina, The Howellite Church and the Emergence of Rastafarian

Traditional Music in Jamaica', *Jamaica Journal* 19:3 (1985), p. 25
5. Sebastien Clarke, *Jah Music: The Evolution of the Popular Jamaican Song*, p. 53
6. Peter Manuel, *Caribbean Currents: Caribbean Music from Rumba to Reggae*, p. 159
7. Liner notes- 'Tougher Than Tough'
8. Stephen Davis and Peter Simon, *Reggae International*, p. 39
9. *The Beat* 13:2 (1994)
10. Liner notes – 'Tougher Than Tough'
11. Liner notes – 'Tougher Than Tough'

SKA, SKA, SKA

1. Interview
2. Interview with Frankie Campbell
3. Liner notes – ' Ska Bonanza', Heartbeat Records, 1991
4. Stephen Davis and Peter Simon, *Reggae International*, p. 38
5. Peter Manuel, *Caribbean Currents: Caribbean Music from Rumba to Reggae*, p. 159
6. Sebastien Clarke, *Jah Music: The Evolution of the Popular Jamaican Song*, p. 69
7. Timothy White, *Catch A Fire: The Life of Bob Marley* (UK: Corgi Books, 1983) p. 38
8. Colin Larkin, ed. *The Guinness Who's Who of Reggae*, p. 56
9. Adrian Boot and Chris Salewicz, *Bob Marley: Songs of Freedom*, (London: Bloomsbury, 1995) p. 64
10. Stephen Davis and Peter Simon, *Reggae Bloodlines*, p. 103
11. Interview
12. Interview
13. Timothy White, *Catch A Fire: The Life of Bob Marley*, pp. 154-155
14. Sebastien Clarke, *Jah Music: The Evolution of the Popular Jamaican Song*, p. 63
15. *Sunday Gleaner*, October 30, 1983
16. Interview
17 Sebastien Clarke, *Jah Music: The Evolution of Jamaican Popular Song*, pp. 65-66
18. *Sunday Gleaner*, February 7, 1965
19. Timothy White, *Catch A Fire: The Life of Bob Marley*, p. 157
20. Sebastien Clarke, *Jah Music: The Evolution of the Popular Jamaican Song*, p. 75
21. *Black Music*, (1975)
22. Sebastien Clarke, *Jah Music: The Evolution of the Popular Jamaican Song*, p. 61
23. Ibid., pp. 77-78
24. Ibid.
25. Ibid.
26. Ibid.
27. *Sunday Gleaner*, April 27, 1965

GET READY FOR ROCKSTEADY

1. Interview
2. Interview with Frankie Campbell
3. Stephen Davis, *Bob Marley: Conquering Lion of Reggae*, pp. 67-68
4. Interview
5. Interview
6. Interview
7. Interview
8. Interview

DO THE REGGAE

1. Interview
2. Stephen Davis, *Bob Marley: Conquering Lion of Reggae*, pp. 77-78
3. Stephen Davis and Peter Simon, *Reggae International*, p. 48
4. Ibid., p. 45
5. Sebastien Clarke, *Jah Music: The Evolution of the Popular Jamaican Song*
6. Stephen Davis and Peter Simon, *Reggae International*, p. 43
7. Liner notes – 'Tougher Than Tough'
8. Stephen Davis and Peter Simon, *Reggae International*, pp. 52-53
9. Interview

REGGAE INTERNATIONAL: THE HARDER THEY COME AND BOB MARLEY

1. *The Beat* 11:3 (1992), p. 41
2. Stephen Davis, *Bob Marley: Conquering Lion of Reggae*, p. 96
3. Ibid., pp. 109-110; Malika Lee Whitney and Dermott Hussey, *Bob Marley: Reggae King of The World* (Kingston Publishers, 1984) pp. 74-75
4. Malika Lee Whitney and Dermott Hussey, *Bob Marley: Reggae King of the World*, pp. 74-75

DUB AND ROOTS

1. Interview
2. *The Beat* 7:3 (1988)
3. Interview
4. Interview

INNA THE DANCEHALL

1. Stephen Barrow, liner notes – 'Tougher Than Tough'
2. *Sunday Gleaner*, November 20, 1994
3. Liner notes – 'Tougher Than Tough'
4. *The New Beats*, p. 48
5. *Reggae Report* 7:8 (1989)
6. Interview

DANCEHALL MASSIVE

1. 'Gleaner Top Ten', *Jamaica Journal* 21:4 (1988)
2. Liner notes – 'Tougher Than Tough'
3. *The New Beats*, p. 35
4. Stephen Davis and Peter Simon, *Reggae International*, p. 33
5. Louise Bennett, *Jamaica Labrish*, (Kingston: Sangsters Bookstores, 1966)
6. *Toronto Star*, February 16, 1996
7. Louise Bennett, *Jamaica Labrish*, p. 9
8. Ibid., p. 9
9. Rex Nettleford, *Caribbean Cultural Identity: The Case of Jamaica*, (Kingston: Institute of Jamaica, 1987)

THE PIONEERS: COUNT MATCHUKIE AND KING STITT

1. *The Star*, December 2, 1994
2. Ibid.
3. *The New Beats*, p. 39
4. *The Observer*, December 2-4, 1995
5. 'U-Roy: Words of Wisdom', *The Beat Magazine* (1989)

U-ROY THE ORIGINATOR

1. 'U Roy: Words of Wisdom', *The Beat* (1989)
2. Dave Marsh, *The First Rock & Roll Confidential Report* (US: Pantheon Books, 1985) pp. 79-80
3. Afrika Bambaataa 'The Rap Attack', *The Beat* 5:4 (1986)
4. *The New Beats*, p. 10
5. Ibid., p. 44
6. Ibid.
7. Ibid., pp. 7-8
8. Ibid., p. 8
9. *The Beat* 5:4 (1986)
10. Dave Marsh, *The First Rock & Roll Confidential Report*, pp. 79-80
11. *The New Beats*, p. 32
12. Stephen Davis and Peter Simon, *Reggae International*, p. 189
13. Ibid., p. 191
14. *The New Trouser Press Record Guide*, p. 300

RIDDIM WILD

1. *Black Music* (1976)
2. Ibid.
3. Stephen Davis and Peter Simon, *Reggae International*, p. 105
4. Interview
5. Stephen Davis and Peter Simon, *Reggae International*, p. 130
6. Ibid., p. 53
7. 'Gleaner Top Ten', *Jamaica Journal* 21:4 (1988)
8. Stephen Davis and Peter Simon, *Reggae International*, p. 53

TALKING GLEANERS

1. 'Gleaner Top Ten', *Jamaica Journal* 21:4 (1988)
2. Howard McGowan, '10 Best Deejays', *The Gleaner*, 1991
3. Ibid.

NOTES & REFERENCES TO THE SOUNDS

EASY SNAPPIN' *p. 84*

Liner Notes: Tougher Than Tough, page 32
The Star, June 29, 1995, page 14, interview with Theophilus Beckford by Andrew Clunis

TELL ME DARLING *p. 84*

Jah Music, page 64
Liner Notes, Ska Bonanza (*Heartbeat*)
Dermot Hussey, *Lifestyle Magazine*

OH CAROLINA *p. 86*

Jah Music, page 62
Roger Steffens, 'Folkes Tale', *The Beat* 13:2 (1994)

SAMMY DEAD OH / OIL IN MY LAMP *p. 90*

Liner Notes, Clancy Eccles Presents His Reggae Review

CARRY GO BRING COME *pp. 91*

Reggae Report, 9:10, (1991)
Black Music (1975)

MUSIC IS MY OCCUPATION/EASTERN STANDARD TIME *p. 94*

Jah Music, pages 65-66; *Catch A Fire*. pages 195-6
Liner Notes, Matador Records. Heartbeat Records
Interview
The Star, May 31, 1995

JAMAICAN SKA *p. 98*

Jah Music, p. 62

TIME IS LONGER THAN ROPE

Liner Notes, Tougher Than Tough. page 32

007/SHANTY TOWN *p. 102*

Liner Notes, The Best of Desmond Dekker, Rhino Records
The Beat 11:6 (1992)
Reggae Report, 10:7

HOLD THEM *p. 112*

Black Music, 1976

ON THE BEACH *p. 110*

Reggae Report, 10:7, (1992); 9:7 (1991)
Interview

DON'T STAY AWAY *p. 113*

Reggae Report, 6:2 (1988)

IT'S HARD TO CONFESS *p. 116*

Liner Notes, Musical Feast, Mrs. Pottinger's High Note and Gayfeet Label

LET THEM TRY *p. 118*

The Beat, 13:3 (1994)

54-46 *p. 119*

Black Music (1976)

BABY WHY *p. 122*

Liner Notes, Studio One
Interview
The Beat, 11:6 (1992)
Jah Music, p. 79
Reggae International, p. 130
Reggae Bloodlines, p. 123

ISRAELITES *p. 122*

Daily Gleaner, August 1969
Reggae Bloodlines, p. 2
Catch A Fire, p. 40
The Heart of Rock and Soul, p. 541

STEPPING RAZOR *p. 125*

The Beat, 5:5 (1986)
Catch A Fire, pp. 172-3
Reggae Bloodlines, pp. 95-97
Black Music, (1975)
Reggae Report, 7:4 (1989)

PRESSURE DROP *p. 130*

The Heart of Rock and Soul, p. 155

DUPPY CONQUEROR *p. 134*

'An Approach to the Study of Jamaican Popular Music'. *Jamaica Journal*. 6:4, (1972)

RIVERS OF BABYLON *p. 134*

Reggae International, p. 48

SATISFACTION *p.135*

Howard McGowan, *Sunday Gleaner*, January 28, 1996

MANY RIVERS TO CROSS *p. 137*

Reggae International, p. 150

CHERRY OH BABY *p. 139*

Liner Notes: From Bam Bam to Cherry Oh Baby

SMALL AXE/BATTLE AXE *p. 139*

Black Music, (1975)

TRENCHTOWN ROCK / SIMMER DOWN / NO WOMAN NO CRY *pp. 92, 95, 139*

Toronto Star, April 26, 1991
Black Music, (1975); August (1976); October 1976
Bob Marley 50th Anniversary Supplement, February 6, 1995
Liner Notes: 'One Love' (Heartbeat)

Liner Notes: 'Jamaica's Golden Hits by
  Byron Lee: Vol 2'
Bob Marley : Songs of Freedom, p. 172
Bob Marley: Conquering Lion of Reggae, pp. 109-110
The Rolling Stone Record Guide, p. 402
Black Music, (1976)
The Complete Guide to the Music of Bob Marley, p. 61
Bob Marley: Conquering Lion of Reggae, p. 93
The Heart and Soul of Rock and Roll, p. 395

MAWGA DOG *p. 139*

Reggae Report, 6:1 (1988); 6:2 (1988); 5:5 (1987)
The Beat, 6:5 (1987)
The Beat, 5:1 (1986)

JOHNNY TOO BAD *p. 145*

'The Truth About Johnny Too Bad', Leroy Pierson, *The
  Beat* Magazine, 7:5 (1988)

BOOK OF RULES *p. 145*

The Heart of Rock and Soul, p. 500
Reggae Bloodlines, p. 109
Reggae International, p. 95-96
The Heart of Rock And Soul, p. 332

MOVE OUT A BABYLON *p. 156*

Catch A Fire
Marley and Me. xxxiii-xxxiv

DREAMLAND *p. 164*

Liner Notes, *Bob Marley and The Wailers: Birth of a
  Legend*

POLICE AND THIEVES *p. 166*

Black Music, (1975)

NATTY REBEL *p. 171*

Black Music, (1976)

FADE AWAY *p. 171*

Liner Notes: Channel One – Hit Bound: The
  Revolutionary Sound.

THE COOL RULER *p. 173*

Reggae International, p. 145
Reggae Report, 6:8 (1988)
The Beat, 12:1 (1993)

STEPPING OUT OF BABYLON *p. 176*

Reggae International, p. 139

PASS THE KUTCHIE *p. 180*

Sibbles Extract
The Gleaner, October 24, 1994
The Weekend Star, February 10, 1995

UNMETRED TAXI *p. 183*

Reggae International, pp 134-5
Reggae Report, 7:8 (1989)
The Beat, 7:1 (1988)

PRINCESS BLACK *p. 182*

Interview with Basil Walters, *Sunday Observer*, January
  28, 1996

SOLIDARITY *p. 187*

Liner Notes, Black Uhuru – Liberation: The Island
  Anthology

GREETINGS *p. 187*

Liner Notes, Tougher Than Tough, p. 57

WILD GILBERT *p. 191*

'Gilbert Songs'. *Jamaica Journal*. 22:2
Ibid.

TELEPHONE LOVE *p. 194*

Reggae Report

STRANGE *p. 202*

The Beat, 11:4 (1992) p. 52

BOOM BYE BYE *p. 204*

Milton Wray, 'A Performance in Justice' *Jamaica Herald*,
  January 31, 1996

ONE DAY *p. 207*

Reggae Island
'Tony, Tony, Tony', *The Beat*, 12:6 (1993)

DANCEHALL SOCA *p. 210*

Jah Music, p. 62
Ibid. p. 75

ACTION / SWEAT *p. 203*

The Gleaner, January 20, 1996. p. 2

CAN'T EVEN WALK *p. 209*

Caribbean Currents, p. 172
Howard McGowan, *Sunday Gleaner*, January 28, 1996

BIBLIOGRAPHY

Magazines
Reggae Report Magazine
The Beat
The Jamaica Journal

Newspapers
The Gleaner
The Herald
The Observer
The Star
X-News
Toronto Star

Abrahams, Roger D and Szwed, John F. *After Africa*
  (New Haven and London, Yale University Press,
  1988)
Barnes, Winston, Series in the *Sunday Gleaner Magazine*,
  May 2, 9, 16, 23, 30, 1982 [Provides part of the

framework for the history. Occasional direct quote]

Barnet, Sr Leonard E. *The Rastafarians* (Boston: Beacon Press, 1988)

_____ *The Sun and the Drum* (Kingston, Heinemann, 1996)

Bayer, Marcel *Jamaica : A Guide to the People, Politics and Culture* (Kingston: Ian Randle Publishers, 1993)

Bennett, Louise *Jamaica Labrish* (Kingston: Sangsters Bookstores, 1966)

Bisnauth, Dale *History of Religions in The Caribbean* (Kingston Publishers Ltd, 1989)

Black, Clinton V. *History of Jamaica* (Kingston: Longman Caribbean, 1993)

Boot, Adrian and Salewicz, Chris *Bob Marley: Songs of Freedom* (London: Bloomsbury, 1995)

Bronson, Marsha *Bob Marley* (Kingston: Sangsters Bookstores, 1993)

Broughton, Simon, et al. *World Music: The Rough Guide* (London: Rough Guides Ltd, 1994)

Bryan, Patrick *The Jamaican People: 1880-1902* (London: Macmillan Caribbean, 1991)

Burnett, Michael, *Jamaican Music* (Oxford University Press, 1982)

Charters, Samuel *The Country Blues* (New York: Da Capo, 1975).

_____ *The Roots of the Blues: An African Search* (New York: Da Capo, 1981)

Chevannes, Barry *Rastafari: Roots and Ideology* (Syracuse University Press, 1995)

Christgau, Robert *Christgau's Record Guide: The '80s* (New York: Pantheon, 1990)

Clarke, Donald *The Rise and Fall of Popular Music* (London: Viking, 1995)

Clarke, Sebastien *Jah Music: The Evolution of the Popular Jamaican Song* (London: Heinemann Educational Books Ltd, 1980).

Cooper, Carolyn *Noises in the Blood: Orality, Gender and the 'Vulgar' Body Of Jamaican Popular Culture* (London: Macmillian Caribbean, 1993).

Crewe, Quentin *Touch the Happy Isles: A Journey Through the Caribbean* (London: Michael Joseph Ltd, 1987)

Davis, Stephen *Bob Marley: Conquering Lion of Reggae* (London: Plexus, 1988).

Davis, Stephen and Simon, Peter *Reggae International* (London: Thames and Hudson, 1983).

_____ *Reggae Bloodlines: In Search of the Music and Culture of Jamaica* (USA: Anchor Books, 1977)

Davis, Francis *The History of the Blues* (New York: Hyperion, 1995)

Erlewine, Michael, All Music Guide (San Francisco: Miller Freemann Books, 1994)

Ewens, Graeme (London: Guinness Publishing., 1991)

Fernando Jr., S. H. *The New Beats: Exploring The Music, Culture and Attitudes of Hip Hop* (New York: Anchor Books, 1994)

Floyd, Barry *Jamaica: An Island Microcosm.* (Macmillian: London, 1979)

Frith, Simon and Goodwin, Andrew *On Record: Rock, Pop & The Written Word* (New York: Pantheon Books 1990)

Gambaccini, Paul and Rice, Tim and Rice Jo. *British Hit Singles* (London: Guinness Books, 1989).

Guillermoprieto, Alma *Samba* (New York: Vintage Departures, 1991)

Gunst, Laurie *Born Fi Dead* (New York: Henry Holt, 1995)

Guralnick, Peter *Feel Like Going Home* (New York: Perennial, 1989)

Hart, Mickey *Drumming On The Edge Of Magic*

Hebige, Dick *Cut 'N' Mix* (London: Comedia Books, 1987)

Hounsome, Terry and Chambre Tim *Rock Record* (New York: Facts On File Inc., 1981)

Hussey, Dermott 'The Red Hot Rhythms of Reggae' in *Insight Guides* (Kingston; Singapore: APA Publications; Houghton Mifflin, 1995)

Jahn, Brian and Weber, Tom *Reggae Island: Jamaican Music in The Digital Age* (Kingston Publishers Ltd, 1992)

Larkin, Colin ed. *All the Top 100 Albums* (London: Guinness Publishing, 1994)

_____ *The Guinness Who's Who of Reggae* (London: Guinness Publishing, 1994)

Lazell, Barry *Marley* (London: Hamlyn, 1994)

Lomax, Alan *The Land Where The Blues Began* (New York: Methuen, 1993)

Manuel, Peter *Caribbean Currents: Caribbean Music From Rumba To Reggae* (Philadelphia: Temple University Press, 1995)

Marriott, Louis *Who's Who & What's What in Jamaican Arts and Entertainment 1996* (Kingston: Talawa 1995).

Marsh, Dave *The First Rock & Roll Confidential Report* (United States: Pantheon Books, 1985).

_____ *The Heart and Soul of Rock and Roll: The 1001 Greatest Singles Ever Made* (London: Penguin 1989)

Marsh, Dave with Swenson John, *The Rolling Stone Record Guide* (New York: Random House. 1979)

McCann, Ian *Bob Marley: In His Own Words* (London: Omnibus Press, 1993)

_____ *The Complete Guide to the Music of Bob Marley* (London: Omnibus Press, 1993)

Mordecai, Pamela, ed. *From Our Yard: Jamaican Poetry Since Independence* (Kingston: Institute of Jamaica Publications, 1989)

Mulvaney, Rebekah Mahele, *Rastafari and Reggae: A Dictionary and Sourcebook* (New York: Greenwood Press, 1990)

Nagashina, Yokimo S. *Rastafarian Music in Contemporary Jamaica* (Kingston: Institute of Jamaica, 1978)

Nettleford, Rex *Caribbean Cultural Identity: The Case for*

Jamaica (Kingston: Institute of Jamaica, 1978)

Oliver, Paul *Blues Off The Record* (New York: Da Capo, 1984)

Owens, Joseph *Dread – The Rastafarians of Jamaica* (Kingston: Sangsters Bookstores, 1976)

Palmer, Robert *Deep Blues* (New York: Penguin, 1981)

Payne, Robert *Politics in Jamaica* (London: C. Hurst & Co, 1988)

Petrie, Gavin *Black Music* (London: Hamlyn, 1974)

Robbins, Ira, A. *The New Trouser Press Record Guide* (New York: Collier Books, 1989)

Small, Geoff *Ruthless: The Global Rise of the Yardies* (London: Warner Books, 1995).

Stapleton, Chris & May, Chris *African Rock: The Pop Music of a Continent* (New York: Obelisk, 1990).

Stein, Judith *The World of Marcus Garvey: Race and Class in Modern Society* (Baton Rouge and London: Lousianna State University Press, 1966)

Stone, Carl *Class Race and Political Behaviour in Urban Jamaica* (Kingston: Institute of Social and Economic Research, University of the West Indies, 1973).

Taylor, Don *Marley and Me: The Real Story* (Kingston Publishers Ltd, 1994).

Waters, Anita M. *Race, Class and Political Symbols* (Oxford: Transaction Books, 1985)

Whitbourne, Joel *The Billboard Book of Top 40 Hits* (New York: Billboard Books, 1989).

White, Timothy *Catch A Fire: The Life of Bob Marley* (UK: Corgi Books, 1983).

Whitney, Malika Lee and Hussey, Dermott *Bob Marley : Reggae King of the World* (Kingston Publishers Ltd, 1984).

INTERVIEW SOURCES

Other than direct interviews

Bob Andy
Black Music (1976)
Interview with Tomlin Ellis, KLAS radio
The Beat 14:6 (1995)

Ken Boothe
Reggae Report 6:2(1988)
Interview with Tomlin Ellis, KLAS radio

Jimmy Cliff
Reggae Bloodlines, pp. 83-89
Reggae International, pp. 150-151
Reggae Report 10:7 (1992)
The Beat 5:4 (1986)
Interview with Tomlin Ellis, KLAS radio

Coxsone Dodd
Reggae International, p. 48
Jah Music, pp. 57-97
Catch A Fire, pp. 159-163

Reggae Report 9:7 (1991)
The Sunday Gleaner, September 30, 1990
The Beat 13:3 (1994)
Liner notes – 'Ska Bonanza', Heartbeat Records

Desmond Dekker
Liner notes – 'The Best of Desmond Dekker', Rhino Records
The Beat 6 (1992)
Reggae Report 10:7 (1992)

Alton Ellis
Reggae International, p. 43
Reggae Report 7:6-7 (1989)
The Beat, 8:4 (1989)
The Beat, (1984)
Interview with Tomlin Ellis, KLAS radio

Marcia Griffiths
Reggae International, p. 138
Reggae Report 10:6 (1992)
Reggae Report 6:7 (1992)
Interview with Tomlin Ellis, KLAS radio

Frederick 'Toots' Hibbert
Reggae Bloodlines, pp. 89-93
Black Music (1976)
Reggae Report 10:7 (1992)

John Holt
Black Music (1976)
Reggae Report 9:7 (1991)
The Beat 8:4 (1989)

Bob Marley
Carle Gayle, *Black Music* September (1975)
Carle Gayle, *Black Music* June (1976)
Carle Gayle, *Black Music* August (1976)

Leroy Sibbles
The Beat 5:5 (1986)
Black Music (1976)
Reggae Report 8:5 (1990)
Toronto Star, April 26, 1991
The Weekend Star, February 10, 1995

Sly Dunbar and Robbie Shakespeare
Reggae International, pp. 134-5
Reggae Report 7:8 (1989)
The Beat 7:1 (1988)

Steelie and Clevie
(Wycliffe Johnson and Cleveland Brown)
Reggae Report

U-Roy
Black Music (1976)
Reggae Report 10:7 (1992)
The Beat 8:1 (1989)

The originating impulse of the Rastafari millenarian vision is often said to be Marcus Garvey's stirring directive: 'Look to Africa where a divine black king shall be crowned, for the day of deliverance is near' – a prophecy supposedly fulfilled by Haile Selassie's coronation as emperor of Ethiopia in 1930. Yet there is no evidence that Garvey ever uttered such words. A somewhat similar message was addressed to a United Negro Improvement Association (UNIA) convention on September 1924 by the Rev. James Morris Webb, a Chicago associate of Garvey's. Webb was quoting from his 1919 book entitled *A Black Man Will Be The Coming Universal King, Proven by Biblical History.* Yet Webb's prophecy does not appear to have reached Jamaica or achieved any popular currency.[1]

In his book, *Rastafari Roots and Ideology,* Barry Chevannes gives a possible source of the 'divine black king' legend. In 1929 Garvey held a UNIA convention in Jamaica for the first time. In addition to his political activities, Garvey also held non-denominational religious services and organised cultural activities, including plays. One of these was entitled 'The Coronation of the King and Queen of Africa', a dramatisation of UNIA work which mixed fact and fiction and ended with the crowning of an African king. It is not surprising that many saw a connection between this play and Selassie's coronation only a year later, especially as most poor Jamaicans were then illiterate, and there was no radio or television to interpret events.[2] Yet Rastafarians who insist that Garvey was their prophet are correct in spirit, if not in letter. For he did speak of a black God in his *Universal Negro Catechism.*

Q. What is the colour of God?

A. A spirit has neither colour, nor other natural parts, nor qualities.

Q. If then, you had to think or speak of the colour of God, how would you describe it?

A. As black; since we are created in his image and likeness.

Q. On what would you base your assumption that God is black?

A. On the same basis as that taken by white people when they assume that God is of their colour.[3]

It required only a minor extrapolation of this eminently reasonable argument to see the earthly representative of this black God in the newly crowned emperor of Ethiopia. For Ethiopia, an independent sovereignty for at least 2,000 years and the only traditional African empire to survive the colonial partition, was a symbol of African dignity and independence long before Selassie's crowning. The battle of Adowa, where Emperor Menelik II destroyed the invading Italian army on March 1, 1896, was a key rallying point not only for African blacks but their descendants in the new world.[4]

Ethiopia's ancient Christian tradition and biblical symbolism enhanced its mystique – 'Princes shall come out of Egypt; Ethiopia shall soon stretch out her hands unto God' says the oft-repeated thirty-first verse of the sixty-eighth Psalm. Practically all forms of black redemptive ideology have been suffused with Ethiopianism. Haile Selassie's coronation on 11 November 1930, provided a new justification for political and spiritual faith in Ethiopia, which fused with Garvey's doctrine of racial redemption, black unity and a free Africa.[5]

Selassie claimed to be 225th in a line of Ethiopian kings which could be traced all the way to Menelik, the son of Solomon and Sheba. His honorific titles included 'King of Kings', 'Lord of Lords' and 'Conquering Lion of The Tribe of Judah'. When some Jamaican preachers began expressing a belief in Selassie's divinity, they used biblical references to buttress their opinions, including Revelation 5: 2-5 – 'Weep not; behold, the Lion of the Tribe of Judah, the root of David, hath prevailed to open the book . . .'; and Psalm 68: 31 – 'Princes shall come out of Egypt, and Ethiopia shall stretch forth her hands unto God'.

Among the earliest Rastafarian exponents were Joseph Nathaniel Hibbert, Archibald Dunkley and Leonard Percival Howell. (Hibbert had lived in Costa Rica, where he joined the Ancient Mystical Order of Ethiopia and become a Master Mason, before returning to Jamaica in 1931. Dunkley had worked as a seaman plying the fruit boat routes between America and the Caribbean. Howell had also been a sailor and for a time lived in America.) All had travelled widely and undoubtedly came in contact with pan-African ideas. Many themes that became important to Rastafarians had been explored by black writers like Ottobah Cugoano and P. K. Isaka Seme.[6]

Rastafarian ideology seems to be based on two books, *The Holy Piby* and *The Royal Parchment Scroll of Black Supremacy. The Holy Piby* otherwise known as 'the Black Man's Bible', was published by Robert Athlyi Roberts in New Jersey in 1924. It provided the doctrinal basis for Roberts' 'Afro-Athlican Constructive Gaathly' which had a Jamaican branch called the Hamatic Church. *The Royal Parchment* was published in Jamaica in 1926 by Fitz Balintine Petersburgh who described the work as 'Ethiopia's Bible Text'. In 1935 this work was extensively plagiarised in 'The Promised Key' by Leonard Howell, who in time became the central figure in Rastafarianism's development.[7, 8]

Howell was born June 16, 1898 in Clarendon. Details of his early life are hazy, but he claimed to have joined the Jamaican war contingent in Panama in 1918, served on American merchant ships, and then resided in the U.S. His return to Jamaica in November 1932 coincided with a marked upsurge of religious revivalism and he held his first public meetings in Kingston on 'Ras Tafari, King of Abyssinia' in January 1933. Citing Selassie's coronation attended by 72 nations paying homage and bearing gifts, Howell spoke of Selassie as 'Christ returned to earth to kill Nebuchadnezzar's image'. Blacks in the west, he said, were really Jews, the biblical lost tribe of Israel.[9] (Ras Tafari, the emperor's pre-coronation name, translates as 'Prince of Peace'. Haile Selassie means 'Power of The Trinity'.)[10]

Many of Howell's initial converts, including his lieutenant, Robert Hinds, were former disciples of the preacher Alexander Bedward. Bedward was not merely the leader of a Revival band but of a movement with affiliated groups all over Jamaica and in Colón, Panama. At one time a migrant worker in Panama, he first came to public attention in 1895 and commanded a large following centred around August Town near Kingston.[11, 12] Bedward's preaching mixed orthodox religion with the African-Jamaican revivalist tradition.

He became famous as a healer and attracted huge crowds, baptizing throngs in the 'healing stream' of the Hope River.

While not overtly political, Bedward was often critical of whites, describing them in 1895 as 'Pharisees and Sadducees'. Not surprisingly his activities were viewed with concern by the authorities and eventually he was placed in a lunatic asylum.[13] On release he continued his activities in August Town until in 1921 he organised a march to Kingston 'to do battle with his enemies'. He and 800 of his followers, who included Robert Hinds, were arrested and put away. It would be simplistic to see Howellism as a continuation of Bedwardism, but there is undoubtedly a connecting thread.[14]

Howell's early proselytising met with little success and in April 1933 he transferred his efforts to Trinityville in the parish of St Thomas. The African originated Kumina-Revivalist cult is prominent in St Thomas, and Howell used and sanctioned Kumina drumming and customs in his ceremonies.[15] Although the rejoicing, spiritual dancing and possession trance features of Revivalism were rejected by Rastas, most aspects of Rastafarian music can be traced directly to Kumina.[16]

But if Rastafarianism borrowed much from the Kumina-Revivalist tradition, there was one crucial distinction. Revivalists' main concerns remained personal salvation and ritual observance. In contrast Rastafarians protested loudly about economic hardships and racial discrimination. Rastafarianism was not a movement isolated from place, time and history. Rather it was an integral aspect of a continuous matrix of black nationalism, folk religion and peasant resistance to the Jamaican plantation economy.[17]

The Rastafarian movement was infused with the same spirit that provoked the Tacky slave rebellion in 1760, the Sam Sharpe slave Rebellion in 1831 and Paul Bogle's Morant Bay Rebellion in 1865. (Interestingly Tacky, Sam Sharpe and Paul Bogle were all religious leaders.) During the same period that Rastafarianism was gaining prominence, Jamaica was undergoing fundamental social upheaval. This unrest culminated in the Frome riots of 1938, a main spark of the movement for independence from Britain. Rastafarianism is perhaps best understood as a differing expression of the same continuing demand for freedom, a spiritual emancipation from what they perceived as mental slavery.

Colonial authorities definitely saw the Rastafarian cry for black liberation as a political threat, and in January 1934 Leonard Howell was charged with sedition and blasphemy for allegedly selling postcards of Emperor Haile Selassie as passports to Ethiopia and imprisoned for two years.[18] Police continued to harass the movement and in 1940 Howell moved his Ras Tafari followers to an old estate in the mountains of St Catherine called Pinnacle, which was maintained as a Rastafarian commune and ganja plantation.

Howell styled himself as a prophet and took the name 'Gong' or 'Gangunguru Maragh'. 'Gangunguru' was a combination of the Hindi words *gyan, gun, guru* meaning 'wisdom', 'virtue', 'teacher'. *Maragh* translates as 'great king' or 'king of kings'. This East Indian adoption is another indication of the Revivalist influence on Rastafarianism. (Revivalists have certain magical beliefs, called obeah or science, which are based on a number of books published by the de Laurence Company of Chicago, U.S.A.. The most popular of these is *The Great Book Of Magical Arts, Hindu Magic And Indian Occultism.* In Jamaican folk memory this 'obeah bible' was written by a man named de Laurence.)

In due course Howell expanded his ritual identity to that of the returned messiah.[19] At first Rastafarian doctrines were obscure, but a firm core of beliefs emerged — Selassie was the living God, his crowning foretold African redemption, and Marcus Garvey was his prophet. Ironically Marcus Garvey, who emphasised black upliftment through education and presented himself neither as preacher nor prophet, was no friend of Rastafarianism. In early 1933 he refused to allow Rastafarian leader Howell to distribute Selassie's picture in Garvey's Kingston headquarters in Edelweiss Park.[20] The August 25 issue of the *Jamaica Times* reported that in his opening address at a session of the 1934 United Negro Improvement Association (UNIA) convention 'Mr. Garvey also referred to the Ras Tafari cult . . . speaking of them with contempt'.[21] Garvey was also highly critical of the Emperor during the Italian invasion of Ethiopia in 1936, blaming him for his country's lack of preparation.[22]

It's often said, though no definite date is ever cited, that Selassie himself denied his divinity. Former senator and *Gleaner* editor, Hector Wynter, tells of asking him, during his visit to Jamaica in 1966, when he was going to tell Rastafarians he was not God. 'Who am I to disturb their belief?' replied the emperor.[23]

The Pinnacle commune, the largest Rastafarian movement of its day, grew ganja and baked bread and marketed both in Kingston. So there was a considerable intercourse and exchange of ideas between Howell's followers and other Rastas. Howellites are thought to have originated and disseminated several important features of modern Rastafarian religious practice, including the sacramental use of ganja.[24]

There are varying stories about the origin of 'dreadlocks', the long, uncombed braids of hair which are the most visually distinguishing feature of Rastafarians (and incidentally one of Jamaica's few contributions to the English lexicon). Some say the style was inspired by news photos of Ethiopian warriors fighting the Italian invasion in 1936. Others state it was copied from the East African Masai who became prominent in the media during the Mau Mau rebellion of the early 1950s.

Barry Chevannes says the dreadlock trend had its beginnings in the late 1940s when a group of young Rastafarian converts formed the Youth Black Faith in Trenchtown.[25]

Rastas cite biblical admonitions against the use of the razor as reason for not cutting their hair. As Tony Rebel sang in his 1994 hit, 'Nazarite Vow':

Mi check Sampson and John The Baptist
Them grow them natty dread, mek it long like wiss
Who, me start fi grow mi dread some more
When me read Ezekiel forty-four . . .
So me people a spread propaganda 'bout long hair is a sin
But me challenge anyone but me know them can't win
Cause any day them show me inna the Bible say man fe trim
Me give them scissors and comb
And mek them cut off everything

Rastafarians shunned alcohol and observed many food taboos of the ancient Hebrews, eating only fruits, roots, grains, vegetables and sometimes fish. Their food was always unsalted, or 'ital'. This salt avoidance has been linked to a belief among the indentured BaKongo, who came to Jamaica after emancipation, that eating salt prevented them from flying back to Africa.[26]

Rastafarians also considered the smoking of ganja a spiritual rite, but 'the sacrament of the herb' often brought conflict with the law. Howell was apparently the island's first large-scale ganja farmer and Pinnacle became famous throughout Jamaica for the quality and quantity of its product, much of which was marketed in Kingston.[27] In 1954 the police raided and closed down Pinnacle. In her poem 'Pinnacle', Louise Bennett gave a contemporary common man's view of the Ras Tafari:

Mass John come back fram Pinnacle
Yuh want see him head Mumma
Yuh kean tell ef it meck o'hair
Or out o' constab-macka
Him tell we dat him get wey
When de police meck de raid;
Him crawl pon him belly like worm
Fe four mile, him so fraid . . .
Po 'ting! Me sorry fe se dat
All o'him hopes dem fail,
Him say him was gwine to Paradise
An lickle most him ketch jail

Many of the Pinnacle Rastas moved to the Kingston slums, mostly into Back-a-Wall and Moonlight City. Ken Boothe remembers: 'Those days you had Back-a-Wall, which they call Tivoli Gardens now, and that's where most of the singers went . . . My brother was a Rasta and end up at Back-a-Wall Most men who say them was Rasta them days end up at Back-a-Wall, because them parents usually fight it or don't want them go dread.'[28]

In time Howell and a few of his followers drifted back to Tredigar Park, a few miles from Pinnacle. In his later years, as Rastafarianism became prominent worldwide, Howell gained a minor sort of fame. In 1980 CBS news correspondent Dan Rather visited the camp and shot footage of Howell and his congregation, some of which was included in the CBS television programme '60 Minutes' on Sunday, December 7, 1980 in a segment entitled 'The Rastafarians'. Howell died only a few months later in February 1981.

Whatever his personal failings, Howell's legacy was a positive one. Rastafarianism may have its irrational aspects, but which religion is without a mystical side accessible only to true believers? Some say Haile Selassie as a man did not prove altogether worthy of the veneration accorded him, but in the end he was only a symbol. In essence Rastafarianism replaced the traditional white Christian image of the Saviour with a black one. Ethiopia and Africa became not so much physical destinations as conceptions of paradise. And given the physical and mental oppression they endured and the sense of hopelessness in which their creed evolved, Rastafarians must be admired for not only creating a lasting sense of black pride, but for developing one which did not revile other races. Despite a strong anti-papal streak, which ironically was partly a legacy of British rule, Rastafarianism is an essentially tolerant faith and must be given some credit for the relatively good race relations which Jamaica enjoys today. The avoidance of racial animosity in Rasta beliefs was not inevitable. And the great

triumph of Rastafarianism is to have channelled understandable feelings of frustration, resentment and dispossession not into a creed of hate, violence and destruction but into one preaching peace, love and the brotherhood of man.

Notes

1. 'Yet there is no evidence . . .': *Jamaica Journal*, 16:1, 1983. 'Leonard P. Howell and Early Rastafari' by Robert Hill, p. 25
2. 'In his book . . .': *Rastafari Roots and Ideology*, p. 94
3. 'What is the colour of God? . . .': ibid. p. 4
4. 'Ethiopia had been . . .': *Encyclopedia Britannica*. 1993, vol 4, p. 581
5. 'Practically all forms of . . .': *Jamaica Journal*, 16:1, 1983. 'Leonard P. Howell and Early Rastafari', p. 26
6. 'Two other early . . .': *History of Caribbean Religions*, pp. 185-186
7. 'The basis of Rastafari . . .': *Jamaica Journal*, 16:1, 1983. 'Leonard P. Howell and Early Rastafari', p. 27
8. 'Howell was born . . .': ibid., p. 27
9. 'Citing Selassie's coronation . . .': *The Guinness Who's Who of Reggae*, p. 223
10. 'Ras Tafari, was Selassie's . . .': *History of Caribbean Religions*, p.188
11. ' . . . made contact with . . .': *Jamaica Journal*, 16:1, 1983. 'Leonard P. Howell and Early Rastafari', p. 38
12. *Rastafari Roots and Ideology*, p. 39
13. 'Bedward's preaching had mixed . . .': *The Jamaican People : 1880-1902*. pp. 41-45
14. *Rastafari Roots and Ideology*, p. 39 (Bedward was immortalised in the classic Jamaican folk song 'Sly Mongoose' which contains the verse *Mongoose go inna Bedward kitchen / Thief out one of him righteous chicken* referring to a con man who lured away one of the prophet's supposedly virginal followers.)
15. 'Howell used and sanctioned . . .' : *Jamaica Journal*, 19:3, 1985. 'Kumina, The Howellite Church and the Emergence of Rastafarian Traditional Music in Jamaica', Bily and Leib, p. 25
16. 'Rastafarian music can be . . .': Some Reflections on the Rastafari Movement in Jamaica: West Kingston in the early 1950s. *Jamaica Journal*. 25:2, 1995, p. 7
17. 'Rastafarianism was not a movement . . .': *Jamaica Journal*, 16:1, 1983. 'Leonard P. Howell and Early Rastafari', p. 38
18. 'In 1933 he was . . .': *History of Caribbean Religions*, p. 185
19. 'Howell styled himself . . .': *Jamaica Journal*, 16:1, 1983. 'Leonard P. Howell and Early Rastafari', Robert Hill, p.age 35
20. 'In early 1933 he refused . . .': ibid., p.32
21. 'The August 25 issue . . .': Marcus Garvey : Anti-Colonial Champion, p. 89
22. 'Garvey was also highly . . .': ibid., p. 172
23. 'Who am I to disturb . . .': Touch The Happy Isles, p. 286
24. 'Several important features . . .': *Jamaica Journal*, 19:3, 1985. 'Kumina, The Howellite Church and the Emergence of Rastafarian Traditional Music in Jamaica', p. 25
25. 'Barry Chevannes says the dreadlock . . .': *Rastafari Roots and Ideology*, p. 152
26. 'This salt avoidance . . .': ibid., p. 34
27. 'Howell was apparently the . . .': ibid., p.122
28. 'Those days you had Back-a-Wall . . .': interview